Theories of Ugliness

ALSO AVAILABLE FROM BLOOMSBURY

Aesthetics of Ugliness, Karl Rosenkranz
Ugliness: The Non-beautiful in Art and Theory, Andrei Pop and Mechtild Widrich
The Aesthetics of Imperfection in Music and the Arts, eds. Andy Hamilton and Lara Pearson

Theories of Ugliness

An Unseemly Aesthetic History

Mark William Roche

BLOOMSBURY ACADEMIC
LONDON • NEW YORK • OXFORD • NEW DELHI • SYDNEY

BLOOMSBURY ACADEMIC
Bloomsbury Publishing Plc
50 Bedford Square, London, WC1B 3DP, UK
1385 Broadway, New York, NY 10018, USA
29 Earlsfort Terrace, Dublin 2, Ireland

BLOOMSBURY, BLOOMSBURY ACADEMIC and the Diana logo are trademarks of Bloomsbury Publishing Plc

First published in Great Britain 2025

Cover image: Maxim Kantor, The Temptation of St. Anthony
The imprint page needs to be in the new style and layout please.

A catalogue record for this book is available from the British Library.

A catalog record for this book is available from the Library of Congress.

ISBN: HB: 978-1-3504-2559-0
PB: 978-1-3504-2560-6
ePDF: 978-1-3504-2561-3
eBook: 978-1-3504-2562-0

Typeset by Deanta Global Publishing Services, Chennai, India
Printed and bound in Great Britain

To find out more about our authors and books visit www.bloomsbury.com and sign up for our newsletters.

In memory of Laszlo Versényi and for Frank Oakley,
who together introduced me to the history of ideas

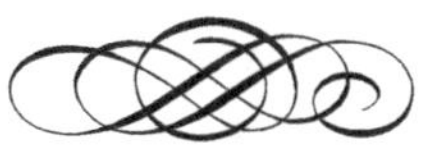

Contents

List of Figures ix
Acknowledgments x
Abbreviations and Translations xi

Introduction 1

Part I Early Reflections 17

1 Plato, Aristotle, and the Ancient World 19
2 The Absence of Ugliness in Medieval Thought 31
3 Maggi, Rocco, and the Early Modern Era 45

Part II The Modern European (and Primarily German) Tradition 61

4 From Lessing to Trahndorff 63
5 Hegel and the Early Hegelians 85
6 Rosenkranz, Schasler, and the Later Hegelians 103
7 Darwin and the Neo-Hegelians 119
8 Nietzsche and the Writers 123
9 The Academic Philosophers: Bolzano to Volkelt 133
10 The Greatness and Limits of Adorno's Aesthetics of Ugliness 155

Part III Contemporary Theories 171

11 Continental Thinkers 173

12 Anglo-American Analytic Philosophers 195

13 An Objective-Idealist Theory 217

Afterword 229

Notes 239

Works Cited 255

Index 273

Figures

Cover. Maxim Kantor, *The Temptation of St. Anthony,* 2015 00

1 Thomas Eakins, *Portrait of Dr. Samuel Gross* (*The Gross Clinic*), 1875 2
2 George Grosz, *Dawn*, 1921 3
3 Mire Lee, Partial view of *Endless House: Holes and Drips*, 2022 4
4 Maxim Kantor, *Socrates*, 2014 22
5 Giotto di Bondone, Detail of *Last Judgment*, c. 1306 32
6 Matthias Grünewald, Detail of *The Crucifixion, Isenheim Altarpiece*, c. 1512–15 33
7 Lucas Cranach, *The Ill-Matched Lovers*, 1531 48
8 *Laocoön and His Sons*, c. 40–30 BC 64
9 Hans Holbein the Younger, *The Ambassadors*, 1533 67
10 Hans Holbein the Younger, *Portrait of the Artist's Wife with the Two Elder Children*, ca. 1528/29 149
11 Lucian Freud, *Benefits Supervisor Sleeping*, 1995 151
12 Kiki Smith, *Tale*, 1992 178
13 Frank Gehry, 8 Spruce Street, New York, 2011 186
14 Kengo Kuma and Associates, M2 Building, Tokyo, Japan, 1990 187
15 Minoru Yamasaki, Pruitt-Igoe Housing Project, St. Louis, 1955 190
16 Hans Schweitzer, Poster for Fritz Hippler's film *Der Ewige Jude* (The Eternal Jew), 1940 208
17 Käthe Kollwitz, *Not* (Misery), 1893–97 221
18 Giuseppe Arcimboldo, *Water*, 1566 222
19 Pablo Picasso, *Guernica*, 1937 223
20 Joseph Beuys, *Fat Chair*, 1963 226
21 Otto Dix, *The Match Vendor*, 1920 230
22 Edvard Munch, *The Scream*, 1893 231

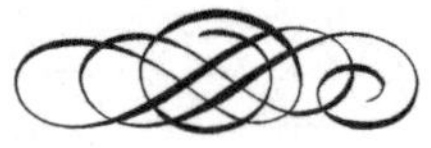

Acknowledgments

A sabbatical from the University of Notre Dame provided me with the necessary time to complete this book, which was initially supported by the Notre Dame Institute for Advanced Study. The book was finalized in late 2024. During my work on the project, I benefited from discussions with Carsten Dutt, Vittorio Hösle, Christian Illies, Cyril O'Regan, and Changjiang Xing. I am also grateful to the faculty and students who participated in my Fall 2023 visit to the University of Bamberg. In addition, the anonymous reviewers for Bloomsbury Publishing provided helpful comments. Keira Stenson ensured that the works cited section matched the manuscript.

I am grateful for the cooperation of many individuals and institutions from around the world, such that I was able to obtain all the images needed for this book. I owe particular gratitude to the contemporary artists and architects—Frank Gehry, Maxim Kantor, Kengo Kuma, Mire Lee, and Kiki Smith—who graciously approved my requests for their work.

My previous book *Beautiful Ugliness: Christianity, Modernity, and the Arts* (2023) includes a chapter titled "Intellectual Resources," which provides brief accounts of a few thinkers examined more thoroughly here. While I borrow from that material, each case is more fully developed in this work. The adapted material is included with the permission of the University of Notre Dame Press.

Abbreviations and Translations

I have used published translations wherever possible. In some cases, all of which are marked "translation modified," I made slight modifications to published translations. In a dozen or so instances, my translation differs so much from the published source that I write "my translation." Accuracy and fluidity were my goals. Where no English translations exist, I offer my own. In these cases, references are solely to the original. Emphasis in quotations, whether they are translations or citations from English, is always taken from the original.

To aid both scholars and general readers, I have, where possible, provided references to works in their original languages as well as in English, employing easily recognizable abbreviations such as Ger. for German, Lat. for Latin, Fre. for French, and Eng. for English. For works with universally identifiable sections, such as paragraph numbers, I have cited those.

Introduction

Studies of truth often develop their arguments by dissecting diverse kinds of fallacies. Similarly, explorations of goodness engage deeply with the nature of evil. Yet for the most part scholarship on beauty has ignored its counterpart, ugliness. Although the British philosopher Frank Sibley recognized ugliness as a concept ripe with "fascination and complexity," he lamented that it was "seldom discussed" (190). This neglect is especially pronounced in the English-speaking world.

Nonetheless, prominent philosophers such as Plato, Hegel, and Adorno have commented on ugliness; forgotten figures such as Vincenzo Maggi, Christian Weiße, and Max Schasler explored ugliness in depth; and a range of writers remembered for their contributions in other fields, such as Antonio Rocco, Eduard von Hartmann, and Hermann Cohen, also offered engaging perspectives on ugliness. *Theories of Ugliness* offers the first historical analysis and philosophical evaluation of theories of ugliness in any language. My book assesses arguments, discusses patterns, and develops new perspectives.

The annals of art and literature are replete with depictions of ugliness, tracing a lineage that stretches back to antiquity. In the mythos of ancient Greece, one encounters grotesque creatures like the Hydra, with its venomous breath and multitude of heads—sever one head, and two more take its place—and the Gorgons, whose hair of living, venomous serpents and petrifying gaze could turn onlookers to stone. Advancing to ancient Rome, we witness a shift as ugliness grounds itself in reality and gives birth to a new literary genre: satire. The advent of Christianity further deepened explorations of ugliness, particularly through stark depictions of human sin and the harrowing visual narratives of Christ's crucifixion.

Figure 1 *Thomas Eakins,* Portrait of Dr. Samuel Gross *(*The Gross Clinic*), 1875, Oil on canvas, Philadelphia Museum of Art / Bridgeman Images.*

Ugly artworks have become even more abundant in modernity. Most readers will be familiar with repugnant images from modern painting, drawing, and printmaking, such as American Thomas Eakins's large and vivid oil painting *Portrait of Dr. Samuel Gross* (*The Gross Clinic*) (1875), which captures the raw brutality of surgical practice (Figure 1), or George Grosz's searing portrayals of Weimar Germany's debauchery, as in his

Figure 2 *George Grosz,* Früh um 5 Uhr! *(*Dawn*), c. 1920, from the portfolio* Im Schatten *(*In the Shadows*), 1921, Photolithograph, Private Collection / The Stapleton Collection / © 2025 Estate of George Grosz / Licensed by VAGA at Artists Rights Society (ARS), New York / Bridgeman Images.*

photolithograph *Dawn*, from his portfolio *In the Shadows* (1921) (Figure 2). Since the Second World War, ugliness has only increased, as we see in Francis Bacon's disfigured portraits and self-portraits, for example, his oil on canvas *Self-Portrait* of 1969, or Jenny Saville's challenge to the idealized (and objectified) female body, as seen in her oil on canvas *Fulcrum* (1999). The

Figure 3 *Partial view of Mire Lee,* Endless House: Holes and Drips, *2022. Mixed mediums, including ceramic sculptures, scaffolding, lithium carbonate, iron oxide glaze liquid, pumps, and motors. 70 9/10 × 78 3/4 x 157 1/2 in (180 x 200 x 400 cm). Exhibition views: "The Milk of Dreams," 59th Venice Biennale, © Mire Lee / Courtesy of the artist and Leeum Museum of Art.*

preoccupation with ugliness permeates virtually all forms of contemporary art. Consider the unsettling installation works of South Korean artist Mire Lee, such as her *Endless House: Holes and Drips* from 2022, which challenge and engage the viewer in profoundly discomforting ways (Figure 3). Through these myriad expressions, ugliness remains a potent and pervasive force in the artistic and literary canon.

Though I am captivated by these vivid portrayals, in this book my focus is on theory, not on artworks themselves, more specifically theories of ugliness that offer fresh perspectives on art, nature, and the world. Consequently, my study excludes artists who merely depict ugliness; instead, it centers on thinkers—primarily philosophers, but occasionally artists as well—who critically reflect on the concept of ugliness. Two further restrictions derive from the extent of my knowledge and the need for concision. Aside from cursory mentions, non-Western theories of ugliness fall outside the scope of this examination.[1] Nor do I endeavor to catalog every reference. Instead, I engage with those thinkers whose ideas are compelling, at least moderately developed, and either original or emblematic of broader intellectual currents.[2]

Previous histories of the theory of ugliness, similar to accounts of ugly art and literature, invariably begin in modernity.[3] I cast a wider historical net, including ancient, medieval, and early modern theories. Further, whereas most accounts of ugliness are purely descriptive, I criticize untenable positions and elevate enduring insights.[4] My analysis gives particular weight to the German tradition, which was deeply immersed in analyses of ugliness. The early Hegelian Karl Rosenkranz wrote the first book on ugliness in 1853, and German philosopher Theodor Adorno centers his entire aesthetics around ugliness and dissonance.

Overview

Part I, "Early Reflections," guides the reader from ancient Greek insights to early modern engagement with ugliness. Chapter 1, "Plato, Aristotle, and the Ancient World," focuses on Plato and Aristotle while also offering comments on the Sophistic *Dissoi Logoi* (*Contrary Arguments*) and subsequent ancient thinkers, Horace, Plutarch, and Plotinus. Virtually no literature exists on ancient ideas of ugliness. Plato, however, offers four original and enduring insights: (1) ugliness and beauty are not binary opposites (one must look more deeply); (2) humans can be drawn to ugliness even against their conscious intentions; (3) ugliness can be defined as an appearance that contradicts essential features of a concept, for example, willful ignorance in a human; and (4) ugliness can (and should) be subdivided into the awful (powerful ugliness) and the ridiculous (ineffective ugliness). Aristotle draws on the last point to develop his famous analysis that the comic is ugliness without pain. Aristotle also praises aesthetic renderings of ugliness for helping us understand the fullness of reality.

Chapters 2 and 3 analyze insights from the medieval and early modern eras. The dominant category in medieval aesthetics is beauty, not ugliness. In Chapter 2, "The Absence of Ugliness in Medieval Thought," I analyze the two primary (and interrelated) medieval claims about ugliness: that the ugly as such does not exist (but is instead a privation of beauty) and that in the long run nothing is ultimately ugly insofar as everything participates in the greater beauty of the universe. Despite differences in time, sources, and perspectives, Augustine, Pseudo-Dionysius the Areopagite, and Aquinas all share these two overarching claims. Even humanity's sinfulness and Christ's ugliness on the cross can be understood as part of a larger, positive narrative. The chapter explores the paradoxical evaluation of ugliness in Bernard of Clairvaux, who is simultaneously repulsed and attracted by monstrous gargoyles. It also analyzes the most focused medieval account of ugliness by Ulrich of Strasbourg.

Chapter 3, "Maggi, Rocco, and the Early Modern Era," delves into the sparse attention given to ugliness in early modern aesthetics, particularly in the Italian Renaissance. The chapter discusses how thinkers such as Leon Battista Alberti adhered to classical ideals of beauty, either avoiding or idealizing ugliness. Most commentary aligns with Aristotle's view that ugliness plays a role in comedy or with the medieval understanding that apparent ugliness is ultimately beautiful. I introduce here the insights of two Italians, Vincenzo Maggi, a translator of Aristotle, whose treatise *De Ridiculis* (*On the Ridiculous*), differentiates kinds of ugliness, and Antonio Rocco, a priest and philosopher, whose satirical essay *Della bruttezza* (On Ugliness) takes the reader through four kinds of ugliness, each of which is the opposite of the beautiful or the good. Rocco then extols the greatness of each type of ugliness. Rocco's essay both buttresses and mocks the medieval argument that evil does not exist, for all that is seemingly evil or ugly does in fact play a positive role within the whole of the universe. Leibniz and Baumgarten develop in different ways many of the ideas previously seen. The chapter concludes with an exploration of early modern British perspectives. It examines contributions from English essayist Joseph Addison, Scottish philosophers David Hume and Adam Smith, Irish statesman Edmund Burke, and Herefordshire landowner Uvedale Price.

By far the longest section of the book, Part II, "The Modern European (and Primarily German) Tradition," details the elevation of ugliness in aesthetic theory. These thinkers stress the dialectical relations between beauty and ugliness; some even go so far as to regard ugliness as superior to beauty. The prominence of the ugly in modern art and literature coincided with a burgeoning theoretical interest, which both influenced, and was influenced by, artistic developments. It wasn't until the 1830s that ugliness finally emerged as a dominant aesthetic category, and of those philosophers who belong to the Western canon, only one, Adorno, a twentieth-century philosopher, made ugliness the center of his aesthetic theory.

The concept of ugliness first began to gain prominence in the late eighteenth and early nineteenth centuries, notably through the works of German writers G. E. Lessing, who analyzed ugliness in the context of the spatial and temporal arts, and Friedrich Schlegel, who contrasted the serenity of ancient beauty with the ugliness of modern art. In Chapter 4, "From Lessing to Trahndorff," I analyze Lessing's argument in *Laocoön* that the temporal arts, such as literature, can better integrate ugliness into a larger aesthetic whole compared to the static arts, which capture only a moment in time. Lessing posits that ugliness must be subsumed within a broader positive narrative to maintain its aesthetic value. Johann Gottfried Herder also plays a role here, particularly through his extensive commentary on Lessing's work. Schlegel's *Über das Studium der griechischen Poesie* (*On the Study of Greek Poetry*) contrasts ancient beauty with modernity's elevation of the interesting and the ugly. The chapter also includes brief reflections on Immanuel Kant, Friedrich Schiller, and some lesser-known figures, including Karl Wilhelm Ferdinand Solger, who recognizes that the ugly is not merely the opposite of beauty. Ugliness goes further: it seeks to overthrow beauty.

Two chapters are devoted to Hegel and the Hegelians, who stress the dialectical relation of the ugly and the beautiful. Chapter 5, "Hegel and the Early Hegelians," explores Hegel's ambivalent relation to ugliness, which was met with a Hegelian turn in aesthetics, where the ugly, the comic, and the sublime became the three dominant aesthetic categories. Most of the early Hegelians—Christian Weiße, Arnold Ruge, Johann Georg Martin (G. M.) Dursch, August Wilhelm Bohtz, Friedrich Theodor Vischer, and Kuno Fischer—are little known, yet these thinkers offer a wide range of intriguing and understudied insights: they analyze the ugly in relation to the sublime and the comic, recognize ugliness as a valuable moment within art, and emphasize the diverse ways in which ugliness is both integrated into artworks but also negated or overcome.[5] No other period placed such a strong emphasis on ugliness. Weiße, in particular, introduces foundational terminology and concepts that future scholars will develop, emphasizing that ugliness must be portrayed in relation to the dynamics of the sublime and the comic. This chapter highlights how these thinkers reconcile ugliness with beauty, providing a more comprehensive view of aesthetics that acknowledges the necessity of ugliness within the dialectical process. Although philosophers who explore ugliness are for the most part now aware of Rosenkranz, few have any idea of the rich discussions of ugliness that predate Rosenkranz's *Aesthetics of Ugliness*; this chapter analyzes those discussions.

The Hegelian tradition does indeed reach an apex with the Hegel biographer Karl Rosenkranz, who was the first to devote an entire book to ugliness. In Chapter 6, "Rosenkranz, Schasler, and the Later Hegelians," I analyze Rosenkranz's elaborate array of categories and assess his strengths and weaknesses. Rosenkranz views ugliness as a necessary element within aesthetics, essential for the full expression of art's dialectical nature. He identifies three main categories of ugliness: formlessness, incorrectness, and deformity. Like his predecessors, Rosenkranz insists that ugliness should be presented in art, but it should always be negated, which is most prominently achieved through comedy. After Rosenkranz, still more Hegelians address ugliness: Max Schasler offers the most capacious definition, and Moriz Philipp Carrière links ugliness with its overcoming in the drama of reconciliation, which is both similar to and different from tragedy.

Because the English language world has undertaken so few explorations of ugliness, Chapter 7, "Darwin and the Neo-Hegelians," which covers British contributions to ugliness in the nineteenth and early twentieth centuries, is comparatively brief. Darwin offers insights into the aesthetic sensibilities of animals. He analyzes human perceptions of beauty and ugliness, noting that both universal and culturally specific elements are at play. He observes that ugliness arises when we experience a lack of variation or deviation from established norms. After Darwin, the chapter returns to the Hegelian tradition. The German engagement with ugliness is so distinctive that even when the ugly appears in early Anglo-American aesthetics, the German influence is apparent, as we see with two British philosophers, the neo-Hegelian Bernard Bosanquet and the Princeton Hegel scholar Walter Terence Stace. Bosanquet, a central figure in British philosophy, introduces the concept of "difficult beauty," arguing that what initially appears ugly may reveal its beauty through deeper engagement and understanding, highlighting the role of sophisticated reception.

Independently of the Hegelians, we can identify in the long nineteenth century two other strands of reflection on ugliness: on the one hand, literary figures, and, on the other hand, academic philosophers who work outside the Hegelian tradition. Chapter 8, "Nietzsche and the Writers," focuses on Victor Hugo, Georg Büchner, Charles Baudelaire, and Friedrich Nietzsche. These writers reflect on ugliness in works that are themselves literary creations. We see a kind of immanent aesthetics at play. Hugo emphasizes the integration of the grotesque and ugly into art as a way of mirroring reality and fostering aesthetic innovation, and he ties this ugliness to a Christian revolution in aesthetics. Büchner argues for the empathetic portrayal of life, including its suffering and ugliness, rejecting idealization and embracing realist Christian art. Baudelaire, in contrast, seeks to transcend reality, promoting the imaginative exploration of ugliness, no matter how monstrous. Nietzsche places ugliness at the core of his aesthetic theory, challenging traditional concepts of beauty and asserting the primacy of ugliness. He argues that we need art to cope with "ugly truth," positioning ugliness as a foundational element that precedes and necessitates beauty. His assessment of ugliness shifts over time: in his early writings, ugliness is linked to tragedy, whereas in later texts he stresses its connection to comedy. These thinkers collectively advance an understanding of ugliness as not only integral to art but also a catalyst for deeper aesthetic and existential insights.

"The Academic Philosophers: Bolzano to Volkelt" is the subject of Chapter 9. None of the thinkers in this chapter are Hegelian. In fact, some like Bernard Bolzano and Adolf Zeising were vehemently anti-Hegelian. Others had loose connections to the Hegelian tradition. For example, Hermann Lotze, who was recognized through the First World War as Germany's leading metaphysician, was influenced by Weiße. Virtually all had some recognition of Hegelian thought on ugliness. Bolzano offers a reception-oriented perspective on beauty and ugliness, asserting that ugliness vexes us because it contradicts our cognitive concepts. Lotze views ugliness not as a lack of beauty but as hostility toward it. Zeising criticizes the Hegelian notion that ugliness can be integrated into beauty, arguing that true beauty cannot tolerate incongruence.

Robert Zimmermann sees ugliness as an appearance that falsely claims to be beautiful and argues that this pretense is inherently comical. Julius Hermann von Kirchmann focuses on ugliness and displeasure, Eduard von Hartmann articulates a series of distinctions within ugliness, Clemens Brentano defends the integration of ugliness into art, and Hermann Cohen relates ugliness to our animal nature. These and others not included in this preview widen the conversation beyond the Hegelian tradition. The most interesting thinker in this chapter is Cohen, who elevates humor for lovingly embracing humanity's ugliness.

The academic tradition of engaging with ugliness wanes for several decades until Theodor Adorno enters the stage. Like Hegel, Adorno elevates artwork aesthetics, but, unlike Hegel, Adorno favors ugliness over beauty. Adorno criticizes all theories and artworks that seek to bring ugliness into harmony with beauty. Chapter 10, "The Greatness and Limits of Adorno's Aesthetics of Ugliness," analyzes and assesses Adorno's contribution. Adorno posits that ugliness and negativity must be preserved in art to reflect the unreconciled and fragmented nature of reality. Adorno asserts that beauty and reconciliation in art obscure the inherent tensions and ugliness of modern life and must be rejected. His theory emphasizes that true art must embrace fragmentation, reject formal harmony, and resist any form of idealization. Adorno's critiques challenge classical aesthetics and present a counter-model, where ugliness is not merely integrated into beauty but is the foundational element of genuine artistic expression. The chapter seeks to recognize the greatness of Adorno, including his account of modernity, but it also uncovers an array of contradictions that render his boldest claims untenable. Adorno is the only thinker to whom I dedicate an entire chapter, not only because he is the most recent major theorist of ugliness, but also because he has defined the parameters for much of contemporary thought. Adorno's *Aesthetic Theory* has been hailed as "the pivotal document of twentieth-century philosophical aesthetics" (Bernstein 139). Even today it continues to receive acclaim (Silverbloom).

The third and final part of the book is devoted to "Contemporary Theories." Chapter 11, "Continental Thinkers," broadens the scope beyond my primary focus on Germany. Here I explore, among others, Georges Bataille, who was fascinated by formlessness and filth, the monstrous and obscene, excrement and death, and Julia Kristeva, who examined the concept of the abject, linking it to disorder, bodily waste, and social rejection. Kristeva offers new insights into ugliness, particularly our instinctive resistance to it. The chapter also explores some well-known figures who engage ugliness peripherally. Jacques Derrida, for instance, uses vomit to highlight the limitations of Kant, who excluded the disgusting from aesthetics. The Slovenian philosopher Slavoj Žižek, like Adorno and Nietzsche before him, resists the traditional definition of ugliness as the negation of beauty. Other figures discussed include British cultural critic Mark Cousins and Cameroonian social scientist Achille Mbembe. Chapter 11 also addresses the aesthetics of ugliness in gardens and architecture, inspired by German philosopher Christian Illies and Belgian architectural theorist Bart Verschaffel. The chapter concludes with an examination of the Italian Hegelian Giacomo Rinaldi.

The long continental tradition, spanning from the earliest German thinkers through Adorno and beyond, unveils a wealth of captivating and largely overlooked insights. Central to this tradition are the intricate dialectical relations between beauty and ugliness, the systematic place of ugliness within aesthetic theory, its multifaceted roles across various art forms, and the myriad ways in which ugliness can emerge within otherwise beautiful works. No other cultural paradigm tackles ugliness with the same depth and breadth as the German philosophical tradition. With few exceptions, these thinkers are united by a profound impulse: an endeavor to contemplate beauty and ugliness not merely as contrasting entities but as interwoven elements of a far more complex aesthetic tapestry.

Whereas thinkers working within the continental tradition often grapple with broader, systematic questions, Anglo-American analytic philosophers favor more isolated insights. In many cases their observations arise indirectly through primary reflections on beauty, into which occasional reflections on ugliness are embedded. What the analytical tradition lacks in extensive reflection and historical awareness, it compensates for with precision. Chapter 12, "Anglo-American Analytical Philosophers," opens with the puzzle: Why has the discourse on ugliness been more vigorous in Europe than in the United States? After comments on John Dewey, I then turn to several early analytic thinkers: Lucius Garvin, Jerome Stolnitz, and Pat Henderson. I examine three of the most prominent twentieth-century philosophers of art: Nelson Goodman, Frank Sibley, and Arthur Danto. In assessing ugliness, Goodman distinguishes between the object depicted and the work's properties. Sibley explores whether ugliness can be defined independently or only in relation to another category. Although Danto never focuses on ugliness, he indirectly addresses it when he argues that something can be good art without being beautiful. His ideas on art can be compared productively, in terms of similarity and difference, with Hegel's. I argue that Danto's theory of beauty and ugliness suffers from an internal contradiction. The chapter also analyzes three philosophers whose topics lie somewhat outside the mainstream of analytic philosophy. Noël Carroll, another notable American philosopher of art, expands the scope of theoretical ugliness to include humor and horror, including hateful images of enemies; and Holmes Rolston, III, and Emily Brady address ugliness in nature, linking it to environmentalism. The chapter concludes with the recent analytic contributions of Panos Paris and Ryan Doran.

In Chapter 13, "An Objective-Idealist Theory," I draw partly on ideas from the tradition, especially from Plato and the Hegelians, but also move beyond them, offering my own perspectives. The chapter criticizes common definitions of ugliness and proposes instead a definition of ugliness as an appearance that contradicts the normative concept of an object. I identify four realms—the physical, emotional, intellectual, and moral—in which ugliness manifests itself. The chapter also introduces new aesthetic concepts, such as "repugnant beauty," "fractured beauty," and the neologism "aischric beauty," to describe various styles of beautiful ugliness, which are based on the distinction between content and form. The chapter concludes by addressing the pitfalls of kitsch and the criteria by which we might separate ugliness from seeming ugliness, introducing the neologism *quatsch* to criticize artworks that are ugly but lack deeper meaning and aesthetic merit, while also recognizing, via the category *prima facie quatsch,* that some seemingly absurd artworks may indeed have hidden merit.

A brief afterward argues that in some cases people are drawn to ugliness, and in others they might initially look away. In either case, art provides a medium to confront and understand the ugly facets of our world. The blending of ugliness with beauty enhances the tension and complexity of artworks, expanding the artist's scope for innovation and challenging the recipient's interpretive capacities. Understanding beautiful ugliness in art can also sharpen our perception of the hidden beauty in life, challenging societal standards and biases. In a broad sense, the chapter discusses the unique role of ugliness in enhancing artistic expressivity and reviews some of the work's major insights. It also explores whether a consistent internal logic can be discerned in the way theories of ugliness have unfolded historically.

Four books in English address the aesthetics of ugliness. The first is the English translation of Rosenkranz's *Aesthetics of Ugliness* of 1853, which appeared with Bloomsbury in 2015. A well-known book written by a prominent follower of Hegel, Rosenkranz's work is important but not easy to read. Many of the examples are arcane, and the conceptual apparatus is almost scholastic in its infinite distinctions of types. I value Rosenkranz's work, but it has its weaknesses and does not itself engage in a history of theory. Two anthologies exist: *Ugliness: The Non-Beautiful in Art and Theory* (2014), edited by the Rosenkranz translators Andrei Pop and Mechtild Widrich; and *On the Ugly* (2019), edited by Jane Forsey and Lars Aagaard-Mogensen. The chapters in both volumes, which mainly focus on modernity, do not seek to engage the history of theory as such. The fourth book is my own *Beautiful Ugliness: Christianity, Modernity, and the Arts* (2023), which includes some theoretical reflections but mainly addresses, on the one hand, historical manifestations of ugliness, focusing on imperial Rome, late medieval Christianity, and modernity, and, on the other hand, the styles and structures of beautiful works that integrate ugliness. In undertaking *Beautiful Ugliness*, I recognized the need for an independent study that would fill a gap by analyzing the history of theories of ugliness.

The English-language world's increasing interest in ugliness is furthermore manifested in a series of additional books on one or another aspect of ugliness, including Sarah Nuttall's anthology *Beautiful Ugly: African and Diaspora Aesthetics* (2005), which explores cross-cultural views of ugliness, and Sianne Ngai's *Ugly Feelings* (2005), which focuses on emotions expressed in works of American literature. Two books give examples of ugliness without a critical or theoretical apparatus: Umberto Eco's *On Ugliness* (2007), a peerless anthology of images and excerpts that awakens interest in the topic but does not offer extended theoretical analysis; and Stephen Bayley's *Ugly* (2012), which differs from Eco's book in being restricted to modernity but is otherwise analogous, an anthology of fascinating images and brief commentary. Gretchen Henderson's *Ugliness: A Cultural History* (2015) is a well-written history of ugliness in popular culture, but it does not delve into theory. The anthology *On the Politics of Ugliness* (2018), edited by Sara Rodrigues and Ela Przybylo, uses connections between "unsightliness" and "gender, ability, race, class, beauty norms, body size, health, sexuality, and age" in order to criticize "visual injustice" (2, 17). Two still more recent books address ugliness in architecture: Timothy Hyde's *Ugliness and Judgment: On Architecture in the Public Eye* (2019) analyzes historical episodes of aesthetic judgment where architecture is viewed as ugly, and Wouter Van Acker and Thomas Mical's anthology *Architecture & Ugliness: Anti-Aesthetics and the Ugly in Postmodern Architecture* (2020) explores more recent architecture. None of these works delves into the history of theory.[6]

Philosophy, Plato said, arose from wonder (*Theaetetus* 155c-d). The object of our wonder is marvelous because it is not only fascinating but also horrifying and awesome, indicative of a force we cannot comprehend. Asking questions to which we don't have satisfactory answers is perplexing, both enchanting and humbling (*Meno* 84c). Our surviving record of conscious theoretical reflection on ugliness begins in ancient Greece, but a sensibility for the ugly and indeed a related sense of wonder presumably arose earlier in human consciousness. The sublime experience of nature—when one is terrified by an animal yet admires its power—engenders a sense of the ugly and the beautiful in one and the same object.

Such experiences of repulsion and fascination, which have aesthetic and religious dimensions, align with what Rudolf Otto termed the numinous. According to Otto, the numinous is the ineffable and overpowering aspect of religion, beyond rational explanation and moral bounds. It encompasses both the holy itself and our awe-inspiring encounter with holiness. The numinous involves a dual experience of the taboo and the consecrated, thereby merging terror and exaltation, dread and delight—what Otto calls *numen tremendum* and *numen fascinans*. In these primordial encounters with the overwhelming power of existence, we find elements that are both frightening and engaging.

For instance, watching a ferocious tiger tear apart a gazelle is an aesthetic experience that both terrifies and fascinates, even if for the archaic human being it is also a religious experience—insofar as an awesome and vital force in being manifests itself. Ugliness and beauty, the repellent and the fascinating, seem connected in such early experiences of awe. The sublime, with its blend of terrifying and inspiring elements, partially mirrors the numinous (Otto 85).

It may be that over time functional magnetic resonance imaging (fMRI) will clarify to what extent the areas of the brain in which religious feelings, such as a sense of divine presence, and in which moral thoughts operate, are as distinct as they are overlapping (Wain and Spinella; Gaw; Fumagalli and Priori). Still, as we seek to make sense of the history of religion, we need to recognize that the moral somehow tames our experience of the religious. When integrated with the moral, the numinous becomes different: it becomes the morally transformed numinous. In archaic religious experiences, good and evil are deeply connected: what is good for my people is bad for another. To be in battle and to kill all the others is a religious experience. God is the god of life for us and the god of death for others.

This religious experience, defined by an emotive encounter with the sublime and a sense of moral exclusivity, undergoes a radical transformation in the so-called axial age (Jaspers). Between 800 and 200 BC and in at least five parts of the world—China, India, Persia, Judea, and Greece—humans no longer accepted this form of the divine. We see instead new and more complex notions of the religious. Humanity becomes conscious of reality as a whole and begins to recognize its specific role and limits, which triggers both radical questions and ambitious ideals. Thought is directed to thought itself. People give reasons for their beliefs and ideas and attempt to convince others. Universality emerges as a category. Reason begins to combat myth, and religion develops in a more rational and ethical direction.

In a world governed by rationality, distinctions emerge: the ugly and the beautiful also become split. Here we can begin our theoretical account of the ugly as a category distinct from the beautiful. Over time, however, the ugly and the beautiful become so separated that Plotinus intimates that the ugly and the beautiful cannot be conceived together, and Augustine suggests that the ugly does not even exist. Today, we are far more conscious, as was humanity at its origin, of the interwoven nature of the beautiful and the ugly. From the nineteenth century onward, thinkers again saw the need to integrate beauty and ugliness. Today we live within that much more complex, dialectical world.

Part I

Early Reflections

1

Plato, Aristotle, and the Ancient World

Comments on ugliness are rare in antiquity. The ancient Greeks had no specifically aesthetic terms. The word *kalos*, which is normally translated as "beautiful," does not equate to beautiful, because it also means "good," "well-done," "virtuous." One might ask, isn't "the good" *agathos*? Not exactly, because *agathos* is always what is useful for another end, whereas *kalos* is what is immediately, intrinsically attractive. So it is not that we have, in the distinction between *kalos* and *agathos*, a contrast between the aesthetic and ethical spheres. The difference is between what is intrinsically attractive and what is useful in achieving a given end. And of course we encounter the combination *kalokagathos*. *Kallos*, which can mean "beauty," is primarily associated with eroticism and is seldom applied to artworks (Konstan).

The situation is not unique to ancient Greece. The Hebrew Bible, which includes fewer descriptions of the ugly than of the beautiful, employs as its term for "the ugly" רע (raʿ), which encompasses a wide semantic spectrum, including, for example, also "bad," "evil," "inappropriate," and "undesirable" (Olyan 22). We see a similar structure in various Sub-Saharan languages, where the overlap of formal and moral beauty is significant (Van Damme 11–15). In the Bantu language Chokwe, which is the national language of the Republic of Angola, the same word, *chibema*, expresses "beautiful" and "good." In Lega, a Bantu language spoken in the Democratic Republic of the Congo, one singular word, *busoga*, designates both formal and moral beauty. Thus, ancient Greek, along with these cultures, shows a close connection between goodness and beauty, as well as evil and ugliness.

The most common Greek word for "ugly" is αἰσχρός (aischros), which entails both physical and moral ugliness. In fact, all of my quotations from Greek sources in this chapter have a version of αἰσχρός (aischros) in the original. The word is used to capture the outward appearance of Thersites, his physical ugliness, as well as his status as ill-favored. In a moral sense, αἰσχρός (aischros) means "shameful," "disgraceful," or "contemptible." Plato's Gorgias, for example, notes that it would be "shameful" (αἰσχρὸν) not to continue the public dialogue that Socrates and Gorgias had begun and from which Gorgias, who had run into difficulties, would have preferred to withdraw (458d). In its meaning as shameful, *aischros* refers to the trespassing of moral virtues in social and political practices.

Presumably, the first Greek text to address ugliness theoretically is an anonymous Sophist (and in some ways Socratic) treatise the ***Dissoi Logoi*** (*Contrary Arguments*). This fragmentary work argues for both sides of multiple issues—good and evil, beautiful and ugly, just and unjust, true and false—such that distinctions between the categories break down. Sickness, for example, is bad for the patient but good for the doctor, so both good and bad or, one could say, neither, since each side is also refuted (1.3). The same logic applies to death, which is bad for the deceased but good for undertakers and gravediggers; as such, death is both good and bad or neither (1.3). One of the longest sections deals with *aischros*, which here is usually translated as "shameful" (because of the often moral considerations at play), but, as I noted above, *aischros* means both "ugly" and "shameful."[1] The treatise argues in essence that the same action, based on circumstance and perspective, is both "beautiful" or "seemly" (kalon) and "ugly" or "shameful" (aischros). For example, when a woman has sex with her husband, the act is beautiful or seemly, but if she has sex with another woman's husband, it is ugly or shameful (2.5). According to the Greek moral code, doing good to one's friends is just, but doing good to one's enemies is ugly or shameful (2.7). The author also dwells on cultural differences: for example, among the Spartans, it is fine and seemly for young girls to engage in athletics and to go around with bare arms and no tunics; whereas for the Ionians, such actions are shameful or ugly (2.9). Thus, everything is beautiful, and everything is ugly; there is no higher form of beauty or ugliness but only divergences in practice, such that what is ugly is also beautiful.

In the section on truth and falsity, the *Dissoi Logoi* gestures toward the transcendence of relativism. The Socratic structure of self-cancellation is at play:

> For if anyone should ask those who say that the same statement is both false and true which of these their own statement is, if they answer "false," then it is clear that the false and the true are two different things; whereas if they answer "true," then this same statement is also false. And if anyone ever says or testifies that certain things are true, then, on that argument, these same things are also false; and if one knows some man to be truthful, one knows him also to be a liar. (4.6)

If we say either "this sentence is both true and false" or "this sentence is false," the statements are self-cancelling, whereas if we say, "this sentence is true," the claim does not suffer the same contradiction. The structure of self-cancellation points toward the priority of the positive (over the negative), which is central to the objective idealism of Plato and Hegel (Hösle, *Wahrheit* 267–304). The self-cancellation of negativity suggests an asymmetry between truth and falsehood, justice and injustice, and beauty and ugliness, with the negative term dependent on, and inferior to, the positive, a position that Plato develops elsewhere, for example, in *Gorgias* and in Book I of *The Republic*, and which will later be central for Hegel and the Hegelians.

If we assume that the *Dissoi Logoi* predates **Plato** (it seems to have been written between 404 and 395 BC, so around the time of Socrates' death in 399 BC), then Plato would not have been the first theorist to address ugliness. However, he was the first to articulate a nuanced, non-relativistic understanding of the concept. In *The Symposium* and *The Republic*, Plato seems to play with the *aischros*-related arguments of the *Dissoi Logoi* (180e–811a; 479a–b). Beauty, one of Plato's most significant categories, is central to his metaphysics and features prominently in *The Symposium* and *Phaedrus*, where it is depicted as the ultimate object of love (210a–212a; 247c–252a). We always love the beautiful, never the ugly (201a, 202d). Although Plato's ideas on art and beauty have been extensively analyzed, discussions on ugliness remain rare.[2] Nonetheless, here, as elsewhere in the history of philosophy, we can view the history of the theory of ugliness—or at least much of it—as little but footnotes to Plato, for Plato offers us multiple enduring insights.

Plato portrays and analyzes the dichotomy between external appearance and deeper essence, which is essential to his thought, from his portrayal of Socratic irony to his metaphysics. This dichotomy also involves ugliness. Socrates, for instance, was famously ugly (Figure 4). Alcibiades comments that Socrates has an ugly, satyr-like body (*Symposium* 215b). According to Theodorus, Socrates is "snub-nosed" and has "bulging eyes" (*Theaetetus* 143e, translation modified). Moreover, Socrates is a nuisance. He is impudent and wraps up his laughable arguments "in just the kind of expressions you'd expect of such an insufferable satyr" (*Symposium* 221e). Not only Socrates' appearance, but his behavior, too, is ugly or shameful, contrary to what is expected in polite society (Figure 4).

Figure 4 *Maxim Kantor,* Socrates, *2014, Oil on canvas, Collection of the University of Notre Dame.*

Socrates is willing to contradict the expectations of his environment and be viewed as an outcast, but it is precisely this shameless questioning of everything that helps lead him to truth. As one digs deeper, one sees that what is uglier than physical appearance or social demeanor are philosophical falsehoods. Just as the beauty of the soul eclipses the beauty of the body (*Symposium* 210b), an ugly body is nothing compared to an ugly soul. In *The Republic*, Plato suggests that opinions without knowledge are "ugly things" (506c). What truly matters are Socrates' ideas, not his appearance. In *The Symposium*, Alcibiades recognizes that Socrates' seeming nonsense contains divine arguments (221e), and Diotima states that "the beauties of the body are as nothing to the beauties of the soul" (210b).

At the end of *Gorgias*, Socrates presents a myth (523a–526d): the just will go to the island of the blessed and the unjust to the prison of retribution and judgment. The decisions must be made by looking at the naked souls, which reveal, for example, that "arrogant power, luxury, and wanton insolence" lead to a "soul full of asymmetry and ugliness" (525a). The naked judgment is essential because, in life, with clothes and property and well-situated witnesses, we cannot know who is beautiful and who is ugly. Beautiful bodies and elaborate trappings can hide ugly souls.

For Plato, recognizing truth requires the grueling effort of working through arguments. Toward the end of *Gorgias*, Callicles has been refuted and refuses to participate further; he is no longer willing to suffer the punishment of being corrected (505c). This scenario illustrates a common Platonic structure: the convergence of theme and performance. While rhetoric is the main discussion topic, the dialogue also addresses the conditions of dialogue and learning, which include the willingness to face correction and be cured of one's errors. Socrates says that Callicles does not want to suffer going through an argument, though such punishment would be advantageous to him. Part of the dialogue is about the benefit of being punished. That is, the dialogue is about the dialectic of finding truth through the admission of error, working one's way to the beautiful via the ugly.

The ugly and impudent Socrates fascinated later thinkers. Erasmus, who saw Socrates as a pivotal figure (Christian), employs Socratic irony in his *Praise of Folly* (1511): most things are different than they appear, such that the beautiful seems ugly, the wealthy appear poor, and the scandalous is thought credible. Later in the sixteenth century, Michel de Montaigne expressed his vexation that Socrates should have had such an ugly face and body that were "so unbecoming to the beauty of his soul, he who was so much in love, so madly in love, with beauty" ("On Physiognomy," 1198). Throughout European history, the deceptive nature of appearances, with its bearing on the beautiful and the ugly, arises again and again.

Even though beauty is wondrously attractive and ugliness deeply repulsive, we can nonetheless be attracted to ugliness.[3] In the fourth book of *The Republic*, Plato describes how we desire to see something unappealing, such as a dead body, even when we consciously do not want to do so. While walking, Leontius becomes aware of corpses that lay at the place of public execution. He is repulsed and at the same time irresistibly drawn to them. He resists at first, covering his face, but is then overpowered. In a beautiful formulation, Plato has him say that his eyes take over his body: "for a time he resisted and veiled his head, but overpowered in despite of all by his desire, with wide staring eyes he rushed up to the corpses and cried, There, ye wretches, take your fill of the fine spectacle!" (439e–440a). Internally split, Leontius apostrophizes his eyes. Reason gives way to desire. Leontius's involuntary action embodies the tension between the notion that we want to know reality and the reflection that some things, like a corpse, should not draw our gaze.[4]

Perverse curiosity will return, with a twist, in Augustine, and then resurface in the modern era: art will become ever more drawn to integrate the superficially repulsive. Plato identifies a facet of the aesthetic realm: our fascination with death and destruction, which are central to tragedy. This morbid impulse is also visible beyond art: in nineteenth-century Paris, for example, the morgue was a major attraction, drawing countless viewers (Schwartz). Similar fascinations date back to ancient Greece and recur throughout popular culture. Freak shows in Europe and the United States, featuring human oddities and deformities, thrived from 1840 to 1940 (Bogdan; Durbach). Matthew Kieran challenges the reigning concept that aesthetic value always involves pleasure, highlighting instead our "human fascination for the freakish or horrific," which leads us to "derive pleasure from and delight in the grotesque, freakish or chaotic" (Kieran 394, 397).[5] An ambivalence, whereby artists criticize moral ugliness but are simultaneously fascinated by it, surfaces intermittently. Still, this ambivalent fascination is superficial. Plato's *Symposium* argues that in the end we love beauty. There is "no such thing as the love of ugliness" (201a).

In the *Sophist* Plato emphasizes that a mindless soul is "ugly" or "deformed," riddled with discord and lacking in measure and symmetry (228a–228d). If we take the argument to a higher level, we could say that Plato implies a definition of ugliness as what is inherently unfitting, an appearance that is contrary to what is appropriate to the nature of something. Ignorance is an aberration or perversion of the mind, a withdrawal from, or negation of, what belongs to the mind as the human organ for knowledge. As a negation of what is intrinsic to the human ideal, ignorance is fundamentally ugly. Among the various forms of ignorance, Plato seems most interested not in the ignorance that requires technical instruction, but instead in the stupid vanity of claiming knowledge when one lacks it. This type of ignorance is best cured through philosophical discussion. The elenchus, the methodical questioning that Socrates adopts to uncover contradictions and refute positions, cures the soul's ugliness, much as gymnastics and medicine work to heal physical ugliness and disease.

In the *Philebus*, Socrates describes "ignorance in the strong" as "hateful and ugly" (49c), whereas ignorance in the weak, because it is harmless to others, is simply "ridiculous" (49c). Plato's distinction, which will be further developed by Aristotle and others, remains relevant today: *harmless ugliness is laughable and powerful ugliness abhorrent.* We hate and fear a murderous dictator but find Homer's Thersites simply ridiculous. Later in the dialogue, Socrates observes that no one would rightly have "a vision of intelligence and reason as ugly" (65e). When someone is consumed by bodily pleasures (devoid of measure, appropriateness, or reason), we see "an element of the ridiculous or of extreme ugliness" (65e–66a). The ridiculous and the ugly contradict the maxim that one should know oneself; they are "the opposite of the inscription at Delphi" (48c; cf. *Sophist* 229c–230e). That is, the ugly and ridiculous are forms of inadequacy that cannot be as they should be because those who are ugly and ridiculous do not even understand what should be. Such persons do not grasp the distinction between what is and what ought to be. Our cognition of the ugly, as with our reception of the true and the good, is based on a normative/descriptive discrimination.

Plato offers four original and valid insights about ugliness: first, ugliness and beauty are not binary opposites; one must look deeper; second, humans can be drawn to ugliness against their conscious will, even though beauty ultimately has a superior pull; third, the ugly is what is contrary to what is appropriate to the nature of something; and finally, weak ugliness is ridiculous, whereas strong ugliness is abhorrent. It is unfortunate that theories of ugliness have largely overlooked Plato, given the depth and richness of his arguments.

Plato's student **Aristotle** offers three enduring insights, though two are variations or echoes of what we have already seen in Plato. More oriented to this world than Plato, Aristotle notes that aesthetic renderings of ugliness have value insofar as they help us understand the fullness of reality. Humans delight in acts of mimesis or imitation, including portraying ugly objects, even dead bodies (Aristotle 1448b). This insight remains relevant today: our fascination with understanding reality drives us to incorporate even what repels us. George Santayana succinctly captures this idea: "Truth is thus the excuse which ugliness has for being" (142).

A second thought of Aristotle's also lasts into modernity. Stemming from his focus on tragedy and reception aesthetics, it can be framed as a question: Why do we find artworks featuring evil, suffering, and ugliness beautiful or rewarding? Specifically, Aristotle asks why we long for the emotions of fear and pity, which in real life we wish to avoid. He posits that fear and pity produce the "pleasure" appropriate to tragedy (1453b). Here we encounter for the first time what later becomes known as the paradox of tragedy. Aristotle's comments inaugurate a tradition of reflection that continues into the present. David Hume formulated the puzzle as the seemingly "unaccountable pleasure" we experience in tragedy ("Of Tragedy" 126).[6] Kant extends the paradox to the sublime, noting in his *Critique of Judgment* that the sublime is "a pleasure that is only possible by means of a displeasure" (§27; B 101). Later, Stace and Goodman call a version of this puzzle the paradox of ugliness.

Aristotle's third insight involves the connection between comedy and ugliness (1449a). In the fifth chapter of the *Poetics*, Aristotle notes that the comic mask is "ugly and distorted" but does not cause "pain" (1449a). This essential insight holds true even today: the disgrace or foible at which we laugh cannot be severe enough to cause "pain or harm to others" (1449a).[7] We can find humor in something otherwise horrific if we know that it is not real and in some sense absurd. For instance, in Aristophanes' *The Clouds*, Strepsiades sets Socrates' house on fire, leading to Socrates' cries of desperation. The audience laughs, knowing the real Socrates did not die this way—in fact, he was in the audience. We laugh at the comic representation of cruelty, not the cruelty itself. When serious pain occurs, comic levity is abandoned. The proximity of the comic and the ugly resurfaces in the Hegelians, including the best early Hegelian study of any single artist, Heinrich Theodor Rötscher's compelling book on Aristophanes, which Rötscher dedicated to Hegel. The idea continues into modernity, with Julia Kristeva noting that "laughing is a way of placing or displacing abjection" (Fre. 15; Eng. 8).

Aristotle's three insights—that beautiful representations of ugliness have value, that we are drawn to (tragic) works that awaken emotional ugliness, and that harmless ugliness belongs in comedy—all endure and are frequently invoked.

*

Further theoretical reflections in antiquity are modest. The Roman theorist and poet **Horace** briefly addresses ugliness. He opens *Ars Poetica* (*The Art of Poetry*) (*c.* 19 BC) with a harsh and mocking critique of artistic creations that are full of contradictions: "Suppose a painter chose to put a human head on a horse's neck, or to spread feathers of various colors over the limbs of several different creatures, or to make what in the upper part is a beautiful woman tail off into a hideous (turpiter) fish, could you refrain from laughing when he showed you his efforts?" (ll. 1–5, translation modified). Horace mocks these deformities as akin to a sick person's dreams—fictitious and vain—and advises that artists instead portray what is simple and uniform. For Horace, art should imitate nature. Implicitly, he draws here on the idea that ugliness is what is not fitting or proper for a given subject.

We also find brief comments on ugliness in the late-first-century *De audiendis poetis* (How the Young Should Study Poetry), written by the Greek philosopher and biographer **Plutarch**. Essentially adopting Aristotle's position, Plutarch emphasizes the distinction between the object of portrayal and the quality of the likeness: "when we see a lizard or an ape or the face of Thersites in a picture, we are pleased with it and admire it, not as a beautiful thing, but as a likeness. For by its essential nature the ugly cannot become beautiful; but the imitation, be it concerned with what is base or with what is good, if only it attain to the likeness, is commended" (18a). Plutarch stresses that the portrayal is not "beautiful" but instead "fitting and proper to the character in hand" (18b). If the imitation is too beautiful in a superficial sense, it will not be truthful or consistent. However, if the imitation accurately renders the object or action, we can admire the artistry. "What we commend," Plutarch asserts, "is not the action which is the subject of the imitation, but the art, in case the subject in hand has been properly imitated" (18b).

In short, the excellence of the object and the excellence of the imitation are not the same; one can effectively imitate an ugly object. One must distinguish the object depicted from the work's artistic properties. Plutarch defends the Aristotelian position by arguing that the image is not in fact ugly, for the drawing underscores the object's ugliness and is thus appropriate. Plutarch's main focus, moral in nature, is to guard against the artist or recipient being seduced into thinking that applauding the portrayal also means commending the ugly object or act. This caution may well have led him away from calling such works beautiful, even if they are not in his eyes ugly.

Plotinus, the last great aesthetician of antiquity, who lived in the third century AD, both echoes and develops Plato's ideas. Moreover, he touches on ideas that have resonance well beyond his era. In Plotinus's *Enneads*, compiled and arranged by his student Porphyry, the Greek philosopher equates ugliness with "self-ignorance" and associates "beauty" with "self-knowledge" (V.8.12). His analysis clearly builds on Plato's account of intellectual ugliness. Above all, Plotinus elucidates the characteristics of an "ugliness of the soul" (1.6.5). He comments: "An ugly soul" is "dissolute, unrighteous: teeming with all the lusts; torn by internal discord; beset by the fears of its cowardice and the envies of its pettiness; thinking, in the little thought it has, only of the perishable and the base; perverse in all its impulses; the friend of unclean pleasures; living the life of abandonment to bodily sensation and delighting in its deformity" (1.6.5). The ugly soul is neither as it should be nor as it would want to be. Such a soul relinquishes all autonomy and is instead driven hither and thither by the objects of its desire: "his ugly condition is due to alien matter that has encrusted him" (1.6.5). This link between ugliness and lack of freedom endures over time and is visible above all in Rosenkranz.

Other characteristics Plotinus associates with the ugliness of the soul, including discordant desires, also surface as distinguishing traits in later thinkers, including Friedrich Schlegel and Georg Büchner. The idea that the ugliness of the soul is defined by aberrant desires is rich; today we see it when discontent individuals move from lethargic indifference to reckless hyperstimulation, including the pursuit of bizarre conspiracy theories, often fueled by internet algorithms. A loss of higher values leads to disorientation and outer-directedness. The Platonic-Plotinian idea of an ugliness of the soul resonates also in modern academic thought, as we see in an analytic philosopher such as Colin McGinn, who defends an aesthetic theory of virtue (92–122).

Plotinus notes that ugliness triggers revulsion and disgust (1.6.2). Just as there is an intuitive attraction to beauty, we are naturally disgusted with ugliness; we turn away. Plotinus's insight is the reverse mirror of Plato's theory that the soul who recognizes beauty is drawn in love and desire to experience ever more of beauty and to share it with others, an insight that likewise has resonance in the present (Nehamas, *Only*).

As the founder of Neoplatonism, Plotinus scorns the material world, viewing its shadows as less than beautiful, if not outright base and ugly (5.8.1 and 6.7.33). While intellect and spirit are beautiful, he considers the body, the earth, and the entire realm of matter sordid (1.6.5). Unlike more dialectical thinkers, Plotinus maintains that beauty cannot consist primarily of ugly parts (1.6.1). Nonetheless, as long as the overarching whole is manifest and the ugly elements are not dominant, *some* ugly moments are permissible. Plotinus embraces "intellectual variety" and writes:

> We are like people ignorant of painting who complain that the colors are not beautiful everywhere in the picture: but the Artist has laid on the appropriate tint to every spot [. . .] we are censuring a drama because the persons are not all heroes but include a servant and a rustic and some scurrilous clown; yet take away the low characters and the power of the drama is gone; these are part and parcel of it. (3.2.11)

Though not as affirming of the material world or as dialectical as later thinkers, Plotinus does exhibit some sensitivity to the relationship between parts and the whole.

2

The Absence of Ugliness in Medieval Thought

Ugliness is not a prominent category in medieval aesthetics. Why? Because medieval thinkers focus on beauty, not ugliness.[1] In the medieval worldview, theology and aesthetics are scarcely separate; theology is the study of God and thus also of beauty, as all beauty stems from God. Pseudo-Dionysius, who influenced later medieval thinkers, argues that goodness and beauty are synonymous with God (*Divine Names* 4.7). Since God created the world and deemed it good, ugliness is considered absent from this world and, therefore, unworthy of significant reflection. Still, the lacuna of reflection on ugliness seems somewhat surprising, given the medieval era's profusion of ugly artworks. Depictions of sin, death, and hell—from Giotto's *Last Judgment* (*c.* 1306) (Figure 5) to Hieronymus Bosch's *The Garden of Earthly Delights* (1490–1500)—represent a radical shift in art. No less revolutionary are gruesome variations on the crucifixion, as we see in the *Crucifixus Dolorosus* in St. Maria im Kapitol in Cologne (*c.* 1304) or in Matthias Grünewald's *The Crucifixion* from his *Isenheim Altarpiece* (*c.* 1512–15) (Figure 6).

During most historical periods, a symmetry exists between art and theory. For instance, in the Renaissance, art and theory largely reject ugliness, whereas in modernity, ugly artworks and theoretical reflections on ugliness abound. There is a reason for the medieval anomaly, with many ugly artworks yet little theoretical reflection on ugliness: medieval theologians recognized a divine purpose behind human sinfulness and Christ's sacrifice. Although these may

Figure 5 *Detail of Giotto,* Last Judgment, *c. 1306, Fresco, Cappella Scrovegni, Padua, Italy / Manuel Cohen / Art Resource, NY.*

appear ugly, they serve a significant role in an ultimately beautiful universe. Punishing sin enacts divine justice, and the crucifixion, though ugly, represents Christ absorbing humanity's sins and expressing solidarity with the lowliest of the low. This self-sacrificial act points toward the resurrection. For medieval thinkers, even ugly works are driven by an overarching holistic beauty.

Two aesthetic ideas are widespread in the medieval era. First, beauty is defined by a combination of symmetry or proper proportion and radiance or brightness, an insight already present in Plotinus (I.6.1), but which gains further prominence among medieval thinkers. Second, and more significant for our study, ugliness is viewed as a deficiency—a privation lacking either symmetry or radiance.[2]

Greek praise of the organic and Roman elevation of symmetry influenced the medieval emphasis on ideal proportions. Augustine asserts that "in all the arts it is symmetry that gives pleasure, preserving unity and making the whole beautiful" (*Of True Religion* 30.55, translation modified). Order, as a form of

Figure 6 *Detail of Matthias Grünewald,* The Crucifixion, Isenheim Altarpiece, *c. 1512–15, Oil on panel, Musee d'Unterlinden, Colmar, France / Bridgeman Images.*

proper proportion, enhances beauty. Aquinas echoes this, stating that "beauty consists in due proportion" (*Summa Theologica* I-I.5.4) or, alternatively, "a fitting arrangement of parts" (*Commentary* 1.13.159), which involves more than mere appearances: if a building's roof leaks, then the materials are "*out of place and incongruous,*" and so ultimately ugly (*Summa Theologica* I-I.5.5; cf Augustine, *De natura boni* para. 23).

Medieval thinkers also extolled light, associating it with color, clarity, and brilliance. In chapter 4 of *Divine Names*, Pseudo-Dionysius treats beauty and light as sister categories. Bonaventure's *De reductione artium ad theologiam* (*On the Reduction of the Arts to Theology*) is structured around a metaphysics of light and opens with light. Anyone who has read Dante's *Paradiso* will have recognized the significance of light.[3] At times, we see both ideas—proportion and light (or color)—together, as in Augustine's observation that the beauty of the body is "the harmony of the parts along with a certain pleasing color" (Letter 3) or throughout chapter 4 of Pseudo-Dionysius' *Divine Names*. Aquinas, too, connects these principles, writing that "the beauty of the body consists in a man having his bodily limbs well-proportioned, together with a certain clarity of color" (*Summa Theologica* II-II.145.2).

An obvious weakness in these theories is that the elevation of color cannot be a universal characteristic of beauty, since it covers a feature not present in some arts. Music has no relation to color.[4] As poetic as such definitions are, and as much as they align with a fascinating theology, we cannot draw on them for analytical precision. Also, the universal elevation of clarity, which is related to brightness as a quality of beauty (*Summa Theologica* I.39.8), is problematic, even if it is shared by other traditions, such as the Bamana and Yoruba of West Africa, who elevate clarity and transparency as marks of sincerity (Van Damme 36–7). Ambiguity, which is contrary to clarity, has great aesthetic value: in fact, one of art's primary functions is indirect communication, which can be enhanced by multiple, complex meanings.[5]

The most prominent and distinctive medieval claim about ugliness is that just as evil is a privation of the good, a "privatio boni" (Aquinas, *De divinis nominibus* 4.14.479, 4.22.587), so is ugliness a privation or failure of beauty, a "defectus pulchritudinis" (Aquinas, *De divinis nominibus* 4.5.345). This analogy builds on the idea that "the good and the beautiful is the same" (Pseudo-Dionysius, *Divine Names* 4.7). Augustine speaks of evil and ugliness in terms of "privation" (*Enchiridion* 4.12). Aquinas, too, argues that goodness and beauty are fundamentally identical, differing only logically (*Summa Theologica* I-I.5.4 and I-II.27). For Aquinas, evil is "the absence of the good," that is, the absence of what ought to be but is not (*Summa Theologica* I-I.48.1).

Despite differences in time, sources, and perspectives, three leading early Christian and medieval theologians, **Augustine, Pseudo-Dionysius,** and **Aquinas**, all share this overarching view. In a generous reading, they seem to be saying not that any absence of beauty is ugly, for some things, such as numbers, are neutral, neither beautiful nor ugly. Instead, ugliness involves a privation, lack, or void where one would have expected to see beauty.

This counter-intuitive claim helps Christian thinkers answer the question: how should we understand evil and ugliness in a monotheistic world? In such a world, evil cannot be a divine counter-force to God, and because God, who is by definition good, could not have created evil, what humans perceive as evil must be reinterpreted as a necessary moment within a larger whole, ultimately part of God's subtle and complex plan; as such, it is not truly evil. In the finite realm, what appears as evil is, from a broader perspective, necessary and even good, integral to the cosmic order of divine purpose. Aquinas notes that evil serves a limited purpose even in bringing forth various goods, among them human virtues and divine grace: "God allows evils to happen in order to bring forth a greater good" (*Summa Theologica* III.1.3, translation modified). Thus, evil "belongs to the perfection of the universe [. . .] by reason of some good joined to it" (*Summa Theologica* I-I.48.1).

This attempt to grasp evil in the light of the divine has its parallel in the concept of ugliness. In God's world, everything is arranged in a hierarchy, with varying degrees of goodness and beauty depending on their proximity to the divine. As Aquinas observes, "all things are arranged according to their degrees of beauty and excellence, and the nearer they are to God, the more beautiful and better they are" (*Three Greatest Prayers* 45, translation modified). Consequently, we can speak of a relative lack of goodness and beauty. Augustine argues that insofar as human beings are more beautiful than apes, apes are comparatively ugly: "In all these things those that are small are, in comparison with greater ones, called by contrary names. In that way, because there is greater beauty in the form of a human being, the beauty of an ape is said to be deformed in comparison with it" (*Nature of the Good* 14, translation modified; cf. *Confessions* 13.20.28).[6] For Augustine contraries are essential to the beauty of the universe (*City of God* 11.18 and 16.8). He contends that God "knows how to weave together the beauty of the whole in the similarity and diversity of its parts. But anyone who is unable to see the whole is offended at what appears to be the deformity of a part, for the person does not know how it fits in or how it is connected with the whole" (*City of God* 16.8; cf. 12.4).

We recognize a twofold conception: first, ugliness is simply a privation of beauty; and second, in the long run nothing is ultimately ugly insofar as it participates in the greater beauty of the universe. In *De vera religione* (*On True Religion*) (*c.* 391), Augustine argues that to appreciate "the beauty of the whole universe," we must look beyond individual parts: "That which we abhor in any part of it gives us the greatest satisfaction when we consider the universe as a whole" (40.76, translation modified). The same principle applies to art: when we "pay exclusive attention to the part, our judgment is itself base. The color black in a picture may very well be beautiful if you take the picture as a whole" (40.76, translation modified). According to Augustine, even seemingly ugly animals—mice, frogs, flies, and worms—are beautiful as part of God's creation (*On Genesis* 1.16.26). The hierarchy and order of creatures, each with varying degrees of value and beauty, ensure the variety and perfection of the whole (*On Free Choice of the Will* 3.9). Contrary to a Platonic vision, this idea affirms all creation and all matter. When Leibniz later connects the best of all possible worlds to principles of plenitude and efficiency, he could draw on these earlier Christian sources. In the *City of God*, Augustine ties his claims to scripture ("God saw everything that He had made, and indeed, it was very good," Gen. 1.31; cf. Gen. 1.25). Augustine supports the organic idea that parts contribute to the whole: "For, just like a painting, when it has dark colors in their proper places, so the entire universe—if anyone could see it whole—is beautiful even when it has sinners, despite the fact that, when sinners are considered in themselves, their ugliness is repulsive" (*City of God* 11.23; cf. 14.11). Parts gain their meaning within the whole, and being and goodness are ultimately one.

In his early dialogue *De Ordine* (On Order), the first book after his conversion, Augustine debates the roles that moral and intellectual ugliness play in the universe. Trygetius, who speaks infrequently but insightfully, suggests that what seems disorderly, ugly, or unappealing on its own still makes sense within the larger whole (2.4.11-13). To the young Licentius, the beauty of the universe is enriched by the clash of contraries (1.18; cf. 2.2). Augustine repeatedly suggests that an essential task in seeking truth is to develop the knowledge that enables one to grasp the role of seeming disorder within the larger whole in which it plays an appropriate part (2.5.17, 2.7.24, and esp. 2.17.46 and 2.19.51). Although the dialogue refers to evil as nothing or a non-entity (2.7.23), the reader gains the impression that evil is not nothing but an active force, a seeming disorder, that has a certain role to play, a role that we must work hard to discern and that ultimately we are capable of reinterpreting as part of the larger, ordered whole and thus not quite evil, a view similar to Stoic thought, as in Seneca's *De providentia* (On Providence).

When the twelfth-century French logician Peter Abelard makes his case for this same idea, he cites Augustine as his authority. All things flow from God, who is good. God wanted plenitude and diversity as well as order; thus all that exists is fitting and appropriate. Evil is not possible unless it is good that there be evil, that is, unless evil has a part to play in a greater good. In making his case, Abelard, too, turns to art: "For as a picture is often more beautiful and worthy of commendation if some colors in themselves ugly are included in it, than it would be if it were uniform and of a single color, so from an admixture of evils the universe is rendered more beautiful and worthy of commendation" (Abelard 56; Arthur Lovejoy's translation at 72).

Despite the medieval Christian language of privation, these thinkers come close to recognizing a dialectical relation of the ugly and beautiful: by playing an appropriately subordinate role, ugliness contributes to the beauty of the larger whole. A part qua part can be seen as deficient, but when this deficiency is viewed from the perspective of the whole, our evaluation is transformed, and the part becomes beautiful. Consider medieval architecture: monstrous gargoyles enhance a cathedral's beauty. These ugly constructs are not only apotropaic, designed to ward off evil; they also affirm that moral and physical ugliness are part of God's creation, part of a harmonious whole. By haunting us and inviting us to enter the security and sanctity of the church, they fit into a positive narrative. Victor Hugo continues this older paradigm in *Notre-Dame de Paris* (1831), where the hideous hunchback Quasimodo, who dwells among such monsters and demons (4.3), rings the bells that call the faithful to church. The ugly figure contributes to the larger harmony.[7]

In his sermons, especially his ninth homily on the First Epistle of John (407), and his twenty-seventh sermon, delivered a decade later, Augustine connects this conceptual argument with the narrative of Christ. Christ became abject and deformed to demonstrate his love for humanity, show solidarity with the lowliest, and offer a path from lowliness to beauty. In the ninth homily, Augustine introduces the idea of Christ's ugliness by suggesting that God can be both beautiful and ugly. God embodies beauty and splendor. In contrast, our wickedness renders us loathsome and "ugly" (9.9). Yet, because Christ assumed human form, he partook of our loathsomeness:

> But, because he took on flesh, he took on as it were your loathsomeness—that is, your mortality—in order to accommodate himself to you and to be suited to you and to arouse you to love beauty inwardly. How, then, do we

> find that Jesus is loathsome and ugly, as we have found that he is beautiful and *splendid in form beyond the sons of men*? How do we find that he is also ugly? Ask Isaiah. *And we saw him, and he had neither splendor nor comeliness* (Is 53:2). (9.9)

Augustine cites Philippians 2:6 and argues that God sacrificed himself to make us beautiful. Christ "*had neither splendor nor comeliness* so that he might give you splendor and comeliness" (9.9). Our soul is loathsome through wickedness, but "by loving God, it is made beautiful" (9.9). Similarly, in his *Homilies on the Gospel of John*, Augustine underscores this theme: Christ "loved even the ugly that he might make them beautiful" (10.13).

In his twenty-seventh sermon, which begins with human sinfulness, Augustine emphasizes Christ's ugliness: "For the sake of your faith Christ became deformed" (Sermon 27.6). Augustine references the book of Isaiah, stating,

> *And we saw him, and he did not have any sightliness or comeliness, but his features were abject* [. . .] *contemptible and deformed his bearing, a man beset with injuries and familiar with enduring infirmities* (Is 53:2-3). Christ's deformity is what gives form to you (deformitas Christi te forma). If he had been unwilling to be deformed, you would never have got back the form you lost. So he hung on the cross, deformed; but his deformity was our beauty (pendebat ergo in cruce deformis, sed deformitas illius pulchritudo nostra erat). (Sermon 27.6)

For Augustine, the deformity of Christ is manifest in his crucifixion—and this ugliness is to be embraced: "Let us not be ashamed of this deformity of Christ" (Sermon 27.6). Augustine is able to draw here not only on biblical sources but also on the earlier Patristic tradition. For example, in section 124 of his *Commentary on Matthew*, Origen, in analyzing Matt. 27:25, describes the crucifixion as "the ugliest death of the cross" (ad mortem turpissimam crucis) (259). The Latin *turpissimus* is the superlative of *turpis* (ugly); it means here ugliest or most vile.[8] Augustine argues that Christ cast away his pure beauty to establish a loving connection with us and our deformed souls. He abandoned his pure existence in the realm of the ideas and forms (forma) and became ugly (deformis)—for us. Ultimately, however, Christ, who appears ugly to us, is alone truly beautiful (Sermon 138.6; Exposition of the Psalms 127.8).

Augustine thinks dialectically: Christ became ugly and shed his blood for those who are ugly in order to make them beautiful (Sermon 62.8). For Augustine, Christ is both deformed and beautiful, though his persecutors saw only the ugliness. Here in the Christian narrative, just as in metaphysics, the Christian grasps ugliness in its full unfolding as part of a larger whole. This is the most significant insight into ugliness that we can take from medieval aesthetics. It builds on Plato's idea that there is a dialectic of beauty and ugliness, but medieval thinkers add a distinctly temporal dimension, framed by Christ's death and resurrection. The idea is vividly illustrated in portrayals of the crucified Christ as truly ugly, such as Grünewald's Crucifixion in his *Isenheim Altarpiece* (Illustration 3). Only a temporal art or a sequence of spatial images can do justice to this Christian narrative, where ugliness is but one moment in a larger narrative. The *Resurrection* is after all part of the same altarpiece.

In reflecting on human weakness and sinfulness, Augustine builds on Plato's recognition that humans are vulnerable to idle curiosity. In Book 10 of the *Confessions,* Augustine elucidates three catalysts for temptations: senses, love of praise, and curiosity. He connects curiosity with vain knowledge and employs the disparaging term "sacrilegious curiosity" (sacrilega curiositate) (3.3.5; cf. 6.8.13, 10.3.3, 13.21.30). Drawing on 1 John 2.16, Augustine associates the "lust of the eyes" (10.30.41; 10.35.54), that is, idle inquisitiveness, with the self-indulgence of bodily appetites. He draws this comparison in other works as well, including *Of True Religion* (38.70). Augustine argues that curiosity misdirects the mind, just as lust leads the body astray, both interfering with prayer and the holy life. He echoes Plato's observation on the morbid attraction to mangled corpses, which serves no purpose and distracts us from God. Augustine asks, where is the divinity in that urge? "What sensual pleasure is to be had in viewing a mangled corpse which sickens you? Yet if there is one lying anywhere, people congregate in order to experience ashen-faced horror" (*Confessions* 10.35.55). Augustine criticizes the exhibition of monstrous sights to satisfy unhealthy curiosity, calling it a "morbid craving" (*Confessions* 10.35.55). He also condemns idle stories, games, and the fascination with insects and wild animals, scolding contemporaries for demanding signs and wonders from God "simply because they crave experience" (*Confessions* 10.35.55). These trivial temptations distract from prayer.[9] In making his case, Augustine remains within a partially Platonic universe. Although for the Christian Augustine, the forms are not the only reality, too much attention to the material world—to what is temporal and mutable, as with alluring music during Mass—can distract worshipers from God; it is thus deformed and sinful (*Confessions* 10.33.50). By turning our gaze to God, Augustine argues, we move from false allure to true beauty (*The Trinity* 15.8.14). Although ugliness unfolding into beauty is at the center of his thinking on Christ, Augustine is uneasy with the distractions of both ugly temptations and temporal beauty.

In a brief but significant reflection in his *Apologia ad Guillelmum Abbatem* (Justification to Abbot William) of 1125, the Cistercian monk **Bernard of Clairvaux** likewise addresses the connections between ugliness and curiosity. He sees curiosity, which can arise from ugly but fascinating art, as the enemy of piety. For Bernard, who predates Aquinas, ugliness can be presented as irresistibly fascinating, but it is inappropriate, particularly in a monastic context. He thus follows Augustine's discomfort with the material world. Bernard opens his reflections on art and beauty with a cautionary note: art can hinder piety because people often "admire the beautiful more than they venerate the sacred" (12.28). Moreover, the investment in religious art and architecture is both extravagant and mad; it comes at the expense of the needs of the poor:

> O vanity of vanities, but no more vain than insane! (O vanitas vanitatum, sed non vanior quam insanior!) The Church is radiant in its walls and destitute in its poor. It dresses its stones in gold and abandons its children naked. It serves the eyes of the rich at the expense of the poor. The curious find what delights them; those in need find nothing to sustain them. (12.28, translation modified)

Bernard then addresses gargoyles, criticizing the deformed figures in monastic churches and cloisters: "What are the filthy apes doing there? The fierce lions? The monstrous centaurs? The creatures, part man and part beast (semihomines)? The striped tigers? The fighting soldiers? The hunters blowing horns? You may see many bodies under one head, and conversely many heads on one body" (12.29). After denouncing the expense, Bernard lingers on the works themselves, condemning the images as non-spiritual, internally contradictory, violent, and secular. Turning to their reception, he criticizes the deformed figures for arousing curiosity. The excesses of art distract the monks from spiritual contemplation, from reading and meditation: "everywhere so plentiful and astonishing a variety of contradictory forms is seen that one would rather read in the marble than in books, and spend the whole day wondering at every single one of them than in meditating on the law of God" (12.29). Although Bernard derides the works themselves, his primary evaluation is tied to reception. As with Augustine, he assesses artistic works based on the resulting gain or loss of piety. And yet Bernard criticizes the images with language that makes them sound appealing. The combination of delight and disgust is manifest in Bernard's paradoxical expression, which introduces his list of objectionable content, beginning with the apes: "what is that ridiculous monstrosity doing, an amazing kind of deformed beauty and yet a beautiful deformity (deformis formositas ac formosa deformitas)" (12.29). The parts are in tension with one another, thus monstrous and deformed, ugly, but the artist's skill is nonetheless evident and lends a certain beauty to the ugliness. Here from the vantage point of reception aesthetics, we see a fascinating set of paradoxes. Bernard criticizes the grotesques as hindrances to spirituality, yet he is undeniably captivated by them.

Also, Aristotle's insight into the beautiful portrayal of ugliness remains relevant for medieval thinkers. Aquinas acknowledges that one can create a beautiful image of an ugly object (*Summa Theologica* I Q39.8). His Franciscan contemporary **Bonaventure** develops the idea further in the first volume of his *Commentary on the Sentences of Lombard.* Bonaventure distinguishes between an image and the object it represents: "An image is said to be beautiful when it represents its object well" (Lib. I, d. 31, p. II, a.1, q. 3). Thus, there can be a "beautiful image of a devil when the image represents well the foulness (foeditatem) of the devil, and then the image itself is foul" (Lib. I, d. 31, p. II, a.1, q. 3, translation modified). Bonaventure praises the extent to which the image embodies the ugliness of the depicted object. The very success of the representation renders the abhorrent image paradoxically beautiful.

A contemporary of Bonaventure and Aquinas, **Ulrich of Strasbourg** was a German Dominican theologian and scholastic philosopher who for four years studied alongside Thomas in Cologne. Both were close to their teacher Albertus Magnus. Thomas had followed Albert from Paris to Cologne, and Ulrich maintained an extensive correspondence with Albert after moving to Strasbourg, where he lectured on theology. Ulrich is known for his *De summo bono* (*On the Supreme Good*), initially conceived as a series of eight books. He managed to write six between 1262 and 1272, but his duties as provincial of the German province prevented him from completing the work. The significance of *De summo bono* is evident from the numerous manuscripts and contemporary citations (Grabmann, *Studien* 318–20, 621–7). Strongly influenced by the Neoplatonist Pseudo-Dionysius, whom he quotes frequently, Ulrich writes in a looser, more poetic style than Thomas.

The second book of Ulrich's *De summo bono* is devoted to God's essence. The third tractate of this second book deals with divine goodness, and the fourth chapter therein addresses beauty. As with Thomas, who viewed beauty and goodness as the same in subject (subiecto) but different in notion (ratione), Ulrich analyzes beauty in the context of goodness. *De pulchro* (*On Beauty*) is arguably the most thorough account of beauty (and ugliness) in the High Middle Ages. It continues many of the major ideas we have already seen. For example, as with Augustine, it acknowledges ugliness as playing an appropriate role within a larger order, and as with Pseudo-Dionysius and Bonaventure, it celebrates light. Ulrich's account was not published until 1926 (Grabmann, *Des Ulrich Engelberti von Strassburg*), but its significance is further evident in its having been translated into English within a decade.

Ugliness appears early in the chapter's first sentences, where Ulrich argues that a deficiency in form is ugly, yet "the ugly (turpe) desires what is good and beautiful" (Lat. 54; Eng. 36).[10] Because beauty emerges from divine light, the more an object is removed from light, the more it becomes "hideous and formless" (Lat. 55; Eng. 38-9). The beauty in this world mirrors the beauty of the divine without, of course, reaching that level. Ulrich notes that appearances may deceive: "many sensually delightful things" are "ugly (turpia)," for they lack sufficient goodness (Lat. 56; Eng. 39). We are reminded here of Bernard's earlier commentary. Ulrich provides a detailed account of proportion, noting that ugliness arises when proportions are not harmonious. He states, "whatever lacks any member is not beautiful, but is defective and a deformity, and the more so the nobler is that part as to which there is privation, so that the want of any facial organ is a greater deformity than the want of a hand or finger" (Lat. 57; Eng. 41). Also, larger heads with smaller bodies or vice versa show poor formal proportion: "the harmony of the parts as measured amongst themselves" is missing, rendering the body ugly (Lat. 57; Eng. 40). In contrast, symmetry is associated with beauty.

Ulrich adds that nothing in the realm of being is completely devoid of beauty. Thus, the "ugly" (turpe) is in truth simply "imperfectly beautiful" (Lat. 58; Eng. 43). This can involve either absolute imperfection (as when something is corrupt and foul) or relative imperfection (as when something is lacking in comparison with a more perfect being). Ulrich distinguishes ugliness into two further categories: a "deforming defect," which is an aesthetic matter, and a "voluntary and culpable defect," which involves an ethical transgression (Lat. 58; Eng. 43). The further a beautiful object is from divine beauty and the closer it is to nothingness, the uglier it is. Beauty itself, that is, divine beauty, cannot be ugly; indeed, in comparison with divine beauty, even the most beautiful created being is ugly.

In the end, ugliness is incompatible with the beauty of the universe, which Ulrich discusses at the end of his chapter. What appears ugly, even a physical monstrosity, is at least imperfectly beautiful, and the ugliness of moral evil is, when being punished, no longer ugly. Ugliness elevates its opposite, beauty, by contrast: "what is diminished in one part is increased in another, either intensively when goods are seen to be the more beautiful when contrasted with their opposite evils, or extensively in that the corruption of one thing is the generation of another and the deformity of guilt is repaired by the beauty of justice in the penalty" (Lat. 62-63; Eng. 47). According to Ulrich, the tyrant's injustice gives rise to the martyr, and the punishment of the damned accentuates by contrast the joy of the holy.

One reason why medieval aesthetics tends to be viewed more historically than systematically is that few signature ideas endure into modernity. The simple link between symmetry and beauty does not last, nor does the concept of ugliness as a privation. The related idea that being and goodness are one disappears almost entirely. And the concept that ugly parts find their fulfillment in a beautiful whole is also challenged by later thinkers.

However, if we consider modest variations on these ideas, we can identify some continuing threads that have been underplayed in historical accounts of theories of ugliness. The link between symmetry and beauty, if we understand it in a more complex and dialectical way, can be said to resurface in modernity: think of the meta-symmetry we see in Krzysztof Penderecki's *Threnody* between dissonant music and horrific subject matter. Although the concept of privation as such does not survive, it is intertwined with a more compelling idea: the apparent ugliness of a part can be both accepted and overcome in a larger whole. The dialectic negates the part, which is insufficient and often ugly, but it also preserves the part and lifts it up within a larger whole. Even this more expansive version of the equation of beauty and goodness and of ugly part and beautiful whole will be strongly challenged in modernity. Still, the one medieval idea that endures the longest is indeed this claim that when seen from the perspective of the whole, an ugly part can become beautiful.

3

Maggi, Rocco, and the Early Modern Era

In the Italian Renaissance, as in the ancient and medieval worlds, comments on ugliness were uncommon. **Leon Battista Alberti**, the author of *De Pictura* (*On Painting*) (1450), an important treatise on the theory and practice of painting, draws on the tradition of the beautiful and the ugly as comparative categories. He cites Virgil, noting that Euryalas, the most beautiful man, is ugly compared to Ganymede. Alberti quotes Plutarch on Agesilaus the Lacedaemonian, who, aware of his ugliness, refused to allow any likenesses for posterity. Alberti recommends an ancient practice, implicit in Aristotle (1454b), where if the subject of a painting has a physical defect, the painter should slightly modify or embellish the trait to improve on reality while still preserving the likeness (18, 25, 40). For Alberti, there is no question that the painter should choose to portray what is "most beautiful and worthy" (56). The two approaches he mentions—either idealizing or avoiding ugliness—align well with the classical and idealizing tendencies of the Italian Renaissance (Wölfflin). However, these ideas are largely left behind as we move toward modernity, even if we do observe occasional anomalies. Franz Marc, for example, avoids ugliness by turning to abstraction (Marc 141), an idea we revisit in Chapter 10.

The Aristotelian link between comedy and ugliness resurfaces during the Renaissance. Most discussions of ugliness appear in publications on comedy. Beginning in 1536 and continuing through the end of the century, a series of thinkers translated Aristotle into Latin and Italian. In Latin commentaries, they elaborated on the authoritative Aristotelian concept, using Plautus and Terence as models. According to Francesco Robortello, a Renaissance humanist who prepared the first critical edition of Aristotle's *Poetics*, with a Latin translation and commentary (1548), we laugh not at what is clearly evil or obscene, but at what is only slightly disgraceful or slightly ugly (subturpiculum) (26). Aristotle's argument that comic ugliness cannot involve pain is often cited.[1] Also common is a continuation of the tradition that speaks of an ugliness of the soul, which can arise from either stupidity or wickedness: "the proper objects for Comedy to imitate are stupid or ugly persons who are neither harmed nor pained by their stupidity or ugliness" (Castelvetro 88).

An exception to the Renaissance neglect of ugliness was the Italian philosopher and humanist **Vincenzo Maggi**. In 1550, Maggi and Bartolomeo Lombardi translated Aristotle's *Poetics* into Italian. Appended to the published translation was Maggi's Latin treatise *De Ridiculis* (*On the Ridiculous*) (1550), in which ugliness features prominently. Maggi draws on and extends not only Aristotle but also Plato and Cicero. For Maggi, the ridiculous is not simply equivalent to painless ugliness. For something to be ridiculous, it must also be novel and laughable. Aristotle and others in his wake derive the ridiculous from a kind of ugliness or baseness (turpitudo) that is not painful (Lat. 93; Eng. 64). Maggi argues that this is too vague. The ridiculous must also include an element of wonder or surprise (admiratio) (Lat. 98; Eng. 69). Maggi writes: "No ridiculous saying is so witty or clever that, when it is heard frequently, it does not beget more aversion than delight" (Lat. 98; Eng. 69). According to Maggi, ugliness can continue, but we do not laugh once we become accustomed to it, after the novelty of either the content or the mode of expression has passed. For example, we do not laugh at the same joke repeatedly, especially if it is told by the same person in the selfsame way. Laughter depends on novelty or wonder. When his focus is the risible, not the ridiculous, Maggi's comments are compelling. He adds to our understanding of comedy and laughter. However, his specific argument that the ridiculous is not ridiculous unless novelty is included is less convincing. Anything that is ugly and weak is, in fact, ridiculous. Indeed, to tell the same joke again and again is not funny, but it is certainly ridiculous. Maggi enriches our understanding of laughter and in this way takes us beyond Aristotle, but he does not erase Plato's argument that weak ugliness is ridiculous.

Seeking to fill yet another gap in Aristotle, Maggi explicates various kinds of ugliness: ugliness of the body, as with a distorted face; ugliness of the mind, as with ignorance; and ugliness of circumstances, which arises from external origins, such as being born a pauper.[2] This sensible threefold distinction follows a pattern of objectivity, subjectivity, and intersubjectivity, even if the first two are more focused on the object itself, with the third having more to do with causality.

Maggi extends his distinctions by proposing for each of the three modes three levels of reality: real, feigned, or accidental (Lat. 96; Eng. 66-67). The ugliness of the body, for instance, can be real, as with a hunchback; pretended, as when someone imitates a limp to mock another; or accidental, as when someone falls but is not thereby hurt. Similarly, both the ugliness of the soul and the ugliness of external origins can be true, feigned, or accidental. Maggi also delves deeper in other ways. He is fascinated by the ugliness of the mind that Plato discussed in the *Sophist* (Lat. 96-97; Eng. 67-68). Maggi introduces what he calls the ignorance of negation, which occurs when someone fails to grasp something. This can involve things hidden in nature, which only experts know, such that our ignorant pronouncements are perceived as ridiculous only by those in the know. Or our ignorance can be of commonly known things, which seem evident to everyone but one person, such as a rich old man who enjoys the affections of a young woman and assumes she adores him because of his qualities, not his money—a common subject of contemporary paintings, as in Quentin Matsys's *Ill-Matched Pair* (*c.* 1525) or several such works by Lucas Cranach, including *The Ill-Matched Couple* (1522), *The Unequal Couple (Old Man in Love)* (*c.* 1530), and *The Ill-Matched Lovers* (1531) (Figure 7). Maggi contrasts the ignorance of negation (which one can subsume under intellectual ugliness) with what he calls deformed disposition, which involves unappealing attitudes, such as arrogance, cowardice, or dishonesty. Here we move into emotional and moral ugliness, which Maggi appropriately links with the mind.

However, the slipperiness of Maggi's categories is evident: the rich old man may misjudge reality precisely because of his arrogance. That is, his error may

Figure 7 *Lucas Cranach (the Elder),* The Ill-Matched Lovers, *1522, Oil on panel, Museum of Fine Arts (Szepmuveszeti) Budapest, Hungary / Bridgeman Images.*

derive as much from a deformed disposition as from an ignorance of negation. Intellectual and emotional ugliness are often interwoven, as the latter easily surfaces when one does not know oneself. Moreover, Maggi's recurring distinctions among real, feigned, and accidental operate on different levels. Real (or one might say genuine) and feigned are opposed to one another and mutually exclusive, but real and accidental are not. To be consistent, Maggi would need two sets of contrasts: (1) real (either intended or accidental) versus feigned and (2) intentional (either genuine or feigned) versus accidental.

Maggi's distinctions, while partly intriguing and partly inadequate, offer an interesting attempt to categorize types of ugliness. Equally engaging is his claim that the ridiculous is more than just painless ugliness; by adding the element of surprise, Maggi enriches our understanding of the comic. Although Maggi is the first to systematize kinds of ugliness, he does not discuss forms of ugliness in art, and his categories sometimes lack analytic precision.

No Renaissance treatise is devoted to ugliness. Given the artistic works of the Italian Renaissance, which rarely immerse themselves in ugliness, the theoretical lacuna is not surprising. References beyond the comic and ridiculous tend to be occasional and incidental. Julius Caesar Scaliger, whose voluminous work on aesthetics was published posthumously in 1561 and who openly disagrees with Aristotle on selected points, including the relative importance of plot and character in tragedy, notes that ugliness is permissible in artworks as long as it serves an instructive purpose (147). As elsewhere during this era, we see the subordination of ugliness to other categories.

A generation later, the French Renaissance philosopher Michel de Montaigne delimits ugliness in his essay *D'un enfant monstrueux* (*On a Monster-Child*) (1578–80). He argues that what seems aberrant to us is harmonious with nature and thus part of God's plan: "what we call monsters are not so for God who sees the infinite number of forms which he has included in the immensity of his creation" (808). Montaigne bridges the lingering Christian belief that all of God's creation is good with the emerging Enlightenment ideal that we should be tolerant toward those who are other or different. This fascinating combination has more or less disappeared in modernity. Tolerance of diversity continues to be a rallying cry, but few recognize that the appeal to tolerance aligns with the Christian idea that everything that exists has dignity and is ultimately good. Instead, tolerance is often equated with the shedding of a religious—and necessarily exclusive—frame of reference, and many religious persons today are the opposite of rational and tolerant.[3]

Yet, surprisingly, given aberrant forms of Christianity in contemporary America, including those who elevate hate over love, both the Protestant and Catholic traditions have brought forward seminal thinkers who understood how to bridge religious engagement and openness. Lessing, a German Protestant, wrote the world's most compelling play on religious tolerance, *Nathan the Wise* (1799). A generation later, Friedrich Schleiermacher, the greatest Protestant theologian between Luther and Kierkegaard, called Christianity "the religion of religions" (Ger. 172; Eng. 123) but only insofar as Christianity privileges love and so reaches out to other religious traditions. Toward the end of the fifth and final address of *Über die Religion: Reden an die Gebildeten unter ihren Verächtern* (*On Religion: Speeches to Its Cultured Despisers*) (1799), Schleiermacher writes: "just as nothing is more irreligious than to demand uniformity in humanity generally, so nothing is more unChristian than to seek uniformity in religion" (Ger. 172; Eng. 123).

Closer to our time, Pope Francis extolled as a favorite work Friedrich Hölderlin's poem about his grandmother, which describes Christ in inclusive terms: "None of the living was excluded from his soul" (Keines der Lebenden war aus seiner Seele geschlossen) (1:214).[4] Disability studies shares much with an aesthetics of ugliness that recognizes the ugliness of Christ and refuses to strip the designation "beautiful" from any human being. The politics of tolerance shares more with this moral and aesthetic tradition than most contemporary theorists recognize.

The only other early modern thinker besides Maggi to have reflected deeply and imaginatively on ugliness was the Italian priest and philosopher **Antonio Rocco**, born six years before Montaigne's death. Rocco, who came onto the scene after the Renaissance had ended, is best known for *Alcibiades, the Schoolboy*, a dialogue written in 1630 and published anonymously in 1652. This work presents a mix of serious and mocking philosophical arguments that defend homoerotic love and seduction. In 1635 Rocco wrote a satirical essay *Della bruttezza* (*On Ugliness*), which is less known and has never been translated into English.[5] The Italian opens his early modern work by lamenting that everyone praises beauty and no one ugliness. He, in contrast, will break free of the crowd and take on the important task of writing "an ugly address in praise of ugliness" (46). His witty and playful essay takes the reader through four kinds of ugliness, each of which is the opposite of beauty or goodness: deformity, the opposite of grace; ignorance, the opposite of knowledge; vice, the opposite of virtue; and indecorum, the opposite of decency. The essay then extols the greatness of each type of ugliness. Rocco seeks to prove that in each case the ugly is superior to the beautiful or the good.

The first two concepts, deformity and ignorance, cover physical and intellectual ugliness respectively. Beautiful women, according to Rocco, are useless, as they are too difficult to win over. Moreover, they are more trouble than they are worth, as they arouse jealousy and cause havoc, as with Helen of Troy. In one of several misogynistic gestures, Rocco suggests that ugly women, in contrast, give themselves freely. The unknowingness of the Garden of Eden was superior to the knowledge that led to expulsion, and the Bible rightly mocks worldly wisdom as foolishness. When we are oblivious to problems, we can at least enjoy some level of contentment. And others' knowledge, for example, concerning secrets in one's own house, is hardly appealing.

The third and the fourth modes, vice and indecorum, capture aspects of moral ugliness. Little that we find appealing, Rocco suggests, could exist without wickedness: "Religion itself, including the most holy sacraments, rests unshakeably on vices" (58). He continues: "Religion is supposed to lead to the human being becoming pious, devoted, and good, for which he must first have been impious, blasphemous, and villainous" (59). One cannot have the one without the other. Sin serves an essential purpose. Without sinners the incarnation would make no sense. Also, government, including its laws and princes, exists only insofar as there are criminals and enemies who must be overcome. Venice itself, where Rocco worked as a teacher of philosophy, "owes its greatness to vice" (58). The city would be a non-entity if it had nothing and no one to combat. When it comes to decency, Rocco argues that calling someone out is far superior to fawning. The former can act as bitter medicine; the latter simply puffs someone up with emptiness.

Rocco concludes his essay by turning to the ugliness of nature, "putrefaction, deaths, famine, poverty, etc." (60). In Rocco's eyes, poverty is welcome. If we were all rich, he asks, "who would cultivate the fields and who would build the houses" (61)? Contrary to popular belief, death itself is not at all ugly, for it frees us from so much misery. Whenever one thing passes away, another takes its place—and that is good for the cycle of life. If we were immortal, we would all be as crowded together as "plants in the forest" (62), and we would be reduced to eating roots in the ground and then presumably one another: "And here you are," he says, returning to the promise of an ugly speech, "devoured and alive, immortal and carved up into mouthfuls" (62).

Rocco cannot make his argument against the good without engaging in partial truths and sophistries and without presupposing the good: for example, he tries to argue that vice is *better* than goodness. The argument cancels itself. But in truth, Rocco is engaging in rhetorical play, not serious argumentation, which underscores how interwoven ugliness and experimentation are. To defend the ugly is to be free of restraints. Celebrating ugliness is enjoyable and entertaining, as it gives one the license to argue absurdities. The essay is partly a rhetorical exercise in proving the opposite of what is valid. Partly, it is an effort to suggest that simplistic abstractions and evaluations overlook the world's complexity. With the latter suggestion, the satirist Rocco inadvertently buttresses the medieval argument that there is no evil in the world, for all that appears evil or ugly actually plays a positive role in the universe as a whole.

*

A recurring theme also in the early modern era is that the ugly can be explored in the arts insofar as it is rendered beautiful.[6] This idea, part of the continuing reception of Aristotle, arises more often as a brief insight than a developed theory. It tends to have two moments: the attraction of ugly content and the capacity of art to render such content beautiful. In the early modern era, the first moment surfaces in Martin Opitz, who writes in his *Buch von der deutschen Poeterei* (*Book of German Poetry*) (1624):

> However, human beings not only enjoy looking at things that are in themselves a source of delight: beautiful meadows, mountains, fields, rivers, graceful women, and the like. People also enjoy listening to stories about things they do not desire to see: how Hercules murders his children, how Dido takes her own life, how towns and cities are set on fire, how the plague ravages entire countries, and other such things that can be found in the works of poets" (12).

In the eighteenth century, Moses Mendelssohn emphasizes the artistic transformation of ugliness: everything, even the most unpleasant, can be rendered beautiful through skillful depiction, where the parts and whole are organically interwoven (1:175-76). In France, the idea that the ugly is legitimate if beautifully depicted surfaces in Nicolas Boileau-Despréaux's didactic treatise *L'Art poétique* (*The Art of Poetry*) (1674), Charles Batteux's influential *Les beaux-arts réduits à un même principe* (*The Fine Arts Reduced to a Single Principle*) (1746), and Denis Diderot's *Lettre sur les sourds et muets* (*Letter on the Deaf and Dumb*) (1751). For instance, Boileau-Despréaux opens Canto 3 of his work by defending Greek tragedy: "There is no serpent, or hateful monster, who, by imitating art, may not please the eye."

The recurring medieval claim that the truth of the part lies in the whole continues as Christianity moves further into the early modern era. **Gottfried Wilhelm Leibniz**, who championed the great chain of being and conceived the idea of the best of all possible worlds, draws a compelling comparison between the universe and a painting. In *De rerum originatione radicali* (*On the Ultimate Origination of Things*) (1697), Leibniz argues that if we cover most of a beautiful painting and look only at a single, isolated part, that singularity may seem arbitrary and unappealing, perhaps even ugly. But when we view the entire painting, we realize that the part has a much different meaning in the work as a whole. So it is with the universe: what in life appears to be only unfortunate or dissonant may in fact be a necessary element of a much larger, ultimately harmonious whole, of which we can see only fragments (*Philosophical Essays* 153–4). For Leibniz, uniformity does not bring pleasure. Instead, we should recognize that a part "can be disordered without detracting from the harmony of the whole" (*Philosophical Essays* 154). Although the idea of a harmonious whole will be vociferously challenged in modernity, it is possible to separate out two distinct points: we can understand evil as more than simply a privation, yet still argue that evil and its parallel, ugliness, are necessary. The notion that evil is a necessary part of the universe is perfectly compatible with the idea that we have a moral obligation to combat any and all particular evils. From the perspective of the German polymath Leibniz, evil and ugliness are a function of finitude, which is necessary for the plenitude of creation.

Alexander Gottlieb Baumgarten, who hovers between early modern and early Enlightenment, coined the term "aesthetics." The son of a pietist minister, Baumgarten studied in Halle and was influenced above all by

Leibniz and Christian Wolff. Baumgarten, in turn, was prominent enough that Kant repeatedly lectured on his *Metaphysica* (1739). In his unfinished but still substantial *Aesthetica* (1750–8), which set the stage for aesthetics as a discipline, Baumgarten offers a series of mixed reflections on ugliness. The German thinker follows Aristotle in noting that ugliness can be portrayed beautifully (§18; §676). Further, for a truly great artist or orator, depraved actions can serve as fitting material, provided that other parts of the work, including formal elements, are grand, and that the thoughtful recipient is moved to recognize the depravity (§204). Baumgarten gives as examples Cicero's *Catilinarian Orations* (63 BC) and Sallust's *War of Catiline* (43–40 BC).

Baumgarten has no patience for obscurity or ambiguity. For him, the goal of aesthetics is "the perfection of sensuous knowledge as such," which he equates with "beauty." Conversely, "imperfection of sensuous knowledge as such," or "the ugly" (deformitas), should be avoided in the thoughts, material (res), combinations of thoughts, and form of a work (§14; §21).[7] Baumgarten follows Horace in excluding chimera and other deformed or impossible creatures. In a section entitled "Aesthetic Falsehood" (§445–77) Baumgarten criticizes absurd combinations. Beyond physical ugliness of this kind, he includes under aesthetic falsehood incoherent forms and he criticizes contradictions (intellectual ugliness) and vice (moral ugliness).

On moral grounds, Baumgarten admonishes those who endorse the poet's freedom to create imaginary worlds rife with vice, even when the tone is mocking (§183–4). Ugliness seems to be permitted only in a clearly pedagogical context. Baumgarten acknowledges the legitimacy of exercises in which ugliness predominates over beauty as long as the process is accompanied by the knowledge that ugliness is a form of aesthetic falsehood and the understanding that engaging with ugliness is merely a stage for the developing artist, who should later abandon the practice. Although Baumgarten inaugurates aesthetics as a discipline, his views on ugliness look backward, not forward.

Before we continue our analysis of continental (and primarily German) reflections on ugliness, it makes sense to integrate here the earliest theoretical reflections that surface in Great Britain. These emerge during the eighteenth century, so essentially between Leibniz (whom we just explored) and Karl Friedrich Eusebius Trahndorff (who will conclude the next chapter).

Among the earliest reflections on ugliness in the English-speaking world are those of English essayist **Joseph Addison**, who claims in *The Spectator* (June 30, 1712) that "not only what is Great, Strange or Beautiful, but any Thing that is Disagreeable when looked upon, pleases us in an apt Description" (no. 418). Hardly original, the claim nonetheless reinforces the recurrence of an insight we have traced back to Aristotle.

In his early work *A Treatise of Human Nature* (1740), Scottish philosopher **David Hume** explores ugliness and architecture, a topic that resonates into the present. In a section entitled "Of beauty and deformity," Hume claims that a functional building that appears to be dysfunctional is ugly. He elevates not only solidity but also its appearance: "the rules of architecture require, that the top of a pillar shou'd be more slender than its base, and that because such a figure conveys to us the idea of security, which is pleasant; whereas the contrary form gives us the apprehension of danger, which is uneasy" (2.1.8). For Hume, beauty gives pleasure, while deformity causes discomfort. He later adds: "When a building seems clumsy and tottering to the eye, it is ugly and disagreeable; tho' we be fully assur'd of the solidity of the workmanship. 'Tis a kind of fear, which causes this sentiment of disapprobation; but the passion is not the same with that which we feel, when oblig'd to stand under a wall, that we really think tottering and insecure. The *seeming tendencies* of objects affect the mind: And the emotions they excite are of a like species with those, which proceed from the *real consequences* of objects, but their feeling is different" (3.3.1).

Hume recognizes here a complex form of ugliness: a functional building that nonetheless challenges our perception of stability. Imagine a building that works well because computer modeling successfully laid out an effective structure, yet the building looks as if it will collapse at any moment. For Hume, such a building would be ugly because its seeming instability would evoke unease—a form of emotional ugliness. Hume's analysis stems from his belief that aesthetic appreciation is reception-oriented, based on what he calls "sentiments," which are reflective responses to sensory impressions and "not to be controlled or altered by any philosophical theory or speculation whatsoever" (7.2.80). In *An Enquiry concerning Human Morals* (1751), Hume extends this argument to other arts. He contends that in observing a sculpture or painting, one should not gain the impression of instability: "There is no rule in painting or statuary more indispensible than that of balancing the figures, and placing them with the greatest exactness on their proper centre of gravity. A figure, which is not justly balanced, is ugly; because it conveys the disagreeable ideas of fall, harm, and pain" (6.2.200).

Until the late eighteenth century, the expectation existed that although painting could integrate ugliness, sculpture should not. The presumption for sculpture was for both graceful artistry and lofty subject matter. In his early, undated, and posthumously published essay *On the Nature of that Imitation which takes place in what are called the Imitative Arts*, Scottish economist and philosopher **Adam Smith** argued that sculpture should restrict its subject matter to what is beautiful and noble: "The picture of a very ugly and deformed man, such as Aesop, or Scarron, might not make a disagreeable piece of furniture. The statue certainly would. Even a vulgar ordinary man or woman, engaged in a vulgar ordinary action, like what we see with so much pleasure in the pictures of Rembrandt, would be too mean a subject for statuary" (5:250). A close friend of Hume (Rasmussen), Smith provides a rationale that goes beyond simple adherence to tradition: in sculpture, there is little distinction between the imitated object and the artwork itself, whereas in painting, the disparity between object and form is greater. This separation allows for pleasure in the painter's craft of imitation, even if the object is ugly (5:249). In sculpture, however, we find it more challenging to distance ourselves from the object and reflect on the act of creation. Interestingly, Smith was a contemporary of G. E. Lessing, who likewise but independently, as we will see in Chapter 4, sought to reflect on the ways in which ugliness relates to diverse arts.

In the English language, beauty was traditionally contrasted with deformity. The frequent use of deformity, not ugliness, is present throughout the seventeenth and eighteenth centuries, as in Francis Bacon's *On Deformity* (1625) and in Addison's contributions to *The Spectator* (June 23, 1712, no. 412). The Irish philosopher Francis Hutcheson uses "ugly" and "deform'd" interchangeably (71), and in Hume, too, the primary opposition is "beauty and deformity" (*Treatise* 2.1.8). This is likewise the case in William Hay's

Deformity: An Essay (1754), which offers a meaningful enlightenment challenge to the link between physical and moral deformity. But Anglo-Irish statesman **Edmund Burke,** who follows all of these thinkers and is the first English-language writer to comment extensively on ugliness, inaugurated a successful turn away from deformity and toward ugliness as the primary counter-term to beauty. In *A Philosophical Enquiry into the Origin of Our Ideas of the Sublime and Beautiful* (1757), Burke argues that proportion is not the cause of beauty nor disproportion the source of ugliness. Therefore, he claims, the "true opposite to beauty is not disproportion or deformity, but *ugliness*" (95). He elaborates: "though ugliness be the opposite to beauty, it is not the opposite to proportion and fitness. For it is possible that a thing may be very ugly with any proportions" (108). Desirable proportion is variable, and a given proportion can be beautiful or ugly based on other factors—a point previously made by Plotinus (1.6.1), whose analysis Burke does not cite and may not have known. Since ugliness is not solely defined by proportion, ugliness—and not deformity—becomes the more efficacious term. Burke argues further—and in ways that parallel later developments in Germany—that when combined with qualities that excite terror, ugliness can contribute to the sublime (109).

In his *Essay on the Picturesque, as Compared with the Sublime and the Beautiful* (1794), **Uvedale Price** occasionally touches on ugliness. A wealthy English landowner, Price adopts an unconventional notion of ugliness as what is unattractive and without distinctive qualities. "Ugliness, like beauty, has no prominent features—it is in some degree regular and uniform, and at a distance, and even on a slight inspection, is not immediately striking" (153). Because ugliness represents for Price insipidness, he argues that the "ugliest buildings are those which have no feature, no character" (152). What Price calls ugly, later thinkers will consider one type of ugliness, an uninteresting regularity. Price applies his restricted principle not only to architecture but also to music: "ugly music is what is composed according to rule and common proportion, but which has neither that selection of sweet and softly varying melody and modulation which answers to the beautiful, nor that marked character, those sudden and masterly changes, which correspond to the picturesque" (153). Price equates ugliness with facelessness and distinguishes it from deformity. For him, the ugly is disagreeable, but when it is combined with deformity, the effect is heightened: "Ugliness alone is merely disagreeable—by the addition of deformity it becomes hideous—by that of terror it may become sublime" (148). Price captures a single aspect of ugliness that had previously surfaced ex negativo in William Hogarth's mid-century *Analysis of Beauty*, where Hogarth argues that variety is a necessary condition of beauty (27–8). The idea that ordinariness is one pole of ugliness, with monstrosity as the other, is widespread in contemporary architectural theory and has partial origins in Price.[8]

*

Even though little attention has been given to theories of ugliness before modernity, many themes that will recur in modernity surfaced earlier. One overarching idea with various manifestations is that the ugly and the beautiful have a complex relationship; they may, but need not, be opposed. If we look more closely, what appears ugly may actually be beautiful. We recognize this structure in Plato's account of Socrates and in the medieval view that ugly parts, when seen from the perspective of the whole, can be beautiful. Additionally, Aristotle's assertion that accurate renderings of ugly objects can be beautiful is endorsed by figures from Plutarch and Bonaventure to Mendelssohn and Boileau-Despréaux. If one looks more sharply, understands the fuller context, or focuses on form, at a deeper level, the ugly may be beautiful. This premodern insight remains central in modern ideas of ugliness. Another complex idea that extends into modernity is the notion, first advanced by Plato, that even against our conscious intentions, we are attracted to, and fascinated by, ugliness. Plato and Aristotle treat this concept more or less objectively, whereas a medieval thinker like Bernard of Clairvaux finds the idea abhorrent—even as he himself succumbs to it. Modernity, however, will embrace this idea.

Early definitions and distinctions also deserve our attention: Plato's account of the ugly as what is not fitting—an appearance contrary to what is appropriate to the nature of something—may be the most promising definition of ugliness we know, much richer in fact than the simplistic ideas that the ugly is what is opposite the beautiful or what we find repugnant (Roche, *Beautiful Ugliness* 25–33). Plato's account aligns with Horace's and Baumgarten's critiques of mixed figures, but it can be understood in a more complex way than what we see in these dualistic thinkers. Significant and enduring is Plato's idea that ignorance (or intellectual ugliness) combined with strength is hateful, whereas weak ignorance is simply ridiculous, an idea that contributes to Aristotle's lasting insight into the link between ugliness and comedy. Also compelling are detailed analyses such as Plotinus's account of the ugly soul as not stable but driven by arbitrary restlessness. The attempt to differentiate types of ugliness, an endeavor that engages a number of modern thinkers, is first visible in Maggi.

The goal of rendering reality better than it is, a position advanced by Alberti, resurfaces in early modern utopias. This idea is not dialectical but instead a straightforward assertion that beauty is preferable to ugliness. In modernity, we encounter its opposite: some topics cannot be rendered beautifully and instead demand ugliness in content and form.

Part II

The Modern European (and Primarily German) Tradition

4

From Lessing to Trahndorff

The concept of ugliness gains prominence in the late eighteenth and early nineteenth centuries, especially in Germany. Aesthetics during this period, even apart from considerations of ugliness, is dominated by the German tradition, as Paul Guyer notes in his monumental history of modern aesthetics (*History* 3:7).[1] The prominence of ugliness during this era begins with two well-known German writers, G. E. Lessing and Friedrich Schlegel. Lessing analyzes ugliness within the context of different arts, and Schlegel calls for an aesthetics of ugliness. Here is where most histories of theories of ugliness commence.

Lessing was the greatest dramatist of Enlightenment Germany and its sharpest wit. An acquaintance of Voltaire and a close friend of Mendelssohn, Lessing contributed to contemporary debates in aesthetics and theology. In *Laokoon oder Über die Grenzen der Malerei und Poesie* (*Laocoön: An Essay on the Limits of Painting and Poetry*) (1766), Lessing posits the importance of time and thus action as a meaningful way of integrating ugliness. For Lessing, ugliness cannot be an end in itself; it must be part of a larger whole. Integrating ugliness is more difficult in sculpture and painting, which capture only a moment in time, than in the temporal arts, for example, literature.

For the archaeologist Johann Joachim Winckelmann, Germany's most influential interpreter of ancient Greece, the essence of sculpture is beauty. Lessing follows his lead, acknowledging that Winckelmann was right to see "noble simplicity and quiet grandeur" (17) in the Hellenistic sculpture

Laocoön and His Sons (Figure 8), but not because the work embodied Stoic thought. Instead, because the rules of sculpture do not permit the integration of ugliness. Discovered in 1506 and created in the second century BC, the sculpture—drawing on Virgil's *Aeneid* (2.199–227)—depicts the hopeless struggle of the Trojan priest Laocoön, who had warned against accepting the

Figure 8 Laocoön and His Sons, *c. 40–30 BC, Marble, Vatican Museums and Galleries, Vatican City, Photo Copyright © Governorate of the Vatican City State—Directorate of the Vatican Museums.*

wooden horse that concealed Greek soldiers. In this magnificent sculpture, the priest and his sons try in vain to fend off two gigantic sea snakes sent by the gods to suffocate them in their coils. The work captures both the dramatic tension and Laocoön's heroic composure. According to Lessing, the hero's quiet grandeur is a result of formal, not thematic, constraints. Ancient sculpture avoids "the most hideous distortions" (die häßlichsten Verzerrungen) (Ger. 26; Eng. 15, my translation). Emotions like rage are hidden from view or recast as earnestness, while lamentation is presented through the less extreme emotion of sorrow (Ger. 27–30; Eng. 15–17).

To Lessing, the ancient world was not devoid of extreme suffering and corresponding cries of pain. Indeed, such moments are abundant, but their proper outlet is literature, where they can be absorbed into a larger, more harmonious whole. This is evident in Virgil's account of Laocoön: the hero's cries are wretched but transitory, part of a larger narrative that conveys also his virtues as a patriot and a father (Ger. 36; Eng. 24). Similarly, the agony of Sophocles' Philoctetes, compounded by his hunger and isolation, is presented in full: "He moans, he shrieks, he falls into the most horrible contortions" (Ger. 43; Eng. 27, translation modified). However, this wretchedness is tolerable because it exists within a drama that, while vividly and powerfully depicting these moments, ultimately treats them as secondary to the hero's moral greatness and the work's moments of reconciliation (Ger. 44; Eng. 29).

Lessing underscores that Homer barely describes Helen and other beautiful figures; he simply gives them the appropriate epithets, but Homer delineates in detail the ugliness of Thersites (Ger. 164–5; Eng. 121–2). According to Lessing, the beauty of the language softens the effect of ugliness (Ger. 165; Eng. 122). Ugliness is presented as ugly only in order to be transformed—into either the ridiculous or the awful, as we saw in Plato. Lessing writes: "harmless ugliness" is "ridiculous" (Ger. 167; Eng. 123). In contrast, "harmful ugliness" is "awful" (Ger. 167; Eng. 124, translation modified). For Lessing, as for earlier thinkers, Thersites is ridiculous: his ugly body and ugly character contradict his self-importance (Ger. 165–66; Eng. 121–2). Lessing does not argue that sculpture and painting cannot engage ugliness. Instead, he makes the more modest claim that integrating ugliness into the plastic arts is more challenging than in literature, where it can become part of a larger narrative (Ger. 171–2; Eng. 128–9). In literature, emotions elicited by the horrific or the ridiculous diminish over time; however, in painting or sculpture, the lasting impression of ugliness is more dominant and confronting (Ger. 172; Eng. 128–29).

The brief appearance of ugliness within a temporal frame mitigates its severity. Literature, music, and film have the capacity to integrate ugliness within a temporal horizon, thus rendering it less overpowering. Pain and ugliness gain legitimacy when presented as part of a larger aesthetic whole. Lessing himself realizes this principle in his plays, for example, his comedy *Minna von Barnhelm* (1767) and his drama of reconciliation *Nathan the Wise* (1779). In each case, we see multiple aberrant paths, which are for the most part corrected, and the possibility of tragedy, which is, however, avoided. This submergence of ugliness within a larger, more positive whole is very much in the spirit of Lessing's Enlightenment optimism.

According to Lessing, the ugly cannot easily become part of a painting since the unerring focus on visual ugliness is at tension with beauty. Although Lessing's general point holds, one way for an artist to both exhibit and soften the ugliness of the static arts is to fold ugliness into a narrative of multiple images. In Hogarth's *Four Stages of Cruelty* (1751), abuse of animals leads to further crime and culminates in murder, but the process ends in punishment. The work is ugly, but its purpose is moral. Hogarth manages to hold diverse moments in tension because he creates a narrative out of a sequence of images. A pictorial narrative in which evil is condemned and punished can vividly portray ghastly events as well as their gruesome consequences.

If one accepts the idea that ugliness should not consume a work, the temporal arts do have an advantage, even if the claim modestly underplays the ways in which even a singular work, such as Hans Holbein the Younger's *The Ambassadors*, can effectively present ugliness as a part (Figure 9). After all, the ugliness of the anamorphic skull can be resolved by a radical shift in the viewer's perspective. What appears as a distorted, oblong smear when we view the painting straight on reveals itself as an exquisite rendition of a skull when we see it from an oblique angle, to the right of the canvas and close to the plane of the work. The painting even contains a nearly hidden crucifix in the upper left-hand corner, which recalls not only death, but also what lies beyond. Moreover, Christian Weiße's critique of Lessing seems cogent. Weiße argues that when an ugly object is presented beautifully, even painting has little

Figure 9 *Hans Holbein the Younger,* The Ambassadors, *1533, Oil on oak, © National Gallery, London / Art Resource, NY.*

difficulty absorbing ugliness: "One sees easily, that, if one talks of artistically depicted ugly figures, their ugliness takes on the meaning of a *sublated* ugliness simply by virtue of its objective representation" (Weiße 2:217). The immediacy of ugliness in the real world is dissolved through artistic mediation.

Lessing's *Laocoön* is a thoroughly modern work, a break from the past. The work would hardly have been conceivable in an earlier era, for one can attempt to distinguish one art from another only after a general concept of art has been formed. Hegel notes in his *Aesthetics* that any division of the arts presupposes a concept of art (*Werke* 13:40). The Greeks lacked an elaborated concept of the fine arts, and medieval efforts were likewise limited. A coherent concept of the arts begins to take shape in the sixteenth century and achieves a certain richness in the eighteenth when common principles are articulated and the discipline of aesthetics is founded (Kristeller). Beforehand the problem Lessing addresses simply did not exist for human consciousness, and no language was available to address the problem. Only when a general concept that encompasses all the arts is developed do we see an interest in differentiation, including how the various arts engage ugliness. In modernity, as systematic interest in the arts gives way to more historical approaches, the question of how ugliness functions in the different arts once again recedes.

Lessing's argument that integrating ugliness into painting makes beauty more difficult to discern will be both embraced and challenged in modernity when a less harmonic worldview takes hold, which no longer values overcoming ugliness, for it sees little conflict between aesthetic excellence and ugliness. Within this new framework, the static arts become privileged territory for dwelling in ugliness, both confirming and reversing Lessing's claims. Because painting arrests time, any presentation of the ugly in painting is more difficult to bear, yet in modernity, where ugliness is preferred, painting allows ugliness to become more intense and powerful.

Another challenge to Lessing emerges from the fact that in the temporal arts a reverse movement is possible and in modernity present: instead of a moment of ugliness embedded within the arc of a positive whole, any of the temporal arts can portray moments of beauty that are swallowed up within a narrative whole defined by ugliness. In German choreographer Kurt Jooss's ballet *Der grüne Tisch* (*The Green Table*) (1932), the beauty and sacrifice of the soldiers and their loved ones are framed on both sides by ugly and futile peace negotiations.

A further reversal of Lessing's claim is one he could hardly have imagined. In film, we see that temporality not only minimizes ugliness, but it can also amplify it. Drawing on the *vanitas* tradition, with its depiction of flowers past full bloom and fruit starting to turn, British director Sam Taylor-Johnson's (née Taylor-Wood's) short film *Still Life* (2001) shows apples, peaches, and pears that decay in minutes, turning dark as mold and bacteria consume the fruit, which rots and collapses in on itself. Similar in style, though more dramatic and violent, is Taylor-Johnson's *A Little Death* (2002), which shows the decomposition of a hare on a table, its leg propped against a wall. Within minutes, the hare loses its form, turns dark, and completely dissolves as insects devour the body. Although the film is about death and decay, the hare symbolizes life and reproduction, suggesting that death is part of life. Beauty and ugliness combine in both sequences, which are as diverse as they are similar. Whereas the living fruit decays quietly and almost gracefully—if also repulsively—the already dead hare seems to come to life in the energetic dynamism of its decomposition. Although we have understood time (in the sense of a longer temporal sequence) as advantageous in softening the effect of ugliness, which thereby becomes a mere moment, here we see via technology that a rapid temporal process can do the reverse: it can enhance ugliness.

One of Lessing's interlocutors was **Johann Gottfried Herder**, one of the most fertile minds in German letters, whose creativity ranged from historical linguistics to the philosophy of history. Herder addressed various aesthetic topics, and two of his early works touch on ugliness. In the first part of *Die Kritschen Wälder zur Ästhetik* (*Critical Groves on Aesthetics*) of 1769, he offers a running commentary on Lessing's *Laocoön*, focusing on conceptual distinctions and examples. Like Lessing, Herder recognizes that Homer's Thersites is morally and physically ugly: "According to Greek notions of honor there can be no uglier soul" (*Werke* 2.224; *Selected Writings* 161). Herder adds: "from a Greek point of view such an ugly soul must also inhabit the ugliest body" (*Werke* 2.225; *Selected Writings* 162).

Yet Herder contests Lessing's claim that Thersites is ridiculous. For Herder, such an evil figure—someone with "*the blackest soul of all those gathered before Troy*"—can hardly be called ridiculous (*Werke* 2.223; *Selected Writings* 161). Although the Greeks laugh at him, their laughter is not the superficial, playful mockery associated with the ridiculous; it is scorn directed at a hated person: "Even when the Greeks laugh at him it is *Schadenfreude*, it is laughter born of hatred, not innocent joy at an amusing buffoon who is innocently ridiculous" (*Werke* 2.226; *Selected Writings* 163). The truth seems to lie between Lessing and Herder: Thersites is ugly and weak and, therefore, ridiculous, but he is also despised (*Iliad* 2.220). He is neither powerful nor innocent. *Schadenfreude*, with its derisive laughter, seems to capture what Homer has in mind. Thersites is both ridiculous and hated.

After distinguishing strictly between the ridiculous and the horrific (das Schreckliche), Herder remarks that when something initially perceived as horrific turns out to be non-threatening, it becomes ridiculous. Conversely, the ridiculous, when revealed to be more dangerous than initially thought, turns into the horrific. Essentially, Herder continues Plato's distinction in the *Philebus* and Lessing's in *Laokoon*: harmless ugliness is ridiculous, whereas dangerous ugliness is horrific (2.233).

But Herder elaborates further: the horrific can arise without being inherently ugly. He cites as examples a raging storm and a threatening lion, both of which evoke terror without necessarily being ugly. Whereas the brutality of Richard III elicits fear, his ugly body and ugly soul awaken revulsion. Thus, Herder seeks to refine Lessing's claim: for Lessing, dangerous ugliness is horrific, but according to Herder, not because it is ugly but because it is dangerous. Herder grasps the kind of complexity that will later arise with a figure such as Dorian Gray, who is physically attractive but malicious and horrific. Herder's main point in chapter 22 is that danger, not ugliness, elicits terror and horror. One can accept Herder's distinctions but still argue that our reception differs depending on whether we encounter simply danger (e.g., the lion), danger along with physical and moral ugliness (e.g., Richard III), or danger combined with physical beauty and moral ugliness (e.g., Dorian Gray). Certainly, Herder is correct that a sense of horror does not presuppose ugliness, but ugliness, depending on its power, does give rise to either the ridiculous or the horrific. Moreover, the examples of Richard III and Dorian Gray have in common moral ugliness. The horror of nature can arise without ugliness, but even when such horror is triggered by the beauty of a lion or a lightning storm, the resulting devastation can easily include physical ugliness, including potentially death.

In 1778, Herder published *Plastik: Einige Wahrnehmungen über Form und Gestalt aus Pygmalions bildendem Traume* (*Sculpture: Some Observations on Shape and Form from Pygmalion's Creative Dream*), which includes considerable reflection on ugliness. The purpose of the book is to continue to develop, as in the first and fourth of his *Critical Groves*, the distinctive nature of the individual arts. A further goal is to contribute to contemporary debates that engage the relative importance of sight and touch (Norton 205). Whereas painting is driven by sight and music by hearing, sculpture is determined by touch, that is, by our creative engagement with three-dimensional objects, our tactile experience of tangible physicality, our sensuous awareness of form. For Herder, to see a formed body in space is to render the eye akin to a hand; the viewer imaginatively, and sometimes literally, touches the work. Herder writes: "Sight gives us *dreams,* touch gives us *truth*" (Im Gesicht ist *Traum*, im Gefühl *Wahrheit*) (*Werke* 4:250; *Sculpture* 38). Whereas most paintings can be appreciated from a single viewpoint, sculpture requires that we explore a work's full physical space and craft a unified impression of that space.

In Part Two of *Sculpture,* Herder asks four questions. The second and third address ugliness. The second asks, why would color render sculpture ugly? Herder's response: color does not belong in sculpture, because color is for arts that are determined by sight, not touch. (The myth that ancient sculptures were white and not in truth vividly painted had gained considerable currency by the time Herder wrote on sculpture.) The third question asks, does ugliness belong in sculpture? Herder argues that whereas painting can and at times should portray ugliness, sculpture should not.

Although Herder was a revolutionary in recognizing historical and cultural differences, he was traditional in his expectations for sculpture, even if his specific arguments were novel. He cites Aristotle, who values ugliness for our minds, noting that ugliness awakens new ideas. However, touch or feeling, the determining sense for sculpture, is the slowest of the aesthetic senses to transition to ideas. Sculpture is more immediate in the feelings it awakens, including sympathy and antipathy. Here, ugliness has no place: "A ravaged, ugly, or distorted form, *Itys* torn to pieces, *Hippolytus* in Euripides' play, *Medea* contorted with rage, *Philoctetes* in the worst convulsions of his illness, someone in the throes of death, or a decomposing corpse struggling against the worms—all these are repugnant when encountered by the feeling hand as it advances" (*Werke* 4:272; *Sculpture* 57). Herder warns against: "atrocious art that bestows form upon deformity!" (*Werke* 4:272; *Sculpture* 57). He argues that ugliness is allowed in sculpture only when it is secondary to the primary portrayal of beautiful human bodies (*Werke* 4:274; *Sculpture* 58–9). In painting, ugliness is permitted, for sight is more cerebral than touch (*Werke* 4:275; *Sculpture* 59).

Thus, Herder embraces ugliness as an artistic subject, but not in sculpture, where reception is oriented to the less cerebral, more visceral sense of touch.

Though Herder's argument, with its prohibition of ugly sculptures, would have few, if any, adherents today, we can modify it and suggest that if his arguments, even if not fully compelling, capture a moment of truth—that the sense of touch is central to sculpture and is both less cerebral and more visceral and impressionable than sight—then, if one wanted to emphasize ugliness, as many contemporary artists do, the most powerful and enduring forms of ugliness would arise in sculptures and installations.[2] Consider the sculpture *Great Deeds Against the Dead* (1994), by Jake and Dinos Chapman, which is more viscerally unnerving, because it is less mediated, than Goya's *Plate 39* from his *Disasters of War* (1810–20), on which it is based. Perhaps, then, with the help of Herder, we can understand, against his own intentions, why we see (1) a dramatic turn to ugliness in sculptures and installations and (2) an emphasis on sculptures and installations as vehicles for expressing ugliness.

Two Swiss contemporaries who commented on ugliness were **Johann Georg Sulzer** and **Johann Kaspar Lavater**. In his popular *Allgemeine Theorie der schönen Künste* (*General Theory of the Beautiful Arts*) from 1771–4, Sulzer includes an entry on "Häßlich (schöne Künste)" (ugly (fine arts)) (1:504–05). Along with endorsing the idea that ugly objects and ugly actions can be portrayed in beautiful works, Sulzer emphasizes that ugliness can also refer to formal distortion. For Sulzer, the ugly functions as a negative example. Additionally, he notes that the simple absence of beauty is not ugliness but indifference, as ugliness has sensuous power. In 1755, Sulzer had translated Hume's *Enquiry Concerning Human Understanding*. Sulzer understood that sentiment can be understood as both a psychological and a moral category, so it is not surprising that in his entry on *Empfindung* or sentiment, Sulzer recognizes the valuable role ugliness plays in cultivating emotional aversion to evil (1:311–16).

Lavater is best known for his studies in physiognomy, particularly his *Physiognomische Fragmente, zur Beförderung der Menschenkenntniß und Menschenliebe* (*Essays on Physiognomy, for the Promotion of the Knowledge and the Love of Humanity*) (1775–8). Physiognomy is the long-discredited attempt to read psychological traits from physical characteristics, especially facial features. Although Lavater did not develop a theory of ugliness per se, he is worth mentioning as the most pronounced representative of a tradition, prevalent in the medieval and early modern eras, which posited that evil character reveals itself through physical deformities. He writes: "The beauty and ugliness of the countenance has a true and precise relation to the person's moral beauty and ugliness. / The more moral, the more beautiful. / The morally worse, the uglier" (Ger. 1.63; Eng. 1.183, translation modified). Lavater tried to counter objections to his claims by conceding that virtue is not the sole cause of human beauty. Nevertheless, he maintained that "virtue beautifies, vice deforms" (macht häßlich) (Ger. 1.64; Eng. 1.184). The lack of dialectical thinking is evident here, as is the reductionism.

Immanuel Kant was the first to develop a systematic philosophy in which aesthetics plays a major role. Like many others, Kant embraces the beautiful portrayal of ugly objects. In his *Critique of Judgment* (1790) he writes: "Fine art shows its excellence in beautifully describing things that in nature would be ugly or displeasing (häßlich oder mißfällig). The Furies, diseases, devastations of war, and the like, can (as evils) be very beautifully described and even represented in painting" (§48, my translation). Kant then introduces a limiting principle to the portrayal of ugliness: "Only one kind of ugliness (nur eine Art Häßlichkeit) is incapable of being represented conformably to nature without destroying all aesthetic pleasure, and therefore the beauty of art: namely, that which arouses disgust (Ekel)" (§48, translation modified).

Kant explains his rejection of disgust: "For, as in this strange sensation, which depends purely on the imagination, the object is represented as insisting, as it were, upon our enjoying it, while we violently resist it. In our sensation, the artistic representation of the object is no longer distinguishable from the nature of the object itself, and so it cannot possibly be considered beautiful" (§48, translation modified). Kant emphasizes how brutally and powerfully disgust obtrudes upon us. The representation of the disgusting is such that we cannot distinguish the nature of the object from its formal representation, and this renders disinterested aesthetic contemplation impossible. Kant's argument is oriented toward reception: in the case of the disgusting, we struggle to distinguish the object from its representation. What we find disgusting, however, changes over time; we can become accustomed to what was initially intolerable or shocking, such that works that once aroused disgust no longer overwhelm us. We can learn to react cerebrally, distinguishing the object from its representation. Nonetheless, I agree with Kant that there is an objective limit to what can and should be considered beautiful, even if that limit is determined as much by moral and aesthetic considerations as by a powerful sensuous experience in which object and representation are indistinguishable. I return to this topic in Chapters 11 and 13.

In paragraph 48, Kant makes another observation on ugliness: sculpture, which is closer to nature than are painting and literature, generally excludes "the immediate portrayal of ugly objects" (die unmittelbare Vorstellung häßlicher Gegenstände) (§48). The parallel to Herder is obvious. Exceptions occur when, for example, death or martial valor is represented in allegorical or visually pleasing ways. Such representations, Kant argues, are linked to reason and so transcend aesthetic judgment.

The brevity of Kant's commentary on ugliness has spawned at least twenty-five attempts by contemporary philosophers to puzzle through what Kant might or should have said about the topic. Some argue, in analogy to the pure aesthetic judgment of beauty,[3] that a pure (or in some cases impure) aesthetic judgment of ugliness is possible, while others contend that no aesthetic judgment of ugliness is possible.[4] The sequence of studies, taken as a whole, is more interesting for shedding light on Kant than for developing new insights into ugliness, so I do not lift this focused philological debate into my main narrative.[5] I do note, however, how fascinating it is that, although the issue arises just a few years after the publication of Kant's third critique, in Karl Heinrich Heydenreich, it then dies down, but in the past twenty-five years the topic of Kant and ugliness has resurfaced with one publication after another, as ugliness comes to the forefront of our consciousness.

In the end, that Kant says so little about ugliness and that Karl Rosenkranz, who assumed Kant's chair less than thirty years after his death, wrote an entire aesthetics of ugliness reveals much about developments in early nineteenth-century aesthetics: in the span of one generation, we move from an aesthetics that brackets ugliness to one that places ugliness at its core.[6]

Kant's third critique was instrumental in encouraging the following generation to reflect further on the sublime as a form of art distinct from beauty. Kant's work paved the way for philosophers to discuss other aesthetic concepts beyond the beautiful, including the ugly. In early nineteenth-century

German aesthetics, in fact, the two categories most frequently linked with the ugly were the sublime and the comic.

Friedrich Schlegel was a poet and theoretician of German Romanticism. Before becoming the primary advocate of transcendental or self-reflective poetry, Schlegel weighed in with a fascinating essay on ancient and modern art, in which ugliness plays a defining role. In *Über das Studium der griechischen Poesie* (*On the Study of Greek Poetry*) (1795), Schlegel discusses the role of ugliness in aesthetics and even calls for a "theory of ugliness" (Ger. 311, 315; Eng. 68, 70). Whereas classical Greek art was beautiful, modern works often include "representations of the ugly" (Ger. 219; Eng. 18). Schlegel extols Greek beauty, especially the writings of Homer and Sophocles: "Only in one nation did fine art correspond to the great dignity of its destiny" (Ger. 275; Eng. 48, translation modified). Schlegel adds: "For this greatness I know of no more appropriate name than *supreme beauty.* Not simply a beauty about which nothing more beautiful could be thought; but instead the complete example of the unattainable idea that as it were becomes here utterly apparent" (Ger. 287–88; Eng. 55, translation modified). Among the qualities Schlegel elevates in Greek art are its completeness and balance (Ger. 279; Eng. 50). Another is organic unity (Ger. 293; Eng. 58). When Homer integrates evil, it is not isolated but "*prepared* and *resolved*" (Ger. 281; Eng. 52).

For Schlegel, not the beautiful but the interesting, the individual, and the characteristic define modern art: "Nothing can better explain and confirm the artificiality of modern aesthetic development than the vast *preponderance of the individual, the characteristic, and the philosophical* throughout the entire mass of modern poetry" (Ger. 241; Eng. 30–31, translation modified). Modern art tends to serve an external, often philosophical or didactic purpose, whereas beautiful art is "free play without determined goal" (Ger. 240–41; Eng. 31). Precisely within this modern context, Schlegel elevates the idea of an aesthetics of ugliness and offers initial reflections on the topic. The ugly, according to Schlegel, is unpleasant, attacking the senses and awakening moral pain. It fills us with disgust and pulls us in contradictory directions, oscillating between dull languor and disordering rage (Ger. 311–12; Eng. 68). Schlegel identifies a dialectic between complete lethargy and utter recklessness. He uses various terms to capture aspects of ugliness, noting emptiness, monotony, uniformity, and banality in contrast to the rich fullness of beauty. He sets the harmony of beauty against disproportion and conflict. One of his main points is that ugliness, as the negation of aesthetic excellence, can be associated with either "infinite deficiency" or "infinite disharmony," depending on whether the deficit represents a lack of richness (a kind of privation) or a lack of harmony (a kind of discord) (Ger. 313; Eng. 69). For Schlegel, "*beauty* in the *strict* sense is the appearance of a finite diversity in a conditioned unity" (Ger. 312; Eng. 69). The sublime, in contrast, embodies "infinite abundance or infinite harmony" (Ger. 313; Eng. 69). Schlegel argues that "the necessary prerequisite for ugliness" is "a deluded expectation, an aroused and then frustrated yearning" (Ger. 313; Eng. 69, translation modified). He continues: "The feeling of emptiness and struggle can grow from mere discomfort to the most raging despair" (Ger. 313; Eng. 69).

Schlegel's essay lacks conceptual clarity and is more suggestive than systematic, offering an impression of contemporary tendencies and a broad set of characteristics associated with ugliness. Schlegel does not offer a dialectical analysis, as will the Hegelians; Schlegel simply contrasts beauty and ugliness (Oesterle 255). Nonetheless, he identifies a distinctive feature of modern art—the individual and the interesting—that endures into the present.

Moreover, Schlegel recognizes the great potential in modern art, including the possibility of an aesthetic revolution and an awakening sense of beauty (Ger. 269; Eng. 45). In this context, he praises selected modern artists, above all Shakespeare and Goethe, but also Friedrich Gottlieb Klopstock, Christoph Martin Wieland, Lessing, and Schiller. Schlegel further recognizes that the subject matter of modern literature pushes artists into new territory:

> beauty is so far from being the dominant principle of modern poetry that many of the most splendid modern works are clearly portrayals of ugliness, so much so that one is obliged to admit unwillingly that an immense richness of reality exists at the peak of its disorder and there is a desperation caused by the excess of energies and the conflict between them, whose portrayal requires an equal, if not a greater creative power and artistic wisdom than that which is required for the portrayal of that richness and those energies when they are in perfect harmony. (Ger. 219; Eng. 18, translation modified)

Schlegel is one of the first theorists to recognize what will eventually become common: the extent to which ugliness, conflict, and disorder unleash new creative capacities.

Only a few years later, Schlegel reverses his ambivalence toward modernity. In fragment 124 of his *Athenäumsfragmente* (*Athenaeum Fragments*), he reevaluates the aesthetic portrayal of eccentricity. In his essay on Greek poetry, he described eccentricity as sick and degenerate (Ger. 255; Eng. 36), but it is now taken to be fully appropriate for modernity. For Schlegel, the novelist who delves into psychology should not hold back from offering "even the most painstaking and thorough analysis of unnatural pleasure, horrible tortures, revolting infamy, and disgusting physical or mental impotence" (*Athenäums-Fragmente* 185; *Philosophical Fragments* 34). No longer content with critically assessing the interesting as the mark of modern poetry, Schlegel becomes its advocate. This shift represents a remarkable development and transformation of his views, even if his earlier ambivalence had planted the seeds.[7]

Like Schlegel, the great poet, dramatist, and philosopher **Friedrich Schiller** wrote an important essay on classical and modern art, *Über naive und sentimentalische Dichtung* (*On Naive and Sentimental Poetry*) (1795). The work contains an engaging analysis of satire, a genre deeply linked to ugliness, insofar as, according to Schiller, satire presupposes a break between the ideal and the real; and unlike the elegiac and the idyllic, which dwell on the attractiveness of the ideal, satire focuses on the inadequacies of reality. If we understand ugliness as what should not be, satire dwells in ugliness.

Still, Schiller's more explicit reflections on ugliness appear elsewhere, in a series of essays on tragedy, sublimity, and related topics, where one of Germany's greatest dramatists wrestles with the paradox of tragedy, including our attraction to ugliness and suffering. In *Über die tragische Kunst* (*On Tragic Art*) of 1792, Schiller is clear about the pull of horror: "the sad, the terrible, the horrible itself attracts us with an irresistible charm [. . .] we feel repelled and attracted again with equal force by appearances of misery and horror" (8:251). Despite sometimes drastic differences among Schiller's various essays on the tragic and the sublime, a recurring theme, even more significant than our attraction to suffering, is his argument that suffering is never an end in itself but always a means to reveal human dignity in the face of suffering. Schiller emphasizes moral resistance to suffering, including the character's assertion of human freedom, which helps viewers become more aware of their own moral capacities. Here, as elsewhere in Schiller's writings, one sees the legacy of Kant's ethics.

According to Schiller, authors must often delve into moral ugliness. In *Gedanken über den Gebrauch des Gemeinen und Niedrigen in der Kunst* (*Thoughts on the Use of the Common and the Low in Art*), written in the early 1790s but not published until 1802, Schiller discusses the "common" and the "low." The "common" is banal and unimportant, but it can and should be included in art if it is necessary for the whole and connected to something great; through aesthetic portrayal, the common can be ennobled. The "low," which is worse than the "common," is unappealing and even evil; it violates capacities that are justly expected of everyone. The low can be artistically portrayed via comic laughter (though the depiction should not go so far as to arouse disgust) or as a catalyst for horror and its consequences, thereby finding its place in tragedy. This double gesture, which finds the ugly acceptable via the comic and the tragic (or its analogue, the sublime), anticipates a common nineteenth-century phenomenon, even as it harkens back to Plato's distinction between harmless and horrific ugliness.

Like Schiller, **Karl Heinrich Heydenreich** developed his ideas by wrestling with Kant's various writings. Heydenreich was a poet and philosopher, known for trying to complement Kant's ethics by elevating emotions and for writing an early work on atheism, *Briefe über den Atheismus* (*Letters on Atheism*) (1796). In his essay "Ideen über Schönheit und Häßlichkeit" ("Ideas on Beauty and Ugliness") from 1796, Heydenreich is the first to identify Kant's neglect of ugliness as a major gap in his work. Heydenreich responds by developing a theory of ugliness analogous to Kant's theory of beauty. Heydenreich stresses the reception context, emphasizing the necessary and universal feeling of displeasure when we experience the "form" of ugliness. As with our encounters with beauty, we seek here to exclude from our judgment peripheral factors, such as personal feelings. Although Heydenreich's reflections are suggestive, they are too brief to serve as a compelling extension of Kant. Heydenreich is among the first to view the ugly as not merely a lack of beauty, not solely the "*non-beautiful*" (214). Instead, he describes the ugly as "*downright contradicting beauty*" (214).

In addition, he makes the valid point that, though a simply pretty face is not beautiful, it is not, in its lack of beauty, therefore ugly (214). For Heydenreich the most extreme form of ugliness is caricature, for it pushes ugliness to the point where the human is so distorted as to be barely recognizable (228). In a move that almost anticipates the humanism of Hermann Cohen, Heydenreich suggests that the essence of humanity is not easily compatible with ugliness. A soul, he argues, can never be entirely ugly (230).

Friedrich Wilhelm Joseph Schelling engaged deeply with Kant's philosophy and in his lectures on the philosophy of art frequently quoted Schiller. Early recognized as a genial thinker, Schelling elevated art (and nature) like few other philosophers. Though five years younger than Hegel and Hölderlin, Schelling shared a room with them when he attended the Protestant seminary in Tübingen. During his tenure as a professor in Jena from 1798 to 1803, Schelling became involved in Romantic circles and delivered multiple lectures on diverse aspects of art. In 1802–3, he lectured on the philosophy of art and then repeated the series in a modified form when he was in Würzburg in 1804–5. Though student lecture notes were widely circulated, Schelling himself never published these lectures. It wasn't until 1859, five years after his death, that a version appeared as part of Schelling's complete works, edited by his son Karl F. A. Schelling.

Schelling's lectures seldom comment on ugliness, and his remarks on the subject are not particularly innovative. He describes ugliness as a "privation" (*Philosophie* 30; *Philosophy* 31) and contends that, as the opposite of beauty, ugliness is both dependent on, and part of, the universe of beauty (*Philosophie* 42; *Philosophy* 40). He also notes that ugliness can be neutralized through comedy (*Philosophie* 212–13; *Philosophy* 160–1). In his renowned Munich address of 1807, "Über das Verhältnis der bildenden Künste zu der Natur" (On the Relationship of the Visual Arts to Nature), he observes that artists are often drawn to, and enjoy, portraying ugliness (6).

Schelling's ideas become more intriguing when he delves into concepts that he does not explicitly label ugly, but which later thinkers will associate with ugliness, above all formlessness that passes over into monstrousness and exaggerated particularity that veers into aberrant mannerism. He primarily explores implicit ugliness through his reflections on the sublime. For Schelling, art is "the *real* manifestation or presentation of the absolute" (*Philosophie* 102; *Philosophy* 83) or, alternatively, "the synthesis of the absolute with the particular" (*Philosophie* 118; *Philosophy* 94). Art gives the absolute particular form; it is a synthesis of the infinite and the finite. The informing of the infinite into the finite is the sublime, whereas the informing of the finite into the infinite is beauty (*Philosophie* 105; *Philosophy* 85). Our encounter with nature's vastness or power evokes the sublime, an experience that is both "terrible and great" (*Philosophie* 108; *Philosophy* 87). Form is finite, but in the sublime, form appears infinite; insofar as the sublime negates the form of the finite, the sublime is interwoven with formlessness. Attuned to dialectical structures, Schelling adds, however, that absolute formlessness is precisely the highest or absolute form (*Philosophie* 109; *Philosophy* 87). Here one finds an "identity of absolute form with formlessness, for that chaos within the absolute is not *mere* negation of form, but rather formlessness within the highest and absolute form and, in a reverse fashion, absolute form within formlessness" (*Philosophie* 109; *Philosophy* 88). In the sublime, the limited categories of understanding, the categories of determinate being, pass over into a perception of the absolute and its ability to absorb seeming contradictions (*Philosophie* 110; *Philosophy* 88).

In contrast, beauty reconciles the infinite and the finite from the outset (*Philosophie* 112; *Philosophy* 90). Yet Schelling acknowledges a higher unity of the sublime and the beautiful, viewing their difference as quantitative rather than qualitative. Taken absolutely, beauty and sublimity cease to be opposed. Without beauty, the sublime degenerates into the "monstrous or adventurous" (*Philosophie* 112; *Philosophy* 90). Whereas for Schelling, sublime formlessness is beautiful, later thinkers will view formlessness as the negation of beauty and a central category of ugliness. The implicit contrast to the monstrous is for Schelling "mannerism in the objectional sense" (im verwerflichen Sinne) (*Philosophie* 120; *Philosophy* 95). Here we see an embrace of the particular (affectation) at the expense of the universal. At its extreme, this focus on particularity becomes exaggerated and inorganic, thus losing its claim to beauty (*Philosophie* 121; *Philosophy* 96). This, too, hints at what later thinkers will call ugliness. For Schelling, then, the aberrant sublime is monstrous, and exaggerated particularity is unattractively manneristic. Schelling does not express himself in the language of ugliness, focusing instead on art as the successful integration of the conscious and unconscious, the infinite and the finite, the universal and the particular, but later thinkers will turn their attention away from synthesis and become more and more absorbed in categories of negativity, including ugliness.

The last two figures to address ugliness in advance of the Hegelian discussions are **Karl Wilhelm Ferdinand Solger** and Karl Friedrich Eusebius Trahndorff. Solger mentions ugliness in his dialogues on beauty, *Erwin* (1815), and in his lectures on aesthetics, which he delivered in 1819, the year of his death. As a student, Solger had attended Schelling's lectures in Jena and Fichte's in Berlin. At the newly founded University of Berlin, Solger was an early faculty member, served as Rector in 1814–15, and played a significant role in bringing Hegel to Berlin. His central position in German intellectual life is underscored by his having delivered the eulogy at Schleiermacher's funeral. Like Schleiermacher, Solger translated ancient Greek texts; in fact, his translations of Sophocles remained in print through the second half of the twentieth century.

Solger writes that the ugly is an appearance that is contrary to the idea (or essence) but which presents itself as, and is mistakenly taken to be, the idea or essence (*Vorlesungen* 101; *Erwin* 180 and 329). This fundamental insight—that the ugly is not simply the opposite of beauty, but also seeks to usurp beauty—will become increasingly prominent in the nineteenth century. In *Erwin*, Solger describes beauty as a unity formed from diversity, whereas the rupture and mutilation of unity is ugliness (179). In his lectures, he draws parallels between ugliness and evil, continuing a long tradition: "The ugly is indignation against the beautiful, as evil is against the good" (101). Important for Solger is the shamelessness with which one substitutes the ugly for the beautiful (*Erwin* 180; *Vorlesungen* 102), an insight that we will find also with later thinkers, such as the Hegelian Dursch (430).

Karl Friedrich Eusebius Trahndorff, a minor yet prolific figure in philosophy and theology, studied in Königsberg, arriving four years after Kant's retirement.[8] Trahndorff wrote sixteen books and left behind another forty-one unpublished manuscripts (Eckardt 5–10). Despite having a scholarly record, he never taught at the university, mainly being employed at a Berlin Gymnasium, a not overly unusual situation in German intellectual life at the time and indeed for many generations to come, an indirect signal of Germany's high regard for education and scholarship, even if the level of Trahndorff's research productivity was certainly unusual for such a teacher. At the time, Trahndorff was known for elevating faith over reason, a position he defended against Hegel, whom he criticized in his book *Wie kann der Supernaturalismus sein Recht gegen Hegel's Religionsphilosophie behaupten?* (*How Can Supernaturalism Assert Its Right against Hegel's Philosophy of Religion?*) and his booklet *Schelling und Hegel oder das System Hegels als letztes Resultat des Grundirrtums in allem bisherigen Philosophieren* (*Schelling and Hegel or Hegel's System as the Final Result of the Main Error in All Previous Philosophy*), published in 1840 and 1842, respectively. In contrast, Hegel, one of the tradition's greatest rationalists, disparaged the elevation of faith over reason and provided an ambitious rational account of Christianity.

In 1827, early in his career, Trahndorff published a two-volume aesthetics, *Ästhetik oder Lehre von Weltanschauung und Kunst* (*Aesthetics or the Doctrine of Worldview and Art*), in which he includes a paragraph on ugliness and related categories (§14), a sign of the concept's emerging importance. Although the insights are on the whole modest, one of them stands out as compelling. Trahndorff, who restricts his discussion of ugliness to nature, views ugliness as "the destruction of being" (die Zerstörung des Daseins) (1:85). He elaborates that every destruction in the realm of appearances is ugly; for example, a dying plant is ugly as long as it is in the process of destruction and its form is still recognizable (it is not as it should be), after which it is no longer ugly. It then becomes closer to non-being than to the temporal destruction of being. This is a discerning insight. If I cut a vine at its base because it is climbing where I no longer want it to be, it quickly withers and becomes extremely ugly. After it becomes easier to remove and lies for a while in the compost pile, it is no longer ugly. Here, in nature, as we will see in the Hegelian analysis of art, ugliness is transient.

Although the long stretch from antiquity through the early modern era was not as focused on ugliness as later periods were, German thinkers turned to the past for inspiration. Leibniz looked to Christianity, and Baumgarten drew from Horace. For all his modernity, Lessing developed his analysis of ugliness and the arts by referencing ancient examples, a practice continued by

Herder and Schlegel. But these theorists also paved the way for what emerges under the Hegelians: deeper reflection on beauty and ugliness as more than mere opposites, the roles of the sublime and the comic in relation to ugliness, critiques of ugliness whenever it overreaches its true nature, and ugliness as a necessary element in the larger unfolding of art.

5

Hegel and the Early Hegelians

The next significant chapter in the history of ugliness begins with Hegel and the early Hegelians, in whose writings we find the ugly occupying center stage. The first and greatest sequence of thinkers in the history of aesthetics to reflect on ugliness were the Hegelians and those associated with the Hegelians: Christian Weiße, Arnold Ruge, Johann Georg Martin (G. M.) Dursch, August Wilhelm Bohtz, Friedrich Theodor Vischer, Kuno Fischer, Karl Rosenkranz, Max Schasler, and Moriz Philipp Carrière. With the exception of Rosenkranz, who has recently been translated into English, these figures have largely been forgotten. Only a few studies have been devoted to their work, and almost nothing exists in English.[1] Yet each of these thinkers is worthy of our attention.

Hegel lectured on aesthetics in Heidelberg in 1818 and in Berlin in 1820/21, 1823, 1826, and 1828/29, but he never published his lectures. What has traditionally been used as reference is the so-called Hotho edition of Hegel's Aesthetics compiled from various sources afterward by his student Heinrich Gustav Hotho.[2] In this edition, with its more than 1,500 pages, Hegel seldom speaks of ugliness and for the most part dismisses it. He understands the need for negativity in art, but he views "ugliness" as beneath the aesthetic realm unless it is "elevated and carried by an intrinsically worthy greatness of character and aim" (*Werke* 13:288; *Aesthetics* 222). Hegel also recognizes the inevitable presence of ugliness in caricature (*Werke* 13:35). Not unlike Schlegel and Schiller, Hegel discusses the contrast between Greek and modern art and thereby the special role that negativity must play in modernity, but it is also clear that his praise of Greek art is extraordinary. He remarks that "the withdrawal of subjective inwardness into itself, the inner turmoil, the instability, the whole series, in short, of disunions that produce in their midst the ugly, the hateful, the repulsive" are foreign to Greek culture, but implicitly part of his age (*Werke* 14:24–5; *Aesthetics* 436, translation modified). Hegel cautions that in the end moral ugliness is beyond aesthetic treatment: "evil as such, envy, cowardice, and baseness are and remain purely repugnant. Thus the devil in himself is a bad figure, aesthetically impracticable; for he is nothing but the father of lies and therefore an extremely prosaic person" (*Werke* 13:288–9; *Aesthetics* 222).

Two recent research projects on Hegel's aesthetics have involved, on the one hand, publishing various student transcripts from the lectures and, on the other hand, making the case—partly using these transcripts—that Hegel's view of ugliness shifted over time and was more accommodating than that of his eventual editor, Hotho (Gethmann-Siefert, *Einführung* and "Hegel über das Häßliche"; Iannelli, "Hegel und die Hegelianer" and *Das Siegel*). The overarching thesis is that Hegel was more modern than the Hegelians, for, although the Hegelians focus much more on ugliness, they see it as valid only insofar as it is negated, whereas Hegel seems comfortable with ugliness as such. Evidence from the student transcripts indicates that the concept of ugliness does indeed appear in Hegel's later lectures more so than Hotho captures it in his edition, and it figures more positively. For example, one transcript states that art must sometimes depict "what is not beautiful (Unschönes), for sin and crime and evil must be portrayed" (*Vorlesungen über die Philosophie* 189; *Lectures on Philosophy* 340, translation modified). In another lecture transcript, as Hegel turns from classical art, which he describes as "perfected art," to romantic art, in which subjectivity plays a greater role, he highlights the presence of ugliness: "In this rupture, evil, the opposite of the natural, enters; it is bound up with the nonbeautiful and advances to ugliness" (*Vorlesungen zur Ästhetik* 101).

Still, the overarching case for Hegel's view of ugliness as an end in itself is less convincing. Gethmann-Siefert elevates Schiller as Hegel's ideal. Though ugliness is certainly present in Schiller's dramas, it is not easy to see ugliness as one of the dominant categories, in either his plays or his theoretical essays on drama. In the theoretical works, Schiller extols suffering that passes over into greatness and nobility, not suffering that festers by itself: "The portrayal of suffering—as mere suffering—is never the end of art, but as a means to this end, it is of the utmost importance to art. The ultimate purpose of art is to portray what transcends the realm of the senses" (*Werke* 8:423; Eng. 45, translation modified). Schiller describes tragedy as involving two essential moments, neither of which can be overlooked: "Depicting the suffering nature is the first law of the art of tragedy. Portraying moral resistance to suffering is the second law" (*Werke* 8:426; Eng. 48, translation modified). Tragedy is the expression of a moral will despite already annihilating circumstances. Queen Elisabeth, in Schiller's *Don Carlos* (1787), articulates this resistance to suffering, which Schiller calls the sublime: "How great is our virtue, / If our hearts break in the practice of it!" (1.5.632–3).

Schiller certainly gives us ruthless characters, from the scheming Franz Moor in his first drama *Die Räuber* (*The Robbers*) (1781) to the brutal Vogts Gessler in his final completed play, *Wilhelm Tell* (1804), but he offers mirroring figures of at least relative goodness, and he gestures toward moments of reconciliation. At the end of *The Robbers*, Karl Moor surrenders to the courts, and in *Wilhelm Tell* the hero defeats the tyrannical Gessler. Though *Don Carlos* ends brutally, we see elements of noble self-sacrifice from Elisabeth, Posa, and Don Carlos. Even the brutal Phillip II longs for friendship. In Schiller's works, moral ugliness is present, even vibrant, but it is also exhibited within a wider horizon. Arguably Schiller's darkest tragedy is *Wallenstein* (1799), to which Hegel vehemently objected, for it lacked any hint of reconciliation. In his unpublished essay "On Wallenstein," Hegel writes: "When the play ends, it's all over, the kingdom of nothingness, of death is victorious; it does not end as a theodicy [. . .] Life against life; but only death rises up against life, and incredible! horrific! death triumphs over life! That is not tragic but appalling!" (*Werke* 1:618–20).[3] In the context of Hegel's evaluation of German Klassik, we can also note that even in the transcripts, as Gethmann-Siefert concedes, Hegel praises Goethe's *Iphigenia* (1779), a work that is richly conciliatory (*Einführung* 321). Already in his discussion of tragedy in the as yet unpublished Heidelberg lectures, Hegel makes clear the importance of overcoming one-sidedness and moving toward reconciliation, even if only after disaster occurs: "The reconciliation of principles is the main thing in tragedy [. . .] Reconciliation must be achieved" (*Heidelberger Vorlesungen* über *die Ästhetik* 608–9). Hegel never wavers from the position that tragedy must include a moment of reconciliation.

Nor is it easy to read Hegel as completely avoiding an aesthetic evaluation of modern art and as being solely interested in cultural history, as Gethmann-Siefert contends (e.g., *Einführung* 299). Hegel's consistent praise of *Iphigenia* and his evaluations of multiple other modern works make this clear (*Heidelberger Vorlesungen* über *die Ästhetik* 611; *Werke* 13:297). Francesca Iannelli, a student of Gethmann-Siefert, argues via the example of the crucified Christ that Hegel recognizes the value of ugliness ("Hegel und die Hegelianer"). Yet even in the Hotho edition, Hegel acknowledges that beauty is not the proper category for the crucified Christ: "Christ scourged, with the crown of thorns, carrying his cross to the place of execution, nailed to the cross, passing away in the agony of a torturing and slow death—this cannot be portrayed in the forms of Greek beauty" (*Werke* 14:153; *Aesthetics* 538).[4] Even in the Hotho edition, then, Hegel integrates the value of artistic negativity. And in one of the lecture transcripts, which supposedly elevate ugliness for they give us a more authentic Hegel, we read, for example, that, though Christ on the cross cannot represent a classical ideal, "ugliness may not be admixed with this figure" *(Vorlesungen* über *die Philosophie* 186; *Lectures on Philosophy* 337, my translation). In another transcript, this one from the last set of lectures where Iannelli argues that Hegel has moved on to a clearer embrace of ugliness as such, we read: "Christ on the cross does not embody the concept of ideal classical beauty, but the profound inwardness of the transfiguration of spirit is expressed therein" (*Vorlesungen zur* Ästhetik 116). In this final set of lectures, Hegel later adds that even in paintings of Christ, when he is isolated and mocked, or in depictions of his supporters, who are on the brink of despair, fearing that salvation may be a subjective illusion, there is "anguish, in which at the same time the objective, reconciliation, is certain" (*Vorlesungen zur Ästhetik* 169). In the passage (from one of the unpublished manuscripts) that Iannelli cites to underscore Hegel's emphasis on the ugliness of Christ, the expression Hegel uses is not simply ugly but "häßlich-verklärt" ("ugly-glorified") (Iannelli, *Das Siegel* 151), that is, a coincidence of opposites that hints at transfiguration.

According to Hegel, in the Christian narrative there is never mere ugliness, but always also ambiguity, and thus beauty.[5] In a transcript of the 1826 lecture, Hegel notes that with Christ "the unbeautiful" enters art, but Hegel then moves on, elevating the pietà for its "reconciliation" *(Philosophie der Kunst* 160). And, of course, not only in the aesthetics but also in his lectures on the philosophy of religion Hegel underscores that the negativity of the cross is part of a fuller Christian narrative that does not end with ugliness; Iannelli does not mention this larger horizon. When Hegel notes the need for art's portrayal of sin, crime, and evil, the larger context for Hegel is that the human being conquers "sin and wrongdoing" (*Vorlesungen über die Philosophie* 189; *Lectures on Philosophy* 339). That is, the ugly is present, but only as a moment in a larger dialectical process. Hegel elevates the portrayal of Maria Magdalena, for she combines both negativity and reconciliation (*Vorlesungen über die Philosophie* 189; *Lectures on Philosophy* 340). In short, Hegel seems to have stressed ugliness more than did his conservative student Hotho, but even in the student transcripts, Hegel does not argue that the ugly is valuable simply as an end in itself. On the contrary.

Also independently of religion, Hegel shies away from pure ugliness. Quoting Schiller, Hegel describes art as involving "Heiterkeit"—serenity or more literally brightness—which Hegel paraphrases as sovereign composure even in difficult circumstances: "Serenity is smiling in tears, a reconciliation with oneself in anguish in spite of the unreconciled nature of existence" (*Vorlesungen zur Ästhetik* 42). Following Schiller, Hegel notes that when tragic heroes are forced into impossible situations, they retain their freedom and composure. In modernity, negativity and suffering increase, but, according to Hegel, heroes—even when internally torn, even when sacrificing their lives—do not lose themselves: "In this pain, however, one should hold oneself together and remain free in total dependence. A person who lacks self-possession is repellent and ridiculous" (*Vorlesungen zur Ästhetik* 42).

The paradox of Hegel and ugliness is that Hegel is not the person to whom one should turn for a detailed analysis of ugliness, but one can find in Hegel, as did his followers, extraordinarily productive categories for understanding ugliness, including his emphasis on dialectic and his view that "the summit of art" is comedy, the genre closest to ugliness (*Heidelberger Vorlesungen über die Ästhetik* 629).[6] Ultimately, for Hegel, great art integrates the beautiful and the ugly and is not simply one or the other. For Hegel, every position calls forth a counterposition that calls into question the initial position. Out of their interaction develops ideally a more stable and coherent synthetic category. For Hegel, only art that unites beauty and ugliness, as with the conflict in Antigone, is truly great. How that evolves in particular is more fully represented by the Hegelians than by Hegel himself.

*

In his *System der Ästhetik als Wissenschaft des Schönen* (*System of Aesthetics as the Science of the Beautiful*), published in 1830—a year before Hegel's death, and well before the posthumous publication of Hegel's aesthetics—**Christian Hermann Weiße** introduces the concept of ugliness to systematic aesthetics. Weiße, who in 1823 had heard Hegel lecture in Berlin, makes clear that he belongs to the Hegel school (x–xviii). Weiße elevates above all the Hegelian method, but he adds that he does not agree with all that has been published in the name of the school. In his diverse writings, Weiße took issue not only with other members of the school but also with much of Hegel, even as Weiße adopted aspects of Hegel's approach.[7] At the time of publication, Weiße was an außerordentlicher Professor in Leipzig, having completed his first Habilitation there in 1823 (he later did a second Habilitation in theology) and having taught aesthetics, Hegel, or related subjects more than a dozen times before his work appeared.[8] He became a full professor there in 1845.

Weiße is important for three reasons. To begin with, Weiße was the first in the history of aesthetics to address the ugly in a sustained and systematic way. He devotes a substantial section of his *System der Ästhetik* to ugliness and revisits the topic throughout his study (1:173–207). As had Schlegel, he consciously demands that art and aesthetics deal with ugliness. Weiße insists on "watchful immersion in the contradiction itself" and praises works that integrate and overcome ugliness (1:176). He writes: "If an art form is able to represent ugliness objectively without being contaminated by a poison and succeeds in glorifying beauty by thus triumphing over the archenemy of all beauty, this should be considered a merit and not at all a deficiency or degradation" (2:217–18). Above all, Weiße goes beyond

Lessing in seeking fully to elaborate the essential attributes of ugliness and its role in aesthetics.

Second, Weiße introduces much of the foundational vocabulary that the early Hegelians will develop and refine. He conceptualizes ugliness within the contexts of the sublime and the comic, and he introduces the important structure of ugliness as a moment within a larger dialectical process, which becomes in some ways the signature post-Hegelian move, even if Lessing had loosely anticipated the process. Weiße describes the moment of ugliness as "fleeting and vanishing" (1:198). In its finitude, beauty deals with contrast and contradiction. Within this framework, Weiße recognizes three relevant categories: the sublime, the ugly, and the comic (1:137). Whereas the sublime lifts us beyond the beautiful to the concepts of the good and the divine, resulting in the mediation of the infinite and the finite, the ugly involves a recalcitrant fixation on finitude alone (1:163–64). Weiße describes ugliness as "inverted beauty or beauty placed on its head" (1:179; cf. 1:144 and 1:157). Articulating a perspective that amounts to a dialectical negation of negativity, he argues that the concept of ugliness belongs to art, but "only in the dialectical unfolding of the idea of beauty" (1:203). Art portrays ugliness in a way that demonstrates its ultimate invalidity, a process achieved primarily through comedy (1:207–14).

Although the proximity of the ugly and the comic finds its first formulation in Aristotle's *Poetics* (1449a), the structure of the comic as a negation of the negation, a rendering of the ugly as ugly, which indirectly affirms the positive, is a theoretical innovation of the Hegelians. Weiße describes comedy as "superseded ugliness (die aufgehobene Häßlichkeit), or [. . .] the reconstitution of beauty out of its absolute negativity, which is the ugly" (1:210). These two insights—that the ugly is a negation that is itself negated and that this negation occurs primarily via the comic—continue through the early Hegelians. Although Weiße is parsimonious with examples, Aristophanes' comedies readily illustrate his point.

Third, although Weiße is aware of the traditional view of ugliness as privation, he is also familiar with Schelling's recent theory of evil as more than a privation, which Schelling developed in his 1809 essay on freedom, *Philosophische Untersuchungen über das Wesen der menschlichen Freiheit* (*Philosophical Investigations into the Essence of Human Freedom*). Schelling offers a perversion, not a privation, theory of evil. He insists on rendering justice to the phenomenological reality of deliberate, willful ugliness and seeks to avoid both the privation theory (whereby evil does not exist) and the non-monotheistic idea of two competing forces, which would limit God and indicate, moreover, the "self-rupture and despair of reason" (Ge.r 66; Eng. 24, translation modified). In creating the world, God separated the real from the ideal. As such, evil, with its horrific potential, is an inherent possibility. Human freedom involves the "capacity for good and evil" (Ger. 64; Eng. 23).

In his *System der Ästhetik* Weiße follows Schelling's essay on freedom and draws the parallel that the ugly, too, is more than just a lack of beauty, and in doing so, he deviates from Schelling's earlier and still unpublished aesthetics, which, as we saw, still worked with the concept of ugliness as privation (*Philosophie* 30; *Philosophy* 31). Weiße attacks "the widespread misconception that everything that is negative is merely a flaw in something that is positive" (1:174). He later states that his concept of ugliness "corresponds to the definition of *evil* that has been repeatedly put forward in contemporary philosophy. According to this definition, evil is not simply the non-good, but rather seceded goodness, goodness that has been perverted and turned on its head" (1:179; cf. 2:415). The reference to Schelling is unambiguous. Weiße further argues that ugliness can be understood as a "double lie": first, that no higher truths exist; and, second, that the particular replaces the true and enduring (1:182). Weiße's description of the ugly is remarkably prescient in terms of later views that embrace ugliness instead of beauty and, in this process, go so far as to erase the concept of truth and elevate the particular as the only bearer of meaning.

Like all the later Hegelians, except for Rosenkranz, Weiße works more at the conceptual than the phenomenological level; his examples are few. Another gap in Weiße is the complete disinterest in the history of aesthetics. Nevertheless, Weiße does show an architectonic interest in the history of art, identifying three stages: classical, romantic, and modern (1:291–3). These stages follow a dialectical pattern and are in that sense superior to Hegel's linear sequence (1:258–320). It is telling that Vischer follows not Hegel's but Weiße's understanding of the history of art (2:492–625).

Arnold Ruge, the next Hegelian to analyze the ugly, does so in his book on comedy, *Neue Vorschule der Ästhetik* (*New Introduction to Aesthetics*), published in 1837. Ruge was active not only as a philosopher but also as a political writer, often using pseudonyms, and as a literary writer, trying his hand at prose, poetry, and drama. He also worked as a translator. A political liberal, Ruge served prison time for his views and was well acquainted with both Feuerbach and Marx, with whom he collaborated. In 1849, he emigrated to England.[9]

Ruge refers explicitly to Weiße, praising him for being the first to analyze ugliness, "this rich and infinitely important aesthetic concept" (88). Ruge builds on Weiße, articulating more fully the dialectical structure of the ugly, the idea of a negation of a negation. Ruge calls ugliness "the *first negation*" and "the finite contradiction" (92). Ugliness lives within finitude, which seeks to assert its own particular validity and negate truth without negating itself, thus holding on to contradiction and stagnating in negativity (93; 96). "The finite spirit itself suffers this defeat by not ascending, but instead by wanting in its finiteness to be sufficient unto itself" (91). The student of Hegel will recognize here echoes of Hegel's arguments in his *Wissenschaft der Logik* (*Science of Logic*) (1812–16, with revisions in 1832), particularly in the second chapter where Hegel analyzes finitude and emphasizes that the finite, instead of recognizing its own finitude, stubbornly takes itself to be absolute (Hegel, *Werke* 5:115–73). Indeed, Hegel calls the finite "the most stubborn category (die hartnäckigste Kategorie) of understanding," which is saying much, since understanding is itself already the moment in the dialectic defined by one-sidedness and stubborn opposition (Hegel, *Werke* 5:140; *Science of Logic* 129, translation modified; cf. *Encyclopedia Logic* §79–81).

Although for Ruge the ugly is mired in finitude, resisting any mediation with beauty or truth, it is in the nature of ugliness to be unaware of its own insufficiency (98). Intriguingly, Ruge insists that ugliness is more prominently visible and dramatic not in the material but in the spiritual realm, where one encounters not simply the ugly but the ugly in its unshakable fixation on finitude. In a sense, Ruge not only echoes Hegel; in terms of ugliness, he modulates an insight we saw before, in Solger and Weiße, that the ugly stubbornly seeks to replace the beautiful and insert itself in its stead.

Ruge also explores the interconnectedness of concepts, noting analogies between ugliness, falsehood, and evil:

> When the finite spirit in its finitude holds firm and asserts itself against its truth, that is, against the absolute spirit, then the finite spirit, in its striving for self-sufficiency, is transformed. As cognition, it becomes *falsehood*; as volition that renounces itself and in its finiteness intends only itself, it becomes *evil*; and when both evil and falsehood *manifest themselves*, the finite spirit becomes *ugly*. (93)

Ugliness denies any form of the spirit apart from finitude: the "denial of God, of immortality [. . .] of beauty, of enthusiasm, of love as a spiritual good—this is the rebellion of the spirit against itself, of the finite spirit against its truth" (97). Emphasizing that ugliness refuses to be moved by truth, Ruge defines it as "the appearance of the false spirit that opposes spirit's truth" (110). Ugliness requires a further negation—"the negation of the negation or the absolute contradiction"—to participate in truth (92). To recognize the ugly as ugly is to transform it. In contrast, avoiding the double negation and seeing ugliness as self-sufficient is to dwell in a condition of stasis, what Ruge calls "the *non-realization of spirit*" (105); in another passage, he calls ugliness "vapid spirit" (den geistlosen Geist) (110).

For Ruge the ugly can be resolved also via the sublime, as, for example, with the sinner or criminal who voices regret at the moment of death (111). Death is ugly insofar as we consider the corpse in its finite form as final, as the dissolution of spirit, where the light of intelligence no longer shines in the face of the dead. Death is sublime, however, when we consider that death means moving beyond the earthly self and toward the resurrection of spirit (98). Whereas the sublime is conscious of its truth, the ugly remains unaware of its lingering in falsehood.

Despite noting that ugliness can be transformed via the sublime, Ruge associates the ugly most prominently with comedy. Ruge agrees with, and reformulates, Weiße to the effect that "ugliness is the first negation, the comic the second negation" (60). For Ruge comedy is not simply a negation of tragedy but a negation of the negation of tragedy; it is not merely a portrayal of finitude but a negation of a position that seeks to render finitude what it is not, absolute. We see the ugly as less than ideal and laugh at it. The negation (of the beautiful) is itself negated. Therefore, caricature contains the seeds of the ideal within it, even if it does not explicitly reveal the ideal.

In his *Aesthetik oder die Wissenschaft des Schönen auf dem christlichen Standpunkt* (*Aesthetics or the Science of the Beautiful from a Christian Perspective*) (1839), Johann Georg Martin (G. M.) **Dursch** devotes dozens of pages to the subject of ugliness. Dursch, a priest with a doctorate in philosophy and theology from Tübingen, wrote extensively on religious topics. After studying for two years in Paris, he translated into German the *Hitopadesha*, an early collection of Sanskrit fables and maxims in prose and verse. However, Dursch's most extensive work was in Christian aesthetics. Although Dursch is sometimes counted among the Hegelians (e.g., Zelle, "Das Häßliche" 1318) and occasionally uses a dialectical structure (e.g., 434), his Hegelianism is less pronounced than that of other thinkers in this sequence. Nonetheless, he shares with Hegel an interest in linking the beautiful with the true and the good; he follows Hegel's understanding of classical and romantic art; and he is clearly influenced by the Hegelian Weiße, whom he cites.

At the outset of his aesthetics, Dursch underscores the importance of ugliness: "The depiction of the beautiful in the realm of spirit and nature takes into itself the opposite of beauty, ugliness, for the concept of a thing includes in itself also its opposite, and a thing shines forth more clearly by way of its opposite" (4). Each of the two parts of Dursch's work, divided into spirit and nature, includes a chapter on beauty, followed by a chapter on ugliness. Since ugliness manifests itself in appearance and action, ugliness belongs in both realms (305). However, a focus on moral ugliness, which Dursch explores from a Christian perspective, dominates these pages.

Dursch brings forward several interesting points, even if none are original. His definition of ugliness aligns closely with Plato's: "The ugly in the realm of the spirit is the orientation and activity of the spirit toward that which resists its nature and purpose" (305). He defines the beautiful as "the appearance of truth in individual form, or we can say what is beautiful is an individual form that is commensurate with the essence of truth" (306; cf. 426). Ugliness not only deviates from beauty, it seeks to usurp it (307), an insight we have encountered before. In the realm of humanity, ugliness primarily involves our being enmeshed in purely sensual drives and driven by such vices as selfishness and arrogance, hatred and self-hatred, ambition and envy, indifference and coldness, injustice and mercilessness, treachery and betrayal, thanklessness and godlessness. Dursch keeps alive the ancient idea that there is an ugliness of the soul. He recognizes ugliness not as non-beauty but as active opposition to beauty (308). Similar to Schelling, he views our abuse of freedom as the dominant catalyst for moral ugliness (305). A prominent form of ugliness in Dursch's analysis is lying, denying the existence of truth and then offering itself in its stead, a position that could be said to have currency even today (307–8). In the realm of nature, ugliness involves what contradicts or limits vitality: "mutilation, destruction, consumption" (305).

Dursch's work has clear limitations. Because his main concerns are theology and ethics, his comments on art and artworks are modest—remarkably so for a book on aesthetics. Dursch makes it a point to criticize Hegel's definition of beauty as too limited: "the sensuous appearance of the idea" is "one-sided and thus too narrow" (62). Dursch embraces an unusually broad understanding of beauty, reproaching Hegel for not acknowledging "a spiritual beauty in itself" (62). As examples of beauty without any sensuous dimension, Dursch cites the community of saints (59–61), angels (63), and heaven (103). Here he returns to the medieval idea of divine (versus sensuous) beauty.[10] Dursch has in stretches a non-dialectical frame, arguing that the ugly cannot be derived from the beautiful (310) and failing to integrate thinkers who recognized the ugliness of the crucified Christ. For Dursch, God is pure beauty: "In God's essence nothing ugly is conceivable" (311). Conversely, the devil epitomizes ugliness: Satan "is the ugliest" (312). Among the nineteenth-century writers I explore, Dursch is, unsurprisingly, the most forgotten. He provides, however, evidence of the heterogeneity of the tradition, even as his specific analyses of ugliness hone closely to earlier contributions, especially those of Weiße.

In *Ueber das Komische und die Komödie. Ein Beitrag zur Philosophie des Schönen* (*On the Comic and Comedy: A Contribution to the Philosophy of Beauty*) (1844), **August Wilhelm Bohtz** also addresses ugliness.[11] Bohtz, a friend of the poet Ludwig Tieck, had been strongly influenced by Solger and Schelling. Although Bohtz was not technically a Hegelian, I include him here because, like Weiße and Ruge, he had been influenced by Hegel's method, expressed admiration for Hegel, and fits intellectually among the Hegelians (*Die Idee des Tragischen* 68). According to Bohtz, if a work is to result in a beautiful whole, it requires a harmony of many diverse elements, each in its proper place. Ugliness disrupts this harmony; it is a kind of discord. Whenever any one part within a larger whole is out of place, the result is ugliness (28). Bohtz follows Ruge in emphasizing that just as evil is not simply the absence of the good but "a positive element that has become perverted," ugliness constitutes "a fight against the harmony that prevails in the realm of beauty" (29). Instead of recognizing itself as part of the whole, the part fixates on itself and views itself as the whole, thereby destroying the whole: "Such *disjointedness*, *distortion* of totality, is a constant feature of ugliness" (29).

Bohtz prefers spatial over temporal imagery of wholeness, but he retains the basic idea that beauty allows for dissonance, provided it is ultimately resolved: "Yet the dissonances that are struck in beauty do not remain as they are. Instead, they pass over into harmony" (30). When this does not occur, the result is ugliness, which Bohtz calls, in what amounts to almost a quote from Weiße, "the *perverted* spirit, beauty that has been *turned on its head*" (30). In ugliness, in contrast with beauty, "the totality of the idea is smashed to pieces" (30). Not unlike others in this tradition, Bohtz links ethics and aesthetics, asserting that whenever we see evil, we recognize ugliness. However, not all appearances of ugliness are associated with evil (37).

Although the sublime and the ghostly play roles for both Weiße and Ruge, Bohtz is the first since the sixteenth-century Vincenzo Maggi to try to conceptualize types of ugliness. In *Ueber das Komische und die Komödie* Bohtz introduces three categories: (1) the demonic, which borders on, but deviates from, the sublime; (2) the ghostly or spectral, where all positive moments have receded, leaving only unadorned ugliness; and (3) caricature, which evokes laughter (38–9). The demonic has a bizarre force of attraction (41). There "the sublime has been distorted and the divine vilely commingled with the satanic" (44). The demonic violates ethical norms and destroys what should be; thus, it is ugly. As examples, Bohtz cites Richard III and Macbeth (44). However, integrating ugly figures does not render a work ugly, and Bohtz makes the reverse point: an artwork can have beautiful moments and yet, taken as a whole, still be ugly (44).

The ghostly, his second category, lacks the attraction of the demonic and is thus immediately recognizable as ugly. The "ghostly" is not merely a "distortion," but "a true mockery of all life that is real and in the flesh" (46). Bohtz uses examples such as ghosts, that is, appearances of the dead, and wax figures, which resemble corpses. The category of the ghostly has even more heuristic value than Bohtz imagined, for today technology has provided us with ever newer versions of the ghostly, that is, distortions of reality. Literary works can include such elements without being ugly. Bohtz gives as an example Tieck's *Der blonde Eckbert* (*Eckbert the Blond*) (1797). Some of E. T. A. Hoffmann's tales, in contrast, where insanity and reason meld together, exemplify for Bohtz unappealing ugliness. In caricature, finally, the ugly is not threatening but is recognized in its inadequacy. Its deviation from the ideal is obvious to all who receive the work. Because the ugly is recognizable as non-real, it is no longer threatening and becomes ridiculous. Bohtz's three categories are drawn from observation, not a logical framework. Certainly, the ideas of the demonic as evil but enchanting and of caricature as a mode of comic negation will reappear in later discussions. The ghostly, which may have emerged in the context of waning romanticism, does not play a major role in later discussions of ugliness, even if the concept will be included in Rosenkranz's typology and could be said to arise indirectly in the notes of Walter Benjamin.[12] However, if we focus less on the name and the examples and more on the definition—mockery of all that is real—the concept remains relevant even today.

Friedrich Theodor Vischer, who taught in Tübingen and Zürich and later became well known also as a novelist and satirist, addresses ugliness in his systematic exposition of beauty. Contemporaries called Vischer "V-Vischer" to distinguish him from the Heidelberg philosopher Kuno Fischer, who also worked on aesthetics. In the first volume of his aesthetics, *Ästhetik oder Wissenschaft des Schönen* (*Aesthetics or the Science of Beauty*), published in 1846, with the sixth and final volume appearing in 1857, Vischer explicates beauty much in the spirit of Hegel, although the influences of Schelling, Solger, and Hotho are also evident (Oelmüller 135–8; Iannelli, "Das Hässliche"). Vischer, who carefully read Hegel after concluding his studies, is the only early Hegelian to develop a truly comprehensive overview of aesthetics, examining all of its features. Still, Vischer, who studied with Hotho, does not elevate ugliness to any significant degree. Though ugliness appears in his system, Vischer does not devote autonomous sections to it. Like his predecessors, Vischer treats the ugly within the contexts of the sublime and the comic. Whereas Weiße and Ruge, who devote autonomous sections to ugliness, view the ugly as an independent, if transitional, category between the sublime and the comic, Vischer sees ugliness as existing solely within these elements.

We recognize ugliness when power extends beyond its appropriate measure and evokes "dread and horror" in the sublime (1:262). Vischer further describes situations where what we perceive as powerful is itself destroyed. He considers the effects of plague, famine, earthquakes, and large-scale battles (1:265). Contemplating the destruction of the world also illustrates the horror of ugliness (1:265). A singular passion that becomes excessive is likewise ugly: "As soon as it becomes total and habitual, it passes over into ugliness" (1:274). Vischer reflects on bitter and obsessive hatred that exceeds the bounds of defending the good and leads instead to self-destruction (1:274–5). Pure evil—not mere privation, but the willful inversion of goodness—is ugly. Such moral evil can appear in a disfigured person, such as Richard III (1:277), or, more deceptively, in the most beautiful of people. Vischer notes a commonality between moral ugliness and the state of nature: "Moral ugliness pulls human beings back into chaos, transforming them into wolves and bears, and is a mirror of the ugliness in nature" (1:279). In such cases, the contradiction between what one expects from a human being and what one receives is not reflected upon but instead simply terrorizes the observer (1:280).

Vischer returns to ugliness when he discusses the comic, where contradiction remains central (1:358–75). When analyzing the transition from the terrible (or sublime) to the ridiculous (or comic), Vischer describes ugliness as the negative element in each, which itself has no positive standing: "The ugly is located between the terrible and the ludicrous. As a result, it surrenders all its positive characteristics to one or the other of these spheres. It is left with nothing but this surrender, this movement of dissolution (diese Bewegung des Zergehens), such that, as the saying goes, it sits between two chairs" (1:369). In the sublime, the ugly appears as a contradiction between the idea and the image that is driven by, but grossly inadequate to, the idea. In the sublime, we dwell on the idea, ugliness overpowers us, and fear dominates. In the comic, in contrast, the contradiction and its moment of ugliness emerge in our consciousness as we focus not on the idea but on the finite image; comic ugliness invites reflection (1:360).

Vischer follows Ruge: the comic presents the ugly as a nullity in the form of a double negation. Vischer writes: "The comic is the negation of a negation" (1:374). Vischer argues that the ugly must be negated because, while beauty is a concordance of appearance and idea where the particular and the universal merge into one harmonious entity,[13] the ugly represents the contradiction of appearance and idea. This disharmony occurs when the particular usurps and displaces the universal, creating a distortion of perspective: "This contradiction is the ugly" (1:360). The art Vischer has in mind in his second extensive discussion of ugliness involves not images that repel us because of their subject matter but forms that lack harmony, images that are distorted or fantastic, and appearances driven by chance and chaos. He considers such forms appropriate in art as long as they are recognized as ugly and, in the context of comedy, negated.

When commenting on sculpture, painting, and literature, Vischer again returns to ugliness. Like Lessing, he favors its portrayal in literature and even advocates for its depiction, recognizing that art should engage the ugly or "evil in its appearance" (6:38). Vischer adds a compelling argument to Lessing's focus on time: when literature portrays ugliness in the mind instead of in the physical world, the force of ugliness is softened. Vischer notes that poetry "weakens the hideousness of the immediate appearance of the ugly by presenting it solely to the mental eye" (6:36). Words can express so much more than the eye can see; although they can amplify ugliness, they can also attenuate it (6:38). For Vischer, as for his Hegelian predecessors, it is essential that ugliness be overcome. He affirms "the universal aesthetic law that distortion and madness should not take on a life of their own but should instead shade over into one of those contrasting forms of the beautiful," namely, the sublime or the comic (6:39).

Later in life, Vischer reflected critically on his past work and subsequent developments in aesthetics. He acknowledges that Schasler's greater emphasis on ugliness was justified (*Kritische Gänge* 6:115–16; cf. 6:106 and 6:112). Here, Vischer recognizes the importance of ugliness for tragedy (*Kritische Gänge*

6:113–14). And he admits that, in general, he gave ugliness too little attention. Vischer goes so far as to say: "the concept of the ugly must therefore [. . .] be developed much more fully than I have done" (*Kritische Gänge* 6:116). In this late text, Vischer returns to a conception of ugliness we first saw in Plato: "After dealing with the general concept of beauty, we must consider its opposite, and so ugliness must be incorporated, initially simply as what should not be" (*Kritische Gänge* 6:116). Vischer then works dialectically with the term, recognizing that ugliness is "the driving force behind differentiation in the realm of beauty," that is, ugliness makes possible different forms of beauty (*Kritische Gänge* 6:118).

Vischer circles back to ugliness also in his late lectures on aesthetics, *Das Schöne und die Kunst* (*The Beautiful and Art*), where he writes:

> *Ugliness* is simply the opposite of beauty, just as evil is the opposite of goodness, and there are many different kinds and degrees of ugliness. Where ugliness appears, there is a lack of order, an absence of unity in diversity, the parts of the whole are not clearly organized, there are no clear-cut boundaries in space and time, the bounds of moderation are overstepped, norms are infringed, symmetry and proportions are skewed. (173–4)

Vischer adds that ugliness surfaces not in the beautiful (in the narrower sense of pleasing) but in the sublime and the comic, a position consistent across his writings (173).

A weakness throughout Vischer's aesthetics is the sparsity of examples, but he has some good theoretical insights, which are not without contemporary resonance. For instance, studies of ugliness in African art have connected ugliness to what Vischer emphasizes: the evocation of fear and the experience of the comic (Van Damme 57–65). The art movements of Expressionism and New Objectivity, which express revulsion at the horrors of war and mock the corrupt and the wealthy, also resonate with Vischer's dialectic. The link between the ugly and both the sublime and the comic, which Vischer stresses even more than his predecessors, has broad applicability.

Kuno Fischer studied Hegel with the Hegelian J. E. Erdmann in Halle, wrote an influential study of Kant, and later in life published a large two-volume book on Hegel's life and works. In Heidelberg, Fischer garnered a reputation as one of the best teachers of his era. He explores ugliness in his first work, *Diotima: Die Idee des Schönen* (*Diotima: The Idea of the Beautiful*) (1849), which is infused with Hegel's idealism and the Romantic elevation of religion and art.

Fischer views the sublime and the ugly as opposites: "The ugly is the flip side of the sublime" (238). In the sublime, the ideal and sensuous appearance are split, and the ideal triumphs separately. In ugliness, base sensuous appearance eliminates the ideal (238). For Fischer, as with other early Hegelians, contradiction is essential to both the sublime and the ugly: "Ugliness is aesthetic: it is the contradiction in the realm of beauty—the sensuous existence that forgets its ideal nature just as in the sublime the ideal nature forgot its sensuous existence" (238). Like almost all his early Hegelian predecessors, Fischer believes comedy resolves contradictions, overcomes ugliness, and so reintroduces beauty. He asserts that the comic brings about "a dissolution of the ugly" (262–3). Much as comedy confronts the sublime with the justice of sensuous reality, so does comedy force ugliness to recognize the justice of the ideal (265).

The ugly is not simply a mistaken truth or a mistaken good. Ugliness emerges only in the form of the persistently negative: "Error becomes ugly only when it dominates cognition, deliberately holds firm, and so as *prejudice* or *superstition* emphatically denies truth" (252). Fischer stresses this element of obstinacy, the failure to recognize the gap between what is and what should be, coupled with an unwillingness to resolve it. Ugliness thus erases any sense of moral striving and moral dignity: "Thus *flaccid, weary* selfishness would be the form in which immoral spirit in its final phase also accomplishes its final aesthetic role—that of ugliness" (256–7). This resistance and false fixation on finitude is a recurring theme in German reflection on ugliness. Arguably, Ruge and Fischer render it most vividly.

Finally, Fischer introduces a distinction within ugliness based on theory and praxis, thereby reminding us of the category of intellectual ugliness: "Brutality is *ugly sensuousness* and stupidity *ugly consciousness*. The former is the baseness of practice, the latter the baseness of theory" (257). Fischer then reinforces his distinctions with imagery that is both classical and Christian, associating the sublime with "*nearness to the sun*" and the ugly with "*distance from the sun*" (260).

6

Rosenkranz, Schasler, and the Later Hegelians

In 1850, **Karl Rosenkranz** corresponded with Kuno Fischer about *Diotima* and, in return, sent Fischer an outline of his own developing concept of aesthetics, which at the time consisted of three main sections: the beautiful, the ugly, and the comic (Glockner 108–10). Three years later, Rosenkranz published an entire book on ugliness, *Die Ästhetik des Häßlichen* (*Aesthetics of Ugliness*).

When Rosenkranz studied in Berlin, he was not the least impressed when he dropped in on Hegel's lectures; Schleiermacher attracted him far more (*Kritik* vii–viii; *Von Magdeburg* 187). Earlier, while in Heidelberg, Rosenkranz had encountered Hegel's *Encyclopaedia*, which he found difficult. Eventually, he became an enthusiastic reader of Hegel's works. When Rosenkranz finally immersed himself in Hegel, particularly through his earliest book, *The Phenomenology of Spirit*, he described the experience as "a revolution" in his education and a kind of "intellectual ecstasy" (*Von Magdeburg* 290). After his sojourns in Heidelberg and Berlin, Rosenkranz continued his studies in Halle and was taught by Hegel's former student at Heidelberg, Hermann Friedrich Wilhelm Hinrichs. While in Halle, Rosenkranz developed a friendship with Arnold Ruge, whom we discussed in Chapter 5. The practice of studying at several universities was common at the time and connected to the German concept of *Lernfreiheit*, a kind of academic freedom for students, which encouraged independent learning and residencies at multiple universities.

After completing his studies, Rosenkranz was appointed a professor in Halle and then in Königsberg, where he also served as Rector. In 1831, around the time of Hegel's final birthday, Rosenkranz was in Berlin and spent several weeks conversing with Hegel (*Hegel's Leben* vi–vii). He went on to write the first biography of Hegel.

Although *Aesthetics of Ugliness* was not translated into English until 2015, Rosenkranz's immediately preceding book, *Die Pädagogik als System* (*Pedagogy as System*) appeared in English already in the nineteenth century. Translated as *Philosophy of Education*, the book benefited from extensive commentary by William Torrey Harris, a leader among the St. Louis Hegelians, who was the US commissioner of education from 1889 to 1906. Both of Rosenkranz's works share a focus on dialectical structures. For Rosenkranz, estrangement and its sublation are the central moments in any meaningful education.[1]

Many who are unfamiliar with the details of the post-Hegelian period identify Rosenkranz as the thinker who initiated systematic reflection on ugliness (Gigante 584; Schaeffer 328; Bachmetjevas 30; Hammermeister 108; Krečič and Žižek 60.) We have seen that this is false. Nonetheless, it is true that Rosenkranz was until recently the author of the only attempt in the history of aesthetics to give a truly comprehensive and detailed account of ugliness. A sign of contemporary interest in the ugly and of Rosenkranz's standing is that his study has been reprinted at least eight times with four publishers since the late 1960s and has been translated into Romanian (1984), Spanish (1992), French (2004), and Italian (2004).[2] That Rosenkranz's work was not translated into English until recently is a fascinating subject in itself and may have to do with German versus Anglo-American engagement with ugliness, a topic I explore in Chapter 12.

Not only does Rosenkranz devote an entire book to the ugly, in which he seeks to grasp various kinds of ugliness and their overcoming, but the richness of his examples has no parallel before him. These are in many cases relatively obscure works of contemporary art, literature, and music, but his examples are also taken from great writers, such as Sophocles, Dante, Cervantes, and Shakespeare. Rosenkranz, who also published works on literature and was himself active as a writer, is interested in the questions of how ugliness fits into art and what constitutes bad art. He views ugliness as "the opposite of beauty" or "the negation of the former" (Ger. 5 and 7; Eng. 32 and 33). For Rosenkranz, ugliness is ontologically deficient and exists only in relation to beauty: ugliness "is only possible through its reflexive relationship to the beautiful, in relation to which it finds its measure" (Ger. 8; Eng. 33). He argues that beauty is absolute, akin to goodness, while ugliness, like evil, is merely relative (Ger. 8; Eng. 33). Rosenkranz rejects the claim that ugliness deepens our sense of beauty (Ger. 37; Eng. 47), but because art expresses the idea in its totality, art allows for—and even calls for—negativity. Ugliness prevents art from becoming restricted or biased (Ger. 39; Eng. 48) and is essential to comedy (Ger. 9; Eng. 34). As with Hegel, Rosenkranz finds collision and contradiction important not only as logical categories but also as ontological and specifically aesthetic categories; working through contradictions provides a rich terrain for artistic exploration.

Most of Rosenkranz's book addresses ugliness in art, but he opens by discussing ugliness in nature, noting its presence not in plants but in animals, above all creatures that are between types, such as amphibians, and those that deviate from the norm, such as sheep with eight legs (Ger. 28–30; Eng. 43–4). This idea continues a theme visible in German aesthetics. Herder had suggested that creatures straddling spheres, such as land and sea, appear "ugly" insofar as they are either "undeveloped" or appear to us to be "biformed and thus confused" (*Kalligone* 1:174–5). Similarly, Hegel remarked that the platypus seems odd because it defies normal categories, being neither bird nor four-footed animal (*Vorlesungen* über *die Philosophie* 61–2; *Lectures on the Philosophy* 233). Such creatures, once called *mirabilia*, puzzled thinkers until Darwin introduced the concept of evolutionary adaptation.

Before turning to art, Rosenkranz discusses "the ugliness of spirit" (das Geisthäßliche), which he associates with our knowing evil but still pursuing it. He calls this behavior "unfreedom" and "the deepest contradiction of the will with its idea" (Ger. 29; Eng. 43). He also identifies dimensions of spiritual ugliness in drunkenness and insanity (Ger. 34; Eng. 46). Negation of freedom is a recurring thread in his explication of ugliness, with illness being a physical example (Ger. 62; Eng. 59).

In much of the work, Rosenkranz offers a comprehensive set of terms to describe various forms of ugliness, which gives his study, as Bosanquet rightly notes, "a certain tinge of scholasticism" (*History* 393). Rosenkranz's three main concepts are formlessness, incorrectness, and deformity (Verbildung). Formlessness violates the principle of unity essential to beauty. Rosenkranz categorizes formlessness into three types: the amorphous, the asymmetrical, and the disharmonic. He criticizes amorphous forms for lacking external limits or internal differentiation and elucidates the boring nature of such formlessness. The way to deal with this, as with all other forms of ugliness, is via the comic, for example, the idea that a continuing iteration can have a comic effect (Ger. 74; Eng. 66). Asymmetry can give evidence of chance and chaos, as well as of deviation from the norm. All of these can easily be absorbed into the comic realm. Similarly, the asymmetry or odd mixing of tragic and comic action in the same work can itself be comic (Ger. 78–89; Eng. 75). This is a particularly astute comment, as the parody of tragedy within comedy remains even today a modestly underexplored topic. Occasionally, Rosenkranz weaves historical observations into his systematic exposition. In discussing disharmony, for example, he notes that the ancients elevated harmony to such a degree that they tended to undervalue individuality and difference, whereas modernity's elevation of the individual can come at the expense of harmony. Following Schlegel, Rosenkranz calls this elevation of the individual, which can beguile us, "the interesting" (Ger. 105; Eng. 83). This fascination with the material, even as we recognize a lack of coherence, is evident in architecture that amalgamates multiple styles in engrossing but not fully harmonic ways (Ger. 108; Eng. 85). Any attempt to resolve contradiction and disharmony without allowing for immanent refutation, such as in fantastic and improbable endings, is comic (Ger. 109; Eng. 85).

Incorrectness, the second major form of ugliness, represents a kind of imperfection, a deviation from normative expectations. These expectations range from accuracy, such as appropriate distinctions among types of trees in a landscape painting, to conventions, such as the purity of genres and styles (Ger. 116–7 and 138; Eng. 89–90 and 99). Although traditional in his approach, Rosenkranz acknowledges that a great work can absorb in its details many deviations (Ger. 118; Eng. 90). Examples of legitimate deviation include the Flemish school's portrayal of Mary as a Northern European (Ger. 125–6; Eng. 94); Schiller's transformation of the Don Carlos story (Ger. 126–7; Eng. 94); magical elements in fairy tales (Ger. 137; Eng. 99); and violations of unity in drama (Ger. 143; Eng. 104). Rosenkranz also endorses the idea of sublime effects in sculptures that are achieved when the artist diverges from the correct form of the human body (Ger. 152; Eng. 107–8). Here Rosenkranz breaks with his predecessors, who consistently rejected ugly sculptures, most prominently Herder and Kant.

At times, Rosenkranz insists on qualities of correctness that seem more conventional than necessary, such as regularity in poetic composition. A break in meter need not be purely ugly; it can represent foregrounding, as in Heinrich Heine's "Nachtgedanken" ("Night Thoughts") (1844). The middle line of this poem—"Deutschland hat ewigen Bestand" ("The German nation will not fail")—breaks the metrical pattern, which undermines the claim (Ger. 4:432; Eng. 51). The Russian formalists later identified this technique of deviating from harmonious patterns to create disharmony as "defamiliarization" (Shklovsky). It serves a purpose: incorrectness allows us to see the familiar in new ways. Outside of tragedy and comedy, where intermingling is legitimate, Rosenkranz insists that the genres should be strictly separate, a view that today would be justly viewed as unnecessarily limiting (Ger. 155; Eng. 109).

Although Rosenkranz is strict on poetic composition, he does in principle recognize the value of incorrectness, that is, intentional deviation from the expected norm, when the context is comic (Ger. 128–9; Eng. 95). This includes, for example, mixing high and low styles to effect irony or parody (Ger. 141; Eng. 103) or employing "incorrect speech" (Sprachunrichtigkeit) and "mixed-up speech" (Sprachmengerei) to undermine a character (Ger. 161 and 162; Eng. 112 and 114, my translation). For the former, Rosenkranz cites Shakespeare; for the latter, one might think of Riccaut in Lessing's *Minna von Barnhelm*, though Rosenkranz gives the now lesser-known example of Gryphius's *Horribilicribrifax* (Horrible Sieve).

In explicating his third form, deformity or *Verbildung*, to which he devotes a majority of his pages, Rosenkranz follows recent tradition by emphasizing that ugliness is not the simple absence of beauty but its positive negation (Ger. 164; Eng. 115). He introduces three forms of deformity: the base (das Gemeine), the repellent (das Widrige), and caricature.[3] The first form, the base, is linked to a lack of freedom. Rosenkranz describes it as dependence on a vice, which contradicts the idea of humanity (Ger. 168; Eng. 117). Gorging ourselves on food and drink is one of his examples (Ger. 170; Eng. 118). In his elaborate schema of categories, Rosenkranz positions the base as the opposite of the sublime (Ger. 179–80; Eng. 122–23). He further divides the base into the small, specifically a smallness that should not be or is out of place (Ger. 181; Eng. 123); the weak, exemplified by Goethe's Werther (Ger. 193; Eng. 130); and the low, characterized by limiting motives such as chance, pettiness, and egotism, which stand in opposition to the majestic (Ger. 198–199; Eng. 132). The low, in turn, is further subdivided into the trivial, which incorrectly deems itself important; the accidental and arbitrary, which replace necessity and freedom, illustrating how the ugly falsely seeks to replace the beautiful; and the raw, defined by Rosenkranz as "the degradation of freedom under a necessity which is not its own" (Ger. 226; Eng. 146). The raw thus includes dependence on nature, resistance to freedom, and mockery of the highest values, such as friendship or religion (Ger. 226, 264; Eng. 146, 164).

Rosenkranz accepts instances of deformity when they realize freedom. Consider forced or exaggerated rhymes, which can be comical and artificial and so can signal irony. That is, they are ugly by design, an act of freedom, and given the comic context, joyfully executed. Rosenkranz writes:

> Freedom asserts itself as a cheerful game and transfigures ugliness into ridiculousness through the conscious excess of arbitrariness. An incorrect rhyme for instance will not be found beautiful by anyone. A forced rhyme distorts a word to make it rhyme. This mishandling of language is also not beautiful; but because it originates in a freedom that has created language itself and according to which the word could also have this form, we must laugh (Ger. 224; Eng. 145)

One could add to Rosenkranz's comic list also exaggerated rhymes, which in their ridiculousness convey irony. Consider Heine's satire of the Germans in "Zur Beruhigung" (Consolation) (1844) or his mocking of Romanticism in "Das Fräulein stand am Meere" ("The Young Lady Stood by the Sea") (1844).

Within the realm of the raw, which follows the low, in which we found the accidental and arbitrary, Rosenkranz introduces yet further categories, such as the obscene, brutal, and frivolous. According to Rosenkranz, obscenity is linked to shame, which he considers "sacred and beautiful," because it represents the superiority of spirit over nature (Ger. 235; Eng. 150, translation modified).[4]

For Rosenkranz, obscenity "consists in the intentional injury to shame" (Ger. 235; Eng. 150). While animals feel no shame, humans do. Unintentional bodily exposure is not obscene, but the intentional contravention of the value of shame is. Pornography violates shame by intentionally exposing private body parts independently of their connection to spirit. Pornography devalues sexuality by decoupling it from a deeper connection to love, which would otherwise grace sexuality with dignity. Solger similarly viewed shamelessness as a false substitute for a higher idea, namely, love. Therefore, shamelessness is ugly (*Erwin* 180 and *Vorlesungen* 101).

Twentieth-century German philosopher Max Scheler draws on the related concept of dignity to develop the concept of obscenity that Rosenkranz only touches upon. Although Scheler does not cite Rosenkranz, his work follows similar lines. Scheler argues that the metaphysical meaning of the sexual act is not rooted in an external purpose, be it procreation or pleasure, even if these are byproducts. Instead, the sexual act is ideally an expression of love (Scheler 118). According to Scheler, pornography violates this connection to love—and thus to a higher realm of dignity—not by severing it indifferently but by instrumentalizing another's body for pleasure. Even voluntary instrumentalization remains instrumentalization. While eros elevates humans above animals, pornography reduces us to mere animality.

Rosenkranz recognizes that the obscene, which substitutes the body for the soul, is inappropriate because it reduces the subject to an object. The obscene act becomes a means for satisfying lower desires, and this, according to Rosenkranz, must be dealt with comically. Portrayals of Priapus, where the erect penis is often as large as the body, are both obscene and comic. For Rosenkranz, obscenities as a form of moral ugliness belong in the sphere of the comic (Ger. 235–46; Eng. 150–5). The comic mode presents obscenities in their untenability and absurdity, thereby negating them: "This whole sphere of sexual vulgarity (sexuelle Gemeinheit) can only be aesthetically freed through the comic" (Ger. 246; Eng. 155, my translation).

The obscene surfaces more readily when moral restraints are lifted and a connection to the transcendent vanishes. This may explain its prominence in modernity. The obscene can also be triggered by a turn to realism, as in Hellenistic sculpture and Roman satire, where we see comic or satiric distancing. These approaches align with what Rosenkranz endorses, even if, as with other instances of ugliness, a certain fascination and thus ambiguity can also be unveiled, as in Petronius' *Satyricon* and Bosch's *The Garden of Earthly Delights*. Occasionally, the formal fascination overrides the moral moment.

The question arises whether the obscene is defined by the object itself or our reception of the object, given that our concept of what constitutes obscenity fluctuates over time and famously differs by locale. Here, as with ugliness itself, I would argue that the concept does not shift; instead, what changes is what we subsume under the (stable) concept. What we find obscene, what offends us, evolves over time, but the concept of the obscene—as a form of indecency or lewdness that is shameless or ugly and violates the concept of human dignity, thereby contradicting what should be—remains stable.

The repellent is the second major category Rosenkranz elucidates under deformity. He notes that a lack of unity, symmetry, or harmony is ugly, but not necessarily repellent (Ger. 278; Eng. 173). According to Rosenkranz, the repellent comes in three forms. First, "clumsiness (das Plumpe) displeases through the nonform of its mass or the awkwardness of its movement" (Ger. 284–5; Eng. 177). Second, the empty or dead reveals a lack of movement or internal differentiation. Third, the hideous, which moves art into the realm of evil, can itself assume three forms: the theoretically hideous, which Rosenkranz describes as absurd, insane, and internally contradictory; the sensuously hideous or the disgusting, for which he includes examples from life, such as vomit and the smell of excrement (Ger. 314, 321; Eng. 191, 195), and from literature, including Petronius and Hartmann von Aue (Ger. 317, 321; Eng. 193, 196); and the practically hideous or evil. This third form of the repellent, itself a subcategory of deformity, can be manifest in three ways, as the criminal, ghostly, and diabolical. As with other forms, comedy is a privileged mode of negation or dissolution. For instance, the portrayal of a human answering the call of nature can be effectively depicted only in comedy (Ger. 231; Eng. 148). Other examples include the comic incongruity between everyday triviality and the bombastic tone of false pathos (Ger. 208; Eng. 137); forced rhymes, which give evidence of the burlesque or arbitrary (Ger. 224; Eng. 145); the combination of freedom and dependence evident in the drunk

(Ger. 233; Eng. 149–50); and intentional repetition that, via parody, mocks what is boring and lacks spontaneity (Ger. 298; Eng. 183).

The emphasis on the comic is so prominent in Rosenkranz that his final and third category under deformity is caricature, which represents a release from deformity through exaggeration and disproportion.[5] Caricature is, for Rosenkranz, "the peak in the conception of ugliness" and offers the transition to the comic (Ger. 387; Eng. 233) and the ridiculous (Ger. 427; Eng. 256). Caricature is essentially identical in its structure with satire (Ger. 394; Eng. 236), though Rosenkranz favors caricature that does not overly dwell on ugliness but moves beyond it with cheerfulness and serenity (Ger. 412; Eng. 247). In this, he follows Hegel, who writes that only after reading Aristophanes can one truly understand "how a person can be as happy as a pig in muck" (wie dem Menschen sauwohl sein kann) (15:553; *Aesthetics* 1221, my translation). Rosenkranz prizes that form of caricature, "the fantastic" (Ger. 424; Eng. 255), that is deeply imaginative and creative and with its unbridled exaggeration leaves the realm of reality behind. Here comedy triumphs over the negativity of both form and content (Ger. 424; Eng. 255). This appreciation is evident in Rosenkranz's praise for Austrian playwright Ferdinand Raimund, particularly his 1828 play *The King of the Alps and the Misanthrope* (Ger. 427–28; Eng. 257).

The connections Rosenkranz draws between caricature, the non-reality of the fantastic, and the ridiculous are compelling. Caricature involves a distortion—often a comic exaggeration—of the face or body, disrupting a sense of measure and proper proportion and allowing quantity to overwhelm quality. It reduces the human being to an animal, automaton, or object. The goal is not to capture a detailed likeness but to emphasize and exaggerate the most distinctive and often least appealing physical features, which results in a semblance of the whole. Precisely the disproportion and distortion, while superficially inaccurate, capture something deeper and can be, in a surprising sense, more accurate, in comparison with a generic likeness, in grasping a character's essence. The image is thus simultaneously fantastic, ridiculous, and true. As the visual image overtakes the person, reality gives rise to an image, which becomes the new reality. Caricature plays a privileged role for Rosenkranz because it not only depicts the ugly, but through its comic structure and effect, simultaneously negates and transcends it.

While Rosenkranz insists on the importance of ugliness, he emphasizes that it must be subordinate and temporary, "a vanishing moment" (Ger. 40; Eng. 49). To render it full and independent would be contrary to its concept (Ger. 41; Eng. 49). Therefore, it is crucial that ugliness be presented in a state not of being, but of becoming or transformation (Ger. 168; Eng. 117). It belongs to the nature of ugliness to negate itself, and so its subordination results not from the artist's external manipulation. Instead, the artist simply lets the internal contradictions emerge, lets the ugly reveal itself as ugly (Ger. 43; Eng. 50). An isolated depiction of ugliness would grant it too much independence, falsely presenting it as an end in itself (Ger. 49; Eng. 53). Ugliness must be framed within a broader context where it is ultimately negated (Ger. 41; Eng. 49).

Prominent for Rosenkranz as well, then, is the figure of double negation, which he associates primarily with the comic: "The comic is the *dissolution* of the ugly insofar as it *destroys itself*" (*System* par. 831). In another passage, he suggests: "The ugly stands in opposition to the beautiful; it contradicts it, whereas the comical can at the same time be beautiful, beautiful not in the sense of simple, positive beauty, but certainly in the sense of aesthetic harmony, the return out of contradiction into unity. In the comical, something ugly is co-posited as the negation of the beautiful, which, however, it negates in turn" (Ger. 53; Eng. 55, translation modified). Indeed, for Rosenkranz the concept of the ugly is "the midpoint between that of the beautiful and that of the comical" (Ger. iv; Eng. 25). Comedy is built on the structure of portraying what is inadequate, untenable, deviant, and then revealing its inner contradiction and self-cancellation. Any contradiction becomes tolerable when it is viewed through a comic lens or comic turn of events (Ger. 136; Eng. 99). The comic presents inadequate positions in their absurdity and as such negates them. The comic is not the negation of substance but the negation of the negation of substance, or the negation of ugliness as the reduction of truth. In comedy, we laugh at contradictory positions; we don't mistake them as the final truth.

Thus, for Rosenkranz, the ugly is invited into art but only insofar as it is transformed or overcome. In this sense, ugliness can be both a danger to and an ingredient of great art. Satire has always portrayed the ugliness of reality, but it does so to reveal it for what it is, something negative, a reality to be overcome. Obscenities as forms of ugliness are presented only to be mocked, displaced, or relativized. This aesthetic rendering of obscenities indirectly serves a moral purpose. Supporting Rosenkranz's view, one can point to works like Aristophanes's *The Clouds* and Ben Jonson's *Volpone*. Both comic writers masterfully employ the reductio ad absurdum. This comic negation of absurdity results in what Rosenkranz calls "beautiful ugliness" (das schöne Häßliche) (Ger. 301; Eng. 185).

Like the earlier Hegelians, Rosenkranz maintains the long-standing connection between the ugly and the comic. He views the ugly as a necessary condition for comedy, asserting that comedy is not possible without an element of ugliness (Ger. vi–vii; Eng. 26). For Hegel, the comic can involve a critique of positions, such as particularity and subjectivity, which are not one and the same with what many would otherwise understand by ugliness. The early Hegelian concept of the comic works only if one accepts an expansive concept of ugliness as including any untenable position. A definition of the ugly as an appearance that deviates from its normative expectation does fit this model. In contrast, definitions of the ugly as what stands opposite the beautiful or what we find repellent are less persuasive in this context.

Rosenkranz has his limits. He privileges overcoming ugliness through the comic. But ugliness cancels itself in other modes too. In tragedy, for example, powerful but morally repugnant heroes may destroy themselves, as in Shakespeare's *Macbeth* or Camus's *Caligula*. Beyond the sensible triad of formlessness, incorrectness, and deformity, Rosenkranz seems unable to offer any logical or structural rationale for his sequence of terms; the distinctions seem to be invented without being related to any overarching systematic order, even if occasionally reasonable transitions surface, such as the sequence, which takes place within the hideous, from the theoretical or internally contradictory to the sensuous or disgusting and, finally, to the practical or evil. Many of the sequences and transitions seem arbitrary. Also, the slight differences among the dozens of categories are often slippery, at times tedious and even unhelpful. Moreover, in terms of meta-distinctions, Rosenkranz's categorical differentiation is not always at the highest level. He recognizes in principle the important distinction between ugliness in the object depicted and ugliness in the depiction itself (Ger. 357; Eng. 214), but at other times, as in his discussions of the accidental and the arbitrary, of the dead and the empty, and of the hideous and its diverse subcategories, he moves back and forth between what is portrayed and how it is portrayed without being clear about the distinction, which will become highly significant for an analytic philosopher such as Nelson Goodman. Still, one must recognize Rosenkranz's pioneering brilliance, the richness of his examples, and the heuristic value of his abundant distinctions.

*

Max Schasler, who comments extensively on Rosenkranz, had a Hegelian as a teacher already at his Gymnasium in Bromberg: Heinrich Theodor Rötscher, the author of a superb book on Aristophanes that Rötscher dedicated to Hegel. On Rötscher's recommendation, Schasler then continued his studies with Rosenkranz in Königsberg. After submitting his dissertation in Berlin and completing a subsequent book on the philosophy of language, Schasler became a leader in the revolts of 1848, leading to his exile from Prussia and later Baden. Eventually, as long-time editor of the art magazine *Dioskuren*, Schasler became one of Germany's most influential art critics. He addresses the concept of ugliness in both his two-volume *Kritische Geschichte der Ästhetik* (*Critical History of Aesthetics*) of 1872, which he dedicated to Rosenkranz and which had considerable influence, and his less well-received two-volume *Ästhetik* of 1886. Surprisingly, he is neglected in even some of the detailed histories of ugliness in German thought (e.g., by Werner Jung).

In his history of aesthetics, Schasler devotes considerable space to his predecessors who addressed ugliness—above all Schlegel, Weiße, and Rosenkranz. Schasler's astuteness is evident at various moments. He criticizes Ruge for not distinguishing the comic from the ridiculous (2:1016), he notes that Vischer failed to grasp the centrality of the history of aesthetics (2:1048), and he points out that Rosenkranz's concepts of *das Gemeine* (the base) and *das Widrige* (the repulsive) hardly stand in opposition to one another (2:1034). In the preface and later in his criticisms of others, Schasler makes apparent his distinctive position (ix). He offers an expansive concept of ugliness as negativity or "the negative moment" in beauty (2:1036). He argues that beauty is not absolute if it is only positive and one-sided; it requires ugliness, that is, negativity, which is itself negated as beauty emerges (2:791–2, 2:961,

2:1024, 2:1036–7). The ugly is thus broader in his eyes than in those of his predecessors, who saw ugliness as a moment of art but not of beauty. The difference with Rosenkranz is striking. For Rosenkranz, ugliness is part of art but not part of beauty; for Schasler, in contrast, the ugly is embraced as a necessary "metaphysical element" within beauty itself (2:1037).

According to Schasler, negativity gives shape and richness to what would otherwise be mere abstraction. Negativity ensures that the Platonic ideal in its abstraction comes into appearance and is realized. In aesthetics, that necessary principle of negativity is ugliness. Schasler quotes (and modifies) Goethe's Mephisto more than once:

> For beauty's activity can easily abate,
> It soon prefers uninterrupted rest;
> To give it this companion hence seems best
> Who roils and must as Devil help *create*. (cf. *Faust*, ll. 340–3)

In the first line of this passage, Schasler substitutes "beauty's activity" for "man's activity," and then in the final line, he italicizes "create" (2:1028). For him, the negativity of ugliness is "the constructive principle in the concrete development of the beautiful" (*Über einige Prinzipienfehler* 24). Ugliness is not a type of beauty and certainly not a kind of "distortion" (2:1025), but a necessary factor, the "principle of motion," within beauty (2:1028). Without ugliness, beauty would not be possible: "Only through the negation of itself does beauty become realized [. . .] the ugly is the negativity in the process of the aesthetic idea" (2:1035).

Already in the first chapter of his *Ästhetik*, Schasler addresses ugliness, reinforcing common ideas of the age, adding new perspectives, and challenging conventional wisdom. He argues for the centrality of ugliness not as a necessary moment in art or as the opposite of beauty. Instead, Schasler goes further, as he did in his historical work: ugliness is a necessary element of beauty, and beauty must be grasped dialectically. Just as we understand truth by thinking through and refuting erroneous positions, so does beauty emerge through its engagement with ugliness (1:19). The ugly, far from being a mere deficiency, has "a thoroughly substantial meaning" (1:19).

Schasler describes ugliness as reality in its distance from the idea, yet the idea cannot become real without this element of distance or differentiation

(1:21). One sees here, although Schasler does not mention it, another way in which the post-Hegelian discussion of ugliness is compatible with Hegel's aesthetics. What Schasler analyzes as a comprehensive element of art is closely analogous to Hegel's articulation of the origin of tragedy. In order to manifest itself in the world, the absolute or divine must take on definite shape. It must become particular, which engenders a necessary rift in the absolute. In this world, the absolute is no longer one, but split, making collision and tragedy inevitable (Hegel, *Werke* 15:522; *Aesthetics* 1195).

Schasler's reflections are modestly abstract, but he makes intriguing moves: defining ugliness very broadly as negativity and viewing ugliness as a constitutive element not just of art, but of beauty itself. This approach elevates the concept of ugliness, surpassing even Rosenkranz's understanding of its systematic importance.

*

Moriz Philipp Carrière was a professor in Munich who also belonged to the Hegelian school, in his case with a strong theistic orientation. In his *Aesthetik*, first published in the early 1850s and appearing in its third edition in 1885, Carrière includes a section on the ugly, tellingly entitled "Das Häßliche und seine Ueberwindung" (The Ugly and its Overcoming) (1:147–68). Noting earlier writings on the topic by Schlegel, Weiße, Ruge, Rosenkranz, and Schasler, Carrière argues that the ugly belongs in works that seek to portray the richness of the world, but it must be tempered. He identifies a variety of strategies for this, including comedy, tragedy, and humor. Carrière defines ugliness broadly as "the conscious break with the ideal" (1:153). Moral ugliness is an example. He insists that some level of poetic justice be preserved and that ugliness not be elevated for its own sake but instead be overcome. Like earlier Hegelians, he argues that "the ugly [. . .] cancels itself" (das Häßliche [. . .] hebt sich selber auf) (1:159).

Much like Plato, Carrière describes the ugly as "something that should not be (ein Nichtseinsollendes) but which nonetheless pushes its way into existence" (1:159). Were it to become stable and not be dissolved, it would cast beauty from its just throne. Carrière cites Dante and Shakespeare as examples of authors who meaningfully integrate ugliness into their works, where beauty is seen not as given but as becoming: "Thus we obtain the appearance of nascent beauty as something which is not completed in immediate harmony, but instead comes into being only through the resolution of dissonances" (1:168). Carrière stands out as the only nineteenth-century thinker besides Hegel to explore the drama of reconciliation, a genre in which ugliness and dissonance are prominent but eventually overcome or resolved, as in Aeschylus' *Oresteia* or Sophocles' *Oedipus at Colonus* (Carrière, *Das Wesen* 291–304 and *Aesthetik* 2:611–16).[6]

Karl Ludwig Michelet was a student during Hegel's later years in Berlin and an editor of his works, who substituted for Hegel, giving lectures on the "Philosophy of Right" when Hegel was ill in 1830–31. In his five-volume system of philosophy, *Das System der Philosophie als exacter Wissenschaft* (*The System of Philosophy as Exact Science*), published between 1876 and 1881, Michelet includes a brief discussion of ugliness. He identifies the ugly as one of only three aesthetic categories, alongside the beautiful and the sublime (1:292–93). Although his comments are cursory, the legacy of the Hegelian tradition is evident.

*

In uniquely elevating the significance of ugliness, the German tradition underscores the interwoven nature of beauty and ugliness. We see the need to differentiate types of aesthetic ugliness, including the role of ugliness in various arts, a topic previously unaddressed. The simple Aristotelian insight—that one can create a beautiful depiction of an ugly object—gives way to a focus on two more complex processes. First, we see a dialectical structure, evident in Hegel's analysis of satire and further developed by the Hegelians, who emphasize comedy and caricature. They assert that the ugly content of a work cannot remain static but must be negated. This idea of a double negation is more or less universal among the Hegelians. Second, we recognize a more expansive framework, with occasional parallels to the Christ story, which suggests that ugliness is best presented as part of an unfolding narrative that includes but also moves beyond ugliness. We see this structure in Lessing's elevation of the temporal arts and in the drama of reconciliation. This frame is less common in modern theory and practice, though a strong advocate surfaces in the Kantian Hermann Cohen, whose concept of humor is not far removed from this speculative framework, as we will see in Chapter 9.

The German aesthetic tradition, perhaps partly influenced by German art, also argues that some topics, such as Christ's crucifixion, inherently demand the presence of ugliness. The Hegelians view ugliness not as an absence of beauty but as a central and constitutive element, be it of art in general or of beauty in particular. After them, there is no serious return to the idea of ugliness as mere privation. And all of these thinkers, in various ways and to varying degrees, present ugliness as part of a larger structure: the ugly should not have the final word but must itself be negated.

We also see more complex associations between the ugly and other central aesthetic categories. Not only is Aristotle's insight into the links between ugliness and comedy further developed, but several Hegelians also relate the ugly to the sublime. Ugliness involves a recalcitrant fixation on the finite without any higher connection and thus provides us with a contrasting category to the sublime. Ugliness fixates on the real and excludes the ideal, even seeking to usurp it. This structure reinforces the role of ugliness in a modern world that has moved beyond the Platonic and Christian ontology.

No other group of thinkers in the history of aesthetics was as interested in the concept of aesthetic ugliness as were the Hegelians. Their immersion in ugliness and their tackling it head-on showed courage for the time, especially in the case of Rosenkranz, who explicitly detailed aspects of ugliness, including obscenities, that would have offended many contemporaries (Ger. 235; Eng. 150). The influence of the Hegelians lasts through the nineteenth century, even among non-Hegelians. Although ugliness disappears from the theoretical landscape as we move into the first half of the twentieth century, from Adorno onward its prominence returns, and ugliness becomes a significant concept also beyond the German tradition.

7

Darwin and the Neo-Hegelians

While the Hegelian turn to ugliness begins to dissipate in Germany after Schasler, it resurfaces with two British thinkers, Bernard Bosanquet and Walter Terrence Stace. However, the first Anglo-American writer after Burke and Price to address ugliness was not a philosopher, but the biologist **Charles Darwin**. Writing contemporaneously with Schasler and Carrière, Darwin does not comment extensively on beauty or ugliness, but he does offer insightful observations. Darwin notes that the reception-aesthetic category of disgust can be evoked whether the offensive object is "actually perceived or vividly imagined" (*Expression* 231). In *The Descent of Man* (1871), he suggests that some animals possess an aesthetic sense that is manifest in sexual selection: features in male animals, such as bright colors or large feathers with remarkable ornamentation, may hinder survival by drawing predators even though they attract females (*Descent* 1:63–5, 2.91–4, 2.399–401). Darwin adds that the capacity to recognize beauty develops over time and that its presence in nature increases (*Descent* 2.401 and 2.223). He also notes that beauty has both universal and culturally specific dimensions (*Descent* 1:64 and 2.39). When addressing ugliness, Darwin identifies two key elements. We perceive as ugly that to which we are not accustomed, such as a nose or eyes twice as large as the norm.[1] We also find ugly that which lacks any variation. Thus, ugliness is not merely a deviation from the norm; it can also be, as with Hogarth and

Price, a pattern without variety, which itself deviates from the norm of beauty (*Descent* 2.354).

The first English writer to tackle ugliness at length is the neo-Hegelian **Bernard Bosanquet**. Bosanquet, who published on logic, metaphysics, politics, and aesthetics, was a contemporary of the neo-Hegelian F. H. Bradley. Although Bradley's reputation has since eclipsed Bosanquet's, during their lifetimes Bosanquet was considered the more prominent figure. Indeed, Bosanquet was arguably the central figure in British philosophy of his day and appears to have influenced even those who opposed him.[2] In his *History of Aesthetic* (1892), Bosanquet refers to ugliness as a "question of supreme aesthetic importance" and elucidates its development among the Hegelians (*History* 393). Beyond tracing the intellectual-historical importance of ugliness, Bosanquet himself introduces the valuable concept of "difficult beauty" (*Three Lectures* 85).[3] Many will call certain works ugly, but others will—on the basis of education, experience, and imagination along with a willingness and patience to attend to details—come to recognize beauty.

Although the term "difficulty beauty" originates with Bosanquet, the concept was implicitly introduced by the Hegelian Max Schasler. As Bosanquet notes, Schasler was the first to view difficult and displeasing elements in art as not only permissible but essential (*History* 424). Seeming ugliness is understood to be beautiful only when the eyes are seasoned and the categories appropriate. In art, hermeneutics is always at play, but the introduction of ugliness raises the stakes. Bosanquet focuses exclusively on the reception context, emphasizing the need for well-educated, sophisticated, and attuned recipients. However, three moments are at play in evaluating difficult beauty: not only the recipients' capacities, which are essential, but also the extent of the ugliness portrayed and the level of artistry.

A weakness of Bosanquet's theory lies in his focus on reception aesthetics rather than artwork aesthetics; he has no clear categories to distinguish difficult beauty from bad art (*Three Lectures* 97–108). Bosanquet implies that in art there is no such thing as ugliness. If beauty is expressive form, and all art involves expressive form of some kind, he argues, then there is no ugliness: "if it [an object] has no expressive form, it is nothing for aesthetic. If it has one, it is beautiful" (*Three Lectures* 98). This suggests that any failure to appreciate a work lies with the viewer's inability to tolerate unpleasant or unusual content or to recognize deeper connections and patterns. Bosanquet is surely right that the problem often lies with the viewer who may fail to recognize a deeper beauty. But to deny the existence of ugliness implies that all art is inherently beautiful, which is not a defensible claim. One can certainly imagine a work where certain brutal episodes or frivolous parts are not justified within a larger whole.[4]

Even if Bosanquet overreaches by pushing the concept of difficult beauty too far, the concept is one of the most compelling in the tradition. Much of what we initially perceive as ugly is, in fact, beautiful, and making that transition can be difficult. When Goethe visited the Strasbourg Cathedral, he expected to see a disordered, ugly, barbaric work. Accustomed to the elevation of classicism, he was famously taken aback by his unexpected admiration for the Gothic cathedral's splendor, glory, and unity amidst so many complex details ("Von deutscher Baukunst"). Goethe's conversion gives us an instructive example of someone extending their horizon of taste and expanding their level of tolerance and capacity for discrimination ("Von deutscher Baukunst"). Under the concept of difficult beauty, we can recognize historical examples of works that initially met with mixed receptions. The Eiffel Tower faced tremendous resistance at first because it fit no previous style. Instead, its form was derived from its material, iron (Brown 124–54). The challenge of finding beauty in seemingly ugly works becomes even more acute in the century after Bosanquet developed his theory. If we use the category of "difficult beauty" and its analogue "seeming ugliness" without restricting ourselves to Bosanquet's presuppositions, we discover a rich set of aesthetic categories.

As the twentieth century unfolds, further Anglo-American contributions to the concept of ugliness emerge, primarily falling into two types. One consists of thinkers, like Bosanquet, who are influenced by Hegel or the Hegelians and who approach beauty with an understanding of dialectic. The other group comprises those who, with analytic precision, address the seemingly neglected topic of ugliness, but in most cases with no awareness of the German tradition.

Walter Terence Stace, who in 1924 published the first English-language study of the Hegelian system, *The Philosophy of Hegel*, is the most prominent member of the first group. In *The Meaning of Beauty* (1929), Stace gives the ugly considerable space. Born and educated in Great Britain, Stace worked in the British civil service for over two decades before moving to Princeton, where he taught from 1932 to 1955, serving as the doctoral advisor of John Rawls. Already in his book on Hegel, Stace notes that, in contrast to classical art, the ugly becomes prominent in romantic art: "suffering and evil, even the *ugly*, find their place in romantic art. For it is the *torn* soul, the soul in conflict with itself, that is here the subject of art" (*Philosophy* 463). Stace recognizes that Hegel had drawn the break between classical and romantic art with the ugliness of Roman satire. Furthermore, Hegel views Christ as paradigmatic of romantic art, for in romantic art the idea is no longer universal but particular. In its particularity, the idea is severed from blissful repose and must engage in suffering and death, even if it ultimately ends in redemption (*Philosophy* 463–4).

Stace thinks that it is not possible to provide "a precise definition of the ugly" (*Meaning* 77), yet he believes that the ugly can enhance "the strength and profundity of the artistic effect" (68). In analogy to the paradox of tragedy, Stace speaks of the "paradox" of ugliness (72). We experience feelings of "displeasure," aversion, and repugnance when we encounter ugliness, but to the extent that the ugly is "genuinely artistic," it also evokes "pleasure" (*Meaning* 74). Stace comments that since we already regard "the sublime, the terrible, the satirical, and the comic" as species of beauty, including the ugly in this spectrum makes sense (*Meaning* 82).

In searching for terms that capture what is not beautiful, Stace speaks not only of the ugly but also of "the unbeautiful," which refers, on the one hand, to a work of art that is "a failure" (*Meaning* 71) and, on the other hand, to anything that is the "absence of beauty," including the "aesthetically indifferent" (*Meaning* 69). For Stace, the unbeautiful encompasses whatever, through failure or indifference, does not achieve his definition of beauty, the fusion of intellectual content with a perceptual field. Stace substitutes "perceptual" for the Hegelian "sensuous" to encompass a wider sphere beyond physical objects, such as "beautiful characters, emotions, or ideas," which, though not strictly sensuous, can still be perceived (*Meaning* 45). Although Hegel might have countered that sensuousness includes physical expressions and the physicality of language, both of which evoke such emotions and ideas, Stace's use of "perceptual" is an intriguing contribution that helps ensure we think of beauty (and ugliness) as potentially expansive categories.

8

Nietzsche and the Writers

While few English writers were reflecting on ugliness, the continental tradition had no shortage of thinkers engaging with the topic. Many of the continent's nineteenth-century proponents of aesthetic ugliness, including Victor Hugo, Georg Büchner, and Charles Baudelaire, were artists themselves. Hugo published his reflections three years before Weiße, and Baudelaire presented most of his thoughts shortly after Rosenkranz's volume appeared. This parallel literary development complements the scholarly tradition. These writers are not simply practitioners; they also reflect on the idea of ugliness. Some offer commentary, while others create self-reflexive literary works. By doing so, they embody two distinguishing facets of modern literature: self-reflection and immersion in ugliness. Two great writers, who were simultaneously philosophers, Schopenhauer and Nietzsche, conclude the chapter.

In his "Preface to Cromwell" of 1827, the French writer **Victor Hugo** analyzes the distinguishing characteristics of modern art. He elevates portrayals of reality's dramatic tensions, contrasting them with the lyrical evocation of an eternal ideal and the epic recollection of the historically grandiose. We see here Winckelmann's influence, also beyond Germany, as Hugo's reflections on Greek art align with Germany's idealizing model. Hugo advances the idea that Christianity brings forward an aesthetic revolution: Christianity recognizes connections between the beautiful and the ugly, fostering art in which "the grotesque" and "the ugly" play prominent roles (*Préface* 21; "Preface" 363). For Hugo, unlike Alberti, the task of art is not to select, correct, or ennoble nature but to show it in a "concentrating mirror" (un miroir de concentration)

(*Préface* 60; "Preface" 386). Thus art integrates "the deformed, the ugly, the grotesque" (*Préface* 40; "Preface" 374). This immersion in reality is perfectly compatible with aesthetic innovation. The grotesque, including the abnormal and the horrible, becomes aesthetically fascinating, elusive, and new.

The anti-idealist movement in nineteenth-century Europe triggered, as did the realist thrust in ancient Rome, a literary turn to ugliness. In the early post-romantic period, the titular hero of the unfinished novella *Lenz*, written in 1836 by German writer **Georg Büchner**, makes the case that the artist should not idealize reality but rather portray it as it is, without overlooking its ugliness. Before Büchner died at the age of twenty-three, he had written, in addition to *Lenz*, three dramas of tremendous literary value and a powerful political pamphlet critical of political and social injustice, for which he was charged with treason, forcing him into exile. That he had by that time already completed his studies as a medical doctor and researcher and was furthermore preparing lectures on the history of philosophy before his untimely death, only accentuates the loss of a truly brilliant mind.

The central scene and a turning point in Büchner's *Lenz* is a discussion of art, in which Lenz argues that art should not elevate the ideal but affirm life:

> The good Lord has certainly made the world as it should be, and we surely cannot scrawl out anything better, our only goal should be to imitate him a little. In all, I demand—life, the possibility of existence, and then all is well; we must not ask whether it is beautiful or ugly, the feeling that the work of art has life stands above these two qualities and is the sole criterion of art. (Ger. 1:234; Eng. 146)

Lenz thus endorses the inclusion of ugliness:

> One must love humanity in order to penetrate into the unique essence of each individual, no one can be too low or too ugly, only then can one understand them; the most insignificant face makes a deeper impression than the mere sensation of beauty, and one can let the figures emerge without copying anything into them from the outside, where no life, no muscles, no pulse swells and beats. (Ger. 1:235; Eng. 147)

In elevating the underprivileged and the ugly, Lenz rejects the ideal of Greek beauty, which German *Klassik* had resurrected and reinforced. He attacks not only idealization but also stillness, which had been linked to sculpture as the pinnacle of classical art (Roche, *Dynamic Stillness* 126–34). In place of such lifeless ideals, Lenz favors the motion of life and the empathetic portrayal of reality. He privileges works of realistic Christian art that do justice to suffering and loneliness. In this context, Lenz recalls the "divine-suffering features" of Christ himself (Ger. 1:235; Eng. 147). Lenz's affirmation of suffering, with its echo of the Passion, is central to his one homily: "He spoke simply to the people, they all suffered with him, and it was a comfort to him when he could bring sleep to several eyes tired from crying, bring peace to tortured hearts, direct toward Heaven this existence tormented by material needs, these weighty afflictions. He had grown stronger toward the end, then the voices began again

> Burst, o divine woe,
> The floodgates of my soul;
> May pain be my reward,
> Through pain I love my Lord"
> (Leiden sei mein Gottesdienst). (Ger. 1:231; Eng. 144)

The final line reinforces the Christian idea of expressing piety by identifying with God's suffering.

On a metalevel, Lenz's aesthetic views and Christianity's emphasis on the vulnerable justify Büchner's empathetic portrayal of a character who suffers from deep emotional ugliness. Lenz's plight is marked by existential isolation. He struggles to formulate coherent sentences and build human connections. His emotional and metaphysical despair alienates him from even existing relationships. During his crisis, Lenz embodies, in the words of the narrator, the two extremes Schlegel identified in ugliness: "a terrible void (Leere) and a tormenting anxiety (Unruhe) to fill it" (Ger. 1:246; Eng. 156).

Driven by his deep concerns over inexplicable suffering, Lenz challenges the theodicy and ultimately turns to atheism:

> Oberlin talked to him about God. Lenz quietly drew away and looked at him with an expression of endless suffering and finally said: but I, if I were almighty, you see, if I were, and I couldn't bear this suffering, I would save,

> save, I just want nothing but peace, peace, just a little peace and to be able to sleep. (Ger. 1:248–9; Eng. 158)

Lenz's embrace of the world as it is, in all its suffering and ugliness, contradicts his inability to accept a world in which suffering and pain exist. By the novella's end, Lenz falls into complete lethargy, and we cannot help but identify with his immeasurable distress. In this fragmentary novella and his other writings, Büchner condemns unjust conditions while evoking empathy for tortured individuals. We begin to see the ways in which for modern writers Christianity is not only admired for its empathy with the ugly and the outcast but also questioned or abandoned insofar as the reality of modern ugliness seems incompatible with a powerful and loving god.

Like Büchner, the French art critic, essayist, and poet **Charles Baudelaire** reflected on art's role in modernity. As a critic of mimesis and an advocate of artistic autonomy, Baudelaire supported the portrayal of ugliness formed in the artist's imagination, for example, Francisco Goya's fantastic and terrifying images (Fre. 2.564–74; "Some"). In his *Salon* of 1859, Baudelaire argues that art should avoid "the exact reproduction of Nature" (Fre. 2.617; Eng. 152). He believed that imitating nature impoverishes the imagination, which is paramount, and erases art's distinctive personality. Baudelaire laments that the advent of photography heightened painters' tendencies toward positivism: "Each day art further diminishes its self-respect by bowing down before external reality; each day the painter becomes more and more given to painting not what he dreams but what he sees" (Fre. 2.619; Eng. 154). Baudelaire abhors this propensity: "I consider it useless and tedious to portray what *exists*, because nothing that *exists* satisfies me. Nature is ugly, and I prefer the monsters of my fantasy to what is positively trivial" (Fre. 2.620; Eng. 155). Baudelaire's poems in *Les Fleurs du mal* (*Flowers of Evil*) of 1857 layered ugly and macabre images with traditional forms, technical artistry, and beautiful language in ways that reach beyond virtually all previous works. Where Hugo and Büchner affirm the links between unvarnished realism and ugliness, Baudelaire champions the ugliness unleashed by the imagination.

*

Arthur Schopenhauer and Friedrich Nietzsche were distinctive writers who straddled the philosophical and literary traditions. In terms of chronology, the two figures bracket the others in this chapter. Schopenhauer was born in 1788, only a few years after Solger and Trahndorff and less than fifteen years before Hugo. Nietzsche was born in 1844, a generation after Baudelaire.

Schopenhauer belongs to the canon of German philosophers, above all for his pessimism and his extraordinary wit, but he had less standing during his age than he does today. He was neither an academic philosopher nor a Hegelian; in fact, he considered Hegel a "charlatan" and bitterly mocked what he called "Hegelian nonsense" (5:10; cf. 6:18–28). Amusingly enough, during his brief sojourn at the University of Berlin in 1820, Schopenhauer requested that his classes be scheduled to coincide (and conflict with) Hegel's lectures, but Hegel was a popular, if unconventional, lecturer, who attracted more than 200 listeners, while Schopenhauer drew 5.[1] Even today, Schopenhauer's influence on Nietzsche may be better known in the Anglo-American world than his own writings. Given Schopenhauer's profound pessimism, the centrality of aesthetics to his philosophy, and the emerging historical interest in ugliness, one might have expected that Schopenhauer would have written extensively on the subject. But most of his aesthetic attention is devoted to the ideal of beauty, which through its tranquillity and repose releases us from the suffering, strife, and senselessness of the world. Consequently, ugliness plays only a modest role in his aesthetics.

Like Winckelmann and others, Schopenhauer viewed traditional sculpture as the perfect art form for the Greeks. Schopenhauer argues that the Christian era is more at home with painting. For him, painting, unlike sculpture, appropriately engages ugliness. His views align with those of Smith, Herder, and Kant. In the expanded version of *Die Welt als Wille und Vorstellung* (*The World as Will and Representation*) (1819, and then revised and expanded in 1844), Schopenhauer writes: "In sculpture beauty and grace are the main thing: in painting, however, expression, passion, and character predominate; therefore, many of the demands of beauty must subside" (4:493). For Schopenhauer, sculpture requires "a pervasive beauty of all figures," whereas in painting such beauty would detract from the portrayal of character and border on the monotonous (4:493). He continues: "Accordingly, painting may also portray ugly faces and haggard figures; sculpture, in contrast, demands beauty, even if not always perfect beauty, but still in every way the strength and fullness of the figures" (4:493). Applying this concept to Christianity, Schopenhauer notes that "a gaunt Christ on the Cross, a dying Jerome, emaciated by age and disease, like the masterpiece of Domenichino, is a suitable subject for painting" (4:493). Schopenhauer finds inappropriate, however, Donatello's marble statue of John the Baptist, for here the figure is "reduced to skin and bone by fasting" and is, thus, "despite the masterly execution, repellent" (4:493–4).

An intense reader of Schopenhauer, **Nietzsche** differs from him in making ugliness central to his writings, beginning with *The Birth of Tragedy*. In his "Attempt at a Self-Criticism," Nietzsche asks what could possibly have led to the early Greek "*craving for the ugly*" (*Werke* 1:12–13; *Basic* 21). What drives the will "to pessimism, to the tragic myth, to the image of everything underlying existence that is frightful, evil, a riddle, destructive, fatal" (*Werke* 1:13; *Basic* 21). This passage recalls Aristotle's comments on the paradox of tragedy. Nietzsche reformulates the classic question thus: "How can the ugly and the disharmonic, the content of the tragic myth, stimulate aesthetic pleasure?" (*Werke* 1:131; *Basic* 141). He answers that the ugly is already present as the profound and intoxicating Dionysian impulse. Thus, for Nietzsche the ugly is primary: "For what would 'beautiful' be if its contrary had not first been presented to consciousness, if the ugly had not first said to itself: 'I am ugly'" (*Werke* 2:828; *Complete Works* 8:276, translation modified).

According to Nietzsche, we create beauty to endure ugliness. In his inversion of tradition, we recognize the first steps from an aesthetics in which ugliness plays a minor role to one in which ugliness is elevated over beauty. Some of Nietzsche's later fragments reinforce this inversion. For Nietzsche, art rescues us from the ugliness of reality and the horrors of knowledge. Although such thoughts may sound like Schopenhauer, Schopenhauer embraces art to deny the world, whereas Nietzsche affirms art to live in the world (*Werke* 3.496). In another late fragment, Nietzsche inverts the traditional equation of truth and beauty, writing: "Truth is ugly. / We possess *art* lest we *perish of the truth*" (*Werke* 3.832; *Will to Power* 435). Ugliness comes first, after which beauty follows. Nietzsche's argument has two moments: we *need* art to cope with truth, as truth is ugly, but with art, we *can* cope with truth rather than hide from it. This statement is a complex affirmation of negativity, akin to his integration of joy and agony in "The Drunken Song," which marks the climax of *Thus Spoke Zarathustra*.

Greek tragedy gives both joyous and horrific shape to "the ugly and the disharmonic" (*Werke* 1:130; *Basic* 141). Nietzsche elevates this "metaphysical joy in the tragic" (*Werke* 1:92; *Basic* 104). After the Socratic turn to reason, intelligibility, and optimism, the Dionysian abyss—and with it tragedy—recedes from the stage. The primordial unity of the ugly and the beautiful, which I mentioned in the Introduction, closely aligns with Nietzsche's challenge to aesthetics. In *The Birth of Tragedy* Nietzsche advocates for an aesthetics that counters the Western tradition, which, in the wake of Socratic reason, had elevated the Apollonian. Instead, Nietzsche embraces the Dionysian, promoting an indifference between the ugly and the beautiful. According to Nietzsche, Socrates introduces a distinction between good and evil and a corresponding aesthetic that separates the beautiful from the ugly. Nietzsche seeks to return to the merging of the beautiful and the ugly, advocating for a metaphysical indifference between the two.

In *Human, All Too Human* (1878), Nietzsche offers a forward-looking insight that anticipates later developments in music: he argues that contemporaries have an expanding capacity for a purely intellectual reception of ugliness, particularly in music (*Werke* 1:574–5; *Complete Works* 3.144–5). This intellectual reception allows composers to express the sublime, alongside the dreadful and mysterious, enabling listeners to move beyond sensuous ugliness and grasp higher meaning. This observation is significant, as musical ugliness increases in modernity: the unstable harmonies, dissonances, and occasional cacophony in classical music give way to atonal music. In modern compositions, musical ugliness—such as the diminished seventh, the augmented fourth, and the tritone—transitions from being momentary parts of longer works to an end in itself.

In 1907, a generation after Nietzsche wrote these words, composer Felix Draeseke questioned whether beauty might disappear from music entirely (694). Almost twenty years later, Schoenberg elevated "the emancipation of dissonance" (Eng. 258; Ger. 25, translation modified). The shift to musical ugliness that occurred through high art's turn to atonal music eventually surfaced in popular music as well. Opening with a melody of tritones became a signature move in jazz, as in saxophonist Sonny Rollins's *Blues 7* (1956), trumpeter Miles Davis's *Sid's Ahead* (1958), and jazz pianist Thelonious Monk's *Raise Four* (1964). One of Monk's works, a haunting waltz, is aptly titled *Ugly Beauty* (1968).

Similar intellectual tendencies arise in painting. The sensuous gives way to the cerebral; the real gives way to the symbolic. Nietzsche writes: "Meanwhile it is still said: the world is uglier than ever, but it *signifies* a more beautiful world than there has ever been" (*Werke* 1:575; *Complete Works* 3:145; cf. *Werke* 1:4491). In other words, the ugliness of being and performance is transformed into the beauty of meaning and reception. This cerebral processing of ugliness is not accessible to all, so most "in the end are stuck with the ugly," which they of course cannot enjoy (*Werke* 1:575; *Complete Works* 3.145, my translation). These recipients are unable to understand "the meaningful also in the form of sensory ugliness" (*Werke* 1:575; *Complete Works* 3:145, translation modified). Schoenberg seems to reinforce Nietzsche's view of the intellectual reception of ugliness: dissonances are more cerebral and intellectual because they are "more difficult to comprehend than consonances" (*Style and Idea* 282). What is implied in Nietzsche's analysis—the struggles many people have with difficult beauty—is a topic to which I return in Chapter 13, including the question, where does one turn when the basic human need for beauty remains unmet.

True to his reevaluation of values, Nietzsche suggests in *Dawn* that moderation can be ugly: "*Ugly in appearance*—Moderation looks beautiful to itself: it is innocent of the fact that in the eyes of the immoderate it seems coarse and stern, and consequently ugly" (*Werke* 1:1206; *Complete Works* 5:205, translation modified). In *Twilight of the Idols*, Nietzsche comments that our human-all-too-human concepts of beauty and ugliness are relative: we measure beauty according to our human preferences, which lack objectivity (*Werke* 2:1001; *Complete Works* 9:98–9; cf. *Werke* 3:576–7;). Yet he continues that this measure is all we have.

In *Beyond Good and Evil*, Nietzsche exposes his own biases, particularly his denigration of women, by claiming that female independence contributes to the "*uglification* (Verhäßlichung) of Europe" (*Werke* 2:697; *Complete Works* 8:137, my translation). Nietzsche associates ugliness with weakness and degeneracy, anything contrary to the will to power: "everything ugly weakens and distresses the human" (*Werke* 2:1002; *Complete Works* 9.99). Having explored ugliness in detail and linking it, as in the tradition, also with age, Nietzsche continues: "in this hatred there is horror, caution, depth, farsightedness—it is the deepest hatred there is. That is why art is *deep*" (*Werke* 2:1002; *Complete Works* 9:99).

Nietzsche consistently asserts that the world is ugly and that art provides a means to overcome this ugliness without denying it. Other views evolve over time. Initially, he considers tragedy the highest art, a form privileged in wrestling with ugliness (*Werke* 1:120). However, he increasingly adopts a comic frame. Through laughter and dance, we mock the world's ugliness and rise above it. In a telling late fragment, Nietzsche associates various negative categories with ugliness: "decline, impoverishment of life, impotence, disintegration, degeneration" (*Werke* 3:753; *Will to Power* 427). He continues: "The ugly has a depressing effect: it is the expression of a depression. It *takes away* strength, it impoverishes, it weighs down" (*Werke* 3:753; *Will to Power* 427, translation modified). Nietzsche contrasts this limping, stumbling ugliness with the divine "frivolity of the dancer" (*Werke* 3.753; *Will to Power* 427).

In *Thus Spoke Zarathustra*, Zarathustra mocks the ugliest man, who himself recognizes the efficacy of this mockery: "Whoever wants to kill most thoroughly, *laughs*" (*Werke* 2:550; *Portable* 427, translation modified). What does the ugliest man kill? In one of Nietzsche's many theories of the death of God, God took pity on humanity's "concealed disgrace and ugliness," especially on the ugliest man. Unable to bear such "overpitying" witness, the ugliest man kills God (*Werke* 2:502–4; *Portable* 376–9). The death of God and abhorrence of pity—two of Nietzsche's major themes—are thus connected to his concept of ugliness.

The creative spirit advances by rejecting what is and seeing through it as ugly. This is not, as in tragedy, an aesthetic justification of life despite its ugliness. Instead, the creative spirit embodies a non-pitying mode of rejecting ugliness by moving beyond it:

> I took the will to beauty, to persist in *like* forms, for a temporary means of preservation and recuperation: fundamentally, however, the eternally-creative appeared to me to be, as the *eternal compulsion to destroy,*

> associated with pain. The ugly is the form things assume when we view them with the will to implant a meaning, a *new* meaning, into what has become meaningless: the accumulated force which compels the creator to consider all that has been created hitherto as unacceptable, ill-constituted, worthy of being denied, as ugly! (*Werke* 3:496; *Will to Power* 224, translation modified)

One leaves ugliness behind to become creative, to seek alternatives, but commonality with the early Nietzsche resurfaces: even what is rejected must also be embraced as part of what makes this overcoming possible (*Werke* 2:551–8; *Portable* 429–36).

Nietzsche's reflections on ugliness underscore its prominence in nineteenth-century aesthetics. His ideas are fundamentally connected to the origin of tragedy, even as they transcend it. Similar to the Hegelians, despite sharing little else with them, Nietzsche wants to blend the ugly and the beautiful, and the late Nietzsche seeks to overcome ugliness through a form of the comic. That beauty is a response to primal ugliness and that contemporary music shifts from pleasing the senses to satisfying the mind, thus alienating much of the public, are two of Nietzsche's ideas that resurface in the twentieth century, most prominently in Adorno, as we will see in Chapter 10.

9

The Academic Philosophers

Bolzano to Volkelt

Through the end of the century, the Hegelian influence helped sustain interest in ugliness. **Bernard Bolzano**, for example, a Catholic priest and a Bohemian mathematician, logician, and philosopher, cites the Hegelians when he turns to analyzing ugliness. A liberal supportive of the disenfranchised and critical of militarism, Bolzano was removed from his professorship by the Austrian empire and faced a partial publishing ban. Today, he is celebrated for his work in mathematics and logic; his collected works currently total 111 volumes, with another 21 in preparation. His few contributions to aesthetics have received less attention (Livingston). In *Über den Begriff des Schönen. Eine philosophische Abhandlung* (*On the Concept of the Beautiful: A Philosophical Essay*) (1843), Bolzano addresses ugliness.

Although familiar with Hegel and the Hegelian tradition—criticizing Hegel in §54 and Weiße in §55, where he explicitly mentions Weiße's work on ugliness—Bolzano distances himself from anything resembling dialectical thought (§1). Indeed, one has the sense when reading Bolzano that one is reading an analytic philosopher who tries to explain each step of his inquiry. His final sentence rails against contemporary attempts to define beauty; criticizing their lack of clarity, he calls them "models of ugliness" (Muster der Häßlichkeit) (§55). In his essay, Bolzano seeks to define beauty, arguing that "the beautiful must be an object the contemplation of which causes pleasure in all people whose cognitive faculties are sufficiently developed" and that this experience of pleasure should be neither too easy nor too difficult, that is, it should not require the effort or rigor of "*distinct thought*" (§11). We sense a pleasing pattern without needing clear and distinct categories to grasp it; our initial thoughts are "obscure" (dunkel) but nonetheless pleasing (§11). Bolzano is oriented toward reception-aesthetics: "determining whether something is beautiful is not a matter of how the object is in and of itself, but rather only of how it appears to us" (§22).

After stipulating that the ugly is "the opposite of the beautiful," Bolzano continues:

> the *ugly is an object that vexes us (den Verdruss uns verursacht), at least when we do not make the effort to maintain the rigour of clear and distinct thought: it vexes us because every time we apprehend the object's qualities and attempt to develop a concept of it we always find something that contradicts the concept that we have formed of it.* (§18)

His definition of the ugly encounters the same complexities as his definition of beauty: first, he focuses not on the object itself but on its reception and, second, he includes under ugliness everything that makes a pleasurable reception difficult. He gives as examples a poem in which there is a break in the rhyme pattern and a building in which a part deviates so much from the principle of symmetry that we notice the irregularity. However, a break in rhyme can signal irony, and even Bolzano admits that an appropriate modulation and occasional asymmetry can be attractive (§18). He acknowledges that we can find pleasure in perceiving "*ugly things within a beautiful whole,*" as when an ugly person appears at the right place and time in a comedy (§18). Yet it is unclear how this pattern differs from a deviation in rhyme or an asymmetrical moment in architecture, except that these may be less formulaic than, say, a blocking character in a comedy.

In any case, if the ugly is the opposite of the beautiful and if no dialectical transitions are allowed, Bolzano excludes from his canon of beauty much of art. For him, anything initially vexing is ugly. As a result, he opposes the concept of "*difficult*" beauty (§11).

Hermann Lotze, a teacher of Josiah Royce, was recognized through the First World War as Germany's leading metaphysician. Having been influenced by Weiße, Lotze addressed ugliness in his occasional writings on aesthetics, including *Ueber den Begriff der Schönheit* (*On the Concept of Beauty*) of 1845 (33–5) and *Geschichte der Ästhetik in Deutschland* (*History of Aesthetics in Germany*) of 1868 (333–52). As we will see repeatedly, any thorough history of aesthetics that integrates the German tradition after Hegel cannot avoid addressing ugliness.

In his history, Lotze discusses ugliness in a chapter alongside the sublime and the ridiculous. Here he follows not the Hegelians, who spoke of the comic, but Jean Paul, a German writer and esthetician who does not thematize the ugly, but who famously viewed the sublime (the infinitely large) and the ridiculous (the infinitely small) as opposites (*Vorschule* §26–8). Like many in the tradition, Lotze links ugliness and evil, but he adopts the modern view of ugliness not as a lack of beauty but as "hostility toward" beauty (334). For Lotze, ugliness represents more than an innocuous disjunction between idea and appearance; it arises from "the hostile intention [. . .] to destroy what should be" (341). Ugliness can take various forms, from the loathsome and repugnant to the charming and alluring (342), but in each case, it deviates from what should be. Lotze does not see ugliness as a moment within the beautiful. Instead, he views the ugly as necessary only to the extent that it serves as a contrast or perversion that helps us understand the essence of beauty (338–9).

Adolf Zeising, who studied philology and philosophy in Berlin and Halle, became well known thereafter for his work on the golden ratio. In the failed revolution of 1848, he was active as a liberal and consequently had to relinquish his Gymnasium position in Anhalt-Bernburg. He eventually settled in Munich and wrote many scholarly and literary works, though he faced financial challenges until his death.

In one of his early works, *Ästhetische Forschungen* (*Aesthetic Investigations*) (1855), Zeising offers an extensive criticism of Hegel and the Hegelian school (27–44). He contests the idea that the ugly can be an element within the beautiful that is dissolved via comedy. Indeed, he calls the notion that ugliness can be housed within beauty "the most extreme error (Verirrung) that has ever existed in the realm of aesthetics" (146). Zeising argues that ugliness can logically be understood as part of beauty only when it is no longer ugly; when it is still ugly, it stands outside of beauty. If ugliness surfaces in a truly beautiful work, then it has already been transformed by the comic and is no longer ugly. The beautiful, as the congruence of idea and appearance, cannot tolerate incongruence and therefore cannot absorb ugliness. One could analyze Zeising's criticism as a terminological disagreement insofar as all the Hegelians to this point (Schasler was later) believed that ugliness is not part of beauty and that it can only be a moment in art which must be resolved, but it also indicates a movement away from the Hegelian emphasis on complex dialectical processes.

Zeising's second contribution to the theory of ugliness likewise suggests a rejection of dialectical thinking. As Zeising further articulates what constitutes ugliness, he shows that he is both against and with the Hegelians—against them insofar as he sees a rigid distinction between beauty and ugliness but with them insofar as he views ugliness as a concept that seeks to usurp and replace beauty.[1] Zeising recognizes that in comedy lying is widespread, but if a lie is even temporarily mistaken as true, it is not comic, but ugly. He prefers comedies where we know that the lie is a lie, such that it does not compete with truth. He writes: "Ugly is only that which within the borders of beauty rebels against beauty: the vapid, the base, the stunted. In contrast, what with sauciness and cheekiness springs beyond the borders of beauty cannot be considered ugly, for it freely renounces beauty, does not enter into conflict with it, and in no way seeks to debilitate or disrupt it" (293; cf. 396).

Robert Zimmermann was Bolzano's student. He was also a teacher of Rudolf Steiner, who appropriated the term "anthroposophy" from Zimmermann. Zimmermann initially taught in Olmütz and Prague before assuming a chair at the University of Vienna, a position he held from 1861 to 1896. Zimmermann wrote a history of aesthetic theory and a systematic aesthetics, viewing the two independent publications as connected works. His interest in literature is revealed by his co-founding of the Franz Grillparzer Society and writing reports on recent German-language publications in literature and philosophy. The English-language reports, which Zimmermann wrote himself, were published from 1870 to 1893 in the London *Athenaeum*.

Ugliness appears twice in Zimmermann's works: in his history, he analyzes the theories of ugliness advanced by Weiße, Ruge, and Vischer, and he returns to the concept in his systematic aesthetics (§158–64). His comments are consistent and worth noting. For Zimmermann, ugliness purports to be what it is not. In fact, it claims that it is beautiful—and that is comical. In his *Geschichte der Aethetik als philosophischer Wissenschaft* (*History of Aesthetics as a Philosophical Discipline*) of 1858, he asserts that for ugliness to be comical, "the ugly must consider itself the beautiful, that is, it must not only admit that ugliness exists, it must view itself as the beautiful" (*Geschichte* 729). Zimmermann emphasizes that this moment of self-reflection (Selbstbesinnung) is essential, but he does not find it in Vischer, who analyzes the transition from ugliness to comedy. Zimmermann writes of this self-reflection: "By viewing itself as the beautiful, the ugly becomes comical" (*Geschichte* 729–30). He sees in this process a restoration of harmony.

In his *Allgemeine Aesthetik als Formwissenschaft* (*General Aesthetics as a Science of Form*) of 1865, Zimmermann argues that ugliness is an appearance that pretends to be what it is not. Ugliness substitutes appearance for being, but even ugliness does not believe in the validity of its own claims (*Allgemeine Aesthetik* §163). The ugliness that pretends to usurp beauty actually depends on what it purports to be and ultimately wants, true beauty, a clever argument that accentuates the ontological superiority of beauty over ugliness: "The disharmony that impersonates harmony not only knows that it must ultimately give way to true harmony, it also wants to do so, because it is only there in order to make true harmony more salient" (*Allgemeine Aesthetik* §163). Even though Zimmermann was not a Hegelian (he aligned himself with Herbart's realism, in which Zimmermann's history of aesthetics culminates), we recognize three ideas that we saw also with the Hegelians, even if Zimmermann adds his own accents: (1) Ugliness does not simply negate beauty, it claims to be what it is not and stubbornly seeks to usurp beauty. (2) The false claim of ugliness—an appearance (Schein) that tries to pass itself off as being (Sein)—is laughable and so dispelled via the comic. (3) Ugliness cancels itself in its would-be autonomy, for it depends on beauty, and thus returns, via negation, to the supremacy of beauty.

In 1868, **Julius Hermann von Kirchmann**, a prominent jurist, published a two-volume work, *Aesthetik auf realistischer Grundlage* (*Aesthetics on a Realist Foundation*). Although Kirchmann was anti-idealist, his analysis still contains dialectical structures. He associates ugliness primarily with pain: "Ugliness is the image of a reality suffused with pain" (2:37). Kirchmann argues that formal ugliness is merely a residue of its origin—displeasure: "No form is in itself ugly; everything that is ugly originates in pain. It's just habit that gradually causes us to forget this basis, and in the end we find ugliness and beauty in form alone" (2:225). Our attraction to beauty, Kirchmann argues, derives from an original sense of pleasure, as with

> a pure skin, a healthy complexion, ruddy cheeks, white teeth, a small mouth, fresh lips, a round chin, a full bosom, a slender body [. . .]. All these outward appearances are, as a rule, signs of health, youth, strength, and agility, thus signs or sources of pleasure. This association alone was the original reason for considering these things beautiful. However, this consistent association has gradually given the forms in question an independence, which ultimately led us to assume that they are beautiful in themselves. (2:38)

Kirchmann applies the same principle to ugliness:

> An impure, yellow, wrinkled skin is considered ugly because it is a sign of illness and old age, both of which are associated with pain. Small eyes are ugly as signs of stupidity or deceitfulness; thin hair and a bald head are ugly because they signal weakness and declining strength; missing teeth, a pointed chin, a thick neck, pudgy hands, and stumpy feet are ugly because they reveal frailty, old age, inertia. (2:38)

Certain sensuous experiences—for example, seeing gestures of despair, hungry children, dangerous animals, and dead bodies—arouse displeasure (2:98). Kirchmann writes that these and other such examples were originally associated with pain, which is why people came to regard them as ugly (2:37). Non-threatening animals that are awkward and ungainly appear ugly to us because we project those traits onto ourselves and find them unappealing (1:169). For example, the sound of a frog strikes us as odd or nonsensical and therefore unpleasant (1:173).

Reducing ugliness to reception, in particular to displeasure, renders the concept relative.[2] Kirchmann acknowledges that to Europeans, camels are ugly, but to Africans, who find them beneficial, they are beautiful (1:175). Kirchmann is at least partially correct that we find certain sensuous experiences pleasing because of their effects, including their usefulness. For instance, humanity has long been drawn to mosaic ecosystems characterized by trees, grassland, and water—landscapes that were productive for nutrition and advantageous for identifying threats. One sees how close Kirchmann comes to the claims of evolutionary biology, yet Darwin himself, as we saw, recognizes tendencies in sexual selection that function separately from natural selection, indicating that aesthetic attraction can exist independently of, and even contrary to, biological advantage. This view contradicts Kirchmann's account, which seeks to derive all beauty from pleasure and advantage and all ugliness from pain and disadvantage.

Kirchmann repeatedly agrees with the basic thrust of the German aesthetic tradition that ugliness is permitted as a moment within an artwork in which it is submerged or transfigured. He distinguishes between the "ideal-ugly" and the "naturalistic-ugly" (2:89–90).[3] The ideal-ugly occurs when pain surfaces but the mind controls its expression. This cerebral overcoming of pain is an expression of the sublime, which is ultimately pleasurable and so becomes in truth the ideal-beautiful. Kirchmann mentions as an example *Laocoön and His Sons* and praises it for contrasting physical pain with spiritual expression (Figure 5). Note that Kirchmann elevates here not a beautiful depiction of an ugly state but instead a process by which ugliness is encountered and withstood, if not overcome. The idea is not far from Schiller's concept of tragedy.

In the naturalistic-ugly, we experience the reverse: ugliness supplants beauty. Here, an affect, usually pain, overtakes the entire person, enslaving them to emotions. Kirchmann states: "Such conditions harm the essence of the soul" (2:90). He includes as examples of the naturalistic-ugly portrayals of lower-strata individuals, including their unrefined language. However, he acknowledges that a beautiful portrayal of the naturalistic-ugly, such as depictions of the poor or of unrelieved suffering, can transform existing ugliness into what he calls the naturalistic-beautiful (2:40). We see this, for example, in Dutch paintings that beautifully represent peasants. Kirchmann rejects any portrayal of ugliness that is not transformed within the work itself (2:42). He demands an "idealization [. . .] of the ugly" as essential for a pleasurable reception (2:42). To step out of chronological sequence, we can imagine Kirchmann as reenacting Alberti's Renaissance precepts and embodying the opposite of Adorno's theory, which rejects any aesthetic transformation of ugliness.

Eduard von Hartmann was educated for a military career, which he pursued for less than a decade before having to resign for health reasons. He subsequently earned his doctorate in philosophy and gained recognition for his first book, the highly successful *Philosophie des Unbewußten* (*Philosophy of the Unconscious*) (1869), which follows in the tradition of Schopenhauer's pessimism, though the influence of Hegel and Schelling is also evident. In 1872, Hartmann married Agnes Taubert, an impressive philosopher in her own right. Hartmann addresses ugliness in his two-volume *Aesthetik* (*Aesthetics*), published in 1886 and 1887. He provides one of the more thorough analyses of ugliness. After giving in his first volume a general account of the history of aesthetics, which he canvasses from Kant to the present, Hartmann then turns to what he considers the most important specific categories in aesthetics, the very first of which is the ugly. Here Hartmann elevates above all not Rosenkranz's but Schasler's analysis (1:377). The other concepts on which he offers a history include the sublime, the comic, the tragic, and the humorous.

Hartmann's stress on ugliness in his first volume, his historical overview, heralds its importance for his second volume, his systematic aesthetics. Alas, Hartmann's later writings, of which there were many, had little influence compared with *Philosophy of the Unconscious*—which saw eleven editions in his lifetime and was central to the pessimism controversy of the nineteenth century (Beiser 158–215). Nonetheless, Hartmann offers interesting perspectives; foremost among these is his concern with categorical differentiation. He draws a compelling distinction between what he calls "nonbeauty" (Unschönheit), a privation of beauty, and "ugliness," a negation of beauty (2:209). Non-beauty represents a weak or ineffective form, whereas ugliness involves a negation of form, characterized by asymmetry, incommensurability, or lack of due proportion (2:225).

In his systematic aesthetics, Hartmann differentiates between two kinds of ugliness: "formal ugliness," where the form does not do justice to the content, and "content-related ugliness," which refers to material that is internally contradictory or illogical (2:211). Hartmann recognizes that when ugliness is limited, it can play a constitutive role in a beautiful work (2:219). As an example, he notes the feigned piety of Tartuffe: the more beautiful it appears, the uglier it is, but this ugliness serves the larger beauty of the work (2:220). Hartmann advances here an impressive dialectical insight: Molière's brilliant but hypocritical comic character does offer an excellent example of beautiful ugliness.

Although beauty is normally associated with symmetry and regularity, Hartmann recognizes that less symmetrical shapes, which are superficially ugly, can convey great beauty. As examples, he notes waterfalls and ocean waves (2:229). Fire, too, exemplifies asymmetrical beauty: a flame is "characteristically beautiful only because it mocks the demands of a relatively formal beauty" (2:229). In such instances, "characteristic dynamic pleasantness is bought at the price of relatively formal mathematical unpleasantness" (2:229). However, Hartmann's concession that asymmetry is not always ugly introduces an inconsistency in his position. This could have been overcome had he distinguished between the ugly and the seemingly ugly. Although Hartmann asserts that incommensurability represents a negation of form and is thus ugly (2:225), incommensurability is hardly only ugly; the golden ratio, to cite a prominent example, is beautiful, but it is an irrational number and so incommensurable. It is difficult to rhyme the beauty of the golden ratio with Hartmann's understanding of incommensurability as a negation of form. His distinctions are helpful but uneven.

Hartmann is the first to identify as objectively ugly those images that are nomologically impossible, that is, they break the laws of nature, such as heavy construction that has no foundation, support structures that have nothing to buttress them, or architectural structures that hover in the air (2:230). In such cases, we encounter "an ugliness that is not aesthetically justified" (2:230). Hartmann makes a claim that we see repeatedly: if the moment of ugliness serves the larger purpose of uncovering beauty and does not detract from it, it is justified (2:257). He asserts: "Artistic beauty can claim to exist alongside natural beauty only when it offers parts that are like self-contained microcosms in which no aesthetically unjustified ugliness appears" (2:259). In this context, Hartmann notes that some breaks in symmetry, which might seem ugly, are justified insofar as they serve a purpose. For instance, formal beauty would demand that a cup have either no handles or two handles, but "such inappropriateness would be ugly in respect of content, although it would be more beautiful in respect of form" (2:230).[4]

Hartmann offers a broadly interesting set of distinctions focused on nature, identifying three forms of teleological ugliness. First, "*lack of adaptation*" (*Unangepasstheit*) is ugly, for example, organs that no longer serve a purpose (2:231). Second, "*lack of health*" (*Ungesundheit*) is ugly because illness detracts from one's capacity for life (2:233). However, Hartmann acknowledges complexities. For example, a bodily weakness may be compatible with a strength of spirit and mind; a widow who does not suffer but is the image of health is ugly; the self-sacrifice of doctors and nurses presupposes illness; and even death can reveal the profound power of the human spirit (2:234–5). The third form of teleological ugliness is "ineptitude" (Ungeschicklichkeit) (2:231), which Hartmann rephrases as "*functional* ugliness of movement or conduct" (2:236), by which he means inappropriate behavior or action. Examples include too much delay or too much haste, although these, too, can play a role in the larger context of beauty. In each case, we see a violation of teleology. Not surprisingly, some of these categories have parallels in artistic beauty; for example, dramatic action can be affected by too much haste or too much delay.

Hartmann has a very positive view of the potential of art: unlike reality, which appears to us in so many disordered, contingent, and even chaotic ways, art is capable of revealing deeper truths concerning that reality (2:260). This includes showing us via comedy the dissolution of ugliness. Like many of his predecessors, Hartmann views comedy as a privileged mode of showing the self-cancellation of ugliness, including the illogical (2:260). Like Rosenkranz, he views caricature, with its critical impulse, as the height of comedy (2:260), though Hartmann is more consequential than Rosenkranz in ensuring that the distinction between ugly content and ugly form is always clear. In a rich statement well ahead of its time, Hartmann cautions against art that seeks, with a certain level of cynicism, to strive for the extreme effects of disgust and repulsion (2:222). Although often overlooked in aesthetic history and theories of ugliness, Hartmann's work contains detailed and cogent insights.

Not surprisingly, public unease with artistic portrayals of ugliness persisted throughout the century. These concerns were occasionally met with theoretical responses. In *Das Schlechte als Gegenstand dichterischer Darstellung* (*The Bad as an Object of Poetic Representation*) (1892), **Franz Clemens Brentano** addressed these concerns. Brentano was a priest (until after the First Vatican Council when he withdrew from the priesthood) and a professor at the University of Vienna, who had a tremendous influence on German philosophy and psychology (he taught both Edmund Husserl and Sigmund Freud). Brentano counters the lament that contemporary literature is overly immersed in the deformed and pathological. Brentano notes that across time, both comedy and tragedy have engaged ugliness, the ridiculous in the former and misery, crime, insanity, and catastrophe in the latter. He defends this integration of ugliness, commenting that in tragedy, for example, we encounter figures of substantial interest, persons of dignity, who suffer pain. These characters, portrayed with formal excellence, can deeply move viewers, those who have become distant from affects such as fear and pity and those who strongly identify with those emotions. Brentano does not add new insights, but his intelligent lecture reminds us of the ongoing public discomfort with portrayals of ugliness, to which he offers a cogent response.

Jonas Cohn, a member of the second generation of Southwestern Neo-Kantianism who nonetheless stressed in his philosophical and pedagogical writings a version of dialectic, was the only significant member of that school to write on aesthetics. In 1901, when Cohn published his two-volume *Allgemeine Ästhetik* (*General Aesthetics*), he was a Privatdozent in Freiburg. In 1919, he became *außerordentlicher Professor*, loosely analogous to associate professor, a position he held until 1933. That year, Martin Heidegger, the new rector, removed him from his post, after which Cohn emigrated to Great Britain. Cohn had relinquished his faith, but he was by birth Jewish.

In his aesthetics, Cohn introduces the beautiful, sublime, comic, and tragic as the most important categories within the field (x). Noticeably absent is the ugly as a central concept, appearing briefly across only two pages. Cohn argues that conflict is essential in the sublime, and here, the ugly plays a role. As an aside, Cohn notes the continuing force of Hegel and the Hegelians:

> Since there is an inherent conflict within the sublime, whereas beauty in the narrower sense is perfect unity, dialectic, which moves in antitheses and their unification, dictates that in the sublime the opposite of beauty, ugliness, is absorbed into beauty and in the Hegelian sense "sublated." Anyone who refuses to recognize the validity of this dialectic will nonetheless be able to follow the idea expressed here. (188)[5]

In further assessing the ugly, Cohn distinguishes between ugliness that is folded or sublated into the sublime and ugliness that remains ugly and, by contrast, serves to highlight the sublime (189). For instance, the ugly body of Socrates houses a person of great moral integrity, transforming ugliness into the sublime. In contrast, when Heracles battles the Hydra and Cerberus, we see the sublime on one side and ugliness on the other, with no integration or transformation. Here, ugliness is merely a foil, a means for the sublime to shine in battle. Despite the ongoing relevance of dialectic, at the turn of the century, we begin to see the diminishing importance of ugliness; it has less of a constructive, integral, and detailed role in theory.

Theodor Lipps, a well-known philosopher and psychologist, influenced not only Freud but also Scheler and Ernst Bloch. In the first volume of his *Ästhetik* (*Aesthetics*), published in 1903, Lipps concludes his extensive 600-page analysis with chapters on tragedy, comedy, humor, and ugliness. For Lipps, suffering and the comic are "ein Nichtseinsollendes," or what should not be; therefore, they are both ugly (*Ästhetik* 593). He describes the ugly as "an immediately intuited negation of the positive in humanity," encompassing weakness, atrophy, deficiency, inner opposition, antagonism, contradiction, impairment, or restraint (*Ästhetik* 593). Yet in Lipps's view, ugliness serves beauty. Without explicitly using the term "dialectic," Lipps suggests that ugliness invokes a negative empathy in the observer, and this negative reaction—this resistance to ugliness—affirms our human essence as inherently other than ugly, thus highlighting something positive (*Ästhetik* 595). The move has modest echoes of Kant's account of the sublime, where we are initially overwhelmed by nature's vastness or power, but true sublimity arises when we reflect on the moral law within us, which is greater than nature's majesty (*Critique of Judgment* §23–9). For Lipps, not only does ugliness accentuate beauty, but the capacity of the beautiful to emerge in such an environment makes beauty even more impressive and striking (*Ästhetik* 596). For Lipps, ugliness has no independent standing; its sole value lies in being overcome in beauty (*Ästhetik* 598).

Max Dessoir, a philosopher with doctorates in both philosophy (Berlin, 1889) and medicine (Würzburg, 1892), explored psychological themes and coined the term "parapsychology." He also influenced Freud, who cites him favorably (*Drei Abhandlungen* 128–9). However, Dessoir was primarily known for his contributions to aesthetics. In 1906 he founded the world's first journal of aesthetics, *Zeitschrift für Ästhetik und allgemeine Kunstwissenschaft,* and edited it until 1937. The journal still exists today. In 1908 Dessoir established the Society for the Study of Aesthetics and led its first world congress, which met in Berlin five years later. From 1897 until 1934 Dessoir held a chair in Berlin. Under the Nazis, Dessoir faced occasional travel restrictions, and in 1938 his name was dropped from the university directory. The rationale was twofold: although Dessoir had converted to Protestantism, he had at least one Jewish grandparent; and his 1936 publication of *Introduction to Philosophy* was deemed incompatible with National Socialist thought (Tilitzki 609). In 1939 Dessoir lost his publication privileges (Tilitzki 611–12).

Dessoir's main scholarly contribution is *Ästhetik und allgemeine Kunstwissenschaft,* first published in 1906 and followed by a second edition in 1923. Under the auspices of the American Society for Aesthetics, it was translated into English, presumably as a synthesis of German thought, for its number of innovations is modest and its disregard of history striking. Exemplary, however, in *Aesthetics and Theory of Art* is Dessoir's interweaving of theory and examples, including contemporary examples, such as the works of the German Naturalists, who focused on "ugly and shocking events" (Ger. 24; Eng. 39). Presumably thinking of poetic realism (but not writers ahead of their time such as Büchner), Dessoir writes that previously ugliness had been neglected: ugly elements "were either no longer present or were embellished to the point of drastic change" (Ger. 24; Eng. 39). Dessoir not only addresses ugliness in art, he also elevates the technical skill of writers in crafting beautiful art from ugly material (Ger. 24; Eng. 39). Dessoir particularly mentions Gerhart Hauptmann, who used dialect to convey society's lower strata and focused on issues affecting the downtrodden: poverty, unemployment, misery, and alcoholism (Ger. 307; Eng. 313–14). Hauptmann's departure from earlier poetic tendencies exemplifies the effective integration of unpleasant realities into compelling art.

In his fourth chapter, Dessoir deals more systematically with ugliness. He outlines five primary aesthetic forms: the beautiful, sublime, tragic, ugly, and comic. In the chapter's introductory reflections, Dessoir comments on dialectical relations between and among these categories. For example, from the sublime to the ridiculous is only a short step; this shows, he notes, the enduring value of Hegel's dialectic (Ger. 138–9; Eng. 150). The ugly, which is the opposite of the beautiful, lies in close proximity to both the tragic and the comic. Tragedy and ugliness are characterized by disharmony (Ger. 157; Eng. 168). With the comic, the ugly shares a "contradiction-rich flexibility" (Ger. 158; Eng. 168, my translation). In noting the presence of ugliness within the sublime and the tragic, Dessoir draws on an insight we recognize as Plato's: "There are things we cannot see, and yet they draw our eyes to them again and again. The ugly possesses the attraction of the abyss" (Ger. 158; Eng. 168–9, my translation). Whereas the beautiful can sometimes be conventional and inexpressive, the ugly has a tremendous capacity for expression. Ultimately, the ugly passes over into the comic. The gesture is well known to us, though here, Dessoir quotes not the Hegelians but Aristotle: an innocuous deviation from the norm is comic. Dessoir's focus is not on bad art but on the presence of the ugly within works that have positive aesthetic value (Ger. 158; Eng. 169).

Hermann Cohen, the primary founder of the Marburg School of Neo-Kantianism, was for decades a towering figure in German philosophy. Among his students was Ernst Cassirer. Cohen was arguably the most important Jewish philosopher of the nineteenth and early twentieth centuries. An impressive thinker, he linked religion and reason, arguing that monotheism was the original source for ethical universalism. Cohen advocated for universal suffrage, workers' rights and the League of Nations. His greatest impact lies in his interpretations of Kant; his contributions to epistemology, ethics, and philosophy of science; and his religious writings. Cohen, however, also wrote a two-volume aesthetics, entitled *Ästhetik des reinen Gefühls* (*Aesthetics of Pure Feeling*) (1912), devoting one of the three multi-volume books of his philosophical system to aesthetics (the others being logic and ethics). In this work, Cohen prominently integrates ugliness, arguing that mature art must address it (1:58). For him, as for Rosenkranz, ugliness belongs in aesthetics, but only as a moment, not as an independent entity (1:125).

Cohen relates ugliness to our animal nature, recognizing the contradiction between the cerebral and material dimensions of the human being. We do not despise the ugly; instead, we acknowledge it as part of human nature (1:304). This recognition occurs through loving humor, which dissolves ugliness, such that it becomes a moment within beauty (1:288). Cohen writes: "Love would become insincere if it did not want to embrace also the ugly. Love embraces the ugly and transforms it, making it a moment of beauty" (1:289). Whereas Lipps sees our strong *resistance* to ugliness as an affirmation of humanity, Cohen finds this affirmation in the loving *acceptance* of ugliness.

For Cohen, a work of art is beautiful insofar as it represents, in the words of Andrea Poma, "a realisation of the straining towards the infinite" (153). Beauty, however, does not fully reach the infinite. Beauty is real, and in being real, it is deficient, but nonetheless capable of being embraced. Cohen rejects Kant's decision to link only the aesthetic category of the sublime to the ethical and finds also in humor, which is for Cohen the opposite of the sublime, a connection to ethics. Whereas the sublime longs for the divine and greets finitude with irony, humor embraces finitude; as such, it is able to integrate ugliness. In embracing the use of humor to defuse ugliness, Cohen speaks of loving human beings, even in their weaknesses: "Thus the great art of humor seeks out the ugly in human beings in order to portray it as worthy of love" (1:304). It is this love, which is the pure feeling in the title of Cohen's book, *Aesthetics of Pure Feeling* (1:178).

In particular, Cohen elevates portraiture for its capacity to work with humor. According to Cohen, Rembrandt portrays ugliness with humor, thereby overcoming it, rendering it beautiful. Though Rembrandt was capable of extraordinary beauty (Cohen gives as an example *The Holy Family* (1634) in Munich), Rembrandt also integrates ugliness. Cohen writes:

> Compassion bewails the *universal* weakness and nakedness of humanity in those creatures whose beauty is insufficient. This lamentation becomes a kind of indictment of the Creator in whose image humanity is supposed

> to have been made. Such compassion with the ugly is like a vindication of God's goodness and justice in the face of evil's existence [. . .]. Ugly people have a share in systematic beauty, and it is the artist's highest calling to reveal this. (2:386–7)

Cohen writes that the greatness of Rembrandt lies in his ability to transfigure "*ugly people by making their share in beauty apparent* and granting them civil rights in the sphere of aesthetics" (2:387). He continues: "His ugly people are far from being monsters; on the contrary, they are surrounded by the magic of the erotic" (2:387). Rembrandt "*renders his ugly figures all worthy of love*" (2:387). Cohen calls this "the triumph of ugliness" (2:387). He elucidates as an example of such triumph Rembrandt's *Hundred Guilder Print* (c. 1649) (2:388).

When Cohen discusses overcoming ugliness via humor, he gestures toward a beauty that offsets physical ugliness. He praises Raphael's genius in portraying Leo X as ugly but likable: "Raphael made this ugly man endearing. This is the secret of his painting; but it is also the secret of art in general, whose fundamental strength is love of human nature. This love knows no bounds and recognizes no forbidding ugliness" (2:355). Cohen also commends Holbein for beautifully combining ugliness and sympathy (2:375–7). In the *Darmstadt Madonna* (1526–8), the kneeling woman is not beautiful, but she wins us over with her passion. In *The Family of the Artist* (c. 1528), the wife, who is not superficially beautiful, gains our sympathy with the soulfulness of her eyes and the adoring look of her son (Figure 10). In Holbein's other portrait paintings, each figure has moments of physical ugliness tempered with earnestness, stateliness, or other qualities that render the person endearing or at the very least not unlikable.[6]

Cohen praises Shakespeare for succeeding in the courtship scene between Richard III and Lady Anne: we see a human truth in the tyrant's neediness (2:355). New in Cohen is the element of love that is integral to humor versus the severe spirit of negation that is privileged when the Hegelians speak of overcoming ugliness. One sees the difference between Rosenkranz, whom Cohen does not mention, and Cohen: Cohen commends Raphael and Holbein for integrating ugliness without resorting to caricature (2:376–7),[7] precisely the category Rosenkranz elevates as the ideal strategy for overcoming ugliness, even if Rosenkranz, too, prefers a soft edge to caricature.[8] Whereas Rosenkranz

Figure 10 *Hans Holbein the Younger,* Bildnis der Frau des Künstlers mit den beiden ältesten Kindern *(*Portrait of the Artist's Wife with the Two Elder Children*), c. 1528/29, Kunstmuseum Basel, Public Domain / Courtesy of the Museum's Sammlung Online.*

focuses above all on a *logical* analysis of ugliness, for Cohen ugliness invites *ethical* reflection. Nonetheless, we see how much the Hegelian idea—that ugliness must be integrated as a moment—became commonplace even when it was modified or vaguely inherited from tradition. Or, if we want to view the matter more systematically than historically, we could argue that independently of influence, Cohen understands the legitimacy of understanding ugliness as integral to humanity and to art even as it remains subordinate to beauty. Although Cohen elevates ugliness, much as Adorno will later, Cohen invokes the very principle that Adorno will hate: *Verklärung*, that is, "transfiguration" or "idealization," which is achieved by moving from ugliness to beauty.

Cohen's concept of humor has received little recognition, yet it illuminates a mode of engaging with human weakness that differs radically from satire and caricature, two other forms in which ugliness is prominently featured. Humor presents ugliness as a meaningful element in art but only by transforming it via love. Cohen's concept of humor as a loving embrace of ugliness may be the most underrepresented idea in the history of the theory of ugliness. In the few partial histories that exist, Cohen's name scarcely, if ever, appears.[9]

Although Cohen's humanism is admirable, his concept of ugliness has limitations. His analysis focuses on the content, not also the form, of artworks, and he essentially limits his comments to physical ugliness. If we move also into other areas of ugliness, including emotional, intellectual, and especially moral ugliness, we need a more differentiated sensibility than simply loving embrace. For that reason, I would suggest a revision and expansion of Cohen's ideas. We could retain the moment of love elevated by Cohen while adding to it a moment of critique. After all, even if ugliness is part of the human condition, various contingent forms of ugliness should not be; they deserve criticism.

To convey this more complex idea of loving critique, let's take an example from literature. Consider the Swiss writer Gottfried Keller's story *Clothes Make the Man* (1874). Here, a tailor tries to extricate himself from a case of mistaken identity, though he does so only half-heartedly, allowing himself to be treated as a count. Other characters similarly exhibit various foibles. Despite lingering on these weaknesses, Keller portrays most of his characters as good-hearted and steers far clear of cynicism. Humor, understood in this expanded sense as a kind of loving critique, offers a reconciliation that is nonetheless aware of still unresolved tensions; it is tolerant of human weaknesses, for it views them *sub specie aeternitatis*. Thomas Mann's novel *The Confessions of Felix Krull: Confidence Man* (1954) would be another example. Mann mocks his character and narrator Krull, but we enjoy him and his antics, even to some extent his misdeeds. He and his society are gently criticized. Mann's loving critique is far removed from the harsh satire of Heinrich Mann's *Der Untertan* (*The Subject*) (written in 1914 and published in 1918), which offers a bitter critique of unappealing characters and a stern, if nonetheless funny, indictment of Wilhelminian Germany. *Der Untertan* is closer to caricature than to humor.

A cinematic example of loving critique can be found in Alfred Hitchcock's film *Shadow of a Doubt* (1943), where the director criticizes the family for its ignorance but does so gently and humorously. Young Charlie distances herself from the family, for she sees reality more clearly than they do, but she still loves them. Hitchcock's critique of the other family members, along with the neighbor Herb, while clear, is hardly bitter or ruthless—it is layered with humor and respect (Roche, *Alfred Hitchcock* 119–58). Addressing ugliness mildly, with loving critique, is a fascinating aesthetic option, to which Cohen points the way. Indeed, it may well be the best lens to understand the ways in which twentieth-century portraitist Lucian Freud uncompromisingly portrays physically ugly figures but with a dignity that renders them beautiful, as in his oil on canvas *Benefits Supervisor Sleeping* (1995) (Figure 11).

Figure 11 *Lucian Freud,* Benefits Supervisor Sleeping, *1995, Oil on canvas, Private Collection / © The Lucian Freud Archive. All Rights Reserved 2025 / Bridgeman Images.*

Johannes Volkelt was a pioneer in the psychology of aesthetics and a professor, briefly, in Jena, Basel, and Würzburg, and then for almost thirty years in Leipzig. His three-volume *System der Ästhetik* (*System of Aesthetics*) was first published between 1905 and 1912, with a thoroughly revised second edition appearing from 1925 to 1927. A discussion of ugliness concludes the second volume, *Die ästhetischen Grundgestalten* (*The Basic Aesthetic Forms*). For Volkelt, the ugly is no longer a part of beauty that must be integrated in a particular way in order to become beautiful; instead, the "ugly is synonymous with the aesthetically harmful, the aesthetically unsatisfying, the contra-aesthetic" (2:582).

Volkelt introduces four general types of ugly art. First, "*psychological ugliness*," fails to appeal to our imagination, for it appears dry or violates the unity of form and content (2:583). Second, the "*ugliness of content*" negates what is humanly meaningful; it is "vacuous (nichtssagend), trivial, paltry, all too superficial" (2:583–4). Third, the "*ugliness of materiality*" involves content that evokes disgust, anger, or outrage (2:584). Finally, in the "*ugliness of structure*" multiple dimensions of a work are chaotic, wild, or incomprehensible (2:584). Essentially, the first and fourth types derive from bad form, either too little formal appeal or too much for us to process meaningfully; and the second and third types stem from weak content that is either boring or outrageous.[10]

Volkelt's distinctions are not without partial insight. However, Volkelt lacks any sense of dialectic and is thus unable to envision how formal transgressions and horrific material can be integrated into great art. As a result, he cannot distinguish between the seemingly ugly and bad art. His only nod to complexity is the concession that the characteristic, that is, the peculiar, strange, and distinct, though not the ugly, can be integrated into the sublime, the tragic, and the comic (2:24). With Volkelt, we observe a clear and paradigmatic shift in academic aesthetics: the concept of beautiful ugliness gives way to ugliness as a form of bad art.

Volkelt's arguments are indicative of a wider trend. The philosophical tradition of engaging the ugly as an element of beauty begins to dissipate in the late nineteenth and early twentieth century.[11] In arguably the most influential aesthetics of the first half of the twentieth century, *Estetica come scienza dell'espressione e linguistica generale* (*Aesthetic as Science of Expression and General Linguistic*) (1902), Benedetto Croce argues that within the realm of aesthetics the ugly is "without meaning" and can refer only to unsuccessful expression, to "the antiaesthetic or inexpressive" (88). This neglect of ugliness continues from the first decade of the twentieth century until the late 1950s when Wolfgang Kayser highlighted the grotesque and Adorno began writing his aesthetics, thereby lifting ugliness and dissonance to the pinnacle of art. In his aesthetics of 1948, which was translated into English, Friedrich Kainz, for example, does not mention ugliness, nor does he include any reference to Rosenkranz. Likewise, Nicolai Hartmann's aesthetics of 1953 does not address ugliness at all. This trend is not unique to Germany. R. G. Collingwood, a prominent idealist one to two generations after Bosanquet, reduces ugliness to negative aesthetic value, viewing ugly works as those that fail to achieve a harmonious whole (54–5).

10

The Greatness and Limits of Adorno's Aesthetics of Ugliness

The next thinker to focus on ugliness was **Theodor Adorno**, one of Germany's most prominent twentieth-century philosophers and the best-known theorist of dissonant beauty. Accustomed to culture from an early age, Adorno had dual interests in philosophy and music. After completing his doctorate in Frankfurt in 1924, he moved to Vienna, where he studied under Alban Berg for two years and also met Berg's teacher, Arnold Schoenberg. Adorno completed his Habilitation (or second book) in 1931. Three years later, his Jewish heritage and political beliefs made emigration necessary. After initially fleeing to England, he eventually settled in New York and then Los Angeles. In 1949, he returned to Germany and, along with Max Horkheimer, became one of the two founding figures of the so-called Frankfurt School.

Adorno's interest in negativity is evident in his works, including *Negative Dialectics* (1966) and his fascination with atonal music. Adorno elevates dissonance and ugliness as art's most privileged categories. In doing so, he breaks with the academic philosophy of his day. He gained inspiration from his distinct version of dialectic and his understanding of history, particularly the Holocaust. Drawing on his master concept of non-identity, Adorno views "dissonance" as "the technical term" for our reception of ugliness (Ger. 74; Eng. 46).[1] He asserts: "Dissonance is the truth about harmony" (Ger. 168; Eng. 110) and "the seal of everything modern" (Ger. 29; Eng. 15). According to Adorno, the quantitative increase of ugliness in modernity leads to a new quality in art: emancipation from harmony (Ger. 74–5, 154; Eng. 46, 100).

Adorno contests the traditional view of art as a counter-model to dissonant reality, which offers us windows onto alternatives characterized by affirmation and reconciliation (Ger. 10; Eng. 2). He criticizes any form of reconciliation in art, which he believes must come at the expense of "unreconciled life" (Ger. 78; Eng. 48). Adorno states: "That is the sadness of art. It achieves an unreal reconciliation at the price of real reconciliation" (Ger. 84; Eng. 52, translation modified). In this sense, idealistic art, even when counter-cultural, must lose its force as critique. Adorno argues that any reconciliation within art necessarily minimizes tension and obscures negativity; this renders it deficient (Ger. 75, 85; Eng. 46, 53). For Adorno, art must avoid a forgetting of the negative.

Artworks conceived as successful wholes, where parts integrate harmoniously, render those parts lifeless; "the death of the moments in the whole" is the result (Ger. 84; Eng. 52, my translation). The very success we associate with an artwork whose parts contribute to the whole is, in fact, decay (Ger. 84; Eng. 52). For the sake of beauty, understood as aesthetic excellence, we need to relinquish any transcendence of negativity: "Indeed, for the sake of the beautiful, nothing is no longer beautiful; for there is no longer anything beautiful. What can appear only negatively mocks a resolution that it recognizes as false and which therefore degrades the idea of the beautiful" (Ger. 85; Eng. 53, translation modified). For Adorno, the world is so deficient that hope is no longer legitimate. In *Negative Dialectics,* he describes the world spirit "as permanent catastrophe" (Ger. 314; Eng. 320).

The best art, therefore, is not organic but fragmentary: "Art of the highest order compels itself beyond form as totality and into the fragmentary" (Ger. 221; Eng. 147, translation modified). Such art seeks to embody the inconclusiveness that Hegel associated with the so-called bad infinite (Ger. 221; Eng. 147).[2] Calls to humanize art over against the reign of the dissonant result in a falling away of formal excellence (Ger. 80; Eng. 49–50). Although Adorno believes that artworks, in their autonomy, strive to counter reality, they also contain internal discord that mirrors societal tensions. Reconciliation in art frequently results from a forced arrangement (Ger. 78; Eng. 48), an oppressive formalism contrary to the defining form of modernity, which Adorno sees as anti-organic montage (Ger. 233–4; Eng. 155–6). Modern art comes across as gruesome and cruel because reality is so overwhelmingly ugly that it cannot be transfigured into form; reconciliation is no longer possible (Ger. 81; Eng. 50). This break occurs independently of content: "even the seemingly most neutral objects that art has sought to eternalize as beautiful come off as [. . .] hard, unassimilable, indeed ugly" (Ger. 81; Eng. 50, translation modified). For Adorno, even impressionism, with its barbarous method and occasional integration of societal fragments, gives evidence of this ugliness (Ger. 81; Eng. 50).

Adorno completely abandons classical aesthetics. Earlier thinkers had allowed for ugliness, but within parameters. For such thinkers, moments of ugliness contribute to art or even to beauty. Adorno calls that entire discourse into question and posits a counter-model. Ugliness now provides the norm of all discourse. There is no compatibility whatsoever between beauty as classically understood and truth. Truth cannot be beautiful, and beauty cannot be true. Truth is disruptive and non-reconciliatory.

Adorno's unrelenting stress on non-reconciliation has multiple catalysts. Historically, it can be understood in light of the Holocaust. The murder of Jews in Nazi death camps is the most unfathomable event of the twentieth century. This is even more so the case for Jewish thinkers. Consider not only Adorno but also Hans Jonas, who wrote "The Concept of God after Auschwitz." Adorno insists on preserving negativity as negative, refusing to accept alternative voices that might, even inadvertently, leave such negativity behind. For Adorno, the primary color of radical art is "black" (Ger. 65; Eng. 39). He argues that any art that presents an alternative viewpoint is "an injustice to the dead, to accumulated, speechless pain" (Ger. 66; Eng. 40). The elevation of non-reconciliation also serves to counter social realism, which blatantly obscures and overrides, and so distorts, the tensions of reality. Additionally, one might interpret Adorno's insistence on non-reconciliation as a kind of theological gesture: Hohendahl sees in Adorno a negative theology in extremis: the absolute will always elude us (73).

The greatness of Adorno's theory includes—and here he does not differ from Hegel—an elevation of artwork aesthetics and a recognition of art's articulation of truth. Moreover, Adorno grasps, like few others, the increasingly reflective and self-reflective dimensions of modern art. Great as well is Adorno's sense that art is its own end and is partly resistant to conceptual understanding. Additional strengths are his deep engagement with the dissonance of the age and his capacity to recognize in ugliness a signature element of modernity. Further, Adorno's writing embodies the very theory he advocates (even if we might argue that the consistency between theory and approach that results in his cultivating an intentionally difficult and obscure style also has disadvantages). Finally, Adorno places unusual stress on the combination of aesthetic autonomy and social resistance; often thinkers opt for one at the expense of the other.

A central question regarding Adorno's views on ugliness is whether Adorno wants to argue that all great art must be dissonant or that all *modern* art worthy of the name must be dissonant. One could even weigh whether he leaves the question unresolved or even contradicts himself. After all, when Adorno died in 1969, he had not fully completed his *Aesthetics*.

On the one hand, Adorno recognizes with modernity an aesthetic shift. Different themes and forms emerge. Adorno is a deeply historical thinker. The ugly and the beautiful are for him "thoroughly dynamic [. . .] both mock definitional fixation" (Ger. 75; Eng. 46). Adorno suggests that "in accordance with the horrors of reality," "Heiterkeit," which in the published translation has been rendered as "lightheartedness," but which equally means "brightness," "clarity," or "serenity," disappears from the individual artwork (*Noten* 600; *Notes* 2:248). In modernity, the ugly is no longer absorbed into something beautiful: "The harmonious view of the ugly was protested in modern art. Something qualitatively new emerged" (Ger. 75; Eng. 46, translation modified). Because Auschwitz was possible and for the foreseeable future remains possible, Adorno claims that "bright art is no longer conceivable" (*Noten* 603; *Notes* 2:251, translation modified). Some traditional forms of art are beyond the legitimate palette of modernity. Tragedy presupposes "the positive meaning of negativity," but this is no longer possible (*Noten* 606; *Notes* 2:253), and comedy is tenable only insofar as it is transformed into "self-critique" or "self-reflexive comedy" (Komik der Komik) (*Noten* 605; *Notes* 2:252, translation modified). In modernity, the ugly is visible not only in art but also in the environment: industrialized landscapes are immediately perceived as ugly.

On the other hand, Adorno offers again and again apodictic statements about what art is and what makes art effective, not simply modern art. "Kunst ist . . ." or "Art is . . ." is a recurring line and is often associated with some element of negativity or non-identity. "Art is the social antithesis of society" (Ger. 19; Eng. 8). "Art is the promise of happiness that is broken" (Ger. 205; Eng. 136). So, too, the evaluative frame has no historical restriction: "The rank of an artwork is defined essentially by whether it exposes itself to, or withdraws from, the irreconcilable" (Ger. 283; Eng. 190; cf. 221). Adorno's comments on the spuriousness of aesthetic wholeness are not restricted to modernity (e.g., Ger. 84, 168; Eng. 52, 110). Lyric poetry, regardless of its historical context, has "the moment of *discontinuity* in it" (das Moment des *Bruches* in sich) (*Noten* 53; *Notes* 1:40). In the paralipomena to his *Aesthetics,* Adorno writes: "Disintegration is the truth of integral art" (Ger. 455). He argues that even before Auschwitz, ascribing any positive meaning to existence was a lie (Ger. 229; Eng. 152). Reinforcing the idea that ugliness is not distinctive to modernity is his assertion that the ugly does not follow, it precedes the beautiful (Ger. 81; Eng. 50). Art's origins, in archaic and traditional art, are already steeped in ugliness, as in the archaic enactment of terror; ancient subject matter, such as the fauns and sileni of Hellenism; and dynamic tension and equilibrium, which presuppose ugliness (Ger. 76–7; Eng. 47–8).

Gestures to harmony are untenable; that is, they violate a norm Adorno sets not only for modern but also for classical art—that they not be harmonic because harmony cannot be achieved without violating integrity: "Formalistic classicism commits an affront: Precisely the beauty that its concept glorifies is sullied by the manipulative, 'composed' violence of its exemplary works" (das Gewaltsame, Arrangierende, 'Komponierende,' das seinen exemplarischen Werken anhaftet) (Ger. 78; Eng. 48). In the classical era, he identifies a corrupting triad: "Reconciliation as an act of violence, aesthetic formalism, and unreconciled life form a triad" (Ger. 78; Eng. 48, translation modified). Elsewhere, Adorno speaks of "the inadequacy of classicism" (das Ungenügen am Klassizismus) (Ger. 181; Eng. 119).

When Adorno interprets artists from earlier ages, he elevates their moments of dissonance. So, for example, in his study of Eichendorff he highlights "despair" (*Noten* 77; *Notes* 1:62), "dissociation" (*Noten* 79; *Notes* 1:65), and "self-estrangement" (*Noten* 80; *Notes* 1:65). When analyzing Hölderlin, Adorno finds "antipathy toward the aesthetic harmony of the finite and the infinite" (*Noten* 465; *Notes* 2:125); "the untruth of reconciliation" (*Noten* 468; *Notes* 2:127, translation modified); "anticlassical quality, its rebellion against harmony" (*Noten* 473; *Notes* 2:133); and "critique of synthesis" (*Noten* 486; *Notes* 2:144). In Goethe's *Iphigenia*, he emphasizes moments of "irreconcilability" and the work's "fragmentary quality" (Brüchigkeit) (*Noten* 502; *Notes* 2:159). Adorno suggests that the depth of art—not specifically modern art—is measured by the extent to which it allows "lack of reconciliation" (Unversöhntheit) to shine through (*Noten* 601; *Notes* 2:249).

Adorno's tendency to discredit reconciliation extends beyond literature to music. Adorno's most critical comments in his book on Mahler pertain to Mahler's most popular work, Symphony no. 2, the Resurrection Symphony. Intolerably for Adorno, the symphony ends with redemption—the joyous resurrection of all humankind and the celebration of divine mercy and love—which is achieved through markedly complex musical strategies in the fifth movement and which, with its final chorus, echoes Beethoven's ninth symphony. Adorno dismisses the work as "weak" and predicts it will "fade first," describing its final movement as crude and "lightweight" (Ger. 280–1; Eng. 136).

We could perhaps solve this puzzle by inverting a comment Adorno makes about Hegel and applying it to Adorno himself. Adorno says that Hegel, like no one before him, understood the concept of dialectical change and the actual historical development of art, yet Hegel nonetheless preserved the canon of the ancient and the classical (Ger. 309; Eng. 208). Adorno follows Hegel in recognizing historical turning points in art but, unlike anyone before him, Adorno elevates dissonance at the expense of the classical and so restricts, in a reverse way, the canon of aesthetic excellence. Adorno refuses to apply negativity to itself.

In some ways, this is not surprising. As much as Adorno wants to resist his age, he is a child of the twentieth century. He was educated by Alban Berg.

Even if we judge Adorno to be not an especially original composer, he knew the craft of cacophony like few others, as his theory of music makes clear. His knowledge of pre-modern art, however, is limited. It is amazing how few in number his examples are from pre-nineteenth-century art and literature; this contrasts greatly with earlier aesthetic theories (Hösle, *Zur Geschichte* 97). The lacuna helps explain Adorno's preference for the cerebral art of modernity: "Only radically intellectualized (vergeistigte) art is still possible; all other art is childish" (Ger. 142; Eng. 92, translation modified). Adorno elevates challenging, complex, and reflective art, asserting that "genuine aesthetic experience must become philosophy or it is in no sense genuine" (Ger. 197; Eng. 131, translation modified).

One of Adorno's early critics, Hans Robert Jauß, recognized the hubris of Adorno's imposing modern categories onto all art: "The history of art cannot be reduced to the common denominator of negativity" (*Ästhetische Erfahrung* 39; *Aesthetic Experience* 16). Jauß makes three compelling criticisms. First, even works of negativity may lose their negativity as they become classics. When integrated into a tradition, they can be said to move beyond Adorno's obligatory "trajectory of progressive negativity" (Adorno Ger. 239; Eng. 159; *Ästhetische Erfahrung* 39–41). Second, Adorno is unable to make sense of heroic poetry, which, far from being defined primarily by negativity, has played a formative role in shaping various cultures (*Ästhetische Erfahrung* 41–2). Finally, Adorno insists on distance and views readers' identification with characters as taboo, as enacting structures of banality. But such identification can extend the reader's horizon of capacities, including empathy and inspiration, an admirable phenomenon that occurs not only in popular literature, but also in the works of great authors such as Lessing (*Ästhetische Erfahrung* 42–3).

In viewing ugliness as primary and thereby resisting the traditional definition of ugliness as the negation of beauty, Adorno follows Nietzsche and is subsequently followed by the Slovenian philosopher and cultural critic Slavoj Žižek. Nietzsche, Adorno, and Žižek all view beauty as derivative of ugliness—an attempt to shade over the ugliness of the world and thereby deny it (Adorno Ger. 77 and 81; Eng. 47 and 50; Žižek 21). This theory offers us an unstated parallel to Karl Marx's quip that religion is the opium of the masses, which deflects our attention from the dissonance of reality (57). Here, *beauty* is the opium of the masses. Adorno notes that the more aggressively the Nazis tortured people in the basement, the more they insisted on the aesthetic perfection of the roof resting on columns (Ger. 79–80; Eng. 49).

For Adorno, dissonance is the signature of reality. It is also the mark of the artwork, insofar as the successful artwork is necessarily at tension with both society and itself and so not self-identical. The intellectual demands arising from this internal disjunction and art's integration of ugliness emerge together. Any effort to criticize ugliness reveals a lack of intellectual capacity to deal with this challenge: "The primacy of intellect in art and the inroads made by what was previously taboo are two sides of the same coin" (Ger. 144; Eng. 93, translation modified). The chaotic elements of modern art and its intellectual demands resist the tendency to flatten reality (Ger. 144–5; Eng. 93–4). Therefore, criticizing the ugliness of modern art is inherently "anti-intellectual" (geistfeindlich) (Ger. 144; Eng. 93, my translation).

In articulating his theory of ugliness, Adorno succumbs to an interwoven set of internally contradictory stances. He argues that when artists introduce reconciliation, they fail to convey the truth. To be beautiful is to be untrue and to falsify reality, which is full of tensions and contradictions. Instead, art must accommodate itself to ugliness: "Art is modern art through mimesis of the hardened and alienated" (Ger. 39; Eng. 21). Art should not attempt to offer redemption, as religion does. Adorno elevates thereby non-identity, but he simultaneously demands correspondence to the dissonance of reality, which we should not even be able to recognize. Adorno suggests that dissonance is so great that concepts and language necessarily distort reality: "The power of language proves itself insofar as expression and thing separate in reflection. Language becomes a measure of truth only when we are conscious of the non-identity of an expression with that which we mean" (*Negative Dialektik*, 117; Eng. 111, translation modified). The claim is self-cancelling. Adorno contends that our concepts cannot grasp reality. But he cannot defend the claim that there is a break between our concepts and reality without presupposing knowledge of reality as different from our concepts. Here Adorno falls into a pragmatic contradiction. He presupposes a *coherence* of negative reality and truth, which his evocation of *non-identity* does not permit.

A further contradiction in Adorno's thought relates to mimesis. Adorno hates mimesis, because it means adapting to the external world, which he abhors. He prefers resistance and critique over adaptation. Yet ironically his theory, as we will see, unwittingly endorses mimetic adaptation. Adorno's concept of mimesis is much broader than Aristotle's. For Adorno, mimesis involves accommodation to the outside world. Thus, Adorno uses not the genitive but the preposition: "Mimesis an" or "mimetic adaption to" (Ger. 39; Eng. 21). For Adorno, mimesis has deep anthropological roots. This orientation is clear in *Dialectic of Enlightenment* (1944), which Adorno wrote together with Max Horkheimer: "For mimesis, the outside world is a model, to which the inner world must try to conform" (187, translation modified). In modernity, mimesis includes adaptation to the culture industry. It is a survival strategy: we get through by becoming part of the external system, adapting to the external world, and Adorno finds that repugnant. He wants instead resistance. For him, art must reflect the dissonance of reality, not through realism, but through resistance to harmony, as harmony fails to account for the ugliness of reality.

Adorno wants to describe the world in all its ugliness and excoriate it: "Art must take up the cause of what has been attacked as ugly [. . .] in order via the ugly to denounce the world that creates and reproduces the ugly in its own image" [Kunst muß das als häßlich Verfemte zu ihrer Sache machen [. . .] um im Häßlichen die Welt zu denunzieren, die es nach ihrem Bilde schafft und reproduziert] (Ger. 78–9; Eng. 48–9, translation modified). Refusing to convey this ugliness betrays those, including the victims of Auschwitz, who suffered at the hands of history. "As long as the world is as it is, all pictures of reconciliation, peace, and repose resemble the picture of death" (*Negative Dialektik* 374; Eng. 381, translation modified). This presents a serious contradiction. On the one hand, Adorno says, look at all the ugliness in reality (forget about all your ideologies that don't allow you to see what is really going on). He censures idealist philosophers who view the world as a place of harmony while the world is filled with the devastations of the Holocaust. Not by chance, Adorno opens the final section of his *Negative Dialectics* with reflections on Auschwitz. On the other hand, Adorno doesn't want to agree with those who say, look, reality is brutal, and we must adapt to it, because that is giving in to the mimetic impulse in order to survive. This explains his revolt against the ugliness of reality, not based on a clear logical analysis but out of a refusal to align with the mimetic instinct.

The consequences of this view become clear. If the world is a disaster, and if there is no hope of changing it—a hope that, if genuine, would betray the brutality of the world—then cynicism is the result. Adorno's pessimism becomes self-fulfilling. It is no long progression from Adorno's position to one that involves revelry in a world that cannot, in any case, be changed. Adorno has no coherent argument against this view, offering instead a stance filled with internal contradictions and personal preferences.

Another weakness is the faulty argument we see in Nietzsche, Adorno, and Žižek: because the ugly is *prior* to beauty in terms of *genealogy,* it should also hold priority in terms of *validity* or evaluation. This slippage is evident in Adorno and the others, but to argue that the genesis of a concept determines its validity is to fall prey to the genetic fallacy. Moreover, it is not clear that ugliness is necessarily prior, though it can be. Beauty can originate on its own (in the form of an ideal vision), or it can emerge as a counter to the world's ugliness. Similarly, ugliness can begin on its own (we see it in reality), or it can be an aesthetic response to the occasional superficiality of formal beauty, triggering an elevation of dissonance over consonance, ugliness over harmony. The artist who embraces ugliness is, after all, rarely the first artist in a cultural sequence.

Adorno elevates ugliness because of its oppositional character. Hohendahl writes: "The autonomy of the artwork depends on its oppositional force, a quality that is enhanced by the ugly" (81). Adorno is clear on this: "works become beautiful on the strength of their movement against mere existence" (Ger. 82; Eng. 51, translation modified). Art stands in a negative relationship to reality; in a world where everything has a function, the function of art is "functionlessness" (Ger. 336–7; Eng. 227). Adorno believes ugliness is not easily assimilated; it resists commercialization. But this is not always the case, as ugliness itself can become commodified. Although ugly art rarely appeals to the masses, it has found success among collectors. One of the largest amounts ever paid for an American painting was the $110.5 million paid in 2017 for Jean-Michel Basquiat's 1982 painting of a skull, an example of beautiful ugliness (Pogrebin and Reyburn). For many, investments in art are analogous to investments in other marketable goods. Even if the boldness and countercultural rhetoric of Adorno's claims may have wide appeal, such links between artwork aesthetics and reception aesthetics tend to be simplistic.[3] Beyond the economic dimensions lies an amusing political irony: the American government, including the CIA, consciously supported abstract art—much of which was ugly—because it embraced individualism and countered the socialist realism that was popular under communism. Here, too, the capitalist market could endorse the non-social and the ugly (Kammen 103–13).

Although Adorno likes to evaluate and criticize artworks, he does not give us any criteria by which to differentiate good art from bad art, other than asserting that all good art is dissonant. In his framework, no specific criteria emerge to help us discern which dissonant art is good and which is not. One sometimes gets the impression that dissonance is itself the criterion.

Adorno reduces great art to dissonant art instead of viewing dissonant and ugly art as one fascinating type of great art among a wider variety of possible models. Essentially, Adorno would discard works that offer gestures toward reconciliation, including, of course, comic works that contain moments of reconciliation: "Humor" is, for Adorno, "more repulsive than all else that is repulsive" (abstoßender . . . als alles Abstoßende) (Ger. 79; Eng. 48, my translation). Consequently, the entire tradition of European comedy has no place in his aesthetics, except for some modern comedies that take a negative turn.

Adorno also has no place for what I call *radiant beauty*—beautiful works that either exclude ugliness or include it minimally (*Beautiful Ugliness* 18). Consider Albrecht Dürer's watercolor *Hare* (1502) or Renoir's painting *Bridge at Chatou* (*c.* 1875). Viewers have little difficulty finding such works beautiful. One could call such beauty "facile" or "easy," as does Bosanquet (*Three Lectures* 85), but these terms relate to reception, and in describing works themselves, I want to stress artwork aesthetics, thus my preference for "radiant beauty." Moreover, what appears facile to the viewer may actually be complex in its creation, making a term like "facile beauty" misleading from a production context as well. As Pseudo-Longinus noted, great artists often hide complex craftsmanship, conveying the appearance of simple beauty, which is belied by difficult processes of creation (chs. 17, 22, and 38). Seemingly superficial beauty can easily be complex in creation or meaning: for example, the highly technical computer graphic art of Charles Csuri, which, even when radiantly beautiful, involves astonishingly complex processes.

Not only in genesis, but even in form, radiant beauty can be complex. Take Mozart's symphonies, which are instantly recognizable as beautiful yet contain complex elements in their structure. I also avoid the term "pure beauty," insofar as it seems to allow for no moments of dissonance or negativity. Rare is the great artwork that is completely without tension or darkness. "Radiant" seems more fitting insofar as it implies something positive and light-filled, without the dominance of negativity.

To underscore that radiant beauty need not be only a beauty of the past, we can consider the art of German artist Wolfgang Laib, who painstakingly collects yellow pollen grains from wildflowers (such as dandelions) and trees (such as hazelnut) and then exhibits them in patterns. He also makes beautiful works with beeswax and with a combination of marble, sandpaper, water, and milk, likewise laborious processes. Laib notes the necessity of irony and doubt but challenges their supremacy (Tanguy 30–1).[4] He comments: "The work I make is very, very simple, but then it's also very, very complex" (Tanguy 30). British artist Andy Goldsworthy offers another example of complexity in non-ironic art (Schama). His often ephemeral creations—made from leaves, twigs, thorns, feathers, snow, and ice—are beautiful and depend not simply on what his own predilections are but also on what he finds in nature.

In some cultures and subgroups of society, only radiant beauty counts as beautiful. It is a virtue of Adorno to turn our attention to an alternative view. Because theory colors our view of reality, it should not surprise us that at one time mountains were considered ugly: they defaced and blemished what should have been (and once was) a perfectly regular and ordered landscape, in the words of Thomas Burnet, "smooth, regular and uniform" (1:51). For late seventeenth-century European theorists like Burnet, mountains represented the earth's disfigurement, its disorder and chaos. They were viewed as having arisen in the wake of human sins and God's wrath, specifically as a result of the "Deluge" or "Noah's Flood" (1:96). Mountains were "great ruines," "wild, vast and indigested," "heaps of Stone and Rubbish," "broken," "barren," "desolate," "shapeless and ill-figur'd," and nothing but "modes of irregularity" (Burnet

1:140, 1:142, 1:143, 1:144, 1:145). Not until the range of aesthetic categories was extended to the sublime could mountains be integrated into aesthetic theory, notwithstanding that on the experiential level mountains had awakened even for their critics a sense of awe and almost unwilling "Admiration" (Burnet 1:145; cf. 1:139–40). The association between mountains and deformity was so pervasive and persistent that even in the nineteenth century, some theorists still described mountainous regions as ugly (e.g., Weiße 2:439–40).

Adorno reminds us of the limits of such a reductive view. But in seeing the dissonant, fractured, and ugly as constitutive of all art or even simply all modern art, Adorno fails to see how diverse beauty can be. Certainly, all great art must include some level of tension. Extreme avoidance of dissonance, as in contemporary kitsch or earlier works that are almost entirely free of dissonance, such as eighteenth-century German American mystic Conrad Beissel's Ephrata music, are as unsatisfying as unrelenting dissonance.[5] But that need not mean that the work be engaged specifically with ugliness or that the tension remain unreconciled. To exclude radiant beauty, tragedy, comedy, and humor from the realm of positive aesthetic value is mistaken. We recognize in Adorno, as well as in some of his followers, a tendency to reduce great art to ugly art instead of seeing it as a fascinating kind of great art among a wider range of possible models. To accept or appreciate only one kind of art is to truncate the richness of aesthetic experience.

In this context, I note that Adorno himself admired beautiful works when he was still in his twenties and had yet to formulate his distinctive philosophy. In his early essay on Schubert, Adorno commends moments of "hope" and "consolation" in Schubert's lied *Death and the Maiden* (Ger. 27; Eng. 42) and "fulfillment" and "joy" in his Symphony no. 9 in C Major (Ger. 27–28; Eng. 43). Indeed, the young Adorno recognizes the theme of "reconciliation" throughout Schubert's work (Ger. 29; Eng. 46). But no similar tendencies surface in Adorno's later writings.

One instance where the exiled Adorno does experience a kind of catharsis occurs more or less outside of art. Adorno tells the story that Harold Russell, who played Homer in William Wyler's award-winning film *The Best Years of Our Lives*, was leaving an event at a Malibu villa. Unlike Charlie Chaplin, who stood next to Adorno, Adorno absent-mindedly extended his hand to

Russell, who had lost both hands in the war and had iron hooks as prostheses. Surprised and embarrassed, Adorno jerked his hand back and sought to mask his shock with an obliging grimace, which, he says, must have looked even more gruesome. As soon as Russell departed, Chaplin performed a pantomime of Adorno's faux pas, including his hopeless attempt to cover it up. Adorno relates that in the face of something horrible, he experienced the redemptive power of humor ("sein Rettendes") ("Zweimal Chaplin" 366).

Adorno might be right that in our age we are drawn to more negative works, but that need not mean that we accept as valid only negative works. One need not choose. Adorno is right that some examples of radiant beauty can be criticized as escapist. Such a critique would apply to works that slide over problems when they might otherwise be worked through, and so could be said to cultivate a kind of false consolation. Such works can be criticized for insufficiently integrating the ugliness that is part of the world. But there is also a role to be played by exhibiting alternatives, otherness. Art need not be restricted to what is, but can also reflect on what should be. If what humanity needs today is a greater sense of transcendence and insight into human dignity, cynically portraying human banality and baseness as the only options available to humanity is hardly promising. The alternatives evoked in art may be simply formal. Through form alone, organic unity may counter the chaos of the age. The emerging field of neuroaesthetics further confirms the narrowness of Adorno's view: the beauty of nature and of art addresses human needs that dissonance alone can hardly satisfy (Magsamen and Ross).

A related defense of Adorno would be that an age that is truly immoral is not deserving of artworks that are beautiful. Although this argument can be short-sighted or overblown, it is not to be taken lightly. It was a genuine motivating force in Roman satire (Juvenal 1.22–30). Creating beautiful works in such an age may seem to justify the status quo. In "To Those Born Later," the German poet Bertolt Brecht asks: "What kind of times are these, in which / A conversation about trees is almost a crime / Because it involves a silence about so many wrongs!" (Ger. 2:723; Eng. 318, translation modified). Danto also wonders whether an immoral age deserves beautiful artworks (*Abuse* 55, 116). Creating such works can appear to justify existing conditions, consoling us in our miserable present (*Abuse* 115). Those who fashion beauty in an unjust world, instead of confronting that world with disgust, are complicit in its evil. In Danto's view, they are "collaborationists" (*Abuse* 118).

This is an argument from the realm of reception aesthetics and has helped to render beauty taboo. Another reception-aesthetic argument is the fear that aesthetic affirmation will be mistaken for real affirmation; this is Adorno's position in the *Aesthetics* (Ger. 203; Eng. 134). Peter Bürger invokes the idea as well, arguing that while art may represent a better alternative than current reality, the fictional realization relieves existing society of any pressure for change (50). To counter this combination of seduction and quietism, Adorno contends that art must only negate, only resist, only criticize; it must eschew positive meaning (Ger. 229; Eng. 153). The argument recognizes the genuine value in works that portray suffering and unresolved social conflicts. When art includes but then overcomes ugliness, it carries with it the danger of reducing tension to the point of falling into a realm of art that no longer engages ugliness, no longer addresses unsettled problems, and no longer evokes mystery.

A counter-argument to the claim of escapism is that some harmonic works stand apart from their age and, through their difference, may offer an implicit critique or at least a contrast. The playfulness of such a work, a harmony derived in part by its being self-contained, may serve as a counter-model to a reality defined by fragmentation and ugliness. Adorno's insistence on intellection may be partially countered with the claims, first, that the distinction of art vis-à-vis philosophy is precisely the moment of sensuousness, which seems especially prominent in radiant beauty, and, second, that too much intellection can inhibit the creative artist and diminish the artwork's effectiveness as an artwork (Vico §821 and §838). To say that there is a place for such works, for moments of radiant beauty, is not to say that such works capture the most complex form of art or that they encompass all that art can express.

Adorno argues that when artists take as their object the ugliness of the world, the resulting images are necessarily other and so can be seen not to imitate but to denounce the world (Ger. 386; Eng. 260). To show any vision beyond the world's negativity would be to deny that negativity (Ger. 386–7; Eng. 386–7). Adorno's mimetic imperative does not allow for alternatives or a reshaping of reality. Without an alternative vision, however, ugliness itself becomes the norm, diminishing the opportunity for critique. The contemporary artist wants, in some ways, to portray ugliness because the world is ugly, and the artist is motivated to portray reality as it is. So artists strive to become countercultural by shocking audiences with various forms of ugliness. Art wants to be avant-garde, but the irony is that if the world is only ugly, then ugly art is mimetic; it imitates the reality that exists. To truly counter the world, art must at least hint at what transcends ugliness, including forms that engage with ugliness but also move beyond it.

As miserable as the world may be, one way to imagine hope for change is to draw attention to seeds of alternatives, whether submerged in this world or lying beyond it. If one of art's tasks, in Danto's paraphrasing of Hegel, is to "represent ourselves for ourselves" (*Abuse* 118), then it makes sense to represent what our highest aspirations are as well as what aspects of our world deserve loathing. Art encompasses a vast range, and not all art needs to focus on ugliness; the world, even in its ugliness, is hardly only ugly.

Artists such as Wassily Kandinsky and Paul Klee use abstraction not only to experiment with pure form, shape, and color but also to challenge the modern preoccupation with ugliness, suggesting it is insufficient in capturing art's possibilities (Engelmann). Franz Marc belongs in this realm as well, though with a twist: Marc seeks to overcome not the ugliness of modern art, but the ugliness of reality. He wants to offer counterimages. On April 12, 1915, he wrote to his wife: "I sensed *very* early on that the human being was 'ugly'; animals seemed to me more beautiful, purer; but even in them I discovered so much that was emotionally objectionable and ugly, such that my portrayals instinctively (out of an inner compulsion) became more and more schematic, more and more abstract" (141). This tradition of beautiful abstraction continues, for example, with contemporary American artist Richard Diebenkorn, whose *Ocean Park* paintings are beautiful in both senses of the term, pleasing in their play with light, shape, and color and aesthetically excellent.

Part III

Contemporary Theories

11

Continental Thinkers

Adorno was not the last European to analyze ugliness, though no more recent critic has reached his standing. As we turn from the German to the French tradition, **Georges Bataille** comes to the fore, an idiosyncratic intellectual, whose theoretical writings were greatly shaped by Nietzsche and, in turn, contributed to postmodernism. Bataille moves us from the philosophy of art to theory. He does not analyze the ugly as such, though he does occasionally make apodictic statements about ugliness. In *L'érotisme* (*Eroticism*) (1957), for instance, Bataille argues that the sexual act is an arousal through beauty and refinement that culminates in its opposite—an ugly, animalistic act. He asserts: "No one doubts the ugliness of the sexual act" (*Œuvres complètes* 10:144; *Eroticism* 145, translation modified). His modus operandi is not as much argumentative as it is assertive, poetic, associative, suggestive. At times Bataille reads like a clever analytic philosopher's parody of continental thinking. At other times he seems profound.

Bataille was fascinated by objects related to ugliness: filth and gore, the monstrous and obscene, excrement and death. Why? Bataille was harshly critical of the instrumental reason and economic rationality that govern modern life. In contrast, the French thinker elevated what served no ulterior purpose, what stood outside convention. Others might privilege disinterested beauty or intrinsic value. Bataille chose instead "decay as an end in itself" (*Œuvres complètes* 2:65; *Visions* 99). He elevates the "*formless*" (*informe*) along with the obscene, perverse, arbitrary, and meaningless. Bataille values the unavoidable "dislocation of meanings" (*Œuvres complètes* 7:294; *Theory of Religion* 22).

He suggests that "the universe resembles nothing" (*Œuvres complètes* 1:217; *Visions* 31). To say that the universe has no inherent meaning or structure, that it is "only formless amounts to saying that the universe is something like a spider or spit" (*Œuvres complètes* 1:217; *Visions* 31). Bataille's inversions and reversals generate renewed focus on what is otherwise repressed, what lies beyond our sight and outside normality.

Bataille sought to counter utility and convention further by advancing sexual transgression, as in his pornographic novella of 1928, *L'histoire de l'œil* (*Story of the Eye*). Related, he extols the concept of sacrifice: "in sacrifice the offering is rescued from all utility" (*Œuvres complètes* 7:311; *Theory of Religion* 49). Bataille criticizes not only instrumental thinking but also rational comprehension. The world, according to Bataille, is full of complexities that cannot be appropriated or rejected: "*As soon as the effort at rational comprehension ends in contradiction, the practice of intellectual scatology requires the excretion of unassimilable elements*, which is another way of stating vulgarly that a burst of laughter is the only imaginable and definitively terminal result" (*Œuvres complètes* 2:64; *Visions* 99). Where Hegel views reality as constituted by divine categories discernible to intelligence, Bataille sees no higher meaning in this world. A thinker who scorns the idea of higher meaning is perhaps not surprisingly drawn to ugliness, not only the formless but also the obscene. The laughter that Bataille champions throughout his writings is not the laughter that negates ugliness and restores beauty, as with Rosenkranz, but a self-consciously diabolical laughter marked by scorn and cynicism.

For Bataille the sacred, which transcends instrumental reason, is both attractive and repellent. Bataille urges a return to repulsive elements, including sacrifice and death, which are inherently fascinating. Modern society, with its emphasis on rationality and utility, struggles to accommodate these aspects. According to Bataille, we reach the sacred only by transgressing taboos. Characterized by horror and ecstasy, the sacred inherently opposes "reason and the good" (*Œuvres complètes* 7:331; *Theory of Religion* 82). Bataille's writings are difficult, partly because he abhorred coherent discourse and sought to elevate what is beyond exchange value and expression. Although Bataille does not significantly advance our understanding of the aesthetics of ugliness, he is noteworthy as an early twentieth-century thinker who contributed to the shift from beauty to ugliness. He has influenced artists, such as Thomas Hirschhorn (Gingeras and Hirschhorn 34–9) and Jake Chapman (Baker), who are engaged in creating ugly and seemingly ugly works. Bataille joins those who contend that idealism neglects the overlooked elements of society. Despite his frequent and approving citation of Nietzsche's dictum that "God is dead" (*Œuvres complètes* 1:501–2, 1:508, 1:563, 2:102; *Visions* 38, 213–14, 218, 245), Bataille to some extent carries on the early Christian turn to what is beyond elevated discourse, particularly "the lowest strata of society" (*Œuvres complètes* 1:349; *Visions* 144).

In criticizing the useful, Bataille elevates whatever is "heterogenous" and "other," whatever is "impossible to assimilate," which is why we find him extolling, in contrast to "the platitude inherent to *homogenous* society," not only the lowly, but also the disruptive otherness of figures such as Mussolini and Hitler (*Œuvres complètes* 1:340–2, 1:347–8; *Visions* 138, 140, 143). In criticizing calculation and normality, Bataille praises the revelatory significance, the "sovereign monstrosity," of irrational and excessive violence (*Œuvres complètes* 10:286; *Trial* 16). In the abominable fifteenth-century Gilles de Rais, who serially violated and killed hundreds of children, Bataille finds a figure who was "incapable of calculation" (*Œuvres complètes* 10:294; *Trial* 23). Precisely this transcendence of reason renders Rais revelatory, "a summit" (*Œuvres complètes* 10:277; *Trial* 9). As Bataille writes in *Eroticism*, "violence alone . . . can burst the barriers of rational thinking" (*Œuvres complètes* 10:139; *Eroticism* 140). He thus prefers the ugly consequences of violence to rational behavior: "Degradation, which turns eroticism into something foul and horrible, is better than the neutrality of reasonable and non-destructive sexual behavior" (*Œuvres complètes* 10:139; *Eroticism* 140). A thinker such as Bataille who elevates ugliness as such cannot easily distance himself from moral ugliness.

In this same tradition, we can place the comments of German composer Karlheinz Stockhausen. Days after 9/11, he stated that the terrorist attacks on the United States were

> the greatest possible artwork that has ever been [. . .] It is the greatest work of art that exists in the whole cosmos. Just picture to yourself what happened

> there. You have people who are so concentrated on one performance, and then in a single moment 5,000 people are sped into resurrection. I couldn't do that. In comparison with that, we're nothing as composers. ("Tonbandabschrift")

What renders the "artwork" of 9/11 great is the colossal, breathtaking performance. In such art, moral values play no role. Although we can give Stockhausen credit for later retracting his comments, he simply drew the horrific consequences of an idea that had (and still has) contemporary currency.

The celebration of moral ugliness often stems from a formal desire to provoke and transgress limits independently of content. Restrictions are viewed as arbitrary, and violence is to be affirmed. In a 2003 interview with Simon Baker, Jake Chapman was asked if "Bataille's formulation of the concept of transgression" relates to his own work. Chapman responded by invoking Bataille's idea of society's need for violence: "Yes—a good social service like the children who killed Jamie Bulger." Chapman refers here to the abduction, horrific torture, and murder a decade earlier of a two-year-old child, acts undertaken by a pair of ten-year-olds. In a similar vein, French-Algerian artist Adel Abdessemed has turned animal abuse into "art" by showing in *Don't Trust Me* (2008) animals being slaughtered by a sledgehammer blow to the head and in *Usine* (Factory) (2009) a fight among scorpions, snakes, tarantulas, roosters, and dogs. We see and hear the misery. It is difficult to criticize such works if one views art through a purely formal lens.

The ugly as what is ignored, rejected, or expelled mirrors what the Bulgarian-French theorist **Julia Kristeva** calls abjection. In her book of 1980, *Pouvoirs de l'horreur. Essai sur l'abjection* (*Powers of Horror: An Essay on Abjection*), Kristeva, who was deeply familiar with the works of both Jacques Lacan and Bataille, offers the most influential set of continental reflections in the post-Adorno era. Her focus is not the ugly as such, but the abject, which one might reasonably view as a subcategory of ugliness. Not surprisingly, several subsequent thinkers analyze the ugly with the very categories Kristeva uses to examine the abject. For Kristeva the abject is what cannot be assimilated, what disturbs order, that from which we turn away: excrement, disease, corpses, outcasts, whatever is seen to oppose the identity of the self or the order of society. The threat of abjection "lies there, quite close, but it cannot be assimilated" (Fre. 9; Eng. 1). The abject is physically ugly and yet at the same time representative of a threatening disorder. Whereas for Bataille, the abject has no form, Kristeva aligns the abject with bodily waste, which gives the term a specificity that counters Bataille's formlessness (Noys 34). She writes: "The corpse, seen without God and outside of science, is the utmost of abjection" (Fre. 11–12; Eng. 4). Rituals of defilement, as Mary Douglas showed in *Purity and Danger*, draw the borders of civilized society. We exclude the abject in creating our individual and collective identities. The abject, like the ugly more broadly, is (at least initially) rejected as unappealing and inappropriate.

For those who develop Kristeva's concept, the abject becomes not only thematic but also material. In introducing an exhibition at the Whitney Museum, Ben-Levi describes abject art as "a body of work which incorporates or suggests abject materials such as dirt, hair, excrement, dead animals, menstrual blood, and rotting food in order to confront taboo issues of gender and sexuality" (Ben-Levi et al. 7). Practicing artists, especially but not only in the Anglo-American world, who are directly or indirectly influenced by Kristeva, likewise engage the abject. Abject art addresses taboo topics and does so by integrating abject materials—hair, menstrual blood, urine, tears, spit, sperm, and excrement—or by evoking allusions to abject topics, such as anuses. Disgust becomes a desired aesthetic experience (*Mire Lee* 51). As an example of abject art, consider American Kiki Smith's *Tale* (1992), which displays a naked woman, made of beeswax, microcrystalline, pigment, and papier-mâché, who crawls hesitantly and painfully on the floor (Figure 12). Her buttocks are smeared with excrement, and a trail of feces extends outward from her rectum, giving the figure a kind of tail. The image suggests degradation and reverses the patriarchal view of the idealized female body. The theory and practice of the abject move art into uncharted territory, including what would otherwise be considered disgusting.

Kristeva recognizes that we experience revulsion at the abject and that we develop identity through distinction, feeling disgust at what threatens our stable identities. However, she also observes that we have a magnetic, albeit ambivalent, attraction to the initial oneness we sensed before differentiating into distinct identities. This insight is reminiscent of Freud's concept of the

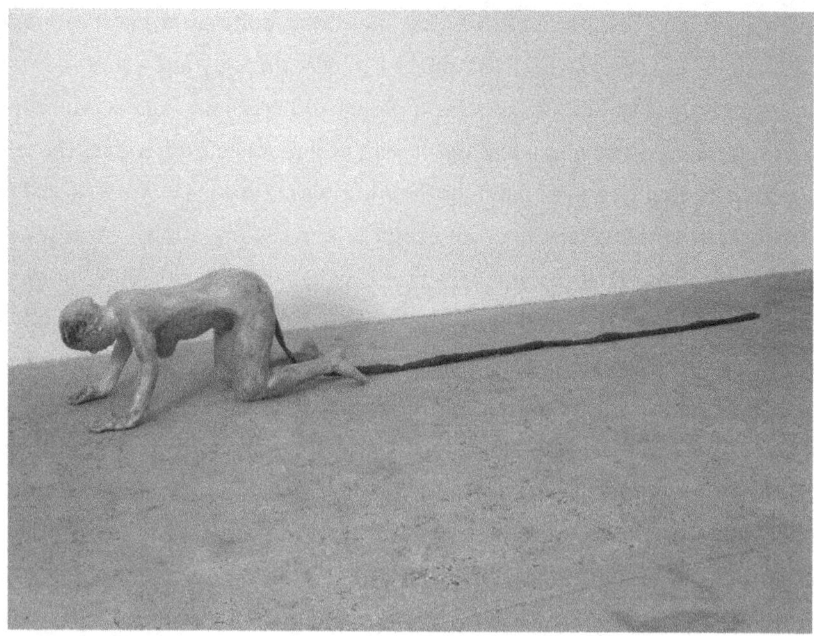

Figure 12 *Kiki Smith,* Tale, *1992, beeswax, microcrystalline, pigment, and papier-mâché, © Kiki Smith, courtesy of Pace Gallery.*

death drive, which he articulated in *Jenseits des Lustprinzips* (*Beyond the Pleasure Principle*) (1920). Thus, the abject is both enticing and disgusting, in Kristeva's phrase "a vortex of summons and repulsion" (Fre. 9; Eng. 1).

For critics today, the ugly and abject are at times taken as synonymous (Koerner 5), though not all that is ugly is abject, and unlike ugliness, the abject hovers between artwork and reception aesthetics. Koerner notes: "unlike objects, which ask to be judged as what they in themselves are, abjection exists in its effects, as a response elicited in the subject" (5). In that sense, the abject is a neighbor of another popular reception-aesthetic category: disgust. The prominence of the abject underscores the contemporary relevance of (the overarching category of) ugliness, and it reminds us that its various manifestations differ across time. Certainly the abject brings forth a distinctive reception, but one can view it not only via reception but also as an object, as a subform of ugliness that has gained prominence in our age, partly because we focus more on the body, partly because we elevate the breaking of taboos.

Though Bataille and Kristeva have had a reception both in Europe and the United States, a thinker who received a still greater response, even if he reflected less frequently on ugliness, is the theorist **Jacques Derrida**. Neither Derrida's integration of the ugly nor his particular take on it is surprising, for Derrida regularly explored the margins, where we often locate ugliness. In his essay of 1981 "Economimesis," Derrida addresses the puzzle of what cannot be assimilated: he reflects on what in Kant's third critique exceeds the realm of the beautiful—the disgusting, which Derrida associates with what we cannot absorb, the limits of digestion, vomit.

Derrida emphasizes that he is speaking not of the *act* of vomiting, which implies a degree of control, but the vomit itself, the expelled matter: "It is indeed vomit that interests us rather than the act or process of vomiting, which are less disgusting than vomit in so far as they imply an activity, some initiative whereby the subject can at least still mimic mastery or dream it in auto-affection, believing that he *makes himself vomit*" (Eng. 21; Fre. 88). Derrida brings forth vomit in order to accentuate the limits of Kant's concept of beauty, yet the physical ugliness of vomit is no longer beyond the bounds of contemporary artistic practice. Still, it would be a mistake to consider all limits inappropriate, for example, the extreme moral ugliness that may even extend beyond our capacity for visualization, as Dante suggests in *The Inferno* (28.1–6; 34.22–4), or the aesthetic (and moral) limits of artworks that praise white supremacy. If aesthetic value requires a connection to truth, then aesthetic expression will have its limits.

In the early 1990s, British cultural critic and architectural theorist **Mark Cousins** published a series of essays on ugliness. Working within the continental tradition, Cousins emphasizes that the ugly is rejected as what is out of place, something that does not belong where it is or should be present but is missing. Facing the ugly requires effort; we intuitively reject it. "Not looking, turning my back, inattention: all betray the fugitive reaction to the ugliness of that which exists" (Cousins 64). For American literary critic Denise Gigante, who writes in the same tradition and cites Cousins, the ugly is defined by "anti-transparency" (578); it is what we cannot comprehend, "something we can't even imagine," for example, the monstrous in Mary Shelly's *Frankenstein* (578). We can recognize great value in the concept of the abject and its associated resonances, though the limits of discarding beauty and of elevating the abject we have already dealt with in evaluating Adorno.

The reception of ugliness contains an aspect of the abject or even monstrous insofar as the abject and monstrous are (at least initially) rejected as unappealing and inappropriate. In *The Abyss of Freedom*, **Slavoj Žižek** argues, similarly, that the ugly becomes "an object that is in the wrong place, that 'shouldn't be there'" (21). Like Adorno and Nietzsche before him, Žižek resists the traditional definition of ugliness as the negation of beauty (Žižek 21). Whereas the ugly is what doesn't belong, Roger Scruton suggests in *Beauty* that beauty gives us "an enhanced sense of belonging" (55), which is not unrelated to the connection between beauty and the organic we find in Plato (264c) and Aristotle (1459a). Today we experience its reverse: when we are surrounded and overwhelmed by an overabundance of arbitrary information and haphazard impressions that have no organic relation to one another and do not constitute anything resembling a meaningful whole, whether in everyday activities or contemporary artworks, we feel disconnected or estranged. It is no surprise, then, that we instinctively want to turn away.

Certainly, theories of ugliness tend to stress aesthetics, but analyses of reality's ugliness date back to Plato. In various essays and in his book of 2000 *De la postcolonie: essai sur l'imagination politique dans l'Afrique contemporaine* (*On the Postcolony: Essay on the Political Imagination in Contemporary Africa*), **Achille Mbembe**, a Cameroonian social scientist, who was trained in France and combines European thought with political analysis of francophone West Africa, reminds us, ala Adorno, that the "ugliness of real life" stands recalcitrantly before us ("La 'chose'" 158; *On the Postcolony* 159).

One of the figures on whom Mbembe draws is the Russian theorist Mikhail Bakhtin, who accentuated the topsy-turvy concept of the carnivalesque. In *Rabelais and His World*, Bakhtin celebrates the lower sphere of the body as ambiguous, a source not only of urine and excrement but also of fertility and life. In the African prominence of "the obscene and the grotesque," Mbembe recognizes a less appealing ambiguity (*De la Postcolonie* 139; *On the Postcolony* 102). Mbembe's political analyses feature a modified version of the carnivalesque: in the contemporary postcolony, power is connected with the lower sphere of the body. Yet, unlike Bakhtin's carnivalesque, where roles are reversed, those who are ruled in the postcolony partake in the symbolic order of power, they do not subvert it.

In Mbembe's account, society's ruling members seek to project and control images of themselves and the world. Power, which is reinforced by the capacity to elicit belief in power, expresses itself in pomp and extravagance and in arbitrary brutality and unrestrained licentiousness. "[D]efecation, copulation, pomp, and extravagance are classical ingredients in the production of power" (*De la Postcolonie* 149; *On the Postcolony* 108).[1] Not only the tyrant, but the subject, too, associates power with excess. Both admire wealth; both embrace pleasure. Rituals of coercion serve to ratify and reinforce power and excess. Power comes from possessions, which enable enjoyment, but power and possessions originate in destruction. Still, the symbolic matrix that elevates wealth and pleasure, and with them corruption and conviviality, is shared by both ruler and subject, thereby sanctioning inequality.

Yet, according to Mbembe, if these common values are exposed as absurd, they can be seen anew, by tyrant and subject alike. Those who can turn the vulgarity of elites into laughter "kidnap power and force it, as if by accident, to examine its own vulgarity" (*De la Postcolonie* 150; *On the Postcolony* 109). In "the postcolony the search for majesty and prestige contains within it elements of crudeness and the bizarre that the official order tries hard to hide, but that the ordinary people bring to its attention, often unwittingly" (*De la Postcolonie* 150; *On the Postcolony* 109). The staged mask of power is exposed, and behind it one sees duplicity and destruction. This unmasking can also occur through caricature and cartoons ("La 'chose'"; *On the Postcolony* 142–72), as autocrats are exposed in their arbitrariness, excess, and vulnerability, but—and this adds to the complexity—to some extent such cartoons merely reinforce the autocrat's all-pervasive presence. Nonetheless, Mbembe returns, perhaps unintentionally, to the implicit Platonic idea that if we can transform ugliness from the horrific to the ridiculous, we can diminish its power.

In the contemporary continental tradition we oscillate between theoretical postmodernism, as in Bataille, and social critique, as in Mbembe, but this wide range is united by an uncommon sisterhood: both aesthetic postmodernism and progressive social critique embrace ugliness. For the postmodernist, the world is broken and fractured, without compass or direction, empty of higher meaning, and in the end not fully intelligible to us. Art must be similar, or it betrays the reality on which it seeks to reflect. Progressive cultural critics favor art that dwells on the ugliness of reality.[2] The goal of such art is not beauty but revelation of what is and has remained hidden, what invites critique, ugliness. Both movements widely embrace the concept of dissonant beauty, prioritizing the revelation of ugliness over traditional notions of aesthetic beauty.

A more recent development of a different kind has involved reflections on ugliness and the arts, in essence a return to the kind of work Lessing initiated when he analyzed ugliness in the spatial and temporal arts. German philosopher **Christian Illies**, who holds a chair in Bamberg and is one of today's most prominent objective idealists, has asked the unconventional question whether modern art's predilection for ugliness has affected gardens. In "Das hässliche Gärtlein? Über die Beharrlichkeit des Schönen in der Gartenkunst" ("The Ugly Garden? On the Persistence of Beauty in Garden Art") (2012), Illies offers several arguments why, beyond simple incompetence and neglect, gardens tend not to be ugly.

First, we have a genetically anchored preference for open landscapes with considerable greenery, trees, and water; these environments benefited early humans, particularly hunter-gatherers, by offering them survival advantages, and so we are naturally drawn to beauty in nature. Although the sublime has a place in nature, the sublime is not ugly, and although there have been transitions in kinds of gardens, most prominently from French to English gardens, these represent different modes of beauty. One could add that, whereas when we go to contemporary museums and performances, we expect to be shocked, we turn to gardens with radically different cultural expectations. Our sense of being at home in such settings is deeply embedded. When we speak of nature, we typically use the word "beautiful" and only rarely its counterpart "ugly" (Gladkova and Romero-Trillo 117, 121). Among contemporary artists whose works are far removed from ugliness, one thinks not surprisingly of nature artists such as Laib and Goldsworthy.

Second, Illies argues that gardens are not fully autonomous but are cultivated for a purpose; our recreation, relaxation, and pleasure. Traditionally, cultivated nature has offered a locus for order and contemplation as well as rest and relaxation. For Stoics such as Seneca and Marcus Aurelius, god, nature, and order are all one. A well-designed and beautiful garden indicates respect for the organic world and a continuing human desire to cultivate what harmonizes with the setting. Interestingly, when it comes to nature, even avant-garde artists seem more positive, less destructive. In 1982 Joseph Beuys, one of twentieth-century Germany's leading avant-garde artists, launched a project at Documenta 7 in Kassel that resulted in the planting of 7,000 oak trees. Related, beautiful gardens often surround even the ugliest postmodern buildings, demonstrating the enduring appeal of natural beauty in contrast to more jarring architectural forms.

Third, Illies observes that, compared to other artistic material, gardens are more difficult to control, thereby limiting the artist's subjectivity. Relatedly, his fourth argument is that since gardens develop over time, they are resistant to shifts in modes, less accommodating to quick human manipulation. Whereas most art allows for a strong stamp of human subjectivity, gardens are less yielding. They result from the collaboration of art and nature; each is there for the other, and together they constitute a remarkable unity (Wandschneider). The transcendence of human subjectivity is not unrelated to the religious sensibilities awakened by gardens, insofar as nature evokes a sense of human limits and a recognition of an otherness beyond our control. When gardens are completely manipulated, as in the case of highly controlled and inanimate gardens, they turn into sculpture.

Finally, Illies argues that while the arts engage us intellectually, gardens are more immediate, bound to the senses. Ugliness is most pronounced in cerebral and complex art forms, an insight that in some ways dates back to Herder. In folk art ugliness has little place, typically arising only from poor workmanship. Innovation is possible with crafts, as with a crazy quilt, but folk art, being for the most part traditional, tends to resist ugliness.[3] Even masks that evoke the devil are often aesthetically beautiful. In the realm of popular art, what is pleasing seems to be valued more highly than what is intellectually demanding. Because gardens are commonly associated with pleasure, if we see an ugly garden, we are likely to say, this is the result not of creativity, but of incompetence and neglect. There may be something healthy and vital in this tendency, which elevates what is pleasing over what is superficially ugly, even if it shortchanges intellection and has difficulties recognizing links between ugliness and deeper meaning.

An example, beyond bad taste and neglect, where we find something analogous to ugliness in gardens arises with poisonous plants. Visitors enter the extensive Poison Garden within England's Alnwick Garden only after passing through large ornate black iron gates, which are adorned with skull and bones and the warning: "These plants can kill." Inside are approximately a hundred poisonous plants. Yet some of the poisons serve medicinal purposes, and the plants themselves are superficially beautiful. Visitors, limited to no more than twenty at a time, are allowed to see but not smell, touch, or taste the plants. We can also consider here anomalous plants, such as the corpse flower, which smells like rotting meat. That such examples are rare says something about the general resistance of cultivated gardens to ugliness.

In the past decade, the topic of architecture and ugliness has garnered considerable attention. Four books have recently appeared on architectural ugliness (Hyde and Van Acker/Mical) or related topics, including the picturesque (Macarthur) and architecture and horror (Comaroff and Ong). In "On Ugliness (in Architecture)" (2020), Belgian **Bart Verschaffel**, a professor of the theory of architecture and of architectural criticism at Ghent University, poses arguably the most interesting questions: Given that ugliness in architecture does exist, what kinds of architectural ugliness can we identify, and what constitutes architectural ugliness?

Verschaffel outlines four types of architectural ugliness. The first two are in a sense opposites of one another. First is the relatively banal case of slapdash and haphazard buildings that were never meant to be beautiful. The second type occurs when an architect tries too hard, which can result in buildings with excessive color, ornamentation, or exaggerated forms, bordering on vulgarity. The third type, essentially a variation of the second, involves a profound lack of organicism, including mistakes and failed jokes—for example, a facade that resembles a human face with eyes, a nose, and a mouth; a garage that is adorned with Doric columns; or a farmhouse that has medieval towers. The fourth type involves inappropriate scale, for example, buildings that come across as enlarged models or as doll houses. Verschaffel's four scenarios of architectural ugliness are more similar than different. Each reveals more amateurish efforts than serious endeavors at architectural ugliness, and all have in common a deficiency in form.

I would revise Verschaffel's typology and subsume all his variations under a type of architectural ugliness characterized by formal deficiency. We could add to his examples tenement housing, which is repulsive by its poor quality and lack of variety, with the two often deriving from a lack of investment. Brutalist architecture, architecture of raw concrete, would be another example. Brutalism was popular from the 1950s to 1970s partly because of its association with transparency (the building materials were visible). Despite this appealing concept, brutalist structures tend toward repetition and inferior quality. Brutalism has been criticized not only for its cold and monotonous appearance, but also for the material itself, which in northern climates often becomes grungy and pockmarked, plagued by stains, decay, and graffiti.[4]

As Verschaffel notes, disunity is one particular manifestation of formal deficiency. A building can mix styles in an unappealing way, such as combining a modernist base with Baroque trim. Or a building whose primary purpose is efficiency may be executed in an overly ostentatious way. As we saw in Chapter 6, Rosenkranz had already identified the problem of using multiple architectural styles without achieving harmony. Featurism, which Robin Boyd identified as the defining characteristic of Australian (architectural) ugliness, exemplifies such inconsistency. Featurism is a mode of design in which a sense of the whole is absent; instead, individual features are accentuated, indecisively and indeterminately, often gratuitous adornments, partly isolated and partly mixed up, without consistency or appropriate subordination to the whole. Traditional architecture, in contrast, integrates the arts. We see such unifying practices through the Baroque era (and occasionally beyond, as with Frank Loyd Wright's concept of organic architecture).

With postmodernism and deconstructionism, fragmentation and discord become intentional design elements. Here is where one finds many creative buildings, and many contemporary theorists celebrate what they call architectural ugliness. An important question with such buildings is whether there is an underlying, perhaps hidden, logic to the design. Consider residential buildings created to evoke vibrant, joyous feelings, such as the Hundertwasser House in Vienna, or to enhance light and evoke variety and dynamism, as with Frank Gehry's 8 Spruce Street in New York (Figure 13). In some cases the form of a building matches the creativity housed within, as in Gehry's Guggenheim

Figure 13 *Frank Gehry,* 8 Spruce Street, *New York, 2011, Courtesy of Frank O. Gehry & Gehry Partners, LLP.*

Museum, Bilboa, Spain or his Walt Disney Concert Hall in Los Angeles. Michael Graves's Portland Building, with its bright, distinctive, and welcoming exterior, serves a municipal purpose, and Ayla-Suzan Yöndel's Kindergarten Die Katze in Wolfartsweier, Germany, playfully resembles a crouching white cat. Finally, Gehry's Cleveland Clinic Lou Ruvo Center for Brain Health in Las

Figure 14 *Kengo Kuma and Associates,* M2 Building, *1990, Tokyo, Japan. Image courtesy of KKAA and photographer Mitsumasa Fujitsuka.*

Vegas reflects the daring and often unexpected nature of scientific discovery. I do not see such buildings as ugly, for in each case the form symbolically fits the purpose; they are instead, like much of modern and contemporary art, unconventionally beautiful, only seemingly ugly. However, innovation can sometimes arise at the expense of the organic, resulting in buildings that seem to elevate disorder and dislocation as ends in themselves, like Kengo Kuma's M2 Building in Tokyo (Figure 14).

I would recognize other forms of architectural ugliness beyond formal deficiency. A building that does not fulfill its function can be ugly. Architecture is defined only partly by its intrinsic value. Functionality plays a role as well. Consider a house whose support structures are inadequate or which includes a gap in the middle of a floor. Though the first is unlikely to be part of a design, in a postmodern world the second could arise intentionally. The elevation of autonomous art that occurred at the end of the eighteenth century led to so-called revolutionary architecture. In 1789 when the French neoclassical architect Claude Nicolas Ledoux first sketched out the idea of a sphere as a building, a new kind of disharmony or ugliness was conceived (plate 254). Architects such as Ledoux experimented with spheres as homes because, from the point of view of a natural object, a sphere is beautiful. For Ledoux, its perfect form mirrored the cosmos. However, a spherical shape contradicts an essential function of domestic architecture: utility. So we can add a further dimension to the ugliness of architecture by saying that a building may be aesthetically beautiful in shape but ugly in terms of functionality. Already Vitruvius demanded such functionality as the middle element of his triad: "soundness, utility, and attractiveness" (*De Architecture* 1.3.2). Hume, too, recognizes this point, when he elevates the importance of utility for shipbuilding and adds: "A building, whose doors and windows were exact squares, would hurt the eye by that very proportion; as ill adapted to the figure of a human creature, for whose service the fabric was intended" (*An Enquiry Concerning the Principles of Morals* 5.1.172).

A related form of architectural ugliness likewise involves function, but in almost the opposite way. A construction is ugly not only if its shape does not match its function, but also if the architectural function or purpose is itself immoral, even if the construction fits the purpose and is effectively executed. The Berlin Wall was hardly beautiful.

Even buildings that appear to be dysfunctional could be considered ugly. We examined this aspect of ugliness in our analysis of Hume. Rosenkranz also addresses this puzzle, arguing that a leaning structure, such as the Tower of Pisa, contradicts "the feeling of safety and permanence," essential to an effective building (Ger. 151; Eng. 107, translation modified). The points raised by Hume and Rosenkranz are significant. If the person in the building loses a sense of security, the perception that the building is not as it should be is hard to overcome. Certainly, a goal of architecture is to foster appropriate emotional sensibilities. The puzzle is not simple, however, for one could make the counter-argument that the ability of an architect to triumph over appearances renders their building beautiful in a deeper sense; it is only seemingly ugly.

Another counter-argument might challenge the inherent value of security and stability. Contributing to this debate is postmodern architecture that challenges traditional expectations. In "The Blue Line Text" (1988) Peter Eisenman makes the case that, with the dissolution of metaphysics, we are no longer at home in the world. Therefore, if architecture is honest, its buildings should reflect and accentuate our existential homelessness, highlighting "the intrinsic uncertainty and alienation of the modern condition" (7). According to Eisenman, the goal of architecture should be "to dislocate that which it locates" (7). With this claim, we see that a proper evaluation of architectural form requires movement into metaphysics.

Architecture is more than simply technique; as an art, it expresses something. A building is judged on its function *and* its expression. Gothic churches, for example, indirectly signal Christian transcendence, the Taj Mahal at Agra invites reflection on remembrance and the meaning of death, the Library of Congress alludes to the value of knowledge, Albert Speer's reviewing stand at the Zeppelin Field in Nüremberg expressed grandiosity and regularity, and Germany's post-unification Reichstag Dome embodies transparency.

In modern architecture, which many find ugly because of the turn away from ornamentation, function itself develops formal features. The form of modernism derives from its function, encompassing economies of various kinds, such as housing more people with greater efficiency. Here there is a consistency and an organic dimension that can readily be seen as beautiful. Thus, the seemingly ugly aspects of modernism become one of its beautiful features. If one wanted to challenge modern architecture, given the size and scale of many such buildings, one might appeal to the criterion that a building should allow occupants to feel at home. In that sense such a building can receive mixed reviews. We are reminded that because of its instrumental value, architecture is more dependent than any other art on reception aesthetics.

Architecture was one of the last arts to adopt ugliness and initially only by wealthy clients. Unlike poetry or music, architecture is deeply influenced by external constraints. In most cultures until recent times, architectural ugliness resulted not from conscious design but from the difficulty of the challenge. Dewey makes the interesting observation that architects, unlike other artists, cannot start afresh or make dramatic revisions, which may explain "why there are so many ugly buildings" (*Art* 53). No less prominently, architectural ugliness has often arisen from expediency, a challenge that persists today. Consider public housing projects that were inexpensively funded, designed, and built with insufficient attention having been given to their effect on residents.

The prevalence of such buildings has diminished, at least in the United States, as governments increasingly recognize the profound impact that space has on moods, ideas, and even behavior. For instance, the transformation of Boston's Columbia Point Housing Project illustrates this shift (Roessner; Herndon). Not only physically ugly, the project was developed in ignorance of the community's needs. The developers neglected the basic infrastructure that sustains a neighborhood—public transportation, a school, a grocery store, a church, and a playground. Moreover, they left a refuse-burning city dump at the project's periphery. Consequently, the project became crime-ridden until it was reconfigured into a new community, Harbor Point. Another example of a failed project was Minoru Yamasaki's Pruitt-Igoe housing development in St. Louis, which became a haven of vandalism and crime (Figure 15). The dysfunctional project was demolished after fewer than twenty years. The failure of this initiative transcends architectural design, for the original plans had been adjusted because of cost constraints and government mandates, which only underscores the economic, social, and political dimensions of public architecture (Bristol).

Figure 15 *Minoru Yamasaki,* The Wendell O. Pruitt Homes and William Igoe Apartments, *public housing, St. Louis, Missouri. Constructed 1951–5; demolished 1972–6. United States Geological Survey, Public domain, via Wikimedia Commons.*

The examples from Boston and St. Louis illustrate the ways in which ugliness can vex not only architecture but also architecture as it merges with city planning. Such ugliness undercuts the higher purpose of urban life. Elements such as unsafe streets, lack of sidewalks, overly long blocks, an absence of neighborhoods, insufficient diversity in age of buildings, little variety among residential, commercial, and industrial uses, dull structures sealed off from urban life, vulgar luxury housing projects, expressways that impede pedestrian traffic, and inadequate mixed-use areas all contribute to poor city planning (Jacobs). Ugly buildings and spaces cultivate a sense of sadness, disillusionment, frustration, and incompleteness, yet Alain de Botton has made the case that architecture can also be designed to inspire and encourage identification with various ideals, from aspiration, reverence, and balance to friendliness, subtlety, and intelligence.

We see then the following types of architectural ugliness, which we can systematize as follows. The simplest type involves a bad purpose, as with the Berlin Wall or a torture chamber. The second or antithetical type is formal deficiency independent of purpose. It is telling that the second type, which involves all kinds of poor execution, misguided functionality, and formal aberration, including disunity, has such variety. It is in the nature of the antithetical to divide itself, for the antithesis is characterized by negativity, difference, and multiplicity—thus Verschaffel's four versions of formal ugliness and the others I have added. The third and final type involves a contradiction between purpose and execution, for example, the Columbia Point Housing Project. Note that some of the examples of beautiful ugliness I gave above involve only seemingly ugly form that is in truth not ugly because form and content merge unexpectedly and beautifully, as with Frank Gehry's 8 Spruce Street in New York.

Despite much of the continental tradition leaning toward contemporary theory and postmodernism, the Hegelian tradition still has its adherents, including those who take their inspiration from Hegel or the wider idealist tradition, even if they criticize certain aspects of it. It is fitting, then, to conclude this chapter with a contemporary Hegelian who has dedicated a part of his aesthetics to examining ugliness (Rinaldi 147–80). In 2021 **Giacomo Rinaldi** published the first conceptual volume of a systematic aesthetics, *The*

Philosophy of Art (2022), in which he engages ugliness, partly with historical commentary, above all by elevating Vischer and criticizing Adorno. Born into a family of Italian schoolteachers, Rinaldi studied in Milan and has devoted his career to exploring Hegel. Since the early 1980s Rinaldi has identified as a neo-Hegelian, with the philosophical ambition to foster a rebirth of idealism in the contemporary world.

A professor in Urbino, Rinaldi recognizes that because art must include "a dialectical unity of opposites," it must engage ugliness (218). Rinaldi considers three forms of aesthetic ugliness (169–71). First is ugliness as deficient art, a subcategory of ugliness he rightly does not wish to lose. His second focus is very Hegelian. In contrast to classical art, where form and content are in harmony, as, for example, in sculptures of the human body, in symbolic and romantic art a disjunction between form and content arises: in the symbolic mode, the idea is still abstract and indeterminate, such that whatever expression is chosen, often strange and distorted shapes, it points toward ideas that are as yet not fully embodied in the art object itself; and in the romantic mode, the spirit being represented is so transcendent that it cannot be fully contained in the sensuous, material world, which is above all the case with Rinaldi's primary focus, Christian art. Because the divine cannot be sensuously represented, the moment of ugliness in Christian art, its inadequacy to the subject portrayed, is "an unavoidable consequence of its very essence" (154). For his third and final point, Rinaldi adopts the Hegelian mode of recognizing ugliness as a moment in the sublime and the comic. The process of double negation elevated by the Hegelians is precisely what Rinaldi finds lacking in Adorno, for whom negation does not turn on itself (94).

Rinaldi is right to point to the ambiguity in the term ugliness, and he justly recognizes that only Hegel's classical mode fully excludes ugliness, but Rinaldi's account of symbolic and romantic ugliness is quite abstract. Left undeveloped is what precisely renders some romantic art beautiful or sublime and other romantic art ugly. Certainly, Rinaldi is right to follow Hegel in arguing that artworks based on false theological doctrines, such as the Crusades, are on content alone deficient, but more needs to be said about the beautiful, the sublime, and the ugly (157–8). Christian art is not only ugly, and the Hegelian true infinite, which is closely interwoven with the idea of the Incarnation, is far removed from the dualism of romantic art.

Moreover, Rinaldi suggests that for Hegel ugliness is legitimate only in the realm of the comic (163), but this seems to derive from Rinaldi's using only the Hotho edition, for in the student transcripts, as we saw in Chapter 5, the non-beautiful and the ugly are legitimate moments within the Christian narrative itself. Rinaldi is right to elevate the early Hegelian interpretation in which both the sublime and the comic can absorb ugliness, but these two modes hardly exhaust the possibilities of ugliness in art, especially in the modern era. In this context, Rinaldi praises Vischer's analysis of the ugly, the sublime, and the comic as "an original and brilliant development of the Hegelian theory of the relationship between the Idea of the Beautiful and the Ugly in Art" (167), but the dialectic Rinaldi describes and praises arose already in full force with Weiße and Ruge, yet Rinaldi seems unaware of their analyses. A final criticism of Rinaldi is that he adds little to our efforts to bridge Hegelian thought with the contemporary world, including its abundance of ugly and seemingly ugly art.

*

The long continental tradition, from the first German thinkers through Adorno and beyond, offers us intriguing and for the most part overlooked insights. The dialectical relations between beauty and ugliness, the position of the ugly in systematic aesthetics, the role of the ugly in the various arts, and the diverse ways in which ugliness can manifest itself in beautiful works are all rich examples of topics central to this tradition. No cultural tradition engages the ugly as deeply and as widely as does the German. With few exceptions, these thinkers embody a common impulse: the desire to think through the ugly and the beautiful as more than simply opposites. Nonetheless, we do not always find in the long German and wider European tradition the same level of analytical precision one recognizes among Anglo-American analytic philosophers, to whom we now turn.

12

Anglo-American Analytic Philosophers

Before we engage with our first American-born theorists, let's step back and ask a broader question: Why is the European, and specifically German, discussion of ugliness more vigorous and extensive than what we find in the United States? While any response must remain speculative, I offer three possible answers.

First, Americans have traditionally been considered more idealistic than Europeans. As early as the nineteenth century, Alexis de Tocqueville commented on American optimism (374). The Hollywood tradition of happy endings stands in stark contrast to the often somber conclusions of European art films. Generally speaking, Americans produce and are drawn to kitsch in ways that Europeans are not. It would be difficult to imagine that in any European country, Thomas Kinkade would be the most collected artist, as he is in the United States (Boylan 1). The US public tends to favor the light-filled impressionists over the darker expressionists; on almost any day at the Art Institute in Chicago, the busiest galleries are those devoted to the impressionists.[1] Not surprisingly, the United States played a leading role in the creation of playful, bright, and superficial art, as with Andy Warhol and Roy Lichtenstein. Americans seem far more open to radiance and reconciliation.

Second, in the United States, there is less immersion in beauty and thus less potential for a radical and conscious break from it. Europeans live amid beautiful works of art. When one walks the streets of Europe, architectural beauty is unavoidable; one needn't even enter the museums. Maxwell Anderson was only slightly hyperbolic when he suggested that the continent itself is a museum (20).

In contrast, the United States has a shorter history, with fewer architectural landmarks and beautiful old buildings. Peter Blake lamented "the flood of ugliness engulfing America," from its billboards and strip malls to its suburban sprawl and destruction of the landscape (11). Consider the difference between the old and beautiful, often incarnational, churches in Europe and those in the United States, especially outside the original colonies and major cities. The churches at the center of virtually every European city and town express verticality and permanence, and in Catholic regions, they are rich in iconography and ornamentation. Conversely, many recent American churches are temporary, horizontal, and unattractive, built or reconfigured minimally to provide practical space for services. Historically dominant in America, Protestantism is associated with communities that can worship in any type of building. American architecture's functionalism and repetition are often accepted without question. In the mid-twentieth century, Mary Mix Foley observed that Americans are "eminently satisfied with the established ugliness. They do not even know that it is ugly" (144). To visibly perceive the difference between beauty and ugliness is to be motivated to reflect on it.

Third, in American philosophy departments, epistemology and metaphysics are the premier fields, whereas the European philosophical tradition is broader and more diverse. In Europe, aesthetics plays a larger role, and a discourse in which ugliness is a central aesthetic category is alive in Germany as well as neighboring countries. Even as reflection on ugliness becomes more prominent in the United States, its history is shorter. I am not aware of any major contributions until the second half of the twentieth century.

The most distinctive American school of philosophy is pragmatism. Among its three leading figures—Charles Sanders Peirce, William James, and John Dewey—only Dewey developed a theory of aesthetics. Before we turn to the analytic revolution in English-speaking aesthetics, it is worth briefly examining Dewey's contributions. Delivered as the inaugural William James Lectures at Harvard, Dewey's major work on aesthetics, *Art as Experience* (1934), influenced American aesthetics for years. Dewey's primary goal was to remove art from "a remote pedestal" and demonstrate its relevance to meaningful everyday human experience (*Art* 4). Ugliness plays little role in Dewey's aesthetically sensitive analysis, but he does recognize its productive potential in art: "Something which was ugly under other conditions, the usual ones, is extracted from the conditions in which it was repulsive and is transfigured in quality as it becomes a part of an expressive whole. In its new setting, the very contrast with a former ugliness adds piquancy, animation, and, in serious matters, increases depth of meaning in an almost incredible way" (*Art* 100). Dewey shows here, and throughout his book, remarkable attentiveness to dialectical structures—the relations of part and whole, flux and rest, discord and harmony, impulsion and resistance, frustration and fulfillment—which reinforces Dewey's observation that his early immersion in Hegelian thought left "a permanent deposit" in his thinking ("From Absolutism to Experimentalism" 154; cf. Good).

Around the end of Dewey's life, at mid-century, analytic philosophers began their first attempts to understand the precise province of ugliness. Whereas Europeans regularly integrate the history of philosophy into their analyses and address larger, systematic questions, American analytic philosophers have tended to offer ahistorical and isolated insights. In many cases, their observations surface indirectly by way of primary reflection on beauty, into which occasional reflections on ugliness are embedded. What these philosophers offer is not insignificant, but often enough it emerges from an ignorance of earlier contributions, which is evident in the lack of engagement with thinkers whose ideas mirror and predate their own. This general neglect of historical context is evident, notwithstanding occasional exceptions.

The first two analytic attempts to engage ugliness stem from 1948 and 1950. In 1948, **Lucius Garvin,** then a philosopher at Oberlin College who later became Provost at Macalester College, published "The Problem of Ugliness in Art." Garvin cites Bosanquet but not any German philosophers, and he contests Croce's view that an ugly artwork is necessarily an artistic failure. But he does not go much further; his goal is simply to defend the conventional view that "the ugly is whatever yields an unpleasant aesthetic response" (404). In one of his earliest essays, "On Ugliness of Art," **Jerome Stolnitz**, who later became president of the American Society for Aesthetics, introduces the concepts of invincible and non-invincible ugliness. According to Stolnitz, invincible ugliness is characterized by overwhelming and intense unpleasantness that compels us to turn away in disgust, whereas non-invincible ugliness still allows for a holistic aesthetic experience. We see here a limit of reception aesthetics. Is a work invincibly ugly because it is received in a certain way, or would it not be more appropriate, given that reception shifts over time, to ask whether the ugly elements are organically integrated into the whole? If ugliness is gratuitous, it justifiably repels us. However, if it is necessary and organically connected, it is not invincibly ugly, no matter how hard it might be to take.

G. P. (Pat) Henderson, a Scottish philosopher and long-time editor of *The Philosophical Quarterly*, primarily worked in logic and metaphysics but also made significant contributions to aesthetics. In his 1966 paper "The Concept of Ugliness," he sought to give greater conceptual precision to the notion of ugliness. Like Rosenkranz, whose work he appears not to have known, Henderson identifies various kinds of ugliness: sensory ugliness, which repels our senses, as with monsters; moral ugliness, such as crime, which offends our moral categories; visceral ugliness, which physically revolts us, as with a decaying corpse; and adjudicative or verdictive ugliness, which requires an extended process of deciphering and thought to recognize.

The terms Henderson introduces seem to allow for overlap and, furthermore, mix the categories of object and reception, and indeed stress reception. Helpful, however, is the idea that ugliness can be an overarching category that captures a family of terms and types (221). He also differentiates ugliness from neighboring categories. For example, he notes that a "sick person can look ghastly or dreadful without looking ugly" in the specific sense in which we typically use the term (222). Exploring our everyday use of the word "ugly," Henderson observes that we speak of beautiful, but not ugly, theorems, and so the beautiful, but not the ugly, is applied to the realm of truth, whereas in the realm of the moral, he sees the reverse: we are more likely to speak of an ugly vice or a hideous crime than we are to suggest that a person's character or disposition is beautiful (223). Whether or not we accept this empirical evaluation, which seems to capture a dominant, but not exhaustive, practice, Henderson aptly revisits the ancient idea that "beautiful" and "ugly" are not limited to aesthetics (224).

With **Nelson Goodman**, we turn to one of the most prominent American philosophers of the twentieth century, known well beyond his contributions to aesthetics. Goodman was steeped in art, having run an art gallery while pursuing his doctorate at Harvard. In *Languages of Art* (1968), Goodman addresses ugliness, even if the topic, perhaps a sign of the times, does not make its way into the book's index. Goodman draws a central distinction, helpful for any analysis of ugliness, between, on the one hand, the object depicted, what the work represents, and, on the other hand, the sort of depiction it is, what kinds of properties it has as an artwork (Goodman 31).[2] The depicted object captures the content, while the depiction itself encompasses the work's form and properties.

Considering this distinction, we can imagine ugly content of various kinds that is nonetheless rendered beautifully. For example, we might say a representation of a corpse is beautiful if it faithfully captures the essence of the corpse, even though the corpse itself is not beautiful. This distinction between the object of the representation and the properties of the representation is relevant for interpreting and evaluating artworks. We can have beautiful depictions of ugly objects, for example, Jenny Saville's *Suspension* (2002–3), an extraordinary oil painting of a slaughtered pig. The aesthetic quality of a work is not diminished in the least by the inclusion of ugly content. This needs to be emphasized against all convention, which in the past has often hesitated to allow certain elements of ugliness into the content of artworks, and against the tendency of recipients not to want to be confronted by ugly content. The question becomes, how is the content shaped in the work as a whole? The distinction between depicted object and depiction is also pertinent to various types of beautiful ugliness, which involve the relation of properties and object, form and content. Gottfried Benn's early poems, for example, give us beautiful depictions of ugly objects, whereas Penderecki's *Threnody* offers an ugly depiction of an ugly object, such that the work is on a meta-level organically beautiful.

Goodman's distinction is significant, but we should not overestimate its originality, even if his language is admirably precise. Earlier thinkers—Aristotle, Plutarch, Bonaventure, Aquinas, Mendelssohn, Boileau-Despréaux, Addison, Batteux, Diderot, Sulzer, Kant, and Weiße—all argued that when the object depicted is ugly, the properties of the work can still be beautiful. Goodman makes another distinction—this time an original one—between depiction and exemplification. In cases such as abstract painting or instrumental music, no object may be represented or depicted. Exemplification arises from the way in which the representation is crafted. For example, a painting may depict flowers, but it may metaphorically express or exemplify sadness. In a sonata, the interaction between the first and second thematic materials may exemplify a tension between the two. A building may not depict an object, but it may exemplify strength or warmth. "To exemplify or express is to display rather than depict or describe" (*Languages* 93). In poetry, meaning may arise from patterns of words and sounds. Goodman argues that exemplification is one of the least noticed and least understood aspects of art (*Ways* 32). It is also one of the most important. Exemplification is part of art's indirection. It refers not to the object depicted but to the mode of depiction, which itself conveys indirect meaning: "An experience is exemplificational insofar as concerned with properties exemplified or expressed—i.e., properties possessed and shown forth—by a symbol, not merely things the symbol denotes" (*Languages* 253). Goodman emphasizes "the primacy of the work over what it refers to" (*Ways* 69).

Vincent van Gogh provides numerous examples of works in which indirect meaning arises more from the way in which an object is portrayed than from what the object is itself. The haunting dimensions of van Gogh's works do not derive from the rooms, buildings, flowers, or landscapes he paints. Instead, they flow from his unprecedented use of brush strokes and stylized patterns, as in *The Starry Night* (1889); exaggerated perspectives, as in *The Bedroom at Arles* (1889); and twisted shapes, as in *The Church at Auvers* (1890). The resulting distortion, with its conscious avoidance of accurate mimesis and superficial beauty, suggests both intensity and disorder bordering in some paintings on an unease we might identify as emotional ugliness.

Drawing on traditional language of the paradox of tragedy, Goodman, like Stace before him, speaks of the "paradox of ugliness" (*Languages* 246). He notes: "We welcome some works that arouse emotions we normally shun. Negative emotions of fear, hatred, disgust, may become positive when occasioned by a play or painting" (*Languages* 246). Goodman elegantly dissolves this paradox by suggesting that it is triggered by a category mistake, a reduction of the art experience to emotions. If we recognize that emotions are not unique to art, that art interests us emotionally, and that aesthetic emotions function cognitively, then the puzzle is easily dissolved.

We are interested cognitively in many positions that repel us and unusual forms that challenge us. Our emotions are intertwined with a sensitivity to the work and our understanding of it: "The horror and revulsion we may feel at *Macbeth* are not lesser means of understanding than the amusement and delight we may find in *Pygmalion*" (*Languages* 250). Goodman links emotional experience with recognition: "Emotion in aesthetic experience is a means of discerning what properties a work has and expresses" (*Languages* 248). We recognize the value of a work and its meaning only by experiencing the work in its fullness. That includes also negative emotions, such as sadness and unease, which continue to linger and affect our recollection and interpretation of a work's richness.

Goodman's insight into the intertwined emotional and cognitive function of art is not without precedent; Schiller and Hegel are among his most prominent precursors. The recognition that ugliness can be a legitimate moment in art and that art can be appreciated sensuously, emotionally, and cognitively makes it possible for Goodman to address the paradox of ugliness: our profound cognitive interest in art means that to appreciate a work, we do not need to shift emotionally from revulsion to delight. The clarity of Goodman's refutation and his insistence on cognition as the primary purpose of our use of symbols render his achievement distinctive. Goodman emphasizes that art helps us strengthen our intellectual abilities, serves as an outlet for the irrepressibility of joy, and fulfills the human desire for communication. But art's ultimate purpose, he suggests, is cognition.

Another prominent analytic philosopher of art who analyzed ugliness was British philosopher **Frank Sibley**. After serving as a tank commander in the Second World War, Sibley studied under Gilbert Ryle at Oxford and later taught both in the United States and England. His 1959 paper "Aesthetic Concepts," which differentiates aesthetic concepts from non-aesthetic concepts, arguing that the former are not reducible to the latter, is one of the most prominent papers in analytic philosophy of art. Sibley was keenly interested in expanding our range of aesthetic categories beyond simply beauty. In this spirit, Sibley devoted a posthumous paper (he died in 1996) to the topic of ugliness, noting its relative neglect despite its fascination and complexity. Sibley shares with Goodman the idea that ugliness need not engender disgust, for our reception of art is not reducible to our emotional response. Pleasure and displeasure do not define reception. Not unlike the idealists, Sibley speaks of ugliness as a departure from a norm, "something out of place, inappropriate" (202).

For Sibley, the beautiful can be beautiful by itself (as a predicative adjective) or in its embodiment of a particular standard or ideal (as an attributive adjective); it is thus, according to Sibley, logically ambifunctional. In contrast, ugliness is ugly only insofar as it deviates from a standard, from an idea of what should be. For Sibley, then, ugliness is logically attributive, a relational category. To call something ugly, to render a negative aesthetic judgment about an object, requires some sense of a norm or standard against which the ugly object is measured.

As with Goodman, who seeks to give clarity to ideas advanced by earlier thinkers he does not cite and presumably does not know, Sibley's main contribution to the theory of ugliness—that an asymmetry exists between beauty and ugliness and that ugliness is always subordinate to beauty—was propounded at length by Hegel's followers, most prominently Rosenkranz, who writes:

> That ugliness is a concept that can be understood only in relation to another concept is not difficult to understand. The other concept is that of beauty, for ugliness can only be insofar as beauty is, which constitutes its *positive presupposition*. If there were no beauty, then ugliness would not at all exist, since the latter only exists as the negation of the former. (Ger. 7; Eng. 33, translation modified)

Sibley does not integrate these earlier claims.

Another weakness is Sibley's inattention to dialectic. We could say, for example, that a norm for beauty is harmonic form, such that if the form is distorted, the work is ugly, but what if the distorted form matches a work's ugly content, creating a higher-level harmony between form and content; in this case, a meta-harmony emerges despite, or because of, the formal distortion.

Such a work would be beautiful and only seemingly ugly. Sibley, using an either-or framework, seems to have no category for such works.

One of the best-known contemporary American philosophers of art was **Arthur Danto**, a practicing artist, long-time art critic for *The Nation*, president of the American Society of Aesthetics, and professor at Columbia University. Danto, who passed away in 2013, stands out among contemporary analytic philosophers for elevating the history of theory and the history of art. Danto never focused on ugliness as such, but he circled around the concept when emphasizing that beauty had disappeared from the contemporary art world. In *The Abuse of Beauty* (2003), Danto argued that some critics cling to the notion of beauty, even as the "Intractable Avant-Garde," starting with Dada, "abjured beauty" and embraced ugliness (xv). For Danto, it is significant that something could be ugly and still be excellent art: "it is important to recognize that the works might still be perceived as ugly even when we have come to see their 'artistic excellence' [. . .] The ugly does not become beautiful just because the ugly art is good" (*Abuse* 107). Danto suggests that a work that is seemingly ugly cannot, through a process of recognition, be considered beautiful, even though many recipients might call such a work beautiful (*Abuse* 88, 107).

Instead, Danto proposes erasing the equation between beauty and aesthetic excellence and instead restricting beauty to the realm of the senses (*Abuse* 92). In this framework, an artwork that is sensuously unattractive would remain ugly, even if it possesses aesthetic merit. By focusing on the sensory dimension, Danto wishes to narrow our concept of beauty, severing its connection to thought, truth, and goodness. Danto recognizes that many good artworks are not at all beautiful in the sense of being sensuously appealing. In fact, he considers "the discovery that something can be good art without being beautiful as one of the great conceptual clarifications of twentieth-century philosophy of art" (*Abuse* 58; cf. *What* 28). However, if beauty means aesthetically excellent, which is one of its common usages,[3] then Danto's statement lacks coherence. And if beauty means, as Danto suggests (*Abuse* 107), pleasing or harmonic, then this insight predates Adorno by more than a century. The German tradition had long recognized that ugliness can play a prominent role in great art. Although the combination of ugliness and aesthetic excellence dominated art practice in the twentieth century, it is hardly a twentieth-century invention, in theory or in practice.

A tension surfaces in Danto. On the one hand, he rejects the everyday usage of the term "beauty." He argues that we *should* not call sensuously ugly works that have aesthetic merit "beautiful." On the other hand, he derives his theory of art programmatically not from any sense of what art *should* be or what we *should* call art, but from our reception of art, what we call art in everyday practice (*Abuse* ix, xvii–xviii). According to Danto, art is not a normative concept (*Abuse* xvii–xviii). For Danto, we do not measure artworks against normative criteria; instead, we measure theory against practice. Danto argues that Plato is wrong about art because his theory cannot accommodate abstract art or readymades (*What* 30). For Danto, Plato's theory is refuted by examples, but an idealist like Plato cannot be refuted by examples. Plato might easily have responded, as Hegel is alleged to have done in a different context, 'So much the worse for the works.' As objective idealists, Plato and Hegel would argue that the world of ideas is the model for this world.

For Danto, who elevates reception, something is art because we call it art, and the task of the philosopher is to ferret out what properties such works have in common. In Danto, we see a link between reception aesthetics, which is prominent in the continental tradition, and the analysis of ordinary language, which is central to analytic philosophy. Danto is interested not in a normative definition of art, such as Hegel's sensuous appearance of the Idea, but in a descriptive definition that matches everyday usage.[4] He wants to capture the philosophical essence behind our social and linguistic practice: "A tenable philosophical definition of art will have to be compatible with whatever art there is" (*Abuse* 19).

Surveying the art world, Danto concludes that works of art are "*embodied meanings*" (*What* 37), more specifically, "x is an artwork if it embodies a meaning" (*Abuse* 25).[5] Even if we were to accept Danto's preference here for the descriptive over the normative, his definition lacks precision. A definition should encompass all entities that fit and exclude all those that do not, as Danto himself acknowledges: "a philosophical definition of art covers all and only works of art" (*Abuse* 19). Yet Danto's formulation includes also what is not art at all (and which few, if any, would call art). Trauma is embodied meaning, yet it is not art. Danto's definition is in need of greater precision, even if we can perhaps understand him to have meant to say that the embodiment must be an artifact that is intersubjectively accessible.

Further, Danto's resistance to calling ugly works "beautiful" reveals a contradiction. Whereas his theory of art rests on social practice, his theory of beauty contradicts social practice. If we call ugly works beautiful, and Danto resists this use of the term "beautiful," his theory of beauty defies social practice—thus his repeated urging that we *should* overcome our practice of calling sensuously ugly works "beautiful" in the sense of aesthetically excellent (92, 107). Recognizing the dual meaning of beauty—beauty as a particular mode of art, like the sublime and the ugly, and beauty as a mark of aesthetic excellence—and endorsing the dialectic at the core of beautiful ugliness would allow us to avoid Danto's dilemma.

Noël Carroll, born in 1947, is a prominent American philosopher of art and a film scholar who earned doctorates in both philosophy and cinema studies. He is well-known for his work on film theory and the philosophy of horror. The sublime, which can be initially threatening or horrific, is ultimately attractive, inspiring feelings of nobility or awe. Physically ugly monsters, in contrast, only evoke horror, fear, and disgust, and so are removed from the sublime. Carroll argues that monsters evoke horror and disgust because they violate traditional concepts of what should be. They threaten us as nonorganic objects (e.g., haunted houses); as hybrids of animal and human (e.g., minotaurs or werewolves); or as mixtures of the living and the dead (e.g., vampires and zombies) (Carroll, "Horror" and "Ethnicity"). Monsters can also be utterly formless. In every case, they frighten us and violate our categories, inducing horror.

In *The Philosophy of Horror* (1990), Carroll not only explores the ways in which monsters evoke fear and disgust but also addresses the puzzle, not unrelated to the paradox of tragedy and the paradox of ugliness, of why do horror films attract so many viewers. In other words, how can monsters be both repulsive and attractive? Carroll's answer centers on our desire for knowledge. The ugly is part of a larger narrative, and our interest is drawn to the question of how the ugly will play out in this particular world: "the locus of our gratification is not the monster as such but the whole narrative structure in which the presentation of the monster is staged" (181). Horror narratives "revolve around proving, disclosing, discovering, and confirming the existence of something that is impossible, something that defies standing conceptual schemes" (181). We become fascinated with the ugly in the form of the horrific and the cognitively disruptive.

Monsters are physically impossible beings and, as such, inexplicable, awakening our desire to understand what seems inherently unknowable. Carroll addresses the concept of disgust: "the disgust that such beings evince might be seen as part of the price to be paid for the pleasure of their disclosure" (184). A monster would presumably not awaken the kind of curiosity driven by conflicting, even impossible categories, if it were not also an object of disgust and even revulsion. Carroll explains: "one way of making the point is to say that the monsters in such tales of disclosure have to be disturbing, distressful, and repulsive, if the process of their discovery is to be rewarding in a pleasurable way" (185). Our curiosity is driven not only by the action but also by the beings that defy our conceptual categories and so belong to the realm of ugliness. Carroll's answer, then, to the paradox of horror has to do with cognitive interests. To gaze upon the unusual even when it is simultaneously repelling is not unusual. As the history of *mirabilia* shows (Daston and Park), humans are fascinated by so-called curiosities, horrific creatures that transgress our standing categories. This insight transcends the ages. In the fifteenth century, Nicholas of Cusa wrote: "Unusual things, even if they be monstrous, tend to move us" (Book I, Prologue, *De Docta Ignorantia*).

Carroll argues that not only horror but also humor involves a violation of categories. Humor is traditionally associated with the incongruous, including the conceptually incongruous. Clowns, for instance, are notoriously too fat or too thin, too short or too tall, or in some other playful way distorted. When hit by clubs, they are unfazed and so inhumanly resilient. Whereas loathsome monsters arouse fear and horror, the comic, including the clown, evokes amusement and mirth. This insight is consonant with Plato's distinction between fearsome ugliness and ridiculous ugliness and with Aristotle's view of comic ugliness as painless.

In "Ethnicity, Race, and Monstrosity," Carroll applies these concepts to a real-world issue: the connections between ugliness and hate. Carroll explores the contrast between beauty as having traditionally referred to nearly perfect instances of the human being (both physically and morally) and ugliness as referring to deficient modes of being human (both physically and morally). Two prominent modes of deviating from the beautiful norm are the horrific, which evokes fear, and the clownish, which elicits laughter. Carroll then shows what the consequences of this dichotomy are in the realm of political rhetoric, giving examples of cultures that have projected monstrous or buffoonish images onto ethnic or racial others: English distortions of the Irish, white portrayals of Blacks, and American images of the Japanese.[6] These portrayals brand the individuals as ugly and morally depraved, "as subhuman and, therefore, as unworthy of the moral concern that befits a human person" ("Ethnicity" 42). This, then, becomes "justification" for discrimination, aggression, and even violence. The enemy can include individuals, social classes, political parties, or ethnic or racial groups. Today we could add sexual minorities to this list of targets.

Carroll highlights an important aspect of ugliness: as much as we like to find redeeming value in ugliness, it can also be simply abhorrent. Sam Keen has extensively documented the manifold ways in which our hostile imagination renders the faces of the enemy distorted and ugly. The Nazis, for example, used the term *Untermenschen* or subhumans as an appellation for Jews. They combined anti-Semitic propaganda with hateful images and narratives to portray Jews as unworthy: materialistic, immoral, uncivilized, parasitic, cunning, conspiring, physically unattractive, and a threat to German unity, pride, and existence (Herf). From campaign posters and the press to radio broadcasts and anti-Semitic films, such as Veit Harlan's *Jew Süss* (1940) and Fritz Hippler's *Der ewige Jude* (*The Eternal Jew*) (1940), Germans were encouraged to see Jews as ugly and threatening (Figure 16). Jews were blamed for Germany's problems. The Nazis argued, for instance, that international Jewry was responsible for the humiliation of the Versailles Treaty. Jews were described as the power behind all of Germany's enemies, aligned with both Bolshevism and the West. This international Jewish conspiracy had to be destroyed for Germany's defense. The appropriate response, according to Nazi propaganda, was extermination and annihilation. Here—against all tendencies to bracket normative reflection—we see a configuration of the ugly that is itself hateful and repugnant.

Figure 16 *Hans Schweitzer, Poster for Fritz Hippler's film* Der Ewige Jude *(*The Eternal Jew*), 1940,* Ein Dokumentarfilm über das Weltjudentum *(*A Documentary Film about World Jewry*), Deutsche Filmherstellungs- und Verwertungs GmbH (DFG) for Reichspropagandaleitung NSDAP, United States Holocaust Memorial Museum Collection, Gift of Helmut Eschwege.*

Dehumanization lays the groundwork for executing and tolerating the torture and eradication of those deemed less than human (David Smith). We recognize here the importance of understanding production context, in this case, ugly images in the hands of abusive power. This is hardly only a historical phenomenon. Right-wing American politicians have used the language of physical ugliness and dehumanization to attack immigrants, describing them as insects that "pour into and infest our country" and blaming them for "poisoning the blood of our country."[7] They use such allusions to garner support for a moral ugliness that strips others, including children, of their dignity. The flip side of this is the presentation of what is morally ugly as beautiful. We see it in fascist aesthetics as well as in cultures that seek out an exclusionary concept of (racial) purity that is nothing other than moral ugliness in disguise.

I now shift my focus from ugliness in art and history to ugliness in nature. With few exceptions, such as Kant and John Ruskin, modern aesthetics has focused on art.[8] Hegel, for instance, regards nature as an inferior subject for aesthetics.[9] A large and influential mid-twentieth-century American anthology on aesthetics doesn't feature a single contribution on nature (Vivas and Krieger). Two more recent collections are similar; aside from Kant's discussion of the sublime, nature is largely absent (Cooper; Tanke and McQuillan). In fact, the renewed interest in nature that emerged at the end of the last century was led not by aestheticians but by philosophers working in metaphysics and ethics.[10] The aesthetic turn to nature is more recent, and, as with the philosophy of art, has focused more on beauty than on ugliness.[11]

As we assess the few contemporary attempts to analyze ugliness in nature, we recognize the resurfacing of an idea prevalent in the Middle Ages: what seems ugly in nature is ultimately beautiful. **Holmes Rolston III**, a pioneer of environmental ethics as an academic discipline, explores this concept in his *Environmental Ethics*, particularly in a section entitled "Ugliness Transformed in Ecosystemic Perspective" (239–43). Rolston argues that seemingly ugly moments enrich the whole of nature. For instance, a dead tree provides nesting cavities, perches, and food for birds as well as nutrients for the soil. In this way, "ugliness is contained, overcome, and integrates into positive, complex beauty" (241). Essentially, nature brings beauty out of ugliness. Rolston, an ordained Presbyterian minister and the son and grandson of ministers, supports his claim from both scientific and religious perspectives (245). Other philosophers, such as Allen Carlson, also embrace the idea that all seeming ugliness in nature is ultimately beautiful, though they do so from a purely scientific standpoint.

Emily Brady, who has published extensively on ugliness in nature, objects to the view that all of nature is ultimately beautiful.[12] An analytical philosopher working in the United States who spent much of her career in England and Scotland, Brady argues: "Ugliness cannot be explained away by a holistic story unless that story can show how the relevant aesthetic qualities themselves are beautiful" ("Ugly Truth" 86). The insight is in a sense justified, but both positions contain elements of truth. In and of itself, a part can be viewed as ugly, but within a larger horizon, the part can be recognized as beautiful. If our aesthetic concepts encompass both sensuousness and cognition—both the isolated object and that same object understood within a wider horizon—we need not adopt an either-or perspective. In essence, ugliness is sublated into beauty, that is, it is in the Hegelian sense preserved, cancelled, and brought into harmony with beauty. This is the way we view ugliness in artworks whenever ugliness is momentary and then sublated within a larger whole. Since parts gain their full meaning only within the whole, a part can initially be viewed as ugly but then ultimately be recognized as beautiful. This larger dialectical and holistic framework allows us to appreciate that not only the immediate beauty of nature can motivate environmentalism; even nature's seemingly ugly parts have a larger role to play in a holistic understanding of the natural world. Therefore, they too can inspire conservation efforts.

In "The Ugly Truth," Brady identifies three types of ugliness: relative ugliness is ugliness in relation to a norm; inherent ugliness is ugliness in itself; and apparent ugliness is ugliness apart from any comparisons or predetermined categories (93–95). These distinctions are not entirely convincing. "Norm" is an ambiguous concept, and it makes a great difference whether the norm refers to what is ideal or what is common. A Nazi is morally ugly by an ideal standard, but the norm in Nazi Germany was to be a Nazi, so the marker deviated from what is ideal, but not from what was common.

Ugliness in itself is still an experience or description of ugliness based on the implicit or explicit categories by which we define ugliness, so it, too, is informed by its relation to a norm of some kind, as Sibley argued. The most we could say is that some ugliness needs to be thought through, whereas other forms of ugliness are immediately manifest, with the latter being more common (Jacobsen and Höfel). Such a distinction would be fair and seems close to what Brady has in mind, but then such a distinction would lie not in the object but in its reception. Pat Henderson already introduced a version of this distinction by contrasting immediate visceral ugliness with delayed adjudicative or verdictive ugliness.

Apparent ugliness suggests overcoming preconceived notions, but it thereby runs into the kind of problem we saw with relative ugliness. Some notions are more coherent than others, so apparent ugliness may be simply that—apparent—or an object may be genuinely ugly, in which case it no longer represents apparent ugliness. If we seek to grasp ugliness in itself, apart from any biases, it is not quite clear how that differs from inherent ugliness. It seems we are left with two reasonable distinctions: first, immediately perceptible ugliness, as with a decaying body, versus ugliness that is fully formed in consciousness only after considerable reflection, as with a difficult artwork that one weighs in various ways before concluding that it lacks the qualities we associate with excellence; and second, ugliness versus seeming ugliness, the latter term the flip side of what Bosanquet a century ago called "difficult beauty." Note that the two structures of immediacy versus reflection and apparent versus genuine overlap at times, as when we say that an object in nature initially appears ugly, but over time and within a wider horizon we recognize its beauty, such that in the end it is only apparently ugly, or—using Hegelian language—we can say that it is ugly (in one sense) and beautiful (in another sense).

In *Aesthetics of the Natural Environment* Brady highlights conflicting orientations toward the aesthetic appreciation of nature. Cognitive thinkers argue that knowledge of ecology and related scientific disciplines provides the proper conceptual framework for an aesthetic approach to nature. This includes not only appreciating nature's value but also understanding its vulnerability and partial destruction. In contrast, non-cognitive theorists elevate a multifaceted sensuous experience of nature characterized by perceptions, imagination, and emotions. These thinkers stress our humility and wonder at the otherness of nature and our active participation in appreciating its richness.

Brady suggests that the two approaches can be integrated, arguing that in diverse ways, the aesthetic appreciation of nature can aid environmental efforts. The point is echoed in the anthology *Nature, Aesthetics, and Environmentalism*, edited by Allen Carlson and Sheila Lintott. I would support Brady's argument and add that the two approaches to nature can also be brought to bear on ugliness: we *experience* disgust and horror at environmental devastation—such as wildfires, flooding, droughts, strip mining, and pollution—and we *recognize* that such devastation is either exacerbated by or directly caused by human actions that are contrary to what should be.[13] Experience and recognition can also be in tension: we may be inspired to protect nature because of its beauty, but in some cases, uglier parts of nature may be more important ecologically than beautiful areas. Understanding this complexity allows for a more nuanced approach to preserving the environment.

We can reinforce the focus on ugliness and nature by alluding to an important insight from an early environmental philosopher, the German-American Hans Jonas, who emphasized, already in 1979, when he published *Das Prinzip Verantwortung* (*The Imperative of Responsibility*), that in a technological world we should reflect on the distant effects of our actions. In particular, Jonas places his emphasis on immoral actions and their ugly consequences. Jonas argues that the consequences of evil actions are easier to perceive than those stemming from goodness; without its contrary, goodness is often invisible, whereas the perception of evil "is more direct, more compelling, less given to differences of opinion or taste, and, most of all, obtruding itself without our looking for it" (*Imperative* 27; *Das Prinzip* 63). The environmental evil Jonas fears is uniquely threatening: first, because the rapid pace of technical change may prevent self-correction, and second, because in the ultimate matter of humanity's continuation, a second chance is not possible. For these reasons, Jonas elevates a "heuristics of fear" (*Imperative* 26; *Das Prinzip* 64). We need to imagine the spatial and temporal, including long-range, effects of our actions, including the ugliness that results from environmental damage. According to Jonas, "the prophecy of doom" should be given more weight than "the prophecy of bliss" (*Imperative* 31; *Das Prinzip* 70). We can live "without the supreme good but not with the supreme evil" (*Imperative* 36; *Das Prinzip* 72). A world that is less than beautiful is tolerable, whereas a purely ugly world would be horrific.

As we conclude this chapter, I turn to two recent contributions from younger analytic philosophers that underscore the contemporary importance of ugliness as an aesthetic category. **Panos Paris**, who was educated in Scotland and currently works in Wales, published "The Deformity-Related Conception of Ugliness" in 2017. The essay, enriched with numerous examples and a proleptic approach, seeks to identify two conditions that, when combined, suffice for us to identify an object as ugly. The first condition is deformity. Paris addresses the vagueness of "deformity" by defining it as a form that frustrates, inhibits, or hinders an object from realizing its proper end or telos (146). Though Paris understands deformity primarily in a physical sense, his theory also accommodates moral ugliness, which can arise from "deformities of human character" (154), and intellectual ugliness, for which he gives examples such as incoherent sentences and ugly mathematical theorems (153, 157). The second condition is displeasure as determined by "good judges" (150). The essay offers a rare and persuasive attempt to isolate conditions for at least some cases of ugliness.

The contribution nonetheless has three limits. First, Paris is seeking not a definition of ugliness but an empirical tool to determine some cases of ugliness. A definition would be more ambitious and useful. Second, because the formula is designed to identify only *some* cases of ugliness, it is again limited in scope. Much that is ugly satisfies one condition but not the other: excrement, for example, displeases us but is not as such deformed, and caricature is deformed but can amuse us. The question remains whether there might be either a definition of ugliness or a formula that would allow us to identify what is necessarily ugly. Third, although the focus on reception is aided by the stipulation that only good judges of displeasure count, the criteria for good judgment are not made clear.

A more recent analytic contribution stems from **Ryan Doran** of the University of Cambridge and the University of Barcelona. Published in 2022, Doran's lengthy essay "Ugliness Is in the Gut of the Beholder" won the 2024 Arthur Danto/American Society for Aesthetics Prize. Doran, who received his doctorate jointly at the Universities of Sheffield, England, and Antwerp, Belgium, seeks in his research, including his interdisciplinary essay on ugliness, to combine theoretical and empirical work. Doran argues that we can identify ugliness empirically: basically, if an object elicits disgust, it is ugly. Doran does not make the case that whatever is ugly, we will necessarily find disgusting. He argues the reverse: because people find something disgusting, it is, therefore, ugly. For Doran, it is "eliciting disgust under standard conditions that *makes* something truly ugly and disgusting, such that there is *no higher court of appeal* about whether something is ugly and disgusting for someone than when the standard conditions hold" (89–90). Drawing on existing literature, Doran explores what elicits disgust, that is, what activates the disgust system, and finds a remarkable concordance with what we consider ugly.

Despite the deep connections Doran notes between disgust and ugliness, he tends to reduce ugliness to physical and moral ugliness. The intellectual ugliness we find in Shakespeare's comedies, for example, the malapropisms of Dull and Costard in *Love's Labors Lost* (1597) and of Dogberry in *Much Ado About Nothing* (*c.* 1598–9), is not in the least disgusting; instead, it is delightful and funny. Emotional ugliness, such as despondency, is likely to be met with sympathy, not disgust. Auguste Rodin's *Despair* of 1890 is emotionally ugly, but not disgusting. As Sibley notes, ugliness need not engender disgust: "In most cases we can make quite cool judgements as to this or that being ugly. We do not have to show or feel disgust, distaste, or revulsion; we do not utter 'ughs' or 'ohs', turn away or avert our eyes" (204). The reason is simple: our reception of art is more than simply emotional; it is also cognitive. For the greater gain of knowledge, we can endure emotional unease, and we can identify ugliness without reacting emotionally or feeling disgust. When we recognize formal ugliness in an artwork, say, incongruity or disharmony, which is a kind of physical ugliness, we need not feel disgust; in fact, such an emotion seems unlikely.

Insofar as the ugly is not always disgusting, Doran's definition is inaccurate. Doran could defend his thesis only by arguing that people do indeed find ugliness, including intellectual, emotional, and formal ugliness, disgusting, or by invoking a circular argument and excluding emotional, intellectual, and formal ugliness from ugliness proper. Though what we call "ugly" can be more capacious than "disgust," the reverse is also true. For instance, someone might find the idea of another person preparing for a colonoscopy disgusting, but it would be far-fetched for anyone to use the word "ugly" in this context.

In addition, the disgust system involves a visceral response; it is purely descriptive. Beauty and ugliness, in contrast, are evaluative terms. To draw a line from disgust to ugliness is to derive an "Ought" from an "Is." Defining ugliness based on what we find disgusting works not from the object but from reception, not from any normative level, as to what we *should* find disgusting, but from a descriptive level. This approach has ethical and political consequences, which Doran acknowledges but does not address (134).

Our society may be conditioned to feel disgust toward foreigners and immigrants, and if, accordingly, we find such foreigners ugly, we dehumanize them, which can lead to horrific consequences, as we discussed earlier in this chapter. If a society is disgusted by gays, then for that society, gays are by definition ugly. We can go further. If the murder of minorities were not repellent in a given society, it would not, according to this definition, be ugly. That itself is an ugly thought. Doran may be concerned about these implications, but to quote his earlier line, "there is no higher court of appeal" (90).

And yet, aesthetic terms such as the ugly and the comic are more than simply descriptive. What is comical is defined not simply by what produces laughter, but also by what should elicit laughter. A mean joke about race or disability is not comical, but ugly. In the realm of the beautiful and the ugly, we recognize the validity of a normative realm. Not everything people find pleasurable encapsulates beauty, as the concept of kitsch illustrates, and not everything we find disgusting is ugly.

I have argued elsewhere that every reception-oriented approach to defining ugliness runs into problems (*Beautiful Ugliness* 25–33, 62–5). Reception is inherently dynamic. After a certain period, the ugliest properties to which we become accustomed, and which become part of our cultural baggage, become less offensive. We begin to tolerate them and may even find them beautiful or, at the very least, no longer repellent. In short, what we consider beautiful and ugly shifts over time. Santayana notes that "the centaur and the satyr are no longer grotesque; the type is accepted" (157).

Differences in reception can even arise simultaneously. In the American South, photographs of public lynchings were received as documents of sublime rituals that reaffirmed white virtue and black degeneracy, while in the North those same images triggered outrage: they were perceived as ugly, dehumanizing, and abhorrent, and so spurred anti-lynching activism (Wood). If we define the ugly according to its reception, according to our sense of disgust, then the ugly shifts not only over time but also according to context.

However, the ugly itself does not change. What changes is what we subsume under the concept of ugliness. This is not unrelated to conventions that shift over time, for example, what belongs in a tragedy, what defines a beautiful body, or what counts as dissonant music. Conventions, like affects, are not stable. But the ugly is not an affect or a convention. It is a concept. Concepts do not change. Concepts are atemporal. They carve out certain spaces in possible worlds.

A final limitation exists in Doran's essay: it offers virtually no insight into art, no categories to help us in deciphering ugly and seemingly ugly art. Given that Doran is interested not in the object, but in its reception, and given that he does not make normative distinctions between the ugly and the beautiful, it is not surprising that he does not give examples from art. If ugliness is simply a matter of reception or taste, then what might have been the province of aesthetics or hermeneutics gives way to the social sciences. Although Doran's study has the philosophical dimension of sorting through terms and the philological value of extensive and thorough social-scientific research, including an impressive proleptic approach akin to Paris's, it is closer to anthropology than to aesthetics or hermeneutics.

13

An Objective-Idealist Theory

A comprehensive theory of ugliness must answer at least four sets of questions. First, how should we define ugliness? What concepts do we need to grasp, and what questions do we need to answer, in order to understand, interpret, and evaluate ugliness? Second, what have previous thinkers said about ugliness, and what are the strengths and weaknesses of their theories? What new perspectives are needed? Third, when and how has the ugly manifested itself in art and literature? What historical, intellectual, and aesthetic factors contributed to its prominence? Finally, what kinds or forms of beautiful ugliness exist, and how are they to be evaluated?

This book has sought to fill a gap by addressing the second question: what have previous thinkers said about ugliness and how are their analyses to be evaluated? In another book, *Beautiful Ugliness*, I sought to answer the remaining three questions, exploring from an objective-idealist perspective what ugliness is, what its history is in art and literature, and what forms of beautiful ugliness exist.[1] I cannot repeat those arguments here, but I do want to offer a few perspectives that complement the historical and evaluative survey we have just completed. Additionally, I introduce some new aesthetic concepts and categories to aid in our understanding of ugliness.

Let's begin with the definition of ugliness. The most common definitions are (1) ugliness is the opposite of beauty and (2) ugliness is what we find repellent. Neither of these is philosophically compelling: beauty and ugliness need not be opposites, as they are often interwoven, and what we find repellent changes over time. To say that the ugly changes over time makes no sense. Instead, as I argued in the previous chapter, what we subsume under the concept of ugliness changes over time. This begs the question: what is ugliness?

In the *Sophist* Plato hints at a definition, implying that ugliness is an appearance that contradicts what is appropriate to the nature of something (228a–228d). Several German philosophers—Bohtz, Vischer, Fischer, Carrière, Lotze, and Lipps—echoed this idea, viewing ugliness as a manifestation of what should not be. In this spirit, I argue that ugliness is an appearance that contradicts the normative concept of an object. Informally, we can say that ugliness is the sensuous appearance of what should not be. Sibley suggests a definition along these lines as well when he discusses the ugly as "some kind of departure from some standard or norm" (200). For Sibley ugliness is a relational value. A relational value can be understood descriptively (as a departure from a dominant or familiar norm) or evaluatively (as a departure from an idealized norm, such as an organic artwork). At times, the ugly represents a departure from both a descriptive and evaluative norm. For example, willful ignorance is ugly because it deviates from the more common desire to know and contradicts the normative concept associated with human intelligence (one should desire to know).

Although a few thinkers offer reflections on the diverse realms in which ugliness surfaces, no one has captured what I think is a fairly simple articulation of the spheres—physical, emotional, intellectual, and moral—in which ugliness is manifest. Physical ugliness is widely recognized; examples include monsters and death. Emotional ugliness, though less apparent, encompasses states defined by inappropriate emotions for a given situation. These can range from indifference and despair to hopelessness and rage. Like physical ugliness, emotional ugliness is richly depicted in artworks. Intellectual ugliness is the least obvious but has been touched upon by various thinkers, including Hartmann, who highlights incongruities, absurdities, and nomological impossibilities. Ignorance combined with arrogance and a lack of curiosity epitomizes intellectual ugliness; it betrays the human capacity for reason. Finally, moral ugliness ranges from modest foibles to acts of cruelty, violence, and betrayal.

In each sphere of ugliness—physical, emotional, intellectual, and moral—we recognize an appearance that deviates from what should be, from what belongs to a normative understanding of something. Particularly fascinating are the various combinations, especially those filled with tension, such as the physical ugliness and intellectual beauty of Socrates and the physical beauty and moral ugliness of Dorian Gray.

Artists often play with these tensions. A striking example of the overlap between intellectual and moral ugliness, which is absurd in its structure and horrendous in its consequences, comes from Heinrich Heine's historical account of religious persecution. According to Heine, Nicholas Rémy, author of *Daemonolatreiae* (*Demonolatry*) (1595) and a criminal judge in the Duchy of Lorraine, convicted no fewer than 800 women of practicing witchcraft and sentenced them to be burned at the stake. How did Rémy know they were witches? Heine explains: "The presentation of evidence usually consisted of the following procedure: one bound their hands and feet together and threw them into the water. If they sank and drowned, they were innocent, if they remained swimming on the surface of the water, they were seen to be guilty and they were burned. That was the logic of those times" (Ger. 3:524; Eng. 18).

Although various thinkers—from Maggi, Bohtz, Rosenkranz, Hartmann, and Volkelt to Pat Henderson, Brady, and Verschaffel—have sought to categorize types of ugliness, only Verschaffel and Rosenkranz sought to identify types of ugliness in artworks. Verschaffel restricts his focus to architecture and offers limited modes of deficient formal ugliness. Rosenkranz is richer beyond bounds. In my chapter on Rosenkranz, I analyzed this creative thinker's strengths and weaknesses. His modes of ugliness, with abundant examples, are in many ways fascinating and engaging, but despite his almost scholastic sensibilities, he does not provide a systematic defense of his distinctions. In *Beautiful Ugliness*, I sought to offer a more systematic typology of forms of beautiful ugliness. I lay out and analyze the different modes in which ugliness can become beautiful. Drawing on the categories of artwork aesthetics, I stress, first, the relation of form and content and, second, the interconnection of part and whole. These two lenses (form and content on the one hand and part and whole on the other) lead in turn to three distinct styles of beautiful ugliness and three diverse structures, each of which follows a dialectical sequence.

The first style, repugnant beauty, interweaves ugly content with beautiful form. Consider Thomas Eakins's *The Gross Clinic*, a masterful yet also gruesome depiction of a surgeon at work, with blood prominently featured throughout the canvas (Figure 1). In repugnant beauty, we see the skillful representation of an unappealing subject. This style of beautiful ugliness is the most widespread and exists across nearly every age and culture. In terms of subject matter, such works cover a full range, from physical to emotional, intellectual, and moral ugliness, in each case portraying what differs from the ideal. The focus on ugly subject matter is often an end in itself, but not always: Käthe Kollwitz's portrayals of hunger and misery, of the poor and disenfranchised, have a certain beauty that is designed to widen our sense of empathy, drawing attention to the abject circumstances of our fellow human beings. Take, for instance, her lithograph *Not* (Misery) (1898), which depicts a grieving mother and her dead child, a scene set in the cramped, dark room of a working-class family (Figure 17). Such art can be understood as subversive beauty, for it challenges our everyday sensibilities.

The second style, fractured beauty, is the reverse of repugnant beauty: here, innocuous content is conveyed via disjointed or fragmented forms. Examples include Picasso's various renditions of *Head of a Woman* and the beautiful yet fractured works of contemporary British painter Flora Yukhnovich, such as *I'll Have What She's Having* (2020). The occurrence of this playful form in premodern periods is uncommon, but we do see it in the portraits of the sixteenth-century Viennese court painter Giuseppe Arcimboldo, who captures human faces by using diverse objects ranging from fruits to fish, frogs, and birds, as in the sea world that populates his oil on panel *Water* (n.d.) (Figure 18). In modernity fractured beauty becomes widespread. Such works tend to underscore the partial and fragmented sense in which modern consciousness perceives the world. As modern art gravitates toward anti-realism and a focus on form as form, fractured beauty gains prominence. Fractured beauty allows for considerable innovation, a category that, along with fragmentation, is very much embraced in modernity.

The third style combines the ugly content we see in repugnant beauty with fractured beauty's formal ugliness. Drawing on the Greek *aischros*, a word that

Figure 17 *Käthe Kollwitz,* Not (Misery), *Plate 1 from the series* Ein Weberaufstand *(Weavers' Rebellion), 1893–97, Image courtesy of the Smith College Museum of Art.*

encompasses both the aesthetic ugliness of form (*deformis* in Latin) and the moral ugliness of content (*turpis* in Latin), I introduce the neologism "aischric beauty" to capture this third style. Aischric beauty encompasses works that are both repugnant in content and dissonant in form. Such works exhibit, paradoxically, a higher unity of form and content.

The episodic structure of Arthur Schnitzler's comedy *Anatol* (1893) formally reinforces the protagonist's lack of progress and is, in this way, paradoxically organic, making it an example of aischric beauty. In a visibly fractured way, Picasso's *Guernica* (1937) depicts the effects of bombing on soldiers, civilians, and animals; the formal distortion effectively matches the horrendous subject matter (Figure 19). Picasso's late work *Rape of the Sabine Women* (1963) also employs distortion and fragmentation to capture

Figure 18 *Giuseppe Arcimboldo,* Water, *1566, Oil on canvas / Kunsthistorisches Museum, Vienna, Austria / Bridgeman Images.*

horrific content. In presenting what is ugly, such works integrate dissonant forms, which then serve the work's meaning and are thus, at a higher level, not dissonant, but organic, that is, form and content ultimately cohere. This hidden organic element offers a new lens for approaching difficult

Figure 19 *Pablo Picasso,* Guernica, *1937, Oil on canvas, Museo Nacional Centro de Arte Reina Sofia, Madrid © 2022 Estate of Pablo Picasso / Artists Rights Society (ARS), New York © Succession Picasso / DACS, London 2022 / Bridgeman Images.*

works and challenges the prevailing model of avant-garde art as necessarily nonorganic (Bürger).

Whereas my initial approach to modes of ugliness draws on content, form, and their interrelation, a second and complementary lens asks to what extent the work identifies with, or distances itself from, ugliness. This question, which focuses on the interaction of parts and whole, leads to what I call diverse structures of ugliness. The first structure, beauty dwelling in ugliness, involves lingering in ugliness without criticizing it or moving beyond it. These works either display an indifference to, or an embrace of, ugliness, even though the work itself may be beautiful, as in Benn's *Morgue and Other Poems* (1912). Although this structure becomes more prevalent in modernity, it is present in earlier periods as well, such as in many of the Biblical psalms. Because styles and structures of beautiful ugliness address different facets of works, we can recognize patterns of frequent overlap. For example, Benn's work exhibits both repugnant beauty and beauty dwelling in ugliness.

In the second structure, dialectical beauty, ugliness dominates the work, but dialectical beauty points to the ugliness of the ugly and so offers an implicit critique. The concept of a negation of a negation as a way of integrating ugliness into art was prominent among the early Hegelians. This mode matches the satiric tradition, from Juvenal to Brecht and beyond. George Grosz, who presents the corruption of modern Germany in ugly ways, offers examples from the visual arts; his artistic portrayals are invariably designed to uncover the ugliness of the ugly (Figure 2). Francisco Goya and Otto Dix use similar strategies: their works negate negativity. The illustration chosen for the cover of *Theories of Ugliness*, Maxim Kantor's oil on canvas *The Temptation of St. Anthony* (2015), presents us with a contemporary example of the ugliness of the ugly. The grotesque dragon, whose features echo Vladimir Putin, alludes to the devil (Rev. 12:3-9). The sickish green and pink evoke poison gas, camouflage, putrefaction, and the glow of bombs. The image is a critique of Putin, his supporters, and his invasion of the Crimean Peninsula.[2] Although dialectical beauty can be integrated with diverse styles, its most frequent pairing, as is the case here, is with aischric beauty.

I conclude the typology with speculative beauty. Here, the ugly, repulsive, or hateful is present, even prominent, but ultimately subordinate within a larger, more complex, and organic unity. The term "speculative" derives from Hegel's elevation of what transcends opposition and negativity, as central as both are within the unfolding of the dialectic. An example is Aeschylus's *Oresteia* (458 BC), which both includes and transcends tragedy. Speculative beauty is most common in literature and other temporal arts, but we find rare, creative instances even in the static arts. For example, Caspar David Friedrich's *Easter Morning* (*c.* 1828–35) is dominated by dead trees, a dirt road, dark clothing, and brown tones, yet it gestures toward what is to come. In our age, speculative beauty is uncommon, though it is notably (and implicitly) the dominant paradigm that environmental analysts use in analyzing ugliness in nature.

What dominates the art world today is not speculative beauty but instead a dwelling in ugliness, which can be challenging for audiences who may not know how to interpret such artworks. Many museum visitors shuffle bewilderedly past exhibits of contemporary art. Dewey lamented that when art becomes remote, the consequences are unappealing: "esthetic hunger is likely to seek the cheap and the vulgar" (*Art* 4). When viewers find contemporary artworks unintelligible and inaccessible, difficult and even ugly, they often turn to kitsch—stereotypical, derivative, and formulaic works that seek to satisfy audiences but lack true beauty. Kitsch is another mode of not being beautiful. In terms of negative aesthetic value, kitsch is in fact ugly. Adorno comments that in its lack of tension and avoidance of contradiction, kitsch is, paradoxically, "the beautiful as the ugly" (*Aesthetics* Ger. 77; Eng. 47; cf. *Noten* 601; *Notes* 2:249). For those who don't know what to make of the kind of cerebral and dissonant art that Adorno prized, their aesthetic impulses remain unsatisfied. The desire for beauty in an age dominated by ugly and incomprehensible art makes kitsch seductively attractive.

A second, almost inverse mode of negative aesthetic value that arises alongside difficult beauty is what I call *quatsch*. The German word *quatsch* means bunk, nonsense, or bullshit with reference to speech. I borrow the term and extend its meaning, as a counterpart to kitsch. In my reformulation and extension, *quatsch* refers to a would-be artwork that is ugly in content or form, has no opening onto deeper meaning, and whose formal accomplishment tends to exhaust itself in innovation. In short, *quatsch* elevates ugliness but lacks aesthetic merit. It is both the opposite of kitsch and its sister category. For an example, think of the Austrian Hermann Nitsch, whose art involved slaughtering and dismembering cows and sheep and then smearing their blood and entrails on human beings. Or think of the American Paul McCarthy, whose art has included placing private parts in contact with various kinds of food, stuffing food into the mouth to the point of excess, and urinating and masturbating on stage. Perhaps only by distinguishing between great art that integrates ugliness and bad art that integrates ugliness can we hope to engage in the difficult task of evaluating controversial art. Ugliness alone, despite its potential for innovation and shock, does not suffice. Works that lack deeper meaning or formal accomplishment demand an expansion and refinement of our categories. When in 2019 Italian artist Maurizio Cattelan duct-taped a banana to a wall and called it art, the work was much discussed, selling for $120,000. By 2024 it had sold for $6.2 million, but it is difficult to make an effective case that the work is more than simply *quatsch*. Part of offering new aesthetic analyses involves proposing new concepts, which help us draw distinctions that were not previously needed or not previously conscious to us—hence the need for neologisms like aischric beauty and *quatsch*.

Of course, not every work that seems nonsensical is truly nonsensical. We must be patient and sensitive with our interpretations. The concept of *prima facie quatsch* captures works that initially appear nonsensical but turn out to be deeper than a first glance suggests. For example, in *Fat Chair* (1963), by

German artist Joseph Beuys, an old wooden chair is embedded with a large mass of fat sculpted into a triangular wedge (Figure 20). Fat is an odd artistic material: "Traditionally associated with excess and waste, fat is supposed to be slimmed, trimmed, and eliminated; it is unseemly, inelegant, and ugly" (Taylor 16). Even though there are contexts in which fat is not considered ugly, the fat in Beuys's work is indeed abject and grotesque.[3] Beuys's sculpture is also a pun: the word for chair (Stuhl) in the German title *Stuhl mit Fett*, is, like the English word "stool," a polite word for excrement. Yet the work is more than

Figure 20 *Joseph Beuys,* Stuhl mit Fett (Fat Chair*), 1963, Space 3 of Block Beuys at Hessisches Landesmuseum Darmstadt, Copyright photo: © Hessisches Landesmuseum Darmstadt/Artists Rights Society (ARS), New York; Foto: Wolfgang Fuhrmannek, Courtesy: Hessisches Landesmuseum Darmstadt.*

a joke. For Beuys, fat, which "embodies life and movement, flux and flow of energy," can be formed (Beuys, Tisdall, and Koepplin 17). It is at once oozing chaos and sculpted form, a coincidence of opposites—a concept elevated by the German idealists whom Beuys admired (Beuys, Bastian, and Simmen 98). As an integral but seemingly unappealing part of the human being, fat is fundamentally organic. It is more than waste, for in such a work, which is not only a metaphor for the human being but also a self-reflexive meditation on art, the lowliest of the low is given shape and meaning. The triangular shape of the sculpted fat alludes to the Trinity, and the lowliest of the low is, at one level, Christ. The work is an embrace of the abject, but formed into art. It is no surprise that Beuys often described art as a form of "resurrection" (Beuys 34; Kuoni 246).

Many ugly artworks violate principles of human dignity. Some mock disability, as with grotesque Hellenistic sculptures of dwarfs and hunchbacks. Others are misogynistic, degrading women to mere objects and seeking to strip them of their humanity. Nationalistic, ethnic, or racial impulses can also produce art that portrays the "other" as subordinate or even subhuman. Broadly misanthropic or cynical works can violate our sense of human value or worth. Some artworks may have innocuous content but challenge our sensibilities for form and our capacities for comprehension. To approach such ugly and seemingly ugly works, we need criteria to guide our interpretations and evaluations. Ugly art becomes seemingly ugly only when it satisfies the conditions of positive aesthetic value, as determined by artwork aesthetics. If we were instead to elevate production, we might end up saying that all works created by a particular type of person are great. If we were to elevate reception instead, we might find ourselves asserting that whatever a group of people considers great art is, indeed, great art.

Drawing on the primacy of artwork aesthetics, I argued in *Why Literature Matters in the 21st Century* and *Beautiful Ugliness* that the excellence of an artwork depends on several factors. The quality of its content is crucial, including its ability to offer an indirect window onto truth, even if that meaning is elusive. In addition, if our criteria for excellence are not purely formal, a great work avoids morally untenable stances, such as misogyny or racism.[4] A formal criterion also exists. Great art has a formal excellence, characterized by innovation or nuance, including a form that fits the content and captivates the recipient. The form should be engaging, coherent, and distinctive, though often in subtle and counter-intuitive ways. Furthermore, great art unites parts and whole such that the parts, though independently interesting, nonetheless gain their full meaning only within the whole. The beautiful, the sublime, and the ugly all meet these criteria whenever they partake of positive aesthetic value. They offer a window onto truth; they are formally intriguing; and the parts and the whole relate to one another meaningfully.

When these criteria for aesthetic excellence are not met, the outcome is either a mixed work or a work with negative aesthetic value. The content may be banal, mediocre, tendentious, or untrue. The moral elements may be untenable or justly reprehensible. The form may be monotonous, pedestrian, simplistic, uneconomical, artificial, haphazard, or otherwise deficient. The meaning and shape may be unrelated or at odds with one another, such that even a meta-harmony of form and content cannot be deciphered. Or the diverse elements or parts may be viewed as unrelated to one another and to the whole and so dissonant or ununified. The result would be not seeming ugliness but ugliness, not positive aesthetic value but negative aesthetic value. However, there is a compelling abundance of works that create positive aesthetic value out of ugliness. Given the complexity of such works, we benefit when approaching them with the rich array of theories of ugliness we have explored from Plato to Adorno and beyond.

Afterword

Ugly works draw us in. Dante's *Inferno* tends to attract more readers than the *Paradiso*. Research has shown that visitors to the Prado Museum in Madrid spend more time studying the disturbing depiction of hell in Bosch's triptych *The Garden of Earthly Delights* than on the other two panels (Jones). Such preferences are tied to the insatiable, even unwilling, human curiosity to explore ugliness.

Yet, ugliness is ambiguous. We are often drawn to it but also compelled to look away, a dynamic captured in artworks like Eakins's *The Gross Clinic* (Figure 1) and Dix's etching *The Match Vendor* (Figure 21). Certain objects and situations we do not want to see. In works that portray ugliness, we must reckon with war and violence, brutality and crime, poverty and sickness, vanity and cowardice, depression and anxiety, pettiness and other such themes. Just as we do not avoid death but confront it via rituals, so does art offer us ways to wrestle with these repugnant or repressed topics. Dissonance and negativity are a part of reality, and their reflection in art is to be welcomed if we want to know and understand what is—also in its deviation from what should be. Ugly art draws our attention to the marginal, the less apparent, the forgotten, the abject, and the denied.

In addition to integrating what might otherwise be overlooked or resisted, the successful fusion of ugliness and beauty has generated many sophisticated and innovative artworks. Such blending adds to the tension that is an almost requisite element of great art. As Leonardo da Vinci suggested, "beauty and ugliness seem more effective through one another" (51; cf. 80). It is rare that an artwork does not benefit from the tension of opposites.

The prominence of ugliness in works of beauty expands our sense of originality and appreciation for innovation. Ugliness extends art's variety.

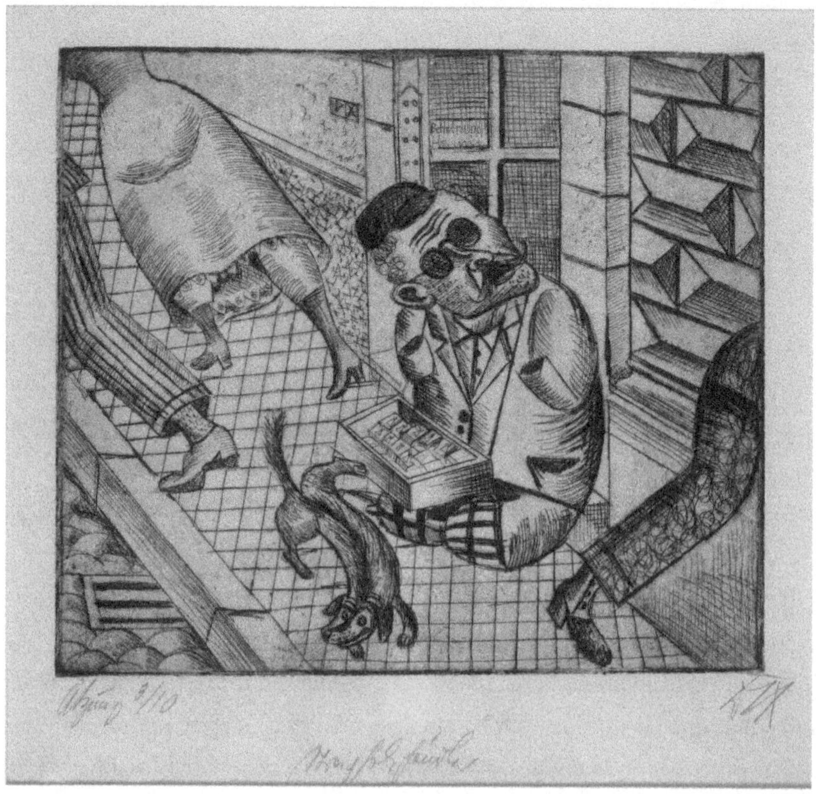

Figure 21 *Otto Dix,* Der Streichholzhändler (The Match Vendor)*, 1920, Etching, © 2025 Artists Rights Society (ARS), New York / VG Bild-Kunst, Bonn / bpk Bildagentur / Kupferstichkabinett / Staatliche Museen / Berlin / Jörg P. Anders / Art Resource, New York.*

An often invoked and indeed ancient insight is that "the beautiful has but one type, the ugly has a thousand" (Le beau n'a qu'un type; le laid en a mille) (Victor Hugo, *Préface* 30; "Preface" 367–8).[1] The diversity of ugliness impacts not only content but also form. Often, ugly art confronts us with unintelligible and distorted forms that are not easy to grasp and may lead to befuddlement or rejection. Such works challenge our interpretive capacities by asking us to identify the often submerged merit of formal innovations. Ugly works stretch our hermeneutic capacities, urging us to discern the hidden meaning of distortion, relate form and content to one another, or integrate various art forms and styles that may initially seem at odds with one another.

Figure 22 *Edvard Munch,* The Scream, *1893, Oil, tempera, pastel, and crayon on cardboard, National Gallery of Norway / © 2025 Artists Rights Society (ARS), New York / Bridgeman Images.*

We see how various formal elements, from color to shape, allow for the beautiful expression of ugly emotions. In Edvard Munch's *The Scream* (1893), the expression of the scream takes over the entire work: the face is distorted, and the gnarled waves of lines reinforce the scream (Figure 22). The juxtaposition of straight and curved lines, all converging on the central figure, adds to the tension. The bold colors seem to express the figure's emotions, while the uneven lines accentuate the curves of the head and hands. To the right, one senses a kind of cliff or abyss. Munch's painting recalls elements of caricature, though the telos is not humor but despair, not critique, but empathy. Fascinating is also the contrast: the two figures walking on seem oblivious to the emotions expressed by the harried and neurotic figure crying out. We, however, cannot turn away. We are inexorably drawn to what might otherwise repel us. Painter Lucian Freud, the grandson of Sigmund Freud, suggests: "The task of the artist is to make the human being uncomfortable, and yet we are drawn to a great work by involuntary chemistry, like a hound getting a scent; the dog isn't free, it can't do otherwise, it gets the scent and instinct does the rest" (Hughes 19).

The critical potential of art—art as a medium through which we see reality anew, including uncovering our own prejudices—is evident in much of dissonant art. In Jenny Saville's *Torso 2* (2004–5), we are simultaneously seduced by the aesthetic quality and repulsed by the specific image: the female body objectified and transformed into a piece of meat. The female body has long been a dominant subject in beautiful art, and to reject this objectification, artists, often female artists, turn to strategies that integrate ugliness. Although ugly images of the female have existed historically, they are almost always comic and derogatory. Saville's images, however, are not comic but confrontational and contemplative. This integration of what society neglects to see or face or recognize reinforces the value of art as a critical force. Art reminds us of the inadequacies of reality and our need to criticize it. Its moment of non-reconciliation allows us to linger with, rather than move beyond or minimize, the disturbing elements of artistic objectification, the dissonant elements of reality, and the various modes of suffering often considered taboo.

If we can perceive the deeper beauty in superficially ugly works, we may sharpen our ability to recognize hidden beauty in reality. Research has documented discrimination against those perceived to be less than beautiful (Hamermesh and Biddle). For example, a dramatic pay gap exists between physically attractive and less attractive individuals (Monk, Esposito, and Lee). Social discrimination based on arbitrary standards of beauty, including race, can lead to issues such as low self-esteem (Pinho). Discrimination extends even to the animal world: ugly animals are less likely to be protected than their more beautiful counterparts (Eveleth).

America no longer has "ugly laws," as we did from the late 1860s to the early 1970s, when local laws often codified that persons who were in any way deformed, so as to be unsightly, must not expose themselves to public view (Schweik).[2] Instead, unease with the superficially ugly has become subtler. Anita Silvers argues that understanding how modern art depicts deformed bodies as beautiful can offer valuable lessons for life. If art has not only intrinsic but also extrinsic value, one of its uses may be to sharpen our gaze beyond simple binaries. The complex hermeneutic categories we learn as we engage beautiful works that integrate moments of ugliness may be not only ends in themselves but also transferable beyond the realm of art.

*

A significant question is whether the history of theories of ugliness reveals an internal logic of development. Plato speaks of ugliness almost in passing, yet he offers insights that suggest an already developed sensibility for the dialectic of ugliness and beauty. In contrast to the relativism of the *Dissoi Logoi*, Plato recognizes that one can distinguish between the ugly and the beautiful. However, he is also aware of complexities. Surface ugliness may belie a hidden beauty. We may be superficially drawn to ugliness, but ultimately only beauty captures our true love. Plato's dialogues arrive at truth by working through and refuting false, intellectually ugly positions, such that beauty and truth are achieved only after passing through ugliness. With just a modest prelude, Plato already achieves a certain synthesis. Medieval thinkers who gave less attention to ugliness could be said to fall back into a more simplistic position: ugliness as such does not exist.

The first sustained focus on ugliness, which emerges in the late eighteenth and early nineteenth centuries, leads to a second synthesis. Lessing and the early Hegelians emphasize ugliness and argue that even though ugliness is an important element of art, it finds its truth only when it passes over into beauty. The dialectical understanding of ugliness is loosely analogous to Plato's recognition of truth as movement beyond the ugliness of error. And, as we saw in Chapter 9, the idea of ugliness as a moment animates even many non-Hegelians. This period of sustained focus provides a second, appealing synthesis. Ugliness is elevated even as it is given a subordinate position vis-à-vis beauty. In contrast to the first, Platonic synthesis, this second synthesis, enriched by the focused studies of the early Hegelians and others, offers a much more detailed account of ugliness.

This overarching structure, with its idea of ugliness as a moment, transitions in the twentieth century to three distinct views of ugliness. First is the position that ugliness belongs outside of beauty, which animates thinkers such as Croce and Nicolai Hartmann and may even have contributed to the early American neglect of ugliness. This view mirrors, in unexpected ways, the medieval framework. Second is Adorno's position, which is often adopted by theorists, critics, and museum directors, that we must dwell much more in ugliness, perhaps infinitely so, in order to do justice to the truths that beauty neglects. This dwelling in ugliness can be seen as a falling back from a synthetic mode or, more positively, as an innovation that insists on lingering in the antithesis, an entreaty that we cannot and should not move too quickly beyond ugliness. A third view, which one might see as a synthesis of the previous two views—no ugliness and only ugliness—and as a partial return to the more dynamic views of the Platonic and early Hegelian frameworks, is the objective idealist position I advanced in the last chapter. Speculative beauty is the synthesis of radiant beauty (no ugliness), beauty dwelling in ugliness (only ugliness), and dialectical beauty (exposition of the ugliness of the ugly). It differs from the second synthesis in giving more space to ugliness; a category such as beauty dwelling in ugliness would have been rejected by even the most radical Hegelians.

One could also argue that many of the individual insights in the tradition are refinements of a half dozen or so dominant, recurring ideas:

- ugliness and beauty can coexist in the same object;
- weak ugliness is ridiculous, whereas powerful ugliness is horrific;
- even though ugliness has a role to play, beauty is ontologically superior to ugliness;
- ugliness is not indifferent to beauty, but stubbornly seeks to replace it;
- ugliness finds its truth when it is included as a moment but only as a moment;
- and if we move beyond ugliness too quickly, we will miss the truths it holds for us.[3]

These overarching positions are complemented by an incredible array of more specific insights, which contribute to a fuller understanding of ugliness. Virtually every thinker covered in this book offers insights worth exploring further:

- Plato recognizes that the same person can be physically ugly and spiritually beautiful, and he distinguishes between weak ugliness, which is ridiculous, and powerful ugliness, which is horrific.
- Aristotle values aesthetic renderings of ugliness because they help us understand the fullness of reality, and he defines comedy as ugliness without pain.
- Plotinus discovers that the ugly soul is not at home with itself but driven hither and yon by discordant desires.
- Augustine advances the theory that, when seen from the perspective of the whole, particular ugliness, which contributes to the beauty of the whole, is no longer truly ugly.
- Bernard of Clairvaux recognizes that ugly art can be so fascinating that we cannot resist it, even when we should. Delight and disgust exist simultaneously.
- Bonaventure distinguishes between the object portrayed, which can be ugly, and the portrayal itself, which can be beautiful, such that if the portrayal is fitting, there can even be a beautiful portrayal of the devil.
- Ulrich of Strasbourg argues that many sensually delightful things are ultimately ugly insofar as they lack sufficient goodness.
- Maggi makes a sensible distinction between the ugliness of the body, as with a distorted face; ugliness of the mind, as with ignorance; and ugliness of circumstances, as with poverty.
- Hume suggests that a perfectly functional building that appears unstable is ultimately ugly and deformed because it challenges our sense of stability.
- Lessing argues that ugliness operates in radically different ways, depending on whether it is integrated into the spatial or the temporal arts.

- Herder contends that ugliness in a painting is easier to process, as sight is cerebral, whereas ugliness in sculpture is more difficult to absorb, as it engages our senses more immediately and viscerally, appealing to our sense of touch.
- Schlegel recognizes that when the concept of the "interesting" displaces beauty as our highest aesthetic category, ugliness increases.
- Weiße illuminates ugliness via its connection to two neighboring categories, the sublime and the comic.
- Ruge considers ugliness a moment in a dialectical process, such that the ugliness of the ugly, the negation of the negation, is the truth of ugliness.
- Vischer makes the case that literature is well-suited to portray ugliness, not only because it is a temporal form in which ugliness can be a moment, but also because ugliness in the mind is much easier to absorb than the physical ugliness depicted in the spatial arts.
- Fischer argues that ugliness is ultimately not only a negative position but one that obstinately holds on to negativity, thereby erasing human striving and dignity.
- Rosenkranz recognizes that ugliness is such a rich category that it is imperative to elucidate diverse types of ugliness.
- Schasler argues that ugliness is not simply a necessary element of art but, as the principle of negativity, a necessary moment within beauty itself.
- Hartmann recognizes that less symmetrical shapes, which are superficially ugly, can convey great beauty, as with ocean waves, waterfalls, and fire.
- Bosanquet accentuates the reception context of ugliness, recognizing that only with sophisticated categories can we understand and fully value the difficult beauty of a work that integrates ugliness.
- Cohen advances the view that ugliness can and should be embraced as part of the human condition, an embrace achieved through loving humor.

- Adorno contends that art that excludes ugliness cannot do justice to social and historical injustice.
- Pat Henderson posits that ugliness can serve as an overarching category that encompasses a family of terms, but it can nonetheless be differentiated from neighboring categories.
- Goodman solves the paradox of ugliness (our surprising attraction to ugly works) by suggesting that the paradox wrongly reduces the art experience to emotions, such as pleasure. He argues that artistic reception also includes cognition, and we are cognitively interested in a wide range of positions.
- Kristeva focuses on the abject, a category related to the ugly, and underscores that we are inclined to turn away from the abject as opposed to confronting it—in both art and life.
- Sibley argues that while the beautiful can be beautiful by itself (as a predicate) or in its embodiment of a particular standard or ideal (as an attribute), the ugly is necessarily attributive, a relational category that deviates from a standard, from an idea of what should be.
- By linking ugliness with hate and racism, Carroll recognizes that as much as we like to find redeeming value in ugliness, it can also be simply abhorrent.
- Rolston and Brady expand our understanding of aesthetics beyond art alone by highlighting the role of ugliness in nature.

One could continue with still further insights beyond this partial selection. I leave out a large number of interesting philosophers and include, for the most part, only one idea from any single figure, but even this truncated list reveals that exploring theories of ugliness gives us rich categories for understanding art, nature, and indeed life itself.

Notes

Introduction

1 Theories of ugliness exist in non-Western cultures, but my lack of expertise restricts me to a few preliminary and pedestrian comments here and occasionally later. Chakrabarti offers an overview of contributions from Indian aesthetics. A major theme in early Indian writings parallels Aristotle's argument, which repeatedly surfaces in the West, that it is possible to have a beautiful rendition of ugly content. *Wabi sabi*, or beauty via imperfection, which is central to Japanese aesthetics, is a significant form of beautiful ugliness. In contrast, the Confucian tradition emphasizes perfection and edification in art, valuing beautiful and elegant rituals, music, and literati paintings, such that it is not surprising that several recent overviews of Chinese aesthetics do not address ugliness (Zhu, Qi, and Goldin). However, Buddhist and Taoist artists, with their focus on the impermanence of this world, have depicted common and even ugly things. Consider one of the greatest Chinese painters, Zhu Da, known by his pen name Bada Shanren, who was a seventeenth-century (late-Ming and early-Qing dynasty) painter, calligrapher, and poet who spent over 30 years as a Buddhist monk. His black-and-white works feature animals with rolling eyes, wilting lotus flowers, and deformed deer bodies. He portrays trees that are withered, at times even "stunted and broken" (Fangyu and Barnhart 17). A contemporary Taoist priest, Fu Shan, deliberately sought an ugly style in his calligraphy, stating that he "would rather be awkward, not skillful; ugly, not pleasing; deformed, not slick" (Bai 118). Fu "embraced 'awkwardness' (zhuo) and 'ugliness' (chuo) as key terms in his aesthetic vocabulary" (Bai 126). *Zhili* (deformity, distortion, or fragmentation) became his stylistic mode and informed even his paintings. Those interested in ugliness in Latin American aesthetics will benefit from integrating Latin American depictions of the tortured Christ, which tend to be unusually dramatic. Readers weighing ugliness in African aesthetics may want to start with Nuttall.

2 The number of major philosophers of art who are left out of this study (because ugliness as such plays little role for them), figures such as Pseudo-Longinus, Giambattista Vico, August Wilhelm Schlegel, Martin Heidegger, and Richard Wollheim, is small, which itself sheds indirect light on the submerged importance of ugliness.

3 See Oesterle, Funk, Jung, Kleine, and Klemme, et al. Menninghaus focuses on the related reception-aesthetic category of disgust. Well-known in German circles is the

Jauß anthology, where the wide-ranging contributions are for the most part historical as opposed to systematic. Zelle is unusual: in two books that touch on aspects of ugliness, he reaches back to the early modern era. Gagnebin discusses Plato (and briefly Aristotle and Plotinus), but then jumps ahead to Nietzsche and the twentieth century. Klicke's encyclopedia entry, arguably the most illuminating overview of the theory and practice of ugliness, is in its historical breadth an admirable exception. Also worthy of note is Tatarkiewicz's three-volume aesthetic history, as it occasionally touches on ugliness, particularly in the medieval era.

4 We see the tendency toward description and paraphrase in broader theoretical studies—Michael Pauen, for example, writes that he wants to avoid any normative and evaluative tendencies (212-13)—and in focused contributions, for example, Schmidt's analysis of Adorno.

5 The early Hegelians have been so forgotten that even Hegel scholars who address ugliness, such as Desmond (150-59), tend to overlook their contributions.

6 In this paragraph I focus on studies available in English, but it is worth noting that Krestovsky's two books in French also align with the dominant pattern found in English-language literature. Her work, like these others, emphasizes not theory but instances of ugliness in literature and the arts.

Chapter 1

1 Sprague (1968) translates *aischros* as "disgraceful"; Robinson (1979), Gagarin and Woodruff (1995), and Dillon and Gergel (2003) use "shameful"; and Graham (2010) uses "wrong," though most employ "ugly" when translating 2.22. In my paraphrases below, I try to capture some of this multiplicity. The translations I cite are from Dillon and Gergel.

2 For studies of art and beauty, see, for example, Murdoch, Janaway, Nehamas ("Beauty"), Hyland, Halliwell (*Between*), Denham, and Sallis. When Halliwell turns from beauty to ugliness, specifically aischrology (that is, ugly, shameful, and offensive speech), he focuses not on Plato but on Aristophanes (*Greek Laughter* 215-63).

3 The temptation toward ugliness that Plato expresses here is at odds with Diotima's glorification of beauty, which draws us in, and her disparagement of ugliness, which pushes us away, a set of insights that Socrates relates in the *Symposium* (210e-212a). The temptation is further at tension with the *Phaedrus* (249d-252c), where Plato evokes the wondrous pull of beauty. The idealist Plato, however, recognized the tripartite nature of the soul, which has impulses beyond (and not always controlled by) reason (*Phaedrus*, 246a-249d). Any account of the Greek discovery of the mind needs to be complemented by the Greek recognition of the irrational, as the twin classics by the German Bruno Snell and the Irishman E. R. Dodds remind us. For other passages in *The Republic* that reinforce the Leontius anecdote, see 352a, 554d, and 603c-d.

4 Plato's insight is especially compelling when one considers that empirical science supports the view that our curiosity and desire to resolve uncertainty can be so powerful that they drive us to expose ourselves to unpleasant information and adverse, even painful stimuli (such as electric shocks). This occurs even when no long-term benefit exists and even when we have the ability to avoid these negative experiences altogether (Hseel and Ruan).

5 From this observation, Kieran concludes that we need to expand our concept of aesthetic value to include not only beauty but also ugliness. Kieran does not develop a theory of ugliness, and his concept of aesthetic value operates independently of moral considerations, that is, he argues that because we find pleasure in the perverse, the perverse has aesthetic value, even when it is morally repugnant. In contrast, I argue that the aesthetic realm should not be reduced to pleasure or sensuous interest alone. Instead, I advocate for a more robust and normative concept of the aesthetic that integrates also cognitive and moral factors.

6 On continuing debates surrounding negative emotions in art, see Levinson.

7 Despite shifts within comic theater, most modern theorists share Aristotle's view. Nicolai Hartmann, for example, writes: "obviously comedy stops where serious suffering and bitter pain begin" (422). Aristotle's insight is not unrelated to our age. In the 2018 Netflix standup special, *Nanette*, Hannah Gadsby moves beyond comedy: during the set she announces that the stand-up routine is over and then articulates the humiliation and violence that lesbians like Gadsby experience in a society that treats them as less than fully human.

Chapter 2

1 The only substantial study devoted to medieval theories of ugliness is Paul Michel's Zürich dissertation of 1976. His focus is less ugliness itself than the ways in which ugliness is overcome, which reflects the medieval understanding of ugliness as subordinate to beauty. Michel's work brings together and explicates central passages, particularly from Augustine and Pseudo-Dionysus, but refrains from evaluating philosophical claims.

2 When Aquinas speaks of beauty and ugliness, he adds to the principles of *consonantia* (proper proportion or harmony) and *claritas* (brightness, clarity, or splendor) also *integritas* (wholeness or perfection), noting that a lack of *integritas* also results in ugliness (*Summa Theologica* 1.39.8), but this third category is less prominent.

3 In *Art and Beauty in the Middle Ages*, Eco offers chapters on these two ideals, "The Aesthetics of Proportion" and "The Aesthetics of Light." The two principles also play a prominent role in his study of Aquinas's aesthetics.

4 That musicians and music critics sometimes borrow terms from the visual arts, including those related to color, ambience, lighting, and so forth (for example, a Neapolitan chord before a dominant chord adds a slightly dark somber stroke before the impending bright conclusion) shows how fascinating the puzzle is and how often we use metaphors to describe the beauty and complexity of instrumental music, but the metaphorical usage does not contradict the basic analytic point that music does not have color.

5 In nature, indirect communication is absent, except among more complex animals, particularly humans. The presence of ambiguity in artworks makes exploring artistic ugliness more challenging and complex, but also more intriguing, than analyzing ugliness in nature.

6 The idea of a sliding scale of beauty and ugliness has a long history. It is central already in Heraclitus's fragment 82: "The most handsome of apes is ugly in comparison with (a member of) the human race." The source for this fragment is *Hippias Major*, where Socrates, citing Heraclitus, refutes one of Hippias's definitions of beauty by noting that the most beautiful of apes is ugly compared with humans and the most beautiful maiden ugly compared with the gods (289a-d). The idea, which plays a central role for Ulrich of Strasbourg, remains prominent in contemporary thought, as with Francis Kovach, who argues that while every being is beautiful, "every being is *more or less* beautiful" (264), and with Andrei Pop, who uses the sliding scale as the center of his argument that the same object can be both beautiful and ugly.

7 Though most medieval thinkers and artists held to the view that what seems ugly contributes to a greater whole and is thus not ultimately ugly, the tradition is not without ambiguities. Aquinas goes so far as to state a position contrary to this dominant view. In his commentary on Aristotle's *Nichomachean Ethics*, he states: "Ugliness, which is a defect of physical beauty, results from any member being unsightly. But beauty arises only when all the members are well proportioned and of a healthy hue" (2.7.320). In other words, ugliness can arise in manifold ways, with a defect in any part, whereas beauty has a much higher presupposition: all the parts must be not only appropriate and integrated but also inherently beautiful.

8 The passage survives in Latin, not Greek.

9 What Augustine counsels against becomes one of Nietzsche's highest values. Curiosity is for the anti-Christian philosopher a mode of exploring what has been suppressed, what lies beneath the surface of traditional morality. In his preface to *Human, All Too Human* Nietzsche praises the free spirit who "full of curiosity, temptation, and experimentation slithers around what is forbidden" (*Werke* 1:440; *Complete Works* 3:8, my translation). Relentless curiosity and unabashed exploration of the forbidden continue in modern art.

10 I cite the critical edition of book 2, tractates 1-4 of *De summo bono,* edited by Alain de Libera.

Chapter 3

1 In his commentary from 1570, Lodovico Castelvetro cites Aristotle's passage on ugliness, pain, and comedy (88). We also see citations in the writings of Bernardo Pino and Alessandro Carriero (Weinberg 1:582, 1:597).

2 Under the influence of his age, Maggi gives as another example of the ugliness of circumstances being born of a perverse religion, by which he means Judaism (Lat. 95).

3 Christianity deserves this secular criticism when it falls victim to elevating the exclusivity of faith over the universality of love. In chapter 27 of *Das Wesen des Christentums* (The Essence of Christianity), Ludwig Feuerbach offers a rich analysis of this tension.

4 Pope Francis stated in a 2013 interview: "I have really loved a diverse array of authors. I love very much Dostoevsky and Hölderlin. I remember Hölderlin for that poem written for the birthday of his grandmother that is very beautiful and was spiritually very enriching for me [...] in that poem Hölderlin compares his grandmother to the Virgin Mary, who gave birth to Jesus, the friend of the earth who did not consider anybody a foreigner" (Spadaro). Not previously translated into English, Hölderlin's poem will appear in English in my forthcoming essay "'None of the living was closed from his soul': A Translation of, and Commentary on, Hölderlin's Poem 'To my Venerable Grandmother. On her 72nd Birthday,'" which will appear in a forthcoming special issue entitled "Hölderlin and Poetic Transport" of the online journal *Humanities*.

5 A sign of contemporary interest in ugliness is that a French translation appeared with Classiques Garnier in 2012.

6 Rocco is an anomaly in the West, but his clever rhetorical praise of ugliness as good and beautiful has a counterpart in a tradition within classical Arabic literature that delights in the perversity of describing ugly things as good and rendering good things ugly. See Van Gelder, who cites, among other works, Al-Thaʿālibi's untranslated eleventh-century anthology *The Beautification of the Ugly and the Uglification of the Beautiful.*

7 Note that for Baumgarten in this passage beauty is associated with cognition, not the object of cognition, as it is in his *Metaphysics* (§662), where he calls "beauty" "the perfection of appearance" and "ugliness" "the imperfection of appearance." Still, it is not immediately apparent that at a higher level the two ideas cannot be reconciled (Solms 51-55).

8 See Venturi, et al., 63-87 and the anthology edited by Van Acker and Mica.

Chapter 4

1 Guyer traces three themes across modern aesthetics: art's relations to truth, play, and emotions. Although he does not focus on ugliness, one could say that ugliness

is deeply intertwined with all three themes: dark *truths* often demand ugliness, not beauty, for their expression; *playful* experimentation can lead to unusual and aberrant forms; and artistic ugliness can shock viewers, thereby intensifying art's *emotional* impact.

2 On the limits of Herder's link between sculpture and touch, see Zuckert 190-222.

3 In §16 of the *Critique of Judgment* Kant differentiates between two kinds of beauty and corresponding modes of appreciating beauty. The pure appreciation of beauty involves a free play of imagination and understanding, a purposiveness without purpose, which avoids any application of determinate concepts. Kant gives as an example instrumental music. In impure or dependent beauty a conceptual or cognitive component is added; we recognize that the object has a deeper meaning or serves a purpose. Kant gives as an example a church.

4 Clewis offers the most comprehensive list, taking account of studies through 2023, although he overlooks at least five studies of which I am aware: a 2013 study by Mary Troxell, essays from 2017 and 2018 by Christopher Buckman, a 2019 essay by Dan Larkin, and a 2023 analysis by Lara Oštarić (which appeared more or less simultaneously with Clewis's book).

5 The most ambitious study of Kant and ugliness is by Mojca Küplen, whose book functions on a different plane than the more philological studies and is one of the strongest reception-aesthetic accounts of ugliness I know. Küplen argues that ugliness is a subjective but universally valid experience of displeasure, which is triggered by a disharmony between the free play of imagination and understanding's need for order. Unlike the transitory displeasure associated with the sublime, this displeasure endures. The weakness of Küplen's interesting study lies in its elevation of reception, which leads to the odd claims that any difficulty or displeasure in interpretation, including ambiguity in an artwork, results in ugliness, and that there can be no movement from ugliness to beauty, even in the process of aesthetic interpretation and evaluation.

6 Rosenkranz was the third successor to Kant's chair. Kant died in 1804 and was followed from 1805 to 1809 by the relatively forgotten Wilhelm Traugott Krug, after which the chair went to Johann Friedrich Herbart, who founded pedagogy as an academic discipline and who argued for the development of character and not simply accumulation of knowledge as the central telos of education. Herbart's works are still in circulation. He held the chair until 1833, when he went to Göttingen, and the position was then assumed by Rosenkranz. Herbart was important enough in the nineteenth century that Hermann Lotze concludes his *Geschichte der deutschen Philosophie seit Kant* (History of German Philosophy since Kant) with a chapter on Herbart, whose chair in Göttingen Lotze occupied after Herbart.

7 Mennemeier makes the case that, despite Schlegel's turn, considerable continuity exists in his theories.

8 A rare contemporary study of Trahndorff, written in Spanish, appeared in 2001. Cornejo opens by noting that Trahndorff "has been eclipsed without a trace in the history of philosophy" (91). When Trahndorff's name does surface, it is usually restricted to his coinage of the term "Gesamtkunstwerk," which he employs when analyzing opera (2:318).

Chapter 5

1 The major exception to the relative neglect of the Hegelians is Bosanquet, who was greatly influenced by the German tradition and in his account of German aesthetics dealt extensively with ugliness. A partial exception is Katharine Gilbert and Helmut Kuhn's *A History of Esthetics*, which devotes a paragraph to Weiße and four pages to Vischer, though it does not mention ugliness (503-07). Beardsley's *Aesthetics from Classical Greece to the Present*, which remains a standard work, allocates only one short paragraph to the Hegelians, including just one sentence to Rosenkranz (239-40). Hammermeister's *The German Aesthetic Tradition* includes only Weiße and Rosenkranz (106-08), and Guyer's three-volume *History of Modern Aesthetics* discusses only Vischer and Rosenkranz, with ugliness surfacing solely in the context of Rosenkranz (2.154-78). Despite Rosenkranz being the best-known figure among them, American philosophers, including Peter Carmichael, who wrote on "The Sense of Ugliness, have rarely demonstrated familiarity with Rosenkranz's work. Even with the recent translation of Rosenkranz, not a single follower of Hegel's is included in a 2021 volume that explores more than 30 key thinkers in the history of aesthetics (Giovannelli). The same omission is evident in a 2012 aesthetics anthology that totals over 600 pages (Tanke and McQuillan).

2 The Hotho edition appeared in 1835 and 1838, followed by a new edition in 1842. Hotho based his compilation on Hegel's *Hefte zur Ästhetik* (notebooks on aesthetics), which Hegel developed for his Heidelberg lecture and then for his first Berlin lecture. These notebooks, along with an array of later notes, save for a small number, are now lost. Hotho also used his own *Vorlesungsnachschriften* (lecture transcripts) of 1823 and 1826 (the latter of which has been lost); three other student transcripts of the 1826 lecture (of which two have been lost); and five transcripts of the 1828/29 lecture (of which four have been lost). Germans at the time distinguished between seminars, where students actively participated, and lectures, where students tried to write down more or less verbatim everything the professor said. Hotho manipulated these materials without having the benefit of today's standards for historical-critical editions. We now have several editions of Hegel's *Aesthetics* based on the transcripts of other students, and these should be used to supplement the larger edition, but they cannot replace its richness. Their main advantage is the supposition that they are truer to Hegel's ideas than the Hotho edition. For more on the issue of Hegel editions, see Roche, "Hegel's Theory of Comedy" 412-13.

3 Hegel's comments on *Wallenstein* seem to be not a sober description of the necessarily ugly nature of modern art, but a critique of Schiller's play. For a contrary view, see Gethmann-Siefert, *Einführung* 130-37.

4 Such a passage makes clear that Iannelli overstates the case when she writes that the Hotho edition offers no evidence of Hegel's interest in ugliness (*Das Siegel* 142).

5 After noting the ambiguity in Christ's death, Hegel suggests, not without some legitimacy, that the two moments in Christ's death, "beauty and hardship," represent the main tendencies of Italian and German painting, respectively (*Vorlesungen zur Ästhetik* 169). The latter leads to paintings that include "the unbeautiful" (*Vorlesungen zur Ästhetik* 169), presumably a middle ground between beauty and ugliness.

6 Hegel also provides us with a rich, proleptic critique of those who treat physical ugliness, for example, disability, as the defining feature of a human being. For more on this, see his essay "Who Thinks Abstractly?" (*Werke* 2:575-81) and my analysis in *Beautiful Ugliness* 79-81, which matches the spirit behind the collection edited by Rodrigues and Przybylo.

7 On Weiße's complex relationship to Hegel and the Hegelians, see Briese 65-77.

8 The *Leipziger Vorlesungsverzeichnisse* list Weiße teaching aesthetics seven times between 1825 and 1830. In addition, already in 1825 and 1826, he offers courses on Hegel's system, Hegel's *Encyclopaedia*, and post-Kantian systematic philosophy.

9 Despite his liberal inclinations, Ruge evidences anti-Semitic tendencies, describing Jews as ugly insofar as they are opposed to the truth of Christianity (95, 97, and 110). We see similar biases throughout these texts. Rosenkranz speaks of the ugliness of Blacks (Ger. 31-32; Eng. 45) and wants to see male and female virtues as absolutely distinct (Ger. 406); Schasler, likewise, sees beauty as involving different characteristics and virtues for men and women (*Ästhetik* 19-20); Hartmann elevates the white race (228) and views homosexual tendencies as ugly (238). As I noted above, my focus is neither a full exposition nor an ideology critique of these writers but simply an attempt to sift the few insights of apparent value. For a critical account of such biases as they surfaced more widely in the nineteenth century, see Gilman.

10 Medieval thinkers identified two types of non-sensuous, non-physical beauty. The first, spiritual beauty, was synonymous with moral beauty. The second, ideal beauty, a concept largely unique to medieval aesthetics, is imperceptible to the senses and was considered the purest and most perfect. See Tatarkiewicz 2:287.

11 In Bohtz's *Die Idee des Tragischen* (The Idea of the Tragic) of 1836, the concept of ugliness appears but plays a minor role. Though ugliness is evident in the darkness of the tragic moment (66, 95), it does not endure. In elevating tragedy as the dialectic of rupture and reconciliation, Bohtz is very close to Hegel. Not surprisingly, like Hegel, he praises Sophocles' *Oedipus at Colonus* (100-103). Bohtz further discusses the difficulty of depicting moral ugliness, noting that many artists portray the daemonic so abstractly, in a manner so removed from the human element, that their creations become "caricatures of ugliness" (163). Because they no longer appear real, they ultimately become harmless, ridiculous, laughable.

12 Benjamin was captivated by the ghostly and spectral nature of phantasmagoria. In his posthumously published collection of notes, *Das Passagen-Werk* (The Arcades Project), Benjamin explores themes that theorists of ugliness often associate with ugliness. These include not only discontinuity and inorganic montage but also phantasmagoria. Originally, phantasmagoria referred to popular magic lantern shows featuring optical effects and illusions. These Parisian exhibitions, which depicted ghosts of both heroes and villains from the tumultuous revolutionary years, utilized mirrors, smoke, projected voices, and music. Their popularity led the term phantasmagoria to evolve into a metaphor for "hallucinatory mental processes that were deluded yet possessed a reality of their own" (Margaret Cohen 207). For Benjamin, "the phantasmagorias of the interior" sustain modern individuals in their "illusions" (*Passagen-Werk* 52; *Arcades* 8-9). According to Benjamin, modernity is dominated by such phantasmagorias, such that disenchantment passes over into enchantment, but at the cost of rejecting any concept of objective reality and displacing it with distortion and wishful thinking (*Passagen-Werk* 77; *Arcades* 26). Bohtz and Rosenkranz would have called these phenomena ugly, but Benjamin is here oriented more toward the descriptive than the normative realm.

13 In describing the harmonic nature of beauty, Vischer writes: "Reality is saturated with the idea, and the idea lowers itself entirety into reality. The highest and harshest contradiction is resolved" (*Über das Erhabene* 67).

Chapter 6

1 Rosenkranz writes: "All education, whatever its specific content may be, must pass through this process of estrangement and its sublation" (§24, my translation).

2 Rosenkranz's study has appeared with Frommann (1968), the Wissenschaftliche Buchgesellschaft (1973, 1979, and 1989), Reclam (1990, 1996, 2007, and 2015), and Inktank (2018).

3 Pop and Widrich translate *das Gemeine* as "meanness," not "the base." Both their translation and mine capture an aspect of the original, which has connotations of both nastiness and commonness. I have chosen "the base" partly because the broader term seems more fitting for Rosenkranz's argument, partly because *das Gemeine* has a tradition of meaning "the base" or "the common" in earlier theories of ugliness, for example, in Schiller and Fischer. Pop and Widrich reserved "the base" for *das Niedrige*, which is also a reasonable choice.

4 It is telling of Rosenkranz's standing that a classic modern work on obscenity by the art historian Peter Gorsen, who had studied with Adorno, returns to Rosenkranz for initial bearings, even if Gorsen is critical of him (16-38).

5 Rose notes that Rosenkranz's elevation of caricature had a liberating effect on an age that preferred to view the form with suspicion. For this broader cultural and political context, see Townsend.

6 For an overview of this fascinating genre, which after Carrière was neglected until the mid-twentieth century, see Roche, *Tragedy and Comedy* 247-79.

Chapter 7

1 Recent research substantiates Darwin via the reverse claim: although the saying "familiarity breeds contempt" is partly true insofar as a closer look at an issue or person tends to reveal flaws, empirical research shows that familiarity also tends to lessen unease and contempt (Finkel, et al).

2 Although the philosopher G. E. Moore opposed idealism (after first having been immersed in it), he was familiar with Bosanquet and the other British idealists, so it is perhaps not by chance that of the tradition's major ethical philosophers, Moore mentions ugliness more than any other ethicist, even if his many comments in *Principia Ethica* (1903), primarily contrasting beauty and ugliness and linking ugliness with evil, do not result in an original theory of ugliness.

3 In one of the most important Indian contributions to the theory of ugliness, K. C. Bhattacharyya examines the concept of difficult beauty. In his 1930 essay "The Concept of Rasa," which loosely translates as aesthetic enjoyment or that which is aesthetically enjoyed, Bhattacharyya—a prominent twentieth-century Indian philosopher well-versed in both Indian and German thought (Lal, 223-24)—captures this concept without explicitly using the term. Most people cannot easily absorb artistic ugliness: "The ordinary spirit is not artistic enough to stand ugliness for any length of time, to maintain the joy of the aesthetic attitude... Yet there are spirits where joy is too deep to be killed by repulsive experience" (362). Bhattacharyya outlines two ways to transform "presented ugliness" into "a beauty rich and strange" (362). The first involves "the feeling of the ludicrous which is just the joy of detaching itself from or shaking off the repulsive experience" (362), often through distancing contemplation or the power of laughter. The second relies on a "patient faith" that what appears ugly can be transformed into something beautiful (362). Here Bhattacharyya emphasizes, much like Bosanquet, the role of aesthetic education in transforming ugliness into *rasa* or aesthetic enjoyment. The first mode of distancing via laughter and reflection is also central in the Western tradition: it is prominent already in Plato and Aristotle and is further developed by the Hegelians. The second strategy of patient faith is promising, but abstract, even if it justly elevates the need for attention and deliberation.

4 In an earlier essay, "The Aesthetic Theory of Ugliness," Bosanquet seems more comfortable with the idea that there can be ugly works (44-48), but in his later deliberations he leaves that idea behind.

Chapter 8

1 On this episode, see Cartwright 362-65. On Hegel's lecture style, see Haym 392-97, Pinkard 611-12, and *Hegel in Berichten* 282-83, 287-88, 377-78. Hegel voted in favor of Schopenhauer's appointment even while knowing that Schopenhauer wanted to schedule his lectures in conflict with Hegel's. Student enrollment at the University of Berlin was at the time only 1,100, which makes Hegel's numbers particularly impressive, even if some of Hegel's listeners were from beyond the university, including business people, officers, government officials, and members of the nobility (*Hegel in Berichten* 200, 282, 287, 364, 398).

Chapter 9

1 The idea that the ugly purports to be the beautiful surfaces already with Solger (*Vorlesungen* 101; *Erwin* 180 and 329) and is echoed, with some modulation, in Ruge and Fischer. We will see it again in Zimmermann. It is a variation of the widespread view that the ugly is not what it should be.

2 Kirchmann's interest in reception is also evident in the intellectual-historical contribution for which he remains best known: his founding in 1868 of the Philosophische Bibliothek, Germany's premier series of classic philosophical works, which still exists today and since 1921 has been overseen by Meiner Verlag.

3 Kirchmann also distinguishes between what he calls "a form-ugliness and an intellectual-ugliness," but he does so only briefly and vaguely (2:98). The former appears to represent ugliness directly (for example, the devil, who is evil), while the latter seems to be more symbolic (as in a skeleton that represents death).

4 Purpose can override symmetry, but in the case of cups, Hartmann seems unaware of the Jewish tradition of using a two-handled cup for ritual hand-washing. The two handles do serve a purpose: they ensure that the hand that is washed first during the ritual cleansing does not touch either the dirty handle or the still unwashed and impure other hand.

5 Both Neo-Kantians in my study, Cohn and Cohen, are, when it comes to aesthetics, not especially close to Kant, as Guyer notes in his essay "What Happened ...".

6 Théodore Géricault's remarkable portraits of the insane also seem to fit Cohen's model. Though the five surviving works, painted in Géricault's later years, are titled according to the maladies depicted, such as *A Woman Addicted to Gambling* (1822), the works themselves present the figures sensitively and with dignity, even if the dark colors and distant gazes are in some ways haunting.

7 Cohen recognizes a satirical (as opposed to humorous) moment in Holbein only in his *Totentanz*, a series of 40 woodcuts (2:377).

8 The complexity of Rosenkranz is evident when he uses the very word "Humor" to elevate Raimund as he concludes his analysis of caricature (428).

9 Cohen is not included even in the otherwise excellent annotated bibliography on ugliness with which Pop and Widrich conclude their anthology (275-99).

10 After presenting these four general types of ugliness, Volkelt makes still further distinctions, which, however, lack systematic interest or conceptual progress. They stress forms that are broken or at tension with themselves and content that is either idiosyncratic and insane or horrific and disgusting (2:586-87).

11 Even though ugliness disappears for a stretch from philosophical debates, it remains prominent on the borders of philosophical discussion, for example, in Max Nordau's *Entartung* (Degeneration) of 1892/1893, and even more so in literature and the arts. See Roche, *Beautiful Ugliness* 201-58.

Chapter 10

1 Unless otherwise indicated, all Adorno quotations stem from his *Ästhetische Theorie (Aesthetic Theory)*.

2 That Adorno's extreme position seems particular to *Western* modernity is evident when contrasted, for example, with dominant currents in modern African aesthetics, where completeness remains a privileged aesthetic principle (Van Damme 41).

3 And yet, Adorno's abstract claim is readily repeated, for example, by Leach, who writes: "What is ugly is situated squarely outside the zone of pleasure, entertainment, or profit" (273).

4 In seeking to create beautiful art, Laib is aware that he is working against the grain of contemporary (in his case German) practice. After an interviewer draws Laib's attention to the fact that he often uses the word "beautiful" to describe his works, Laib responds: "Artists hate that word, especially German artists. If you wanted to be really hated in Germany, then you would say, 'My work is beautiful.' German artists believe in ugliness and nastiness. I think beauty can be something extremely important in our lives. And it's not true that this is naive. This is what is the most needed: inner beauty and outer beauty, which is an incredible challenge for us" (Simonini).

5 As an example of Beissel's avoidance of dissonance, consider his "Mein Herz weiss," "Nun walle Ich im Frieden fort," or "Ich bin ein' Blum' im Rosenthal," which stays harmonic even when the content refers to thorns or the cross (Ephrata).

Chapter 11

1 The attempted insurrection at the U.S. Capitol on January 6, 2021 seems to reinforce Mbembe's argument, as the assault combined weapons of assault with the spreading of urine and feces and a sea of flags, banners, and symbols.

2 Although criticism of reality's ugliness is a dominant mode of social criticism, a complementary trend is evident among those who advance analogous claims via subversive beauty, presenting objects of stigmatization, be it seemingly ugly bodies or seemingly ugly acts, as beautiful (Hickey).

3 Ugliness has not affected the realm of craft in any extensive way, even if rare exceptions exist. For example, Bisa Butler, who makes colorful portrait quilts with fabric from Africa, created *Mannisch Boy* (2018), a beautiful example of emotional ugliness.

4 I have in mind here more unsightly versions of graffiti. Anyone who has been to Berlin knows that graffiti is also a mixed media art form that can be superbly executed. Like other arts, graffiti can be ugly, beautiful, or a complex combination of the two.

Chapter 12

1 It is an amusing footnote of history that although the impressionists have satisfied many generations of viewers seeking beauty, the formal innovations they initiated led contemporary critics, such as Louis Leroy, to call their works ugly.

2 The French philosopher Michel Ribon, who does not appear to be familiar with Goodman, nonetheless makes an analogous distinction: "the question of ugliness in its relation to art is twofold: that of the ugliness *in* the work and that of the ugliness *of* the work" (10). Although I elevate Goodman for his precision in making this distinction, it was first made by Aristotle and has been a recurring insight, as I underscore below.

3 Sibley, for example, takes it as a given that beauty and aesthetic excellence are interchangeable: "Anything with positive aesthetic value is called beautiful" (191).

4 In §213 of his *Encyclopedia Logic*, Hegel defines the Idea as "truth *in and for itself—the absolute unity of Concept and objectivity*" (*Werke* 8:367; *Encyclopedia Logic* 286).

5 Danto's definition of art as embodied meaning has similarities with Hegel's sensuous appearance of the idea, which likewise links meaning and embodiment. Hegel suggests: "The beautiful is the Idea as immediate unity of the Concept and its reality, yet the Idea only insofar as this its unity is immediately present in sensuous and real appearance" (*Werke* 13:157; *Aesthetics* 116, translation modified). Danto himself acknowledges the connection (*After* 194-95), noting that Hegel's *Aesthetics* "became a kind of treasury of philosophical wisdom for me" (*Abuse* 12). Yet in defining art, Danto takes his cue not, like Hegel, from a concept by which works are to be measured but instead from works that are called art and for which the philosopher must find a concept. As a result, Danto removes any reference to an ideal sphere. For Danto the initial impulse was the puzzle of differentiating between the original Brillo boxes and Andy Warhol's *Brillo Boxes (Philosophical Disenfranchisement* ix-x). It is not clear to me that Hegel would have viewed Warhol's creation as art, as the sensuous shining of the idea or of truth. The fact that it is today generally recognized as art is no argument against Hegel, who as an objective idealist would define art not from social practice but from its correspondence to a normative definition.

Our age has undeniably been moving away from normative categories, not just in art but across various spheres. The descriptive realm now dominates. A revealing anecdote illustrates this shift. When asked in December 2016 whether irresponsible tweets from Donald Trump were presidential (Trump had suggested that he would have won the popular vote if millions of illegal votes had not been counted), his advisor Kellyanne Conway responded: "He's the president-elect, so that's presidential behavior" (Gabriel). The meaning of "presidential" shifts from a normative category of what *should* be expected of such an office holder to a descriptive category of what *is,* to whatever the office holder happens to say or do. No longer measured against an ideal, Trump's actions become the norm, effectively erasing the distinction between the normative and descriptive. We are here far removed from Boethius, who still worked within a Platonic frame and insisted on the normative-descriptive divide, arguing: "We can scarcely consider men worthy of respect on account of the offices they hold, if we judge them unworthy of those offices!" (3.4). Here, as later with Hegel, the normative is the measure of the descriptive.

6 For a rich account of examples along these lines, see Eco, *On Ugliness* 185-201.

7 Tweet from Donald J. Trump (@realDonaldTrump) at 9:57 AM on June 19, 2018 and campaign speech of Donald Trump on December 16, 2023 in Durham, New Hampshire (quoted in Arnsdorf).

8 Despite the dominance of art, occasional commentary on nature has surfaced throughout this study, above all in the sections on Rocco, Dursch, Vischer, Rosenkranz, Darwin, Hartmann, and Illies.

9 I have argued elsewhere that Hegel's view of nature as an inferior subject for aesthetics is unconvincing (Roche, "Hegels Relevanz" 77-80).

10 See, for example, Jonas, *Imperative*; Hösle, *Die Philosophie der ökologischen Krise*; and Rolston. A rare focus on the aesthetics of nature arises in Hepburn, whose topic, the "neglect of natural beauty," proves the broader point.

11 Parsons, who assesses different approaches to nature aesthetics, dates the inauguration of analytic philosophy's engagement with nature aesthetics to 1993 (1).

12 See either "Ugliness and Nature" or "The Ugly Truth," which are essentially two versions of the same essay, with most of the material the same. Brady also addresses ugliness in "The Sublime, Terrible Beauty, and Ugliness," chapter 7 of *The Sublime in Modern Philosophy* (166-82), although she does not seem to be familiar with the extensive analyses of the sublime and the ugly in Weiße, Ruge, Bohtz, Vischer, and Fischer.

13 Environmental art that integrates ugliness makes an analogous effort in drawing our attention to human-induced environmental damage, as, for example, with Robert Rauschenberg's *Earth Day* (1990), Olafur Eliasson's *Ice Watch* (2014), or Judy Chicago's *Stranded* (2016).

Chapter 13

1 Objective idealism is the idea that theoretical knowledge is available to us through reason (not all knowledge comes from experience) and that this knowledge has ontological valence. Simply put, reason allows us to discern categories and structures that offer windows onto aspects of reality, including art. Plato and Hegel are its most famous representatives. Hegel's entire project was an attempt to ascertain the complex and interrelated set of categories that constitutes the ideal sphere and to analyze the various realms of reality—nature, history, politics, psychology, art, religion, and philosophy—by way of these descriptive and normative categories. Dialectical thinking, which is universal among objective idealists, lends itself very well to reflection on beautiful ugliness.

2 For a fuller analysis of Kantor's painting, see Roche, *Beautiful Ugliness*, 158-59.

3 "Ugly" would not be the first word that comes to mind when describing the remarkable butter sculptures—of cows, farmers, buildings, and so forth, which are visible at American state fairs. Here, as we saw above, folk art tends to shy away from ugliness.

4 The link between art and morals was dominant until the eighteenth century, whereas their separation is a modern and contemporary artifact. Engaging contemporary defenses of (various versions of) ethical criticism are available in Carroll, "Art and Ethical Criticism"; Gaut; and Eaton. My own argument is not that all great works are moral but that no truly great work is immoral. Although some artworks do not engage ethical issues, others have ethical issues at their core. Carroll draws the helpful analogy that simply because sharpness is not a legitimate criterion for evaluating some kinds

of knives, such as butter knives, it does not follow that sharpness should not be an essential criterion for the quality of other kinds of knives ("Art and Ethical Criticism," 357). Certainly, some earlier works that were once deemed great are in truth banal and boring, and the morality of some truly great artworks consists in subverting traditional moral norms, that is, calling into question or challenging moral conventions that are in fact immoral. My claim here, which is both countercultural and commonsensical, is that if we look at an artwork holistically, we are not free to ignore its moral value (or disvalue) and that this moral value (or disvalue) is also an aesthetic value (or disvalue).

Afterword

1 The idea reaches back to Aristotle, who writes that "men are good in but one way but bad in many" (1106b).

2 Ugly laws, often called unsightly beggar ordinances, were municipal laws partly designed to curb begging and vagrancy, which in effect mandated eviction of selected persons from public places. One such ordinance reads in part: "Any person who is diseased, maimed, mutilated, or in any way deformed, so as to be an unsightly or disgusting object, or an improper person to be allowed in or on the streets, highways, thoroughfares, or public places in this city, shall not therein or thereon expose himself to public view" (Schweik 1-2).

3 At least two of these positions are present to us both in recent history and today, not in art but in politics. Consider a political candidate initially perceived as laughable, an idiot, a buffoon—until the terrifying realization dawns that the candidate could have the power to fulfill his dictatorial ambitions. And think of conspiracy theories, instantiations of intellectual ugliness, that are not simply alternatives to reality; their proponents aggressively seek to overthrow the truth and replace it with lies.

Works Cited

Abelard, Peter. *Epitome Theologiae Christianae*. Ed. F. H. Rheinwald. Herbig, 1835.

Adorno, Theodor W. *Aesthetic Theory*. Trans. Robert Hullot-Kentor. U of Minnesota P, 1997.

Adorno, Theodor W. *Ästhetische Theorie*. Suhrkamp, 2003.

Adorno, Theodor W. *Mahler. Eine musikalische Physiognomik. Die musikalischen Monographien*. Suhrkamp, 1986: 149–317.

Adorno, Theodor W. *Mahler. A Musical Physiognomy*. Trans. Edmund Jephcott. U of Chicago P, 1992.

Adorno, Theodor W. *Negative Dialectics*. Trans. E. B. Ashton. Continuum, 1973.

Adorno, Theodor W. *Negative Dialektik*. Suhrkamp, 1982.

Adorno, Theodor W. *Noten zur Literatur*. Suhrkamp, 2003.

Adorno, Theodor W. *Notes to Literature*. Trans. Shierry Weber Nicholson. 2 vols. Columbia UP, 1991–92.

Adorno, Theodor W. "Schubert." *Musikalische Schriften IV*. Suhrkamp, 2003: 15–29.

Adorno, Theodor W. "Schubert." *Night Music. Essays on Music 1928–1962*. Ed. Rolf Tiedemann. Seagull, 2009: 19–46.

Adorno, Theodor W. "Zweimal Chaplin." *Kulturkritik und Gesellschaft I*. Suhrkamp, 2003: 362–6.

Alberti, Leon Battista. *On Painting and On Sculpture. The Latin Texts of De Pictura and De Statua*. Ed. Cecil Grayson. Phaidon, 1972.

Anderson, Mawell L. *The Quality Instinct: Seeing Art through a Museum Director's Eye*. American Alliance of Museums, 2012.

Aristotle. *The Basic Works of Aristotle*. Ed. Richard McKeon. Random, 1941.

Arnsdorf, Isaac. "Trump Quotes Putin Condemning American Democracy, Praises Autocrat Orban." *Washington Post*, December 16, 2023.

Aquinas, Thomas, Saint. *Commentary on Aristotle's Nichomachean Ethics*. Trans. C. I. Litzinger, O.P. Dumb Ox, 1993.

Aquinas, Thomas, Saint. *In librum beati Dionysii De divinis nominibus expositio*. Ed. Ceslai Pera. Marietti, 1950.

Aquinas, Thomas, Saint. *Summa Theologica*. Trans. Fathers of the English Dominican Province. 2nd ed. 5 vols. Christian Classics, 1981.

Aquinas, Thomas, Saint. *The Three Greatest Prayers: Commentaries on the Our Father, the Hail Mary, and the Apostles' Creed*. Trans. Laurence Shapcote. Newman P, 1956.

Augustine, Saint. *Opera Omnia. Corpus Augustinianum Gissense*. Ed. Dr. Cornelius Mayer. Schwabe, 1995.

Augustine, Saint. *The Works of Saint Augustine. A Translation for the 21st Century*. Ed. Boniface Ramsey. New City P, 1990-.

Bachmetjevas, Victoras. "The Ugly in Art." *Man and the Word* 9 (2007): 29–34.

Bai, Qianshen. *Fu Shan's World: The Transformation of Chinese Calligraphy in the Seventeenth Century*. Harvard UP, 2003.

Baker, Simon. "Jake Chapman on Georges Bataille: An Interview with Simon Baker." *Papers of Surrealism* 1 (Winter 2003): 1–17.

Bakhtin, Mikhail. *Rabelais and His World*. Trans. Hélène Iswolsky. Indiana UP, 1984.

Bataille, Georges. *Eroticism: Death and Sensuality*. Trans. Mary Dalwood. City Lights, 1986.

Bataille, Georges. *Œuvres complètes*. 12 vols. Gallimard, 1970–88.

Bataille, Georges. *The Trial of Gilles de Rais*. Trans. Richard Robinson. Amok, 1991.

Bataille, Georges. *Theory of Religion*. Trans. Robert Hurley. Zone, 1992

Bataille, Georges. *Visions of Excess. Selected Writings, 1927–1939*. Ed. Allan Stoekl. U of Minnesota P, 1985.

Baudelaire, Charles. *Art in Paris, 1845–1862. Salons and Other Exhibitions*. Trans. Jonathan Mayne. Phaidon, 1965.

Baudelaire, Charles. *Œuvres complètes*. 2 vols. Gallimard, 1975–1976.

Baudelaire, Charles. "Some Foreign Caricaturists." *Selected Writings on Art and Literature*. Trans. P. E. Charvet. Penguin, 1972: 232–43.

Baumgarten, Alexander Gottlieb. *Aesthetica*. 2 vols. Meiner, 2007.

Baumgarten, Alexander Gottlieb. *Metaphysica*. Hemmerde, 1739.

Bayley, Stephen. *Ugly: The Aesthetics of Everything*. Overlook, 2012.

Beardsley, Monroe C. *Aesthetics from Classical Greece to the Present: A Short History*. 1966. U of Alabama P, 1975.

Beiser, Frederick C. *After Hegel: German Philosophy, 1840–1900*. Princeton UP, 2014.

Ben-Levi, Jack, Craig Houser, Leslie C. Jones, and Simon Taylor. *Abject Art: Repulsion and Desire in American Art*. Whitney Museum of American Art, 1993.

Benjamin, Walter. *The Arcades Project*. Trans. Howard Eiland and Kevin McLaughlin. Harvard UP, 1999.

Benjamin, Walter. *Das Passagen-Werk*. Suhrkamp, 1982.

Benn, Gottfried. *Morgue und andere Gedichte*. Bücherwinkel, 1923.

Bernard of Clairvaux. *Justification to Abbot William*. In Conrad Rudolph, *The "Things of Greater Importance": Bernard of Clairvaux's Apologia and the Medieval Attitude Toward Art*. U of Pennsylvania P, 1990: 232–87.

Bernstein, J. M. "'The Dead Speaking of Stones and Stars': Adorno's Aesthetic Theory." *The Cambridge Companion to Critical Theory*. Ed. Fred Rush. Cambridge UP, 2004: 139–64.

Beuys, Joseph. *In Memoriam Joseph Beuys. Obituaries, Essays, Speeches*. Trans. Timothy Nevill. Inter Nationes, 1986.

Beuys, Joseph, Heiner Bastian, and Jeanot Simmen. "If Nothing Says Anything, I Don't Draw." *Zeichnungen, Tekeningen, Drawings*. Prestel, 1979.

Beuys, Joseph, Caroline Tisdall, and Dieter Koepplin. *Joseph Beuys: The Secret Block for a Secret Person in Ireland*. Kunstmuseum Basel, 1977.

Bhattacharyya, Krishnachandra. "The Concept of Rasa." *Studies in Philosophy*. Ed. Gopinath Bhattacharyya. Motilal Banarsidass, 1983: 345–63.

Blake, Peter. *God's Own Junkyard: The Planned Deterioration of America's Landscape*. Holt, 1964.

Boethius. *The Consolation of Philosophy*. Trans. Victor Watts. Penguin, 1999.

Bogdan, Robert. *Freak Show: Presenting Human Oddities for Amusement and Profit*. U of Chicago P, 1988.

Bohtz, August Wilhelm. *Die Idee des Tragischen. Eine philosophische Abhandlung*. Kübler, 1836.

Bohtz, August Wilhelm. *Ueber das Komische und die Komödie. Ein Beitrag zur Philosophie des Schönen*. Vandenhoeck, 1844.

Boileau-Despréaux, Nicolas. *Oeuvres poétiques de Boileau Despréaux*. 2 vols. Delarue, 1876.

Bolzano, Bernard. "*Über den Begriff des Schönen. Eine philosophische Abhandlung*." 1843. In *Gesamtausgabe*. Ed. Eduard Winter et al. 132 vols. Frommann-Holzboog, 1969-: 1:18: 87–217.

Bolzano, Bernard. "On the Concept of the Beautiful: A Philosophical Essay" [includes §1-25 only]. Trans. Adam Bresnahan. *Estetika: The Central European Journal of Aesthetics* 52.2 (2015): 229–66.

Bonaventure. *Commentary on the First Book of Sentences of Master Peter Lombard*. Franciscan Archive, 2007.

Bonaventure. *On the Reduction of the Arts to Theology*. Trans. Zachary Hayes. Franciscan Institute, 1996.

Bosanquet, Bernard. "The Aesthetic Theory of Ugliness." *Proceedings of the Aristotelian Society* 1.3 (1889–1890): 32–48.

Bosanquet, Bernard. *A History of Aesthetic*. Macmillan, 1892.

Bosanquet, Bernard. *Three Lectures on Aesthetic*. Macmillan, 1915.

Boylan, Alexis L., ed. *Thomas Kinkade: The Artist in the Mall*. Duke UP, 2011.

Brady, Emily. *Aesthetics of the Natural Environment*. Edinburgh UP, 2003

Brady, Emily. *The Sublime in Modern Philosophy: Aesthetics, Ethics, and Nature*. Cambridge UP, 2013.

Brady, Emily. "Ugliness and Nature." *Enrahonar* 45 (2010): 27–40.

Brady, Emily. "The Ugly Truth: Negative Aesthetics and Environment." *Philosophy and Environment*. Ed. A. O'Hear. Royal Institute of Philosophy Supplements 69. Cambridge UP, 2011: 83–100.

Brecht, Bertolt. *Ausgewählte Werke in sechs Bänden*. Suhrkamp, 2005.

Brecht, Bertolt. "To Those Born Later." *Poems 1913–1956*. Eds. John Willett and Ralph Manheim. Methuen, 1976: 318–20.

Brentano, Franz Clemens. *Das Schlechte als Gegenstand dichterischer Darstellung*. Duncker, 1892.

Briese, Olaf. *Konkurrenzen. Philosophische Kultur in Deutschland 1830–1850: Porträts und Profile*. Königshausen, 1998.

Bristol, Katharine. "The Pruitt–Igoe Myth." *Journal of Architectural Education* 44.3 (1991): 163–71.

Brown, Frederick. *For the Soul of France: Culture Wars in the Age of Dreyfus*. Knopf, 2010.

Büchner, Georg. *Complete Works and Letters*. Trans. Henry J. Schmidt. Continuum, 1986.

Büchner, Georg. *Sämtliche Werke*. Ed. Henri Poschmann. 2 vols. Deutscher Klassiker Verlag, 1992.
Buckman, Christopher. "A Kantian Analytic of the Ugly." *International Philosophical Quarterly* 57.4 (2017): 365–80.
Buckman, Christopher. "Political Ramifications of Formal Ugliness in Kant's Aesthetics." *Idealistic Studies* 48.3 (2018): 195–209.
Bürger, Peter. *Theory of the Avant-Garde*. Trans. Michael Shaw. U of Minnesota P, 1984.
Burke, Edmund. *A Philosophical Enquiry into the Origin of Our Ideas of the Sublime and Beautiful*. Ed. Adam Phillips. Oxford UP, 1990.
Burnet, Thomas. *The Theory of the Earth Containing an Account of the Original of the Earth, and of All the General Changes Which it Hath Already Undergone, or Is to Undergo, till the Consummation of All Things*. 2 vols. Norton, 1684.
Carlson, Allen. "Nature and Positive Aesthetics." *Environmental Ethics* 6.1 (1984): 5–34.
Carlson, Allen and Sheila Lintott, ed. *Nature, Aesthetics, and Environmentalism: From Beauty to Duty*. Columbia UP, 2008.
Carmichael, Peter A. "The Sense of Ugliness." *The Journal of Aesthetics and Art Criticism* 30.4 (1972): 495–8.
Carrière, Moriz. *Aesthetik: Die Idee des Schönen und ihre Verwirklichung im Leben und in der Kunst*. 3rd ed. 2 vols. Brockhaus, 1885.
Carrière, Moriz. *Das Wesen und die Formen der Poesie: Ein Beitrag zur Philosophie des Schönen und der Kunst. Mit literarhistorischen Erläuterungen*. Brockhaus, 1854.
Carroll, Noël. "Art and Ethical Criticism: An Overview of Recent Directions of Research." *Ethics* 110 (2000): 350–87.
Carroll, Noël. "Ethnicity, Race, and Monstrosity: The Rhetorics of Horror and Humor." *Beauty Matters*. Ed. Peggy Zeglin Brand. Indiana UP, 2000: 37–56.
Carroll, Noël. "Horror and Humor." *The Journal of Aesthetics and Art Criticism* 57 (1999): 145–60.
Carroll, Noël. *The Philosophy of Horror or Paradoxes of the Heart*. Routledge, 1990.
Cartwright, David E. *Schopenhauer: A Biography*. Cambridge UP, 2010.
Castelvetro, Lodovico. "From Commentary on Aristotle's Poetics. 1570." *Theories of Comedy*. Ed. Paul Lauter. Anchor, 1964: 87–97.
Chakrabarti, Arindam. "Refining the Repulsive: Toward an Indian Aesthetic of the Ugly and the Disgusting." *Indian Aesthetics and the Philosophy of Art*. Ed. Arindam Chakrabarti. Bloomsbury, 2016: 149–65.
Christian, Lynda Gregorian. "The Figure of Socrates in Erasmus' Works." *The Sixteenth Century Journal* 3.2 (1972): 1–10.
Clewis, Robert R. *The Origins of Kant's Aesthetics*. Cambridge UP, 2023.
Cohen, Hermann. *Ästhetik des reinen Gefühls*. Cassirer, 1912.
Cohen, Margaret. "Benjamin's Phantasmagoria: The Arcades Project." *The Cambridge Companion to Walter Benjamin*. Ed. David S. Ferris. Cambridge UP, 2004: 99–220.
Cohn, Jonas. *Allgemeine Ästhetik*. Engelmann, 1901.
Collingwood, R. G. *The Philosophy of Enchantment: Studies in Folktale, Cultural Criticism, and Anthropology*. Ed. David Boucher et al. Clarendon, 2005.
Comaroff, Joshua and Ong Ker-Shing. *Horror in Architecture*. ORO, 2013.
Cooper, David E., ed. *Aesthetics: The Classic Readings*. Blackwell, 1997.

Cornejo, Manuel Pérez. "La Aesthetik de K. F. E. Trahndorff: Ideas para la fundamentación de un romanticismo cristiano." *Estudio Agustiniano* 36.1 (2001): 91–126.
Cousins, Mark. "The Ugly." *AA Files* 28 (Autumn 1994): 61–4; 29 (Summer 1995): 3–6; 30 (Autumn 1995): 65–8.
Croce, Benedetto. *Aesthetic as Science of Expression and General Linguistic*. Trans. Douglas Ainslie. Farrar, 1966.
Csuri, Charles. *Charles A. Csuri Project*. http://csuriproject.osu.edu/.
Dante. *The Inferno*. Trans. Robert Hollander and Jean Hollander. Anchor, 2002.
Danto, Arthur C. *The Abuse of Beauty: Aesthetics and the Concept of Art*. Open Court, 2003.
Danto, Arthur C. *After the End of Art: Contemporary Art and the Pale of History*. Princeton UP, 1997.
Danto, Arthur C. *The Philosophical Disenfranchisement of Art*. Columbia UP, 1986.
Danto, Arthur C. *What Art Is*. Yale UP, 2013.
Darwin, Charles. *The Descent of Man, and Selection in Relation to Sex*. Princeton UP, 1981.
Darwin, Charles. *The Expression of the Emotions in Man and Animals*. Penguin, 2009.
Daston, Lorraine, and Katharine Park. *Wonders and the Order of Nature: 1150–1750*. Zone, 2001.
de Botton, Alain. *The Architecture of Happiness*. Pantheon, 2006.
Denham, A. E., ed. *Plato on Art and Beauty*. Palgrave, 2012.
Derrida, Jacques. "Economimesis." *Diacrticis* 11.2 (1981): 2–25.
Derrida, Jacques. "Economimesis." *Mimesis des articulations*. Eds. Sylviane Agacinski, Jacques Derrida et al. Flammarion, 1975: 55–93.
Desmond, William. *Art and the Absolute: A Study's of Hegel's Aesthetics*. SUNY, 1986.
Dessoir, Max. *Aesthetics and Theory of Art*. Trans. Steven A Emery. Wayne State UP, 1970.
Dessoir, Max. *Ästhetik und allgemeine Kunstwissenschaft*. 2nd ed. Enke, 1923.
Dewey, John. *Art as Experience*. Penguin, 1980.
Dewey, John. "From Absolutism to Experimentalism." *The Later Works*. Ed. Jo Ann Boydston. Southern Illinois UP, 1984: 5: 147–60.
"Dissoi Logoi." *Contrasting Arguments: An Edition of the Dissoi Logoi*. Ed. and Trans. T. M. Robinson. Arno, 1979.
"Dissoi Logoi." *Early Greek Political Thought from Homer to the Sophists*. Ed. and Trans. Michael Gagarin and Paul Woodruff. Cambridge UP, 1995: 296–308.
"Dissoi Logoi." *The Greek Sophists*. Trans. John Dillon and Tania Gergel. Penguin, 2003: 318–33.
"Dissoi Logoi." *The Texts of Early Greek Philosophy. The Complete Fragments and Selected Testimonials of the Major Presocratics*. Ed. and Trans. Daniel W. Graham. 2 vols. Cambridge UP, 2010: 2: 877–904.
"Dissoi Logoi or Dialexis." Trans. Rosamond Kent Sprague. *Mind* New Series 77.306 (1968): 155–67.
Dodds, E. R. *The Greeks and the Irrational*. Beacon, 1957.
Doran, Ryan P. "Ugliness Is in the Gut of the Beholder." *Ergo* 9.5 (2022): 88–146.
Douglas, Mary. *Purity and Danger*. Routledge, 1966.

Draeseke, Felix. "Der Wechsel im Musikalisch-Schönen." *Signale* 41 (29 May 1907): 689–95.

Durbach, Nadja. *Spectacle of Deformity: Freak Shows and Modern British Culture*. U of California P, 2010.

Dursch, Johann Georg Martin. *Aesthetik oder die Wissenschaft des Schönen auf dem christlichen Standpunkt*. Cotta, 1839.

Eaton, Marcia Muelder. *Merit, Aesthetic and Ethical*. Oxford UP, 2001.

Eckardt, Julius W. von, ed. *K. F. E. Trahndorff: der Bewusstseinsphilosoph. Ein Beitrag zur Würdigung und Hochschätzung eines verklungenen Namens*. Fricke, 1878.

Eco, Umberto. *Art and Beauty in the Middle Ages*. Trans. Hugh Bredin. Yale UP, 1986.

Eco, Umberto, ed. *On Ugliness*. Rizzoli, 2007.

Eisenman, Peter. "The Blue Line Text." *Architectural Design* 58.7 (1988): 5–10.

Engelmann, Ines Janet. *Hässlich?! Eine Diskussion über bildende Kunst und Literatur vom Anfang des 19. bis zum Beginn des 20. Jahrhunderts*. VDG, 2003.

Ephrata Cloister Chorus. *The Songs of the Turtle Dove. A Celebration of America's Musical Heritage*. Ephrata Cloister Associates, 2011. CD.

Eveleth, Rose. "Zoo Illogical: Ugly Animals Need Protection from Extinction, Too." *Scientific American*, December 8, 2010.

Fangyu, Wang and Richard M. Barnhart. *Master of the Lotus Garden: The Life and Art of Bada Shanren (1626–1705)*. Yale UP, 1990.

Feuerbach, Ludwig. *Das Wesen des Christentums*. Reclam, 1969.

Finkel, Eli J., Norton, M. I., Reis, H. T., Ariely, D., Caprariello, P. A., Eastwick, P. W., Frost, J. H., and Maniaci, M. R. "When Does Familiarity Promote Versus Undermine Interpersonal Attraction? A Proposed Integrative Model From Erstwhile Adversaries." *Perspectives on Psychological Science* 10.1 (2015): 3–19.

Fischer, Kuno. *Diotima: Die Idee des Schönen*. Flammer, 1849.

Foley, Mary Mix. "The Debacle of Popular Taste." *Architectural Forum* 106.2 (February 1957): 141–5, 238, 240, 242, 246, 248.

Freud, Sigmund. *Drei Abhandlungen zur Sexualtheorie*. Fischer, 2007.

Fumagalli, Manuela and Alberto Priori. "Functional and Clinical Neuroanatomy of Morality." *Brain* 135 (2012): 2006–21

Funk, Holger. *Ästhetik des Häßlichen: Beiträge zum Verständnis negativer Ausdrucksformen im 19. Jahrhundert*. Agora, 1983.

Gabriel, Trip. "Trump and Clinton Aides Clash During Election Forum." *The New York Times*, December 1, 2016.

Gagnebin, Murielle. *Fascination de la Laideur: L'en-deçà Psychanalytique du Laid*. 2nd ed. Champ Vallon, 1994.

Garvin, Lucius. "The Problem of Ugliness in Art." *The Philosophical Review* 57.4 (1948): 404–9.

Gaut, Berys. "Art and Ethics." *The Routledge Companion to Ethics*. Ed. Berys Gaut and Dominic McIver Lopes. Routledge, 2001: 341–73.

Gaw, Albert C. "Belief at the Level of the Brain." *The Journal of Nervous and Mental Disease* 207.7 (2019): 604–10.

Gethmann-Siefert, Annemarie. *Einführung in Hegels Ästhetik*. Fink, 2005.

Gethmann-Siefert, Annemarie. "Hegel über das Häßliche in der Kunst." *Hegel-Jahrbuch* 2000: 21–41.

Gigante, Denise. "Facing the Ugly: The Case of Frankenstein." *ELH* 67 (2000): 565–87.

Gilbert, Katharine Everett and Helmut Kuhn. *A History of Esthetics*. Macmillan, 1939.

Gilman, Sander. *Picturing Health and Illness: Images of Identity and Difference*. Johns Hopkins UP, 1995.

Gingeras, Alison M. and Thomas Hirschhorn, "Interview." *Thomas Hirschhorn*. Phaidon, 2004: 8–39.

Giovannelli, Alessandro, ed. *Aesthetics: The Key Thinkers*. Bloomsbury, 2021.

Gladkova, Anna and Jesús Romero-Trillo. "Is Ugliness in the Mind of the Beholder? The Conceptualization of 'Ugly' in English." *International Journal of Language and Culture* 8.1 (2021): 106–27.

Glockner, Hermann. "Kuno Fischer und Karl Rosenkranz." *Archiv für Geschichte der Philosophie* 40 (1931): 106–16.

Goethe, Johann Wolfgang von. "Von deutscher Baukunst." *Werke. Hamburger Ausgabe*. Ed. Erich Trunz. Beck, 1981: 12:7–15.

Goethe, Johann Wolfgang von. *Goethe's Faust*. Trans. Walter Kaufmann. Doubleday, 1961.

Goldin, Paul Rakita. *The Worlds of Classical Chinese Aesthetics*. Routledge, 2024.

Good, James A. "John Dewey's 'Permanent Hegelian Deposit' and the Exigencies of War." *Journal of the History of Philosophy* 44.2 (2006): 293–313.

Goodman, Nelson. *Languages of Art: An Approach to a Theory of Symbols*. 2nd ed. Hackett, 1976.

Goodman, Nelson. *Ways of Worldmaking*. Hackett, 1978.

Gorsen, Peter. *Das Prinzip Obszön. Kunst, Pornographie und Gesellschaft*. Rowohlt, 1969.

Grabmann, Martin. "Studien über Ulrich von Straßburg. Bilder wissenschaftlichen Lebens und Strebens aus der Schule Alberts des Großen." *Zeitschrift für katholische Theologie* 29.3 (1905): 82–107, 315–30, 482–99, and 607–30.

Grabmann, Martin, ed. *Des Ulrich Engelberti von Strassburg O. Pr. Abhandlung De pulchro. Untersuchung und Texte*. Verlag der Bayerischen Akademie der Wissenschaften, 1926.

Guyer, Paul. *A History of Modern Aesthetics*. 3 vols. Cambridge UP, 2014.

Guyer, Paul. "What Happened to Kant in Neo-Kantian Aesthetics? Cohen, Cohn, and Dilthey." *The Philosophical Forum* 39.2 (2008): 143–76.

Halliwell, Stephen. *Between Ecstasy and Truth: Interpretations of Greek Poetics from Homer to Longinus*. Oxford UP, 2012.

Halliwell, Stephen. *Greek Laughter: A Study of Cultural Psychology from Homer to Early Christianity*. Cambridge UP, 2008.

Hamermesh, Daniel S. and Jeff E. Biddle. "Beauty and the Labor Market." *The American Economic Review* 84.5 (1994): 1174–94.

Hammermeister, Kai. *The German Aesthetic Tradition*. Cambridge UP, 2002.

Hartmann, Eduard von. *Aesthetik. Erster historisch-kritischer Theil. Die deutsche Aesthetik seit Kant*. Friedrich, 1886.

Hartmann, Eduard von. *Aesthetik. Zweiter systematischer Theil. Philosophie des Schönen*. Duncker, 1887.

Hartmann, Nicolai. *Ästhetik*. de Gruyter, 1953.

Hay, William. *Deformity: An Essay*. Ed. Kathleen James-Cavan. English Literary Studies, 2004.

Haym, Rudolf. *Hegel und seine Zeit: Vorlesungen über Entstehung und Entwickelung, Wesen und Werth der Hegel'schen Philosophie*. Gaertner, 1857.

Hegel, G. W. F. *Aesthetics: Lectures on Fine Arts*. Trans. T. M. Knox. Clarendon, 1975.

Hegel, G. W. F. *The Encyclopaedia Logic: Part I of the Encyclopaedia of the Philosophical Sciences with the Zusätze*. Translated by T. F. Geraets et al. Hackett, 1991.

Hegel, G. W. F. *Hegel's Science of Logic*. Trans. A. V. Miller. Allen and Unwin, 1969.

Hegel, G. W. F. *Heidelberger Vorlesungen über die Ästhetik*. Transcribed by Friedrich Wilhelm Carové in Summer Semester 1818 and as yet unpublished. Archiv und Bibliothek des Erzbistums München und Freising.

Hegel, G. W. F. *Lectures on the Philosophy of Art: the Hotho Transcript of the 1823 Berlin Lectures*. Trans. Robert F. Brown. Oxford UP, 2014.

Hegel, G. W. F. *Philosophie der Kunst. Vorlesung von 1826*. Ed. Annemarie Gethmann-Siefert et al. Suhrkamp, 2005.

Hegel, G. W. F. *Vorlesungen über die Philosophie der Kunst. Berlin 1823*. Nachgeschrieben von Heinrich Gustav Hotho. Ed. Annemarie Gethmann-Siefert. Meiner, 1998.

Hegel, G. W. F. *Vorlesungen zur Ästhetik. Vorlesungsmitschrift Adolf Heimann (1828/1829)*. Eds. Alain Patrick Olivier and Annemarie Gethmann-Siefert. Fink, 2017.

Hegel, G. W. F. *Werke in zwanzig Bänden*. Eds. Eva Moldenhauer and Karl Markus Michel. Suhrkamp, 1978.

Hegel in Berichten seiner Zeitgenossen. Ed. Günther Nicolin. Meiner, 1970.

Heine, Heinrich. *Poetry and Prose*. Ed. Robert C. Holub. Continuum, 1982.

Heine, Heinrich. *Sämtliche Schriften*. Eds. Klaus Briegleb et al. 6 vols. Hanser, 1968–1976.

Henderson, Gretchen E. *Ugliness: A Cultural History*. Reaktion, 2015.

Henderson, G. P. "The Concept of Ugliness." *British Journal of Aesthetics* 6 (1966): 219–29.

Hepburn, R. W. "Contemporary Aesthetics and the Neglect of Natural Beauty." *British Analytical Philosophy*. Eds. Bernard Williams and Alan Montefiore. Humanities, 1966: 285–310.

Heraclitus. *Fragments*. Ed. T. M. Robinson. U of Toronto P, 1987.

Herder, Johann Gottfried. *Kalligone: Vom Angenehmen und Schönen*. 3 vols. Hartknoch, 1800.

Herder, Johann Gottfried. *Sculpture: Some Observations on Shape and Form from Pygmalion's Creative Dream*. Trans. Jason Gaiger. U of Chicago P, 2002.

Herder, Johann Gottfried. *Selected Writings on Aesthetics*. Trans. Gregory Moore. Princeton UP, 2006.

Herder, Johann Gottfried. *Werke in zehn Bänden*. Eds. Martin Bollacher et al. Deutscher Klassiker Verlag, 1985–2000.

Herf, Jeffrey. *The Jewish Enemy. Nazi Propaganda during World War II and the Holocaust*. Harvard UP, 2006.

Herndon, Astead W. "Columbia Point Gives Way to Upscale Harbor Point." *The Boston Globe*, July 13, 2015.

Heydenreich, Carl Heinrich. "Ideen über Schönheit und Häßlichkeit." *Originalideen über die interessantesten Gegenstände der Philosophie: nebst einem kritischen Anzeiger der wichtigsten philosophischen Schriften*. Baumgärtner, 1793–1796: 3:211–31.

Hickey, Dave. *The Invisible Dragon: Four Essays on Beauty*. 1993. U of Chicago P, 2009.
Hogarth, William. *The Analysis of Beauty*. Yale UP, 1997.
Hohendahl, Peter Uwe. *The Fleeting Promise of Art: Adorno's Aesthetic Theory Revisited*. Cornell UP, 2013.
Hölderlin, Friedrich. *Sämtliche Werke und Briefe in drei Bänden*. Ed. Jochen Schmidt. Deutscher Klassiker Verlag, 1992–94.
Horace, *Ars Poetica. Classical Literary Criticism*. Trans. T. S. Dorsch. Penguin, 1965: 79–95.
Horkheimer, Max and Theodor W. Adorno. *Dialectic of Enlightenment*. Trans. John Cumming. Continuum, 1987.
Hösle, Vittorio. *Die Philosophie der ökologischen Krise*. Beck, 1991.
Hösle, Vittorio. *Wahrheit und Geschichte. Studien zur Struktur der Philosophiegeschichte unter paradigmatischer Analyse der Entwicklung von Parmenides bis Platon*. Frommannn-Holzboog, 1984.
Hösle, Vittorio. *Zur Geschichte der Ästhetik und Poetik*. Schwabe, 2013.
Hseel, Christopher K. and Bowen Ruan. "The Pandora Effect: The Power and Peril of Curiosity." *Psychological Science* 27.5 (2016): 659–66.
Hughes, Robert. *Lucian Freud*. Thames, 1987.
Hugo, Victor. *Préface de Cromwell*. Larousse, 2004.
Hugo, Victor. "Preface to Cromwell." *Prefaces and Prologues to Famous Books*. Collier, 1910.
Hume, David. *An Enquiry Concerning the Principels of Morals*. 1748. *Enquiries Concerning Human Understanding and Concerning the Principles of Morals*. Ed. P. H. Nidditch. Clarendon, 1975.
Hume, David. "Of Tragedy." *Selected Essays*. Oxford, 1993: 126–33.
Hume, David. *A Treatise of Human Nature*. Ed. David Fate Norton and Mary J. Norton. Oxford UP, 2000.
Hutcheson, Francis. *An Inquiry Into the Original of Our Ideas of Beauty and Virtue in Two Treatises. Volume I. Concerning Beauty, Order, Harmony, Design*. 3rd ed. Knapton, 1729.
Hyde, Timothy. *Ugliness and Judgment: On Architecture in the Public Eye*. Princeton UP, 2019.
Hyland, Drew A. *Plato and the Question of Beauty*. Indiana UP, 2008.
Iannelli, Francesca. "Das Hässliche: ein Lapsus oder das Ferment der Differenzierung? Zu F.Th. Vischers Diskussion mit H.G. Hotho." *Zwischen Philosophie und Kunstgeschichte: Beiträge zur Begründung der Kunstgeschichtsforschung bei Hegel und im Hegelianismus*. Eds. Annemarie Gethmann-Siefert and Bernadette Collenberg-Plotnikov. Fink, 2008: 205–28.
Iannelli, Francesca. *Das Siegel der Moderne: Hegels Bestimmung des Hässlichen in den Vorlesungen zur Ästhetik und die Rezeption bei den Hegelianern*. Fink, 2007.
Iannelli, Francesca. "Hegel und die Hegelianer über das Häßliche: Eine kontroverse Rezeption." *Kulturpolitik und Kunstgeschichte: Perspektiven der Hegelschen Ästhetik*. Eds. Ursula Franke and Annemarie Gethmann-Siefert. Meiner, 2005: 195–214.
Illies, Christian. "Das hässliche Gärtlein? Über die Beharrlichkeit des Schönen in der Gartenkunst." *uni.vers Forschung: das Universitätsmagazin der Universität Bamberg* 2012: 20–3.

Jacobs, Jane. *The Death and Life of Great American Cities*. Random, 1961.
Jacobsen, Thomas and Lea Höfel. "Descriptive and Evaluative Judgment Processes: Behavioral and Electrophysiological Indices of Processing Symmetry and Aesthetics." *Cognitive, Affective, & Behavioral Neuroscience* 3.4 (2023): 289–99.
Janaway, Christopher. *Images of Excellence Plato's Critique of the Arts*. Clarendon, 1995.
Jaspers, Karl. *Vom Ursprung und Ziel der Geschichte*. Fischer, 1955.
Jauß, Hans Robert. *Ästhetische Erfahrung und literarische Hermeneutik*. Fink, 1977.
Jauß, Hans Robert. *Aesthetic Experience and Literary Hermeneutics*. Trans. Michael Shaw. U of Minnesota P, 1982.
Jauß, Hans Robert, ed. *Die nicht mehr schönen Künste: Grenzphänomene des Ästhetischen*. Fink, 1968.
Jonas, Hans. "The Concept of God after Auschwitz: A Jewish Voice." *The Journal of Religion* 67.1 (1987): 1–13.
Jonas, Hans. *The Imperative of Responsibility. In Search of an Ethics for the Technological Age*. Trans. Hans Jonas with the collaboration of David Herr. U of Chicago P, 1984.
Jonas, Hans. *Das Prinzip Verantwortung. Versuch einer Ethik für die technologische Zivilisation*. Insel, 1979.
Jones, Sam. "Eye-tracking Glasses Show Viewers of Bosch Triptych are Drawn to Hell." *The Guardian*, June 20, 2023.
Juvenal. *The Satires*. Ed. John Ferguson. Bristol Classical P, 1999.
Jung, Werner. *Schöner Schein der Häßlichkeit oder Häßlichkeit des schönen Scheins. Ästhetik und Geschichtsphilosophie im 19. Jahrhundert*. Athenäum, 1987.
Kainz, Friedrich. *Vorlesungen über Ästhetik. Aesthetics the Science*. Trans. Herbert M. Schueller. Wayne State UP, 1962.
Kammen, Michael. *Visual Shock: A History of Art Controversies in American Culture*. Vintage, 2006.
Kant, Immanuel. *Critique of Judgement*. Trans. James Creed Meredith. Oxford UP, 2007.
Kant, Immanuel. *Werkausgabe*. Ed. Wilhelm Weischedel. 12 vols. Suhrkamp, 1968.
Kayser, Wolfgang. *Das Groteske: Seine Gestaltung in Malerei und Dichtung*. Stalling, 1957.
Keen, Sam. *Faces of the Enemy: Reflections of the Hostile Imagination*. Harper, 1986.
Kieran, Matthew. "Beauty, Ugliness and Coherence." *Philosophy* 72 (1997): 383–99.
Kirchmann, Julius Hermann von. *Aesthetik auf realistischer Grundlage*. 2 vols. Springer, 1868.
Kleine, Sabine. *Zur Ästhetik des Häßlichen: Von Sade bis Pasolini*. Metzler, 1998.
Klemme, Heiner F. et al., ed. *Im Schatten des Schönen: Die Ästhetik des Häßlichen in historisichen Ansätzen und aktuellen Debatten*. Aisthesis, 2006.
Klicke, Dieter. "Häßlich." *Ästhetische Grundbegriffe. Historisches Wörterbuch in sieben Bänden*. Eds. Karlheinz Barck et al. Metzler, 2000: 3.25–66.
Koerner, Joseph Leo. "The Abject of Art History." *Res* 31 (Spring 1997): 5–8.
Konstan, David. *Beauty: The Fortunes of an Ancient Greek Idea*. Oxford UP, 2014.
Kovach, Francis J. *The Philosophy of Beauty*. U of Oklahoma P, 1974.
Krečič, Jela and Slavoj Žižek. "Ugly, Creepy, Disgusting, and Other Modes of Abjection." *Critical Inquiry* 43 (2016): 60–83.
Krestovsky, Lydie. *La Laideur dans l'Art. A Travers les Ages*. Seuil, 1947.

Krestovsky, Lydie. *Le problème spirituel de la beauté et de la laideur*. Presses Universitaires de France, 1948.

Kristeller, Paul Oskar. "The Modern System of the Arts: A Study in the History of Aesthetics, Parts I and II." *Journal of the History of Ideas* 12.4 (1951): 496–527 and 13.1 (1952): 17–46.

Kristeva, Julia. *Pouvoirs de l'horreur. Essai sur l'abjection*. Editions du Seuil, 1980.

Kristeva, Julia. *Powers of Horror: An Essay on Abjection*. Columbia UP, 1982.

Küplen, Mojca. *Beauty, Ugliness and the Free Play of Imagination: An Approach to Kant's Aesthetics*. Springer, 2015.

Kuoni, Carin, ed. *Joseph Beuys in America. Writings by and Interviews with the Artist*. Four Walls Eight Windows, 1993.

Lal, Basant Kumar. *Contemporary Indian Philosophy*. 2nd ed. Motilal Banarsidass, 1978.

Larkin, Dan. "Shock and Aw(e)ful: The Ugly Truth of Ugliness in Kant's Aesthetics." *Natur und Freiheit: Akten des XII. Internationalen Kant-Kongresses*. Eds. Violetta L. Waibel, Margit Ruffing, and David Wagner. De Gruyter, 2019: 4: 3055–62.

Lavater, Johann Caspar. *Essays on Physiognomy. For the Promotion of the Knowledge and the Love of Mankind*. 3 vols. Trans. Thomas Holcraft. Robinson, 1789.

Lavater, Johann Caspar. *Physiognomische Fragmente, zur Beförderung der Menschenkenntniß und Menschenliebe*. 4 vols. Weidmann, 1775–78.

Leach, Pamela. "On Adorno's Aesthetics of the Ugly." *Adorno and the Need in Thinking: New Critical Essays*. Eds. Donald A. Burke et al. U of Toronto P, 2007: 263–77.

Ledoux, Claude Nicolas. *Architecture de C.N. Ledoux: premier volume, contenant des plans, élévations, coupes, vues perspectives ... : collection qui rassemble tous les genres de bâtiments employés dans l'ordre social*. Princeton Architectural P, 1983.

Leibniz, Gottfried Wilhelm. *Philosophical Essays*. Trans. Roger Ariew and Daniel Garber. Hackett, 1989.

Leipziger Vorlesungsverzeichnisse 1814/15–1914. Universitätsbibliothek Leipzig (Signatur: Universität 899).

Leonardo da Vinci. *On Painting. A Lost Book*. Ed. Carlo Pedretti. U of California P, 1964.

Leroy, Louis. "L'Exposition des impressionnistes." *Le Charivari*, April 25, 1874, 79–80. In *The New Painting. Impressionism 1874–1886. Documentation. Volume 1. Reviews*. Ed. Ruth Berson. Fine Arts Museum, 1996: 25–6.

Lessing, Gotthold Ephraim. *Laocoön: An Essay on the Limits of Painting and Poetry*. Trans. Edward Allen McCormick. John Hopkins UP, 1984.

Lessing, Gotthold Ephraim. *Laokoon*. Ed. Wilfried Barner. Deutscher Klassiker Verlag, 2007.

Levinson, Jerrold. *Suffering Art Gladly: The Paradox of Negative Emotion in Art*. Palgrave, 2014.

Lipps, Theodor. *Ästhetik. Psychologie des Schönen und der Kunst. Erster Teil: Grundlegung der Ästhetik*. Voss, 1903.

Livingston, Paisley. "Bolzano on Beauty." *The British Journal of Aesthetics* 54.3 (2014): 269–84

Lotze, Hermann. *Geschichte der Aesthetik in Deutschland*. Cotta, 1868.

Lotze, Hermann. *Geschichte der deutschen Philosophie seit Kant: Diktate aus den Vorlesungen*. Hirzel, 1894.

Lotze, Hermann. *Ueber den Begriff der Schönheit*. Vandenhoeck und Ruprecht, 1845.

Lovejoy, Arthur O. *The Great Chain of Being*. Harvard UP, 1976.

Macarthur, John. *The Picturesque: Architecture, Disgust and Other Irregularities*. Routledge, 2007.

Maggi, Vincenzo. *De Ridiculis* [1550]. *Trattati di poetica e retorica del Cinquecento*. Ed. Bernard Weinberg. Laterza, 1970: 2.91–125.

Maggi, Vincenzo. *On the Ridiculous* [excerpts]. Trans. George Miltz. *Theories of Comedy*. Ed. Paul Lauter. Anchor, 1964: 64–73.

Magsamen, Susan and Ivy Ross. *Your Brain on Art: How the Arts Transform Us*. Random, 2023.

Marc, Franz. *Briefe, Schriften und Aufzeichnungen*. Ed. Günter Meißner. Kiepenheuer, 1989.

Marx, Karl. *Early Political Writings*. Ed Joseph O'Malley. Cambridge UP, 1994.

Mbembe, Achille. *De la postcolonie: Essai sur l'imagination politique dans l'Afrique contemporaine*. Karthala, 2000.

Mbembe, Achille. "La 'chose' et ses doubles dans la caricature camerounaise." *Cahiers d'Études Africaines* 36.141/142 (1996): 143–70.

Mbembe, Achille. *On the Postcolony*. U of California P, 2001.

McGinn, Colin. *Ethics, Evil, and Fiction*. Clarendon, 1997.

Mendelssohn, Moses. *Ausgewählte Werke: Studienausgabe*. 2 vols. Eds. Christoph Schulte et al. Wissenschaftliche Buchgesellschaft, 2009.

Mennemeier, Franz Norbert. "Unendliche Fortschreitung und absolutes Gesetz: Das Schöne und das Häßliche in der Kunstauffassung des jungen F. Schlegel." *Wirkendes Wort* 17 (1967): 393–409.

Menninghaus, Winfried. *Disgust: The Theory and History of a Strong Sensation*. Trans. Howard Eiland and Joel Golb. SUNY P, 2003.

Michel, Paul. *"Formosa deformitas": Bewaltigungsformen des Häßlichen in mittelalterlicher Literatur*. Bouvier, 1976.

Michelet, Karl Ludwig. *Das System der Philosophie als exacter Wissenschaft enthaltend Logik, Natur- und Geistespilosophie*. 5 vols. Nicolai, 1876–81.

Mire Lee. Black Sun. Eds. Gary Carrion-Murayari and Madeleine Weisberg. New Museum, 2023.

Monk, Ellis P., Jr., Michael H. Esposito, and Hedwig Lee. "Beholding Inequality: Race, Gender, and Returns to Physical Attractiveness in the United States." *American Journal of Sociology* 127.1 (2021): 194–241.

Montaigne, Michel de. *The Complete Essays*. Trans. M. A. Screech. Penguin, 1987.

Murdoch, Iris. *The Fire and the Sun: Why Plato Banished the Artists*. Viking, 1990.

Nehamas, Alexander. "Beauty of Body, Nobility of Soul: The Pursuit of Love in Plato's Symposium." *Maieusis: Essays in Ancient Philosophy in Honour of Myles Burnyeat*. Ed. Dominic Scott. Oxford UP, 2007: 97–135.

Nehamas, Alexander. *Only a Promise of Happiness. The Place of Beauty in a World of Art*. Princeton UP, 2007.

The New Oxford Annotated Bible with Apocrypha: New Revised Standard Version. 4th ed. Ed. Michael D. Coogan. Oxford, 2010.

Ngai, Sianne. *Ugly Feelings*. Harvard UP, 2005.

Nietzsche, Friedrich. *The Complete Works of Friedrich Nietzsche*. Stanford UP, 1995-.

Nietzsche, Friedrich. *Basic Writings of Nietzsche*. Trans. Walter Kaufmann. Modern Library, 1968.

Nietzsche, Friedrich. *The Portable Nietzsche*. Trans. Walter Kaufmann. Penguin, 1976.

Nietzsche, Friedrich. *The Will to Power*. Trans. Walter Kaufmann and R. J. Hollingdale. Random, 1967.

Nietzsche, Friedrich. *Werke*. Ed. Karl Schlechta. 6th ed. 3 vols. Hanser, 1969.

Nikolaus von Kues [Nicolaus Cusanus]. *Die philosophisch-theologischen Schriften*. Ed. Leo Gabriel. 3 vols. Herder, 1964–67.

Norton, Robert E. *Herder's Aesthetics and the European Enlightenment*. Cornell UP, 1991.

Noys, Benjamin. *Georges Bataille. A Critical Introduction*. Pluto, 2000.

Nuttall, Sarah, ed. *Beautiful Ugly. African and Diasporta Aesthetics*. Duke UP, 2006.

Oelmüller, Willi. *Friedrich Theodor Vischer und das Problem der nachhegelschen Ästhetik*. Kohlhammer, 1959.

Oesterle, Günter. "Entwurf einer Monographie des ästhetisch Häßlichen: Die Geschichte einer ästhetischen Kategorie von Friedrich Schlegels *Studium*-Aufsatz bis zu Karl Rosenkranz' *Ästhetik des Häßlichen* als Suche nach dem Urpsrung der Moderne." *Zur Modernität der Romantik*. Ed. Dieter Bänsch. Metzler, 1977: 217–97.

Olyan, Saul M. *Disability in the Hebrew Bible. Interpreting Mental and Physical Differences*. Cambridge UP, 2008.

On the Ugly: Aesthetic Exchanges. Eds. Jane Forsey and Lars Aagaard-Mogensen. Cambridge Scholars Publishing, 2019.

Opitz, Martin. *Buch von der deutschen Poeterei*. Niemeyer, 1955.

Origen. *Matthäuserklärung II. Die lateinische Übersetzung der Commentariorum Series. Die Griechischen Christlichen Schriftsteller der ersten Jahrhunderte Origenes Elfter Band*. Ed. Erich Kolstermann. Akademie, 1976.

Oštarić, Lara. *The Critique of Judgment and the Unity of Kant's Critical System*. Cambridge University Press, 2023.

Otto, Rudolf. *Das Heilige. Über das Irrationale in der Idee des Göttlichen und sein Verhältnis zum Rationalen*. Beck, 2004.

Pauen, Michael. "Die Ästhetik des Häßlichen. Grauenhafte Probleme und eine schöne Bescherung." *Im Schatten des Schönen. Die Ästhetik des Häßlichen in historischen Ansätzen und aktuellen Debatten*. Aisthesis, 2006: 211–26.

Paris, Panos. "The Deformity-Related Conception of Ugliness." *British Journal of Aesthetics* 57.2 (2017): 139–60.

Parsons, Glenn. *Aesthetics and Nature: The Appreciation of Natural Beauty and the Environment*. 2nd ed. Bloomsbury, 2023.

Paul, Jean. *Vorschule der Ästhetik*. Meiner, 1990.

Pinho, Patricia. "Afro-Aesthetics in Brazil." *Beautiful / Ugly. African and Disapora Aesthetics*. Ed. Sarah Nuttall. Duke UP, 2006: 266–89.

Pinkard, Terry. *Hegel: A Biography*. Cambridge UP, 2000.

Plato. *The Collected Dialogues*. Eds. Edith Hamilton and Huntington Cairns. Princeton UP, 1961.

Plato. *Gorgias*. Trans. James H. Nichols Jr. Cornell UP, 1998.

Plotinus. *The Enneads*. Trans. Stephen MacKenna. Penguin, 1991.

Plutarch. *Moralia*. Trans. Frank Cole Babbitt. Harvard UP, 1927.
Pogrebin, Robin and Scott Reyburn. "A Basquiat Sells for 'Mind-Blowing' $110.5 Million at Auction." *The New York Times*, May 18, 2017.
Poma, Andrea. *Yearning for Form and Other Essays on Hermann Cohen's Thought*. Springer, 2006.
Pop, Andrei. "Can Beauty and Ugliness Coexist?." *Ugliness: The Non-Beautiful in Art and Theory*. Eds. Andrei Pop and Mechtild Widrich. Tauris, 2014: 165–79.
Price, Uvedale, Sir. *On the Picturesque: With an Essay on the Origin of Taste, and Much Original Matter*. Caldwell, 1842.
Pseudo-Dionysius. *The Complete Works*. Paulist P, 1987.
Qi, Zhixiang. *The Spirit of Traditional Chinese Aesthetics*. Palgrave, 2024.
Rasmussen, Dennis C. *The Infidel and the Professor: David Hume, Adam Smith, and the Friendship That Shaped Modern Thought*. Princeton UP, 2017.
Ribon, Michel. *Archipel de la Laideur. Essai sur l'Art et la Laideur*. Éditions Kimé, 1995.
Rinaldi, Giaccomo. *The Philosophy of Art*. vol. 1. Pertinent P, 2022.
Robortello, Francesco. *In librum Aristotelis de arte poetica explicationes. Paraphrasis in librum Horatii qui vulgo de arte poetica ad pisones inscribitur*. Torrentinus, 1548.
Rocco, Antonio. *Della bruttezza. Amore è un puro interesse*. Ed. F. Walter Luppi. ETS, 1990.
Roche, Mark W. *Alfred Hitchcock: Filmmaker and Philosopher*. Bloomsbury, 2022.
Roche, Mark W. *Beautiful Ugliness: Christianity, Modernity, and the Arts*. U of Notre Dame P, 2023.
Roche, Mark W. *Dynamic Stillness: Philosophical Conceptions of Ruhe in Schiller, Hölderlin, Büchner, and Heine*. Niemeyer, 1987.
Roche, Mark W. "Hegels Relevanz für die gegenwärtige Ästhetik." *Das Geistige und das Sinnliche in der Kunst: Ästhetische Reflexion in der Perspektive des deutschen Idealismus*. Ed. Dieter Wandschneider. Königshausen & Neumann, 2005: 67–81.
Roche, Mark W. "Hegel's Theory of Comedy in the Context of Hegelian and Modern Reflections on Comedy." *Revue Internationale de Philosophie* 56 (2002): 411–30.
Roche, Mark W. *Tragedy and Comedy: A Systematic Study and a Critique of Hegel*. State U of New York P, 1998.
Roche, Mark W. *Why Literature Matters in the 21st Century*. Yale UP, 2004.
Rodrigues, Sara and Ela Przybylo, ed. *On the Politics of Ugliness*. Macmillan, 2018.
Roessner, Jane. *A Decent Place to Live: From Columbia Point To Harbor Point: A Community History*. Northeastern UP, 2000.
Rötscher, Heinrich Theodor. *Aristophanes und sein Zeitalter. Eine philologisch-philosophische Abhandlung zur Alterthumsforschung*. Voss, 1827.
Rolston, Holmes. *Environmental Ethics: Duties to and Values in the Natural World*. Temple UP, 1988.
Rose, Margaret A. "Karl Rosenkranz and the 'Aesthetics of the Ugly'." *Politics, Religion, and Art: Hegelian Debates*. Ed. Douglas Moggach. Northwestern UP, 2011: 231–53.
Rosenkranz, Karl. *Ästhetik des Hässlichen*. Wissenschaftliche Buchgesellschaft, 1979.
Rosenkranz, Karl. *Aesthetics of Ugliness: A Critical Edition*. Trans. Andrei Pop and Mechtild Widrich. Bloomsbury, 2015.
Rosenkranz, Karl. *Die Pädagogik als System. Ein Grundriß*. Bornträger, 1848.
Rosenkranz, Karl. *Georg Wilhelm Friedrich Hegel's Leben*. Duncker und Humblot, 1844.

Rosenkranz, Karl. *Kritik der Schleiermacherschen Glaubenslehre*. Unzer, 1836.

Rosenkranz, Karl. *The Philosophy of Education*. Trans. Anna C. Brackett. Ed. William Torrey Harris. 2nd ed. Appleton, 1889.

Rosenkranz, Karl. *Von Magdeburg bis Königsberg*. Heimann, 1873.

Ruge, Arnold. *Neue Vorschule der Ästhetik. Das Komische mit einem komischen Anhang*. 1837. Olms, 1975.

Sallis, John. *On Beauty and Measure: Plato's Symposium and Statesman*. Ed. S. Montgomery Ewegen. Indiana UP, 2021.

Santayana, George. *The Sense of Beauty. Being the Outline of Aesthetic Theory*. Dover, 1955.

Scaliger, Julius Caesar. *Poetics Libri Septem. Faksimile-Neudruck der Ausgabe von Lyon 1561*. Frommann, 1964.

Schaeffer, Jean-Marie. *Art of the Modern Age: Philosophy of Art from Kant to Heidegger*. Trans. Steven Rendall. Princeton UP, 2000.

Schama, Simon. "The Stone Gardener: A Land Artist Comes to Lower Manhattan." *The New Yorker*, September 23, 2003.

Schasler, Max. *Ästhetik: Grundzüge der Wissenschaft des Schönen und der Kunst*. 2 vols. Freytag, 1886.

Schasler, Max. *Aesthetik als Philosophie des Schönen und der Kunst. Erster Teil. Grundlegung. Kritische Geschichte der Aesthetik von Plato bis auf die Gegenwart*. 2 vols. Nicolai, 1872.

Schasler, Max. "Über einige Prinzipienfehler der modernen Ästhetik." *Zeitschrift für Philosophie und philosophische Kritik* 89 (1886): 1–48.

Scheler, Max. *Wesen und Formen der Sympathie*. Bouvier, 2005.

Schelling, Friedrich Wilhelm. *Philosophical Investigations into the Essence of Human Freedom*. Trans. Jeff Love and Johannes Schmidt. SUNY P, 2006.

Schelling, Friedrich Wilhelm. *Philosophie der Kunst*. Wissenschaftliche Buchgesellschaft, 1960.

Schelling, Friedrich Wilhelm. *Philosophy of Art*. Trans. Douglas W. Scott. U of Minnesota P, 1989.

Schelling, Friedrich Wilhelm. *Über das Verhältnis der bildenden Künste zu der Natur*. Meiner, 1983.

Schelling, Friedrich Wilhelm. *Über das Wesen der menschlichen Freiheit*. Ed. Horst Fuhrmans. Reclam, 1977.

Schiller, Friedrich. *Essays*. Eds. Walter Hinderer and Daniel O. Dahlstrom. Continuum, 2005.

Schiller, Friedrich. *Werke und Briefe in zwölf Bänden*. Eds. Otto Dann et al. Deutscher Klassiker Verlag, 1988–2004.

Schlegel, Friedrich. *Athenäums-Fragmente. Kritische Friedrich-Schlegel Ausgabe*. Ed. Hans Eichner. Schöningh, 1967. I.2.165–255.

Schlegel, Friedrich. *Philosophical Fragments*. Trans. Peter Firchow. U of Minnesota P, 1991.

Schlegel, Friedrich. *Über das Studium der griechischen Poesie. Kritische Friedrich-Schlegel Ausgabe*. Ed. Ernst Behler. Schöningh, 1979. I.1.217–367.

Schlegel, Friedrich. *On the Study of Greek Poetry*. Trans. Stuart Barnett. SUNY P, 2001.

Schleiermacher, Friedrich. *On Religion. Speeches to its Cultured Despisers*. Trans. Richard Crouter. Cambridge Univeristy P, 1996.

Schleiermacher, Friedrich. *Über die Religion. Reden an die Gebildeten unter ihren Verächtern*. Meiner, 1958.

Schmidt, Siegfried J. "Der philosophische Begriff des Schönen und des Häßlichen in Adornos 'Ästhetische Theorie.'" *Zeitwende* 43 (1972): 94–104.

Schnitzler, Arthur. *Anatol.* Stuttgart: Reclam, 1977.

Schoenberg, Arnold. "Gesinnung oder Erkenntnis?" *Jahrbuch 1926 der Universal-Edition, 25 Jahre Neue Musik.* Universal-edition, 1926: 21–30.

Schoenberg, Arnold. *Style and Idea: Selected Writings of Arnold Schoenberg*. Ed. Leonard Stein. St. Martin's, 1975.

Schopenhauer, Arthur. *Zürcher Ausgabe. Werke in zehn Bänden*. Diogenes, 1977.

Schwartz, Vanessa R. *Spectacular Realities: Early Mass Culture in Fin-de-Siècle Paris*. U of California P, 1998.

Schweik, Susan M. *The Ugly Laws: Disability in Public*. New York UP, 2010.

Scruton, Roger. *Beauty: A Very Short Introduction*. Oxford, 2011.

Shklovsky, Viktor. "Art as Technique." *Russian Formalist Criticism: Four Essays*. Eds. Lee T. Lemon and Marion J. Reis. U of Nebraska P, 1965: 3–24.

Sibley, Frank. "Some Notes on Ugliness." *Approach to Aesthetics: Collected Papers on Philosophical Aesthetics*. Clarendon, 2001: 190–206.

Silverbloom, Rachel. "The Critical Power of Ugliness." *On the Ugly: Aesthetic Exchanges*. Eds. Jane Forsey and Lars Aagaard-Mogensen. Cambridge Scholars Publishing, 2019: 95–105.

Silvers, Anita. "From the Crooked Timber of Humanity, Beautiful Things Can be Made." *Beauty Matters*. Ed. Peg Zeglin Brand. Indiana UP, 2000: 197–221.

Simonini, Ross. "Beauty and the Bees: Q+A with Wolfgang Laib." *Art in America*, February 27, 2013.

Smith, Adam. *The Works of Adam Smith*. 5 vols. Cadell, 1811–12.

Smith, David Livingstone. *Less than Human: Why We Demean, Enslave, and Exterminate Others*. St. Martin's, 2011.

Snell, Bruno. *The Discovery of the Mind: The Greek Origins of European Thought*. 1946. Trans. T. G. Rosenmeyer. Harper, 1960.

Solger, Karl Wilhelm Ferdinand. *Erwin: Vier Gespräche über das Schöne und die Kunst*. Wiegandt, 1907.

Solger, Karl Wilhelm Ferdinand. *Vorlesungen über Aesthetik*. Ed. K. W. L. Heyse. Brockhaus, 1829.

Solms, Friedhelm. *Disciplina aesthetica: Zur Frühgeschichte der ästhetischen Theorie bei Baumgarten und Herder*. Klett, 1990.

Spadaro, Antonio. *Interview with Pope Francis*. Libreria Editrice Vaticana, 2013.

The Spectator. London, 1711–14.

Stace, W. T. *The Meaning of Beauty: A Theory of Aesthetics*. Richards, 1929.

Stace, W. T. *The Philosophy of Hegel: A Systematic Exposition*. Macmillan, 1924.

Stolnitz, M. Jerome. "On Ugliness of Art." *Philosophy and Phenomenological Research* 11 (1950): 1–24.

Sulzer, Johann Georg. *Allgemeine Theorie der schönen Künste in einzeln, nach alphabetischer Ordnung der Kunstwörter auf einander folgenden Artikeln, abgehandelt*. 2 vols. Weidemann, 1771–74.

Tanguy, Sarah. "Making the Ideal Real: A Conversation with Wolfgang Laib." *Sculpture* 20.4 (2001): 28–33.

Tanke, Joseph and Colin McQuillan, eds. *The Bloomsbury Anthology of Aesthetics*. Bloomsbury, 2012.

Tatarkiewicz, Wladyslaw. *History of Aesthetics*. 3 vols. Ed. J. Harrell et al. Mouton, 1970–74.

Taylor, Mark C. *Refiguring the Spiritual: Beuys, Barney, Turrell, Goldsworthy*. Columbia UP, 2012.

Tilitzki, Christian. *Die deutsche Universitätsphilosophie in der Weimarer Republik und im Dritten Reich*. 2 vols. Akademie, 2002.

"Tonbandabschrift Pressekonferenz Karlheinz Stockhausen." Hamburg: September 16, 2001.

Tocqueville, Alexis de. *Democracy in America*. Trans. George Lawrence. Harper, 1966.

Townsend, Mary Lee. *Forbidden Laughter: Popular Humor and the Limits of Repression in Nineteenth-Century Prussia*. U of Michigan P, 1992.

Trahndorff, Karl Friedrich Eusebius. *Aesthetik oder Lehre von der Weltanschauung und Kunst*. 2 vols. Maurer, 1827.

Troxell, Mary. "Kant and the Problem of Ugliness." *Kant und die Philosophie in weltbürgerlicher Absicht: Akten des XI. Kant-Kongresses 2010*. Eds. Stefano Bacin, Alfredo Ferrarin, Claudio La Rocca, and Margit Ruffing. De Gruyter, 2013: 301–10.

Ugliness: The Non-Beautiful in Art and Theory. Eds. Andrei Pop and Mechtild Widrich. Tauris, 2014.

Ulrich Engelberti. [Ulrich of Strasbourg] *On Beauty*. Trans. Ananda K. Coomaraswamy. In "Mediaeval Aesthetic I. Dionysius the Pseudo-Aeropagite, and Ulrich Engelberti of Strassburg," by Ananda K. Coomaraswamy. *The Art Bulletin* 17.1 (1935): 35–47.

Ulrich von Strassburg. *De summo bono*. Band I, Liber II, Tractatus 1-4. Ed. Alain de Libera. Meiner, 1987.

Van Acker, Wouter and Thomas Mical. *Architecture & Ugliness: Anti-Aesthetics and the Ugly in Postmodern Architecture*. Bloomsbury, 2020.

Van Damme, Wilfried. "A Comparative Analysis Concerning Beauty and Ugliness in Sub-Saharan Africa." *Africana Gandensia* 4 (1987): 1–97.

Van Gelder, Geert Jan. "Beautifying the Ugly and Uglifying the Beautiful: The Paradox in Classical Arabic Literature." *Journal of Semitic Studies* 48.2 (2003): 321–51.

Venturi, Robert et al. *Learning from Las Vegas*. MIT P, 1972.

Verschaffel, Bart. "On Ugliness (in architecture)." *Architecture & Ugliness: Anti-Aesthetics and the Ugly in Postmodern Architecture*. Eds. Wouter Van Acker and Thomas Mical. Bloomsbury, 2020: 39–55.

Vico, Giambattista. *The New Science*. Trans. Thomas Goddard Bergin and Max Harold Fisch. Cornell UP, 2016.

Vischer, Friederich Theodor. *Ästhetik oder Wissenschaft des Schönen*. 2nd ed. Ed. Robert Vischer. 6 vols. 1846–1857. Olms, 1975.

Vischer, Friederich Theodor. *Das Schöne und die Kunst: Zur Einführung in die Aesthetik*. 1898. Cotta,1907.

Vischer, Friederich Theodor. *Kritische Gänge*. 6 vols. Cotta, 1860–73.

Vischer, Friederich Theodor. *Über das Erhabene und Komische und andere Texte zur Ästhetik*. Suhrkamp, 1967

Vitruvius. *Ten Books on Architecture*. Cambridge UP, 1999.

Vivas, Eliseo and Murray Krieger. *The Problems of Aesthetics: A Book of Readings*. Rinehart, 1953.

Volkelt, Johannes Immanuel. *System der Ästhetik*. Beck, 1925–1927.

Wain, Omar and Marcello Spinella. "Executive Functions in Morality, Religion, and Paranormal Beliefs." *International Journal of Neuroscience* 117 (2007): 135–46.

Wandschneider, Deiter. "Zur Metaphysik des Gartens." *Die Philosophie des Gärterns*. Ed. Blanka Stolz. Mairisch, 2017: 111–27.

Weinberg, Bernard. *A History of Literary Criticism in the Italian Renaissance*. 2 vols. U of Chicago P, 1961.

Weiße, Christian Hermann. *System der Ästhetik als Wissenschaft von der Idee der Schönheit*. Olms, 1966.

Winckelmann, Johann Joachim. *Gedanken über die Nachahmung der griechischen Werke in der Malerei und Bildhauerkunst*. Reclam, 1977.

Wölfflin, Heinrich. *Die klassische Kunst: Eine Einführung in die Italienische Renaissance*. Bruckmann, 1914.

Wood, Amy Louise. *Lynching and Spectacle: Witnessing Racial Violence in America, 1890–1940*. The U of North Carolina P, 2009.

Zeising, Adolf. *Aesthetische Forschungen*. Meidinger, 1955.

Zelle, Carsten. *"Angenehmes Grauen". Literaturhistorische Beiträge zur Ästhetik im achtzehnten Jahrhundert*. Meiner, 1987.

Zelle, Carsten. "Das Häßliche." *Historisches Wörterbuch der Rhetorik*. Ed. Gerd Ueding. 12 vols. Niemeyer, 1992–2015: 3:1304–26.

Zelle, Carsten. *Die Doppelte Ästhetik der Moderne. Revisionen des Schönen von Boileau bis Nietzsche*. Metzler, 1995.

Zhu, Zhirong. *Chinese Aesthetics in a Global Context*. Springer, 2022.

Zimmermann, Robert. *Allgemeine Aesthetik als Formwissenschaft*. Braumüller, 1865.

Zimmermann, Robert. *Geschichte der Aesthetik als philosophischer Wissenschaft*. Braumüller, 1858.

Žižek, Slavoj. *The Abyss of Freedom*. U of Michigan P, 1997.

Zuckert, Rachel. *Herder's Naturalist Aesthetics*. Cambridge UP, 2019.

Index

Note: Page numbers followed by 'n' indicate note number(s).

9/11 175–6

Aagaard-Mogensen, Lars 13
Abdessemed, Adel 176
abject, abjection 179–80, 220, 226–7, 229
in Kristeva 37–8, 176–8

The Abuse of Beauty: Aesthetics and the Concept of Art (Danto) 203
The Abyss of Freedom (Žižek) 180
Acker, Wouter Van 14
Addison, Joseph 6, 55–6, 199
on ugliness 55
Adorno, Theodor 1, 7, 10, 140, 153, 157–70, 176, 180
artwork aesthetics 156–8
atonal music 155
and Hegelian bad infinite 156
beauty as secondary to ugliness 161, 164
classical aesthetics 157
dissonance 155–6, 160, 162, 165, 168
and ugliness as art's most privileged categories 155
early admiration of hope 167
evaluation of art 158–60
humor, redemptive power of 168
interest in negativity 155
Jauß's criticisms 161
mimesis 163, 169–70
in modernity an aesthetic shift 158
Negative Dialectics 155, 163
pragmatic contradiction 162
stress on non-reconciliation 156–7, 167
ugly/ugliness
as anti-organic montage 156
increase in modernity 156
is prior to beauty 164
signature element of modernity 158
unreconciled life 156
Aeneid (Virgil) 64
Aesthetica (Baumgarten) 54
aesthetic excellence 68, 76, 156, 160, 203, 205, 251 n.3
criteria 227–8
Aesthetics and Theory of Art (Dessoir) 145
Aesthetics of the Natural Environment (Brady) 211
Aesthetics of Ugliness (Rosenkranz) 8, 13, 103–14
Aesthetic Theory (Adorno) 10

Die Ästhetik des Häßlichen (*Aesthetics of Ugliness*) (Rosenkranz) 8, 13, 103–14, 247 n.2
Aesthetik auf realistischer Grundlage (*Aesthetics on a Realist Foundation*) (Kirchmann) 138
aischric beauty 12, 221, 224–5
aischros 20–1, 220–1, 240 n.1
Alberti, Leon Battista 6, 45, 59, 123

Allgemeine Aesthetik als Formwissenschaft (*General Aesthetics as a Science of Form*) (Zimmermann) 137
The Ambassadors (Holbein) 66–7
ambiguity 34, 54, 89, 110, 242 n.5, 246 n.5
American optimism 195
American versus German conceptions of ugliness 195–6
Analysis of Beauty (Hogarth) 58
Anatol (Schnitzler) 221
Anderson, Maxwell 195–6
Anglo-American aesthetics 8
Anglo-American analytic philosophers 11, 193
anti-idealism 124
anti-Semitic
  films 207
  tendencies 246 n.9
Aquinas 6, 33–5, 40–2, 199
  evil serves a limited purpose 35
  hierarchy of goodness 35
architecture, and ugliness 14, 37, 40–1, 55–8, 106, 184–91, 196
  types of architectural ugliness 191
Architecture & Ugliness: Anti-Aesthetics and the Ugly in Postmodern Architecture (Van Acker and Mical) 14
Arcimboldo, Giuseppe 220, 222
Aristophanes 27, 91, 111, 114
Aristotle 5–6, 25–6, 45–7, 49, 52, 54–5, 58, 71, 128, 146, 163, 180, 199, 235
  beautiful representations of ugliness 26–27
  comedy and ugliness 26–7, 46
  paradox of tragedy 26
Ars Poetica (Horace) 27
Art as Experience (Dewey) 196–7
artwork aesthetics 10, 120, 157, 165, 219, 227–8
  art and morals, link between 253 n.4
Ästhetik (*Aesthetics*) (Lipps) 144
Ästhetik des reinen Gefühls (*Aesthetics of Pure Feeling*) (Cohen) 146–50
Ästhetik oder Wissenschaft des Schönen (*Aesthetics or the Science of Beauty*) (Vischer) 98
Ästhetik und allgemeine Kunstwissenschaft (Dessoir) 145
Ästhetische Forschungen (*Aesthetic Investigations*) (Zeising) 135
Augustine 6, 15, 24, 32–42, 235, 242 n.9
  Christ, deformed and beautiful 37–9
  City of God 36
  Confessions 39
  human sinfulness 38–9
  Ninth Homily on the First Epistle of John 37
  On Order 36
  Twenty-seventh Sermon 37–8
  On True Religion 32, 35–6, 39
axial age 15

Bacon, Francis 3, 56
Baker, Simon 176
Bakhtin, Mikhail 180
Basquiat, Jean-Michel 164
Bataille, Georges 10, 173, 175, 176
  formlessness 173–4
  moral ugliness 176
  objects related to ugliness 173
  the sacred 174
  sexual act 173
  sovereign monstrosity 175
Batteux, Charles 53, 199
Baudelaire, Charles 9, 123, 126–7
  art's role in modernity 126
  painters' tendencies toward positivism 126
Baumgarten, Alexander Gottlieb 6, 53–4, 58, 82
  aesthetic falsehood 54
Bayley, Stephen 13
beautiful ugliness 12–13, 141, 152, 164, 191, 205, 217, 227
  in Rosenkranz 113
  types of 199, 219–24

Beautiful Ugliness: Christianity, Modernity, and the Arts (Roche) 13, 217, 219
Beautiful Ugly: African and Diaspora Aesthetics (Nuttall) 13
beauty
as aesthetic excellence 203–4
and goodness 19–20
as sensuously appealing 203–4
beauty dwelling in ugliness 223
The Bedroom at Arles (Van Gogh) 200
Beissel, Conrad 167
Benefits Supervisor Sleeping (Freud) 151
Ben-Levi, Jack 177
Benn, Gottfried 199, 223
Berg, Alban 155, 160
Bernard of Clairvaux 6, 40, 58, 235
Apologia ad Guillelmum Abbatem 40
on gargoyles 40–1
grotesques as hindrances to spirituality 41
The Best Years of Our Lives (Wyler) 167
Beuys, Joseph 183, 226–7
Beyond Good and Evil (Nietzsche) 130
The Birth of Tragedy (Nietzsche) 128
Blake, Peter 196
Bloch, Ernst 144
Der blonde Eckbert (*Eckbert the Blond*) (Tieck) 98
The Blue Line Text (Eisenman) 188
Blues 7 (Rollins) 130
Bohtz, August Wilhelm 7, 85, 96–8, 218–19
caricature 97–8
categories of ugliness 97–8
demonic 97–8
ethics and aesthetics 97
ghostly or spectral 97–8
Boileau-Despréaux, Nicolas 53, 58, 199
L'Art poétique (*The Art of Poetry*) 53
Bolzano, Bernard 9, 133, 134, 136
contributions to aesthetics 133
definition of the ugly 134
models of ugliness 133–4
opposition to difficult beauty 134
work in mathematics and logic 133
Bonaventure 41–2, 58, 199
image and the object, distinction 41
Bosanquet, Bernard 8, 105, 119–21, 153, 165, 197, 211, 236
difficult beauty 120–1
facile beauty 165
neo-Hegelian 120
reception aesthetics 120
Botton, Alain de 191
Boyd, Robin 185
Brady, Emily 12, 219–21, 237
apparent ugliness 210–11
difficult beauty 211
experience and recognition 212
immediately perceptible ugliness 211
relative ugliness 210
Brecht, Bertolt 168, 223
Brentano, Franz Clemens 10, 143
comedy and tragedy 143
defence of ugliness 143
Bridge at Chatou (Renoir) 165
Buch von der deutschen Poeterei (*Book of German Poetry*) (Opitz) 52
Büchner, Georg 9, 29, 123–6
atheism 125–6
discussion of art 124
God's suffering 125–6
inclusion of ugliness 124
sculpture 125
theodicy 125
Bulger, Jamie 176
Bürger, Peter 169
Burke, Edmund 6, 57, 119
Burnet, Thomas 166–7
busoga 19

caricature 79, 85, 95, 142, 148, 151, 181, 213
in Bohtz 97–98
in Rosenkranz 107, 111, 142, 148, 248 n.5, 250 n.8
Carlson, Allen 209, 211

Carrière, Moriz Philipp 8, 85, 116–17, 119, 218
ugliness, definition 116–17
Carroll, Noël 12, 205–7, 237
dehumanization and physical ugliness 208–9
film theory and philosophy of horror 205
horror 205–6
humor 206
monsters 206
ugliness and hate 206–7
Cassirer. Ernst 146
Catilinarian Orations (Cicero) 54
Cattelan, Maurizio 225
Chaplin, Charlie 167–8
Chapman, Jake 72, 175–6
Charles Sanders Peirce 196
chibema 19
Chinese aesthetics and ugliness 239 n.1
Christ 32, 37–40, 50, 88–9, 96, 122, 125, 227
Christian art 1, 6, 31–2, 196, 239 n.1, 251 n.5
Beuys 227
Gothic churches 189
Hegel on 88–9, 122, 192–3, 246 n.5
and realism 9, 125
Rinaldi on 192–3
Schopenhauer on 128
Christian revolution in aesthetics 9
Christ's crucifixion 1, 31–3, 38–9, 88, 118
The Church at Auvers (Van Gogh) 200
Cicero 46, 54
classicism 121, 159
Clothes Make the Man (Keller) 150
The Clouds (Aristophanes) 27, 113
Cohen, Hermann 1, 10, 79, 118, 146–51
finitude 147
humor 147–8, 150
humanism 150
humor *vs.* severe spirit of negation 148
the sublime 147
the triumph of ugliness 148
ugliness
and animal nature 147
and humor 147–8
as integral to humanity and to art 150
universal suffrage 146
Cohn, Jonas
beautiful 143
comic 143
sublime and ugly 143–4
tragic 143
Collingwood, R. G. 153
color 33–4, 71, 242 n.4
comedy
Adorno on 158, 165, 167
comedy and ugliness, link between 45–6, 79, 117–18, 134–6, 143–4, 158, 192–3
in Aristotle 26–7, 45–6, 59, 241 n.7
in Bohtz 96
in Dessoir 145–6
in Fischer 102
in Hartmann 142
in Hegel 89
in Nietzsche 131–2
in Rosenkranz 103, 105–13
in Ruge 93–5
in Vischer 99–100
in Weiße 91
in Zimmermann 10, 137
comic, the
and derogatory female images 232
as a normative, not simply descriptive, category 215
Commentary on the Sentences of Lombard (Bonaventure) 41
complexity 1, 13, 52, 70, 152, 166, 181, 202, 212, 228
The Concept of Ugliness ((Pat) Henderson) 198
Confessions (Augustine) 39
The Confessions of Felix Krull: Confidence Man (Thomas Mann) 150
Cousins, Mark 11, 179

anti-transparency 179
Critique of Judgment (Kant) 26, 73, 144
Croce, Benedetto 153, 197, 234
The Crucifixion from his *Isenheim Altarpiece* (Grünewald) 31
Crucifixus Dolorosus 31
Crusades 192
Csuri, Charles 166
curiosity 24, 39–41, 206, 218, 241 n.4, 242 n.9
Cusa, Nicholas of 206

da Vinci, Leonardo 228
Daemonolatreiae (*Demonolatry*) (Nicholas Rémy) 219
Dante 33, 104, 116, 179, 229
Danto, Arthur 11, 12, 168–70, 203–5, 213
  art as embodied meaning 204, 252 n.5
  beauty versus aesthetic excellence 203–4
  resistance to calling ugly works "beautiful" 205
  usages of term beauty 203
Darmstadt Madonna (Cohen) 148
Darwin, Charles 8, 104, 119, 139
  capacity to recognize beauty 119
  sexual selection 119
  ugliness 119–20
Das System der Philosophie als exacter Wissenschaft (*The System of Philosophy as Exact Science*) (Michelet) 117
Davis, Miles 130
Dawn (Grosz) 3
De Ordine (*On Order*) (Augustine) 36
De Pictura (Alberti) 45
De providentia (Seneca) 36
De rerum originatione radicali (*On the Ultimate Origination of Things*) (Leibniz) 53
De Ridiculis (*On the Ridiculous*) (Maggi) 6, 46
De vera religione (*On True Religion*) (Augustine) 32, 35–6, 39
Death and the Maiden (Schubert) 167
deconstructionism 184
deformity 28, 35, 41, 55–8, 71
  of Christ 38
  in Horace 27
  and mountains, association between 167
  in Paris 212–3
  in Rocco 50–1
  in Rosenkranz 8, 106–13
  in Ulrich 43
Deformity: An Essay (Hay) 56
The Deformity-Related Conception of Ugliness (Paris) 212
Della bruttezza (*On Ugliness*) (Rocco) 6, 50
Derrida, Jacques 11, 179
  act of vomiting 179
  aesthetic (and moral) limits of artworks 179
  Economimesis 179
The Descent of Man (Darwin) 119
Despair (Rodin) 214
Dessoir, Max 145–6
  contributions to aesthetics 145
  incompatible with National Socialist thought 145
  parapsychology 145
  primary aesthetic forms 146
  on ugliness 146
Dewey, John 11, 189, 196–7, 224
  reflection on beauty 196
  ugliness, understanding of 196
dialectic 23, 39, 93, 121, 143–4, 146, 224
Dialectic of Enlightenment (Adorno) 163
dialectical beauty 223–4, 234
Diderot, Denis 53, 199
Diebenkorn, Richard 170
difficult beauty, concept of 9, 120–1, 130, 134, 211, 225, 236, 248 n.3
dignity 49, 77, 102, 109–10, 151, 209, 227

Diotima: Die Idee des Schönen (*Diotima: The Idea of the Beautiful*) (Fischer) 102
disability studies 50
Disasters of War (Goya) 72
disfiguration 3
disgust 41, 73, 78, 119, 142, 177–9, 198, 200, 202, 205–6, 213–15
Dissoi Logoi 5, 20–1, 233
dissonance 5, 97, 117, 129–30, 155, 158, 160–8, 182, 228–9
  emancipation of 129
Divine Names (Pseudo-Dionysius) 31, 33–4
Dix, Otto 224, 230
Don Carlos (Schiller) 87
Doran, Ryan 12, 213–16
  disgust and ugliness 214–5
  reception focus 215
Douglas, Mary 177
Draeseke, Felix 129
drama of reconciliation 66, 117, 248 n.6
Dürer, Albrecht 165
Dursch, Johann Georg Martin (G. M.) 7, 81, 85, 95–6
  limitations 96
  ugliness, importance of 95
  ugliness of the soul 96
  writings on religious topics 95

Eakins, Thomas 2, 220, 229
early Hegelians 7, 85, 91, 102, 223, 233–4, 240 n.5
Easter Morning (Friedrich) 224
Eisenman, Peter 188–9
emotional ugliness 27, 47–8, 55, 125, 200, 214, 218
emotions 12–13, 26–7, 55, 65, 78, 125, 139, 143, 200–2, 218–20, 231–2, 237
empathy 126, 144, 161, 220, 231–2
Encyclopaedia (Hegel) 103
Endless House: Holes and Drips (Mire Lee) 4
Enneads (Plotinus) 28
An Enquiry concerning Human Morals (Hume) 56
Essay on the Picturesque, as Compared with the Sublime and the Beautiful (Price) 57
evil 53, 72–3, 81, 86, 89, 91–2, 94, 97–9, 110, 248 n.2
  Jonas on 211–12
  as privation 34–7, 43, 52
  Schelling on 91–2
Der ewige Jude (*The Eternal Jew*) (Hippler) 207
Expressionism 101
external appearance and deeper essence, dichotomy 22
The Family of the Artist (Holbein) 148

fascination with ugliness 1, 14, 24–6, 39, 58, 106, 110, 155, 202, 229
featurism 185
fine arts, concept of 67
finitude, and ugliness 91, 93–4, 102, 118
First World War 9, 135
Fischer, Kuno 7, 85, 98, 101–3, 218, 236
  dissolution of the ugly 102
  distinction within ugliness 102
  obstinacy, element of 102
Foley, Mary Mix 196
Forsey, Jane 13
Four Stages of Cruelty (Hogarth) 66
fractured beauty 12, 220
Frankenstein (Shelly) 179
Frankfurt School 155
Franz Grillparzer Society 136
freedom 28, 54, 78, 89, 91–2, 96, 105, 107–8, 110
Freud, Lucian 151, 232, 252
Freud, Sigmund 144, 177, 232
Fulcrum (Saville) 3
The Garden of Earthly Delights (Bosch) 31, 110, 229

gardens 182–4
Garvin, Lucius 11, 197

ugly as unpleasant aesthetic response 197
Gehry, Frank 185–6, 191
German aesthetics 75, 105, 139
Gigante, Denise 179
Goethe 76, 87, 108, 115, 121, 160
Gogh, Vincent van 200
distortion 200
Goldsworthy, Andy 166, 182
Goodman, Nelson 11, 12, 26, 114, 199–202, 237
cognition 201
exemplification 200
object and properties of representation 199
paradox of ugliness 200–1
goodness 1, 20, 31, 34–6, 42–4, 50, 52, 87, 92, 99, 101, 105, 148, 203, 212, 235
Gorgias (Plato) 20–1, 23
Gothic churches 189
Goya, Francisco 72, 126, 224
Graves, Michael 186
Great Deeds Against the Dead (Jake and Dinos Chapman) 72
Greek moral code 20
The Gross Clinic (Eakins) 2, 220, 228, 229
Grosz, George 2–3, 223
grotesque, the 1, 9, 24, 123–4, 153, 180, 215, 224, 226–7
Der grüne Tisch (*The Green Table*) (Joos) 68
Grünewald, Matthias 31, 33, 39
Guernica (Picasso) 221, 223

Hare (Dürer) 165
Harlan, Veit 207
Hartmann, Eduard von 1, 10, 110, 140–1, 143, 153, 218, 219, 234, 236
art 142
artistic beauty 141
asymmetry 141
comedy 142
content-related ugliness 141
formal ugliness 141
forms of teleological ugliness 142
ineptitude 142
lack of adaptation 142
lack of health 142
nonbeauty 140
Hartmann, Nicolai 153
Hauptmann, Gerhart 145
Hay, William 56
Head of a Woman (Picasso) 220
Hegel 1, 8, 10, 13, 21, 27, 67, 79, 81–2, 85–90, 93, 95–9, 101, 103–5, 111, 113–14, 116–17, 121–2, 133, 135, 140, 143, 156, 157, 160, 170, 174, 191–3, 201, 204, 209
definition of beauty 96
editions of his lectures on aesthetics 85, 245 n.2
Greek and modern art, contrast 85–6
negativity of the cross 89
reconciliation 87–9
ugliness
in caricature 85
of Christ 88
views of 86–90
value of artistic negativity 88
Heidegger, Martin 143
Hellenism 159
Henderson, Gretchen 14
Henderson, G. P. (Pat) 11, 198, 210, 219, 237
types of ugliness 198
Herder, Johann Gottfried 7, 69–72, 74, 83, 105, 107, 127, 183, 236
reflection on ugliness 70
ridiculous and the horrific 70
sight and touch 70–1
ugliness as an artistic subject 71–2
Heydenreich, Karl Heinrich 74, 78–9
atheism 78
ugliness not as privation but as opposed to beauty 78–9
hierarchy and order of creatures 65–66

Hinrichs, Hermann Friedrich Wilhelm 103
Hippler, Fritz 207–8
Hirschhorn, Thomas 175
History of Aesthetic (Bosanquet) 120
Hitchcock, Alfred 151
Hoffmann, E. T. A. 98
Hogarth, William 58, 66, 119
Hohendahl, Peter Uwe 157, 164
Holbein, Hans 66–7, 148–9
Hölderlin, Friedrich 50, 79, 160
Holocaust 155, 157, 159, 163, 166, 208
Homer 25, 65, 69, 75, 167
  ugliness of Thersites 20, 25, 27, 65, 69
Homilies on the Gospel of John (Augustine) 38
Horace 5, 27, 54, 58, 62
Horkheimer, Max 155, 163
Horribilicribrifax (Gryphius) 107
horror 12, 39, 70, 77–8, 99, 184, 205–6, 212
Hugo, Victor 9, 36, 37, 123, 126–7, 230
  the deformed, the ugly, and the grotesque 124
  Preface to Cromwell 123
Human, All Too Human (Nietzsche) 129
Hume, David 6, 26, 55–6, 72, 188, 235
  instability in architecture and other arts 55–6
  sentiments 55
humor 12, 26–7, 118, 147–50, 165, 168, 206
  as loving critique 150–1
Hutcheson, Francis 56
Hyde, Timothy 14

idealization 10, 45, 124, 140, 177, 218
ignorance 5, 25, 28, 47–8, 50–1, 59
  combined with arrogance and a lack of curiosity 218
Illies, Christian 11, 182–3, 252
  gardens 182–3
The Ill-Matched Lovers (Cranach) 47
Ill-Matched Pair (Matsys) 47
incommensurability 140–1
Indian aesthetics and ugliness 239 n.1, 248 n.3
installations 4, 72
interesting, the 75–7, 106, 236
In the Shadows (Grosz) 3
Inferno (Dante) 228
intellectual ugliness 28, 36, 47, 51, 54, 59, 102, 213–14, 218, 254 n.3
Introduction to Philosophy (Dessoir) 145
Iphigenia (Goethe) 87
  Book of Isaiah 38
Italian Renaissance 6, 45, 49

James, William 196
Jauß, Hans Robert 161
Jew Süss (Hippler) 207
Jew Süss Poster (Schweitzer) 208
Jonas, Hans 143, 157, 212
  heuristics of fear 212
  the prophecy of doom 212
Jonson, Ben 113
Jooss, Kurt 68

Kainz, Friedrich 153
kallos (beauty) 19
kalokagathos 19
kalos and *agathos* 19
Kandinsky, Wassily 170
Kant, Immanuel 7, 11, 26, 54, 73–4, 78, 101, 107, 127, 140, 146, 147, 179, 199, 209
  aesthetics, role of 73
  commentary on ugliness 74
  objective limit 74
  portrayal of ugliness 73
  rejection of disgust 73
  theory of beauty 78
  and ugliness 244 n.5
Kantor, Maxim 22, 224
Kayser, Wolfgang 153
Keller, Gottfried 150
Kieran, Matthew 24
The King of the Alps and the Misanthrope (Raimund) 111
Kinkade, Thomas 195

Kirchmann, Julius Hermann von 10, 138–40
attraction to beauty 138
ideal-ugly 139
naturalistic-ugly 139
sensuous experiences 138
ugliness
associated with pain 138
emphasis on reception 139
kitsch 224–5
Klee, Paul 170
Klopstock, Friedrich Gottlieb 76
Koerner, Joseph Leo 178
Kollwitz, Käthe 221
portrayals of hunger and misery 221
Kristeva, Julia 11, 27, 176–7, 179, 237
abjection
abject materials 177
threat of 176–7
artwork and reception aesthetics 178
counters Bataille's formlessness 177
revulsion 177
Die Kritschen Wälder zur Ästhetik (*Critical Groves on Aesthetics*) (Herder) 69–70
Kuma, Kengo 187

Lacan, Jacques 176
Laib, Wolfgang 166, 182
Languages of Art (Goodman) 199
Laocoön and His Sons, Hellenistic sculpture 63–5
Laokoon oder Über die Grenzen der Malerei und Poesie (*Laocoön: An Essay on the Limits of Painting and Poetry*) (Lessing) 63
Lavater, Johann Kaspar 72–3
physiognomy 72
on ugliness 72–3
Ledoux, Claude Nicolas 187–8
Leibniz, Gottfried Wilhelm 6, 36, 53, 82
evil as necessary part of the universe 53
Lenz (Büchner) 124–126
L'érotisme (*Eroticism*) (Bataille) 173
Les beaux-arts réduits à un même principe (*The Fine Arts Reduced to a Single Principle*) (Batteux) 53
Les Fleurs du mal (*Flowers of Evil*) (Baudelaire) 126
Lessing, G. E. 7, 50, 56, 63, 65–71, 76–7, 82, 91, 107, 117, 161, 182, 233, 235
language and ugliness 65
dramatist of Enlightenment Germany 63
immediacy of ugliness 67
importance of time and action 63
integrating ugliness into painting 66–8
suffering and pain 65
temporal arts 66–8
visual ugliness 66
Lettre sur les sourds et muets (*Letter on the Deaf and Dumb*) (Diderot) 53
L'histoire de l'oeil (*Story of the Eye*) (Bataille) 174
Lichtenstein, Roy 195
Lintott, Sheila 211
Lipps, Theodor 144–7, 218
ugly, description 144–5
A Little Death (Taylor-Johnson) 68
Lombardi, Bartolomeo 46
Lotze, Hermann 9, 134–5, 218
ugliness as hostility toward beauty 135
ugliness as what should not be 135
love 21, 25, 29, 38, 50, 109, 124, 147–8, 150–1, 160, 243 n.3
Love's Labors Lost (Shakespeare) 214
Lucas Cranach 47–8

M2 Building (Kengo Kuma) 187
Macbeth (Shakespeare) 113
Maggi, Vincenzo 1, 6, 46–8, 50–9, 97, 219, 235
ignorance of negation 47–8
kinds of ugliness 47, 49

levels of reality (real, feigned, or accidental) 47
ugliness 46
comic 46
of the mind 47, 235
understanding of laughter 46
Mann, Heinrich 151
Mann, Thomas 150
Marc, Franz 45, 170, 182
Maria Magdalena, portrayal of 89
Martin, Johann Georg 85, 95
Marx, Karl 161
The Match Vendor (Dix) 229–30
Matsys, Quentin 47
Mbembe, Achille 11, 180–1
power 180–1
unmasking 181
The Meaning of Beauty (Stace) 121
medieval aesthetics 5, 31–44
Christ as ugly and beautiful 37–9
clarity 34
definition of beauty 32–4
evil and ugliness 34–7
Giotto, *Last Judgment* 32
light 33
Matthias Grünewald, *The Crucifixion* 33, 39
Matthias Grünewald, *The Resurrection* 39
order 32–4
relation of part and whole 35–7
ugliness as privation 33–4, 43
medieval architecture 36
Mendelssohn, Moses 52, 58, 63, 199
Metaphysica (Baumgarten) 54
metaphysics 21–2, 33, 39, 120, 188–9, 196, 198, 209
Mical, Thomas 14
Michelet, Karl Ludwig 117
Minna von Barnhelm (Lessing) 66, 107
mirabilia, history of 105, 206
misogyny 51, 130, 227
modern aesthetics 6–7, 63, 75–7, 85–6, 123–6, 155–62, 209, 243–4 n.1
Molière 141
Monk, Thelonious 130
montage 157, 247 n.12
Montaigne, Michel de 24, 49–50
tolerance of diversity 49
ugliness in *D'un enfant monstrueux* 49
moral ugliness 20, 47, 51, 54, 70, 78, 86–7, 95–6, 99, 109, 116, 150, 175–6, 179, 198, 209, 213–14, 218–21
morbid attractions 24, 39
Morgue and Other Poems (Benn) 223
Mozart 166
Much Ado About Nothing (Shakespeare) 214
music, and ugliness 40, 44, 57, 66, 129–30, 132, 160

Nachtgedanken (*Night Thoughts*) (Heine) 107
Nathan the Wise (Lessing) 50, 66
Nature, Aesthetics, and Environmentalism (Carlson and Lintott) 211
nature 12, 14, 27, 49, 51, 73–4, 82, 96, 99, 105, 126, 166, 168, 182–3, 209–12, 224
theories of ugliness in nature 209–12
negation
of beauty 80, 107, 140, 161, 181
comic 91, 98, 113
concept of 223
of freedom 105
of the negation or double negation 91, 93–4, 100, 112, 117, 192, 236
Negative Dialectics (Adorno) 155–6, 163
neologism 12, 221
Neoplatonism 29
Neue Vorschule der Ästhetik (*New Introduction to Aesthetics*) (Ruge) 93
New Objectivity 101
Nietzsche 9, 11, 123–32, 161, 164, 173, 175, 180
beauty and ugliness 128–9

death of God and abhorrence of pity 131–2
and the Hegelians 132
intellectual reception of ugliness 130
metaphysical joy in the tragic 129
musical ugliness 129–30
truth as ugly 128–9
ugliest man 131
ugliness
as primary 128
and negativity 131
as weakness and degeneracy 130–1
Nitsch, Hermann 225
normative and descriptive, relation of 25, 204, 207, 214–16, 240 n.4, 241 n.5, 247 n.12, 252 n.5, 253 n.1
Notre-Dame de Paris (Hugo) 36
numen fascinans 14
numen tremendum 14
Nuttall, Sarah 13

objective idealism 21, 204, 217, 253 n.1
Oedipus at Colonus (Sophocles) 117
On Deformity (Bacon) 56
On the Politics of Ugliness (Rodrigues and Przybylo) 14
On the Ugly (Forsey and Aagaard-Mogensen) 13, 116
On Ugliness (Eco) 13
Opitz, Martin 52
Oresteia (Aeschylus) 117
Die Pädagogik als System (*Pedagogy as System*) (Rosenkranz) 104

pain 26–7, 46, 56, 65–6, 75, 125–6, 138–9, 241 n.7, 243 n.1
painting 2–3, 36, 45, 53, 56, 63, 65–8, 71, 73, 106, 126–8, 130, 148–9, 164, 200, 246 n.5
Paris, Panos 12, 212
deformity 213
focus on reception 213
on ugliness 213
part and whole, relations between 6, 29, 34–9, 43–4, 49, 52–3, 63, 65–6, 69, 89, 97, 118, 121, 156, 197, 210, 219, 223–4, 228, 242 n.7
Paul, Jean 135
Penderecki, Krzysztof 44, 199
Phaedrus (Plato) 21
phantasmagoria 247 n.12
Philebus (Plato) 70
ignorance in the strong and in the weak 25
hateful ugliness versus ridiculous ugliness 25
A Philosophical Enquiry into the Origin of Our Ideas of the Sublime and Beautiful (Burke) 57
Philosophie des Unbewußten (*Philosophy of the Unconscious*) (Hartmann) 140
The Philosophy of Art (Rinaldi) 192
The Philosophy of Hegel (Stace) 121
The Philosophy of Horror (Carroll) 205
physical ugliness 20, 25, 37, 54, 70, 148, 150, 179, 209, 214, 218–19, 236, 246
Plato 1, 5, 12, 14, 20–9, 36, 39–40, 42, 46–7, 58–9, 65, 70, 78, 95, 101, 115–16, 118, 146, 180–1, 204, 206, 228, 233–5
appearance versus reality 22–24
definition of ugliness 25, 218
pull of beauty 21, 24–5, 240 n.3
and the *Dissoi Logoi* 21
synthesis of beauty and ugliness 233
and wonder 14
pull of ugliness 24, 58, 240 n.3
ugliness as powerful or harmless 25, 65
Plautus 46
Plotinus 5, 15, 28–9, 32, 57, 59, 225
beauty and self-knowledge 28
intellectual variety 29
Neoplatonism 29
revulsion and disgust 29

self-ignorance 28
ugly soul 28–9, 59
Plutarch 5, 27–8, 45, 58, 199
ugliness in *De audiendis poetis* 27–8
Poetics (Aristotle) 45, 46, 91
Pop, Andrei 13, 247 n.3, 250 n.9
Pope Francis 50
Portland Building (Graves) 186
Portrait of Dr. Samuel Gross (Eakins) 2
postmodernism 173, 181, 184, 185, 191
Pouvoirs de l'horreur. Essai sur l'abjection (*Powers of Horror: An Essay on Abjection*) (Kristeva) 176
poverty 51, 145, 229, 235
pragmatism 196
Praise of Folly (Erasmus) 23
Price, Uvedale 6, 57–8, 119–20, 141, 156, 206
prima facie quatsch, concept of 12, 225–6
proportion 32–34, 42–3, 57, 101, 111, 140, 188

Wendell O. Pruitt Homes and William Igoe Apartments (Yamasaki) 190–1
Przybylo, Ela 14
Pseudo-Dionysius 6, 31, 33–4, 42
beauty and light 33
goodness and beauty 31

quatsch 12, 225

radiant beauty 165–9, 234
Raimund, Ferdinand 111
Rais, Gilles de 175
Rape of the Sabine Women (Picasso) 222
Raphael 148
Die Räuber (*The Robbers*) (Schiller) 87
Rawls, John 122
relativism 21, 233
Renaissance 6, 31, 45–6, 49–50, 140
The Republic (Plato) 21, 23–4
repugnant beauty 12, 220–1, 223
repulsion 14, 143, 178
Resurrection (Grünewald) 39
resurrection 32, 39, 94, 160, 176, 227
ridiculous, the 5, 25–6, 46–7, 49, 59, 65, 69–70, 98–9, 111, 114, 135, 146, 181, 206, 234–5
Rinaldi, Giacomo 11, 191–3
aesthetic ugliness 192
artworks based on false theological doctrines 192
on Hegel and ugliness 193
ugly, the sublime, and the comic 193
Robortello, Francesco 46
Rocco, Antonio 1, 6, 50–2
Alcibiades, the Schoolboy 50
in praise of death 51
in praise of deformity 50–1
in praise of ignorance 50–1
in praise of indecorum 50–1
in praise of poverty 51
in praise of vice 50–1
in praise of ugliness 50–2
self-cancellation 52
Rodrigues, Sara 14
Rollins, Sonny 130
Rolston III, Holmes 12, 209, 237
beauty out of ugliness 209
environmental ethics 209
on ugly moments 209
Romanticism 75, 98, 108
Rome, ancient 1, 124
Rosenkranz, Karl 5, 8, 28, 74, 85, 103–14, 123, 142, 148, 153, 174
asymmetry 106
caricature 111
comic/comedy 107, 110–12
conversation with Hegel 104
deformity or *Verbildung* 106–111
disharmony 104
distortion 111
double negation 112
formlessness 106
freedom 105, 107–8, 110
not the first German thinker to address ugliness 104
imperfection 106

incorrectness 105–7
"incorrect speech" and "mixed-up speech" 107
intellectual ecstasy 103
legitimate deviation 106
Lernfreiheit, concept of 103
modernity's elevation of the individual 106
obscenities 108–10, 112–13, 118
raw, definition 107
repellent, forms of 110
satire 112–13
strengths and weaknesses 113–4
ugliness
and the comic, connection 111–3
in nature 105
as ontologically deficient 105, 202
as the opposite of beauty 104–5
of spirit 105–6
systematic reflection on 104
three main types 105–6
unintentional bodily exposure 109
Rotscher, Heinrich Theodor 27, 114
Royce, Josiah 135
Ruge, Arnold 7, 85, 93–100, 102–14, 116, 137, 193
ugliness
falsehood, and evil, interconnectedness 94
as the first negation and the finite contradiction 93
in spiritual realm 93
as "vapid spirit" 94
Ruskin, John 209
Russell, Harold 167–8

Salon (Baudelaire) 126
satire 1, 6, 50–2, 77, 108–12, 117, 122, 150–1, 168, 223–4, 250 n.7
Satyricon (Petronius) 110
Saville, Jenny 3, 199, 232
Scaliger, Julius Caesar 49
Schasler, Max 1, 8, 85, 100, 114–16, 119–20, 140, 236
beauty's activity 114
history of aesthetics 114
negativity 114–5
ugliness
definition 115–16
as negativity or negative moment 114–15
Scheler, Max 144
concept of dignity 109
Schelling, Friedrich Wilhelm Joseph 79–82, 91–2, 96, 98, 140
aberrant sublime 80
absolute form with formlessness 80
on beauty 80
essay on freedom 92
implicit ugliness 79–80
ugliness as a "privation" 79
Schelling, Karl F. A. 79
Schiller, Friedrich 7, 76–9, 86–7, 89, 106, 201
common and the low 78
moral ugliness 78
reflections on ugliness 76
tragedy, description 87
Über die tragische Kunst (*On Tragic Art*) 77
Schlegel, Friedrich 7, 29, 63, 75–7, 83, 85, 90, 106, 114, 116, 125, 236
aesthetics of ugliness 75
"infinite deficiency" or "infinite disharmony" 76
modern art 76
role of ugliness in aesthetics 75
Schleiermacher, Friedrich 50, 81, 103
Schnitzler, Arthur 221
Schoenberg, Arnold 129, 130, 155
"the emancipation of dissonance" 129
intellectual reception of ugliness 130
Schopenhauer, Arthur 123, 127, 128, 140
influence on Nietzsche 127
painting 127–8
sculpture 127
Schubert, Franz 167
The Scream (Munch) 231

Scruton, Roger 180
sculpture 56, 63–6, 70–2, 74, 107, 109, 125, 127–8, 183, 225–7, 236, 244 n.2
Second World War 3, 201
seeming ugliness 12, 36, 120–1, 141, 152, 187–9, 191, 193, 203, 209–10, 216, 227–8, 251 n.2
self-cancellation 21, 52, 111–12, 116, 137, 142, 162
Self-Portrait (Bacon) 3
Shadow of a Doubt (Hitchcock) 151
Shakespeare 76, 107, 113, 116, 148, 214
Shelly, Mary 179
Sibley, Frank 1, 11, 12, 201–3, 210, 214, 218, 237
  on beauty 202
  inattention to dialectic 201–3
  ugliness as departure from a norm 202
  ugliness as neglected category 1, 202
Silvers, Anita 233
sin 1, 6, 31–2, 36, 39–40, 51, 166
Smith, Adam 6, 56, 127–8
Smith, Kiki 177–8
Society for the Study of Aesthetics 145
Socrates 20–5, 27, 58, 129, 144, 219
Socrates (Kantor) 22
Solger, Karl Wilhelm Ferdinand 7, 81, 93, 96, 98, 109, 127
  dialogues on beauty 81
  ugly, interpretation 81
Sophist (Plato) 20, 25, 47, 218
Sophocles 65, 75, 81, 104, 117, 246 n.11
speculative beauty 224, 233
Speer, Albert 189
Stace, Walter Terence 8, 26, 119, 121–2, 200
  ugly, interpretation 122
  the unbeautiful 122
  use of "perceptual" 122
The Starry Night (Van Gogh) 200
Steiner, Rudolf 136
Still Life (Taylor-Johnson) 68
Stockhausen, Karlheinz 175–6
Stolnitz, Jerome 11, 197
  invincibly ugly 198
  ugly as overwhelming and intense unpleasantness 198
sublime, the 7–8, 14–15, 57–8, 83, 118, 167, 182, 205, 215, 253 n.12
  in Bohtz 87
  in Cohn 143–4
  in Dessoir 146
  in Fischer 102
  in von Hartmann 140
  in Jean Paul 135
  in Kant 26, 74–5, 147, 209
  in Kirchmann 139
  in Michelet 117
  in Rinaldi 192–3
  in Rosenkranz 107–8
  in Ruge 94
  in Schelling 79–80
  in Schiller 77–8, 87
  in Schlegel 76
  in Stace 122
  in Vischer 99–101
  in Weiße 91, 236
Sulzer, Johann Georg 72, 199
  emotional aversion 72
  ugliness as formal distortion 72
Suspension (Saville) 199
The Symposium (Plato) 21, 23, 25
System der Ästhetik als Wissenschaft des Schönen (*System of Aesthetics as the Science of the Beautiful*), (Weiße) 90, 92, 152

taboo 14, 161–2, 169, 174, 177–8, 232
Tale (Kiki Smith) 177
Taubert, Agnes 140
Taylor-Johnson, Sam 68–9
The Temptation of St. Anthony (Kantor) 224
Terence 46
Theodorus 22
Threnody (Penderecki) 44, 199
Thus Spoke Zarathustra (Nietzsche) 129, 131

Tocqueville, Alexis de 195
tolerance 49–50
Torso 2 (Saville) 232
Tower of Pisa 188
Trahndorff, Karl Friedrich Eusebius 7, 55, 81–2, 127, 245 n.8
  aesthetics 82
A Treatise of Human Nature (Hume) 55
truth 1, 9, 21, 23, 26, 36, 43, 52–3, 69, 71, 72, 92–6, 102, 112, 115, 128, 136, 139, 148, 155, 157–9, 162, 179, 191, 198, 203, 210, 227–8, 233–4
  asymmetry between truth and falsehood 21
Trump, Donald J. 252 n.5, 252 n.7
Twilight of the Idols (Nietzsche) 130

Über das Studium der griechischen Poesie (*On the Study of Greek Poetry*) (Schlegel) 7
Ugliness: A Cultural History (Gretchen Henderson) 14
Ugliness and Judgment: On Architecture in the Public Eye (Hyde) 14
On Ugliness of Art (Stolnitz) 197
Ugliness: The Non-Beautiful in Art and Theory (Pop and Widrich) 13
Ugly Feelings (Ngai) 13
ugly/ugliness
  animals 36
  definitions of 5, 12, 25, 32, 58, 94–5, 113, 116, 122, 134, 158, 179, 213–15, 217–19
  descriptions in Hebrew Bible 19
  diversity of 229
  emotions 231
  harmful versus harmless 25–7, 46–7, 59, 65, 69–70, 234, 246–7 n.11
  laws 232, 254 n.2
  as privation of beauty 34–5, 43
  as what should not be 135, 144, 150, 188, 218
  of the soul 28–9
  as subordinate to beauty 37, 112, 150, 202, 233, 241 n.1
  temptation toward 240 n.3
  truth 9
  as usurping beauty 81, 93, 95, 108, 118, 136–7, 234
Ulrich of Strasbourg 6, 42, 235
  beauty in the context of goodness 42
  De summo bono 41–2
  divine beauty 43
  image and the object, distinction 41
  ugly
    as deficiency 42–3
    imperfectly beautiful 43
The Unequal Couple (*Old Man in Love*) (Cranach) 47
Der Untertan (*The Subject*) (Heinrich Mann) 151

vanitas tradition 68
Versailles Treaty 207
Verschaffel, Bart 11, 184–5, 191, 219
Vischer, Friedrich Theodor 7, 85, 98–101, 114, 137, 192–3, 218, 236
  history of art 92
  self-criticism 100–1
  ugliness
    and the comic 99–101
    and the sublime 99–101
visual injustice 14
Volkelt, Johannes 9, 152, 219
  academic aesthetics 152
  psychological ugliness 152
  types of ugly art 152
  ugly/ugliness
    of content 152
    as an element of beauty 152–3
    is without meaning 153
    of materiality 152
    of structure 152
Volpone (Jonson) 113
Voltaire 63

Wallenstein (Schiller) 87
Walt Disney Concert Hall in Los Angeles 186

War of Catiline (Sallust) 54
Warhol, Andy 195
Water (Arcimboldo) 220, 222
weak ugliness 26, 47, 234–5
Weimar Germany's debauchery, portrayals of 2
Weiße, Christian Hermann 1, 7, 9, 66–7, 85, 90–7, 99, 114, 116, 123, 133, 135, 137, 167, 193, 199, 236
  disinterest in the history of aesthetics 92
  foundational vocabulary 91
  mediation of the infinite and the finite 91
  proximity of the ugly and the comic 91
  ugliness
    as a double lie 92
    in history of aesthetics 87
    as more than privation 91–2
Die Welt als Wille und Vorstellung (*The World as Will and Representation*) (Schopenhauer) 127
Widrich, Mechtild 13, 247 n.3, 250 n.9
Wieland, Christoph Martin 76
Winckelmann, Johann Joachim 63, 123, 127
Wissenschaft der Logik (*Science of Logic*) (Hegel) 93
Wolff, Christian 54
Wyler, William 167

Yöndel, Ayla-Suzan 186

Zeising, Adolf 9, 135–6
  rejection of dialectical thinking 136
  ugliness not a part of beauty 135–6
Zimmermann, Robert 10, 136–7
  anthroposophy 136
  comic untenability of ugliness 137
  superiority of beauty over ugliness 137
Žižek, Slavoj 11, 104, 161, 164
  on ugliness 180